Body,
Subject
&
Power
in
China

The University
of Chicago Press
Chicago & London

Body, Subject & Power in China

Edited by

ANGELA ZITO

and

TANI E. BARLOW

ANGELA ZITO is assistant professor of religion at Barnard College. TANI E. BARLOW is associate professor of Chinese studies at the University of California, Berkeley.

The University of Chicago Press, Chicago 60637
The University of Chicago Press, Ltd., London
© 1994 by The University of Chicago
All rights reserved. Published 1994
Printed in the United States of America
03 02 01 00 99 98 97 96 95 94   1 2 3 4 5
ISBN: 0-226-98726-4 (cloth)
       0-226-98727-2 (paper)

Library of Congress Cataloging-in-Publication Data
Body, subject, and power in China / edited by Angela Zito and Tani E. Barlow.
      p.   cm.
   Includes bibliographical references and index.
   1. China—Civilization.   I. Zito, Angela.   II. Barlow, Tani E.
DS721.B615   1994
951—dc20   93-15596
                                                        CIP

⊗ The paper used in this publication meets the minimum requirements of the American National Standard for Information Sciences—Permanence of Paper for Printed Library Materials, ANSI Z 39.48-1984.

CONTENTS

8 (Re)inventing *Li: Koutou* and Subjectification in Rural
Shandong

Gendering Bodies

9 The Classic "Beauty-Scholar" Romance and the Superiority
of the Talented Woman

10 Theorizing Woman: *Funü, Guojia, Jiating*

A C K N O W L E D G M E N T S

The contributors to this volume were especially patient and dedicated throughout a long process of writing and commenting. They made doing a critical anthology a rare pleasure, and the editors thank them. Miriam Silverberg and another reader for the Press provided excellent editorial advice for which we are very grateful. Judith Farquhar and Ann Anagnost commented most usefully on the introduction. Donald M. Lowe and John Calagione deserve special thanks for support, comradeship, and advice at every stage of the work.

We also gratefully acknowledge Barnard College, which provided a Faculty Grant for aspects of the production of the book.

Body, Subject, and Power in China

The Editors

> Heaven, earth, and humanity are the basis of all things. Heaven gives them birth, earth nourishes them, and humanity brings them to completion. Heaven provides them at birth with a sense of filial and brotherly love, earth nourishes them with food and clothing, and humanity completes them with rites and music.
>
> Dong Zhongshu, ca. 150 B.C.

People often intuit common sense as an imposed regime. Bumping up against the unfamiliar might trigger such a feeling, but even new contexts can trouble older versions of the everyday and prompt re-visions. A vacation after many years of marriage, a visit to a spouse's workplace, meeting a teenage daughter's first love object: these simple encounters easily render contrived things that once seemed natural. The interruption of the quotidian provides us with a useful metaphor because scholars and their versions of common sense operate within the wider domain of the everyday. The same shock of the unnatural can overtake a reader encountering texts from a different time or place. Experiencing reading in this way alters habitual perception just as seeing others living lives different from our own raises new interpretive possibilities. When the problem of interpreting difference intensifies, as it has in the decades since World War II, the troubling of common sense grows more difficult to evade.

Contributors to this volume were keenly aware that we live under regimes of scholarly commonsense truth. Because powerful institutional topographies had situated us and our work, a number of conceptual traps awaited us in thinking about the body. We quickly realized that if we wished to talk about bodies—our own or other people's—and failed to address our own assumptions, we could easily ensnare ourselves. We may imagine that other people's bodies are just like ours, or that they have no bodies at all, or that their bodies are so different that we cannot possibly understand them, trapped as we are in a particularly Western post-

Cartesian body-mind. In this introduction we explore a number of interesting escape hatches that have been provided in the past twenty years. The ones that we open here include poststructuralist techniques, Marxisms, and feminisms: entryways into cultural studies.

Common Sense, Common Problems

We begin with common sense for a reason: as with much modern writing in the United States about human affairs, writing about China has tended to begin with either nature or culture. For example, nineteenth-century explorer-missionary scholars wrote comfortably about Chinese nature (Smith 1894). At the other extreme, Arthur Waley, sitting at home reading classical texts, convinced an entire generation of readers that the Chinese were more "cultural" than we are. But having inherited this split does not mean we ought to perpetuate it forever. Marxism, feminism, and poststructuralism have all generated ways to overcome the nature/culture divide. Each of these methods has wrestled strenuously with the distinction as it has become a kind of common sense for us. Although not everyone in every part of the world in every epoch has accepted the distinction between nature and culture, people do apparently always feel that their own culture's way of doing things is natural. Although in this volume we are moving across historical, canonical, and traditional differences, we can call the way people move within the specifics of their world "common sense."

We must then ask ourselves, How is common sense constructed? This is not simply a matter of "You do your thing, I'll do mine." Common sense doesn't just happen; it is generated under specific conditions of inequity, sustained over long periods, benefiting some people more than others. It is, in short, connected to questions of power.

If power resides in the processes of social construction, intrinsic to the creation of language, people, and things, then scholars who wish to understand power and society cross-culturally must scrutinize sources in new ways. If we assume that power is embedded within social life and not outside it, merely waiting to be mobilized as violence or coercion, we must then recognize that fundamental modes of creating and ordering are implicated in social inequities and imbalances. We are forced to notice uneasily that the most powerful coercion of all lies with the innocuous constitution of reality, which helps people every day to forget the contingency of their experience and to live life as necessity.[1]

In this volume we pursue a double interest. We keep in mind how our own common sense is structured while never forgetting that our interest lies, in fact, in the common sense of others. What are some of the assumptions that have structured China studies in a post–World War II United States?

The influence of the Cold War upon our field cannot be overstated. The specific version for China studies of what has come to be called the self/other problem was communist world versus free world. China was a country of "blue ants," barely human, utterly different from Western democratic society. Or else China held out hope for a utopian egalitarian alternative to a corrupt bourgeois American society. Such thinking reinstates what has come to be criticized by Derrida and others as an "essentializing binary"—an opposition that brings into being two things whose interdependence is then disguised by their seeming substantiality. Self/other, man/woman, and nature/culture are classic examples.[2]

In a sense, the times determine how we think. Cold War politics nurtured the sorts of binary divisions that we subject to criticism in this book. We realize we are not performing the first critique of such oppositions. Founders and contributors to the *Bulletin of Concerned Asian Scholars* courageously interrogated many of these attitudes in the context of the Vietnam War.[3] That the institutional and conceptual centers of the field have not changed as much as any of us might have hoped suggest that many of the ideological underpinnings of the Cold War years persist.

The diplomatic offensive of the Cold War is over, and its closure removes that overarching structuring binary for China studies, communism versus free world. Increased diplomatic, economic, and cultural ties now exist not only between China and the United States, but between China and the rest of Asia. Scholars move freely between China, Hong Kong, and Taiwan, to say nothing of intra-Asian scholarly exchanges with Japan and Korea. However, the ideological offensive of the Cold War still requires dismantling. Having been deeply implicated in that war of ideas, our field is a necessary site of struggle.

The self/other problem undergirds this persisting ideology. Our Cold War commonsense versions of human life and history have often relegated others to being instances of diversity or, worse, obstructed evolutionary stages or partial norms, precluded by the terms of their secondariness from unfolding naturally.[4] The expansion of commodification underlying capital and the collapse of monolithic Cold War ideological polarization open new spaces for contention within Asia. To unravel our Cold War commonsense assumptions, scholars of Asia might begin by reading critiques from the margins (such as those by Gayatri Spivak and Stuart Hall), which may help shift our own ideologized blinders.

In the Cold War past, scholars of China were also quite interested in questions of ideology and power (Pye 1985; Levy 1968; Fairbank 1968; Schram 1973). However, they tended to link their analyses almost exclusively to state power and to see ideology as a project of mystification. Progressive writers in cultural studies such as Harry Harootunian (1988), Stuart Hall (1990), Raymond Williams (1977), and Jean Baudrillard (1989) do not confine themselves to analyses of state ideological control and power. They are also concerned with investigating power as it operates through the practices of everyday life.

Since an entire scholarly worldview was built upon this now vanished Cold War foundation, what alternatives do we now have? We chose to construct our various anthropological, literary, and historical projects around the question of the body. Surely no more plain and powerful commonsense datum exists for corporeal creatures such as ourselves.[5] In fact, there is nothing obvious about "the body"—not even our own bodies, much less bodies in other times or places. Critical scholarship in the history of European literature and art has uncovered a reciprocity between positivist science and canons of realist representations. These paradigms construct the body as universally available for figuring and expression, a "natural ground" that provides ideology's referent (Bryson 1983; Suleiman 1986). The subjection of the body in the European post-Renaissance to discourses of biology provided a naturalized ground for the production of racial, ethnic, and gender inequality (Coward 1983; Stoller 1992; Laqueur 1990). The poststructuralist commitment to rigorous historicizing has allowed a new archaeology of the body to follow upon the long-standing concerns of feminists to denaturalize the bodies they found themselves discursively and materially trapped within.[6]

We agree with these writers that bodies (even European bodies) never escape construction in discourse/power; they hold no extradiscursive privilege. In fact in Europe the concept of one biological body, generalizable to all human beings in all social contexts and produced within regimes of medicine and surveillance, paralleled development of the unitary subject of the individual.[7] Building upon shared critical research into the problematic and powerful status of the body in all societies, we argue that China possesses a multiplicity of "bodies" subject to historical and cultural variation that is as deep and complex as any charted for Europe. With this recognition, spaces then appear for us to place Chinese experiences next to those of Europe and North America. We avoid the temptation of reducing to similarity or confining to the status of exotic data reports from China's past and present. Instead of answering the question, Are we all the same or different? we ask, In what ways are we and they always unfinished products of ongoing processes?

Within the poststructuralist framework of investigating and contesting common sense, we have found new concepts of power, discourse (Macdonell 1986), subjectivity, and difference especially compelling and useful. In the following discussion of these ideas we will amend a purely poststructuralist approach. Marxist and feminist strategies explicitly politicize this useful cultural-critical mode of reading that has too often been accused of having no politics of its own. But even these influential correctives tend to be Eurocentric. We hope that once we have read our Chinese sources with insights borrowed from these new concepts, we can return to these heretofore largely Europe-centered theoretical contexts with concrete suggestions for altering the terms of debate about social life.

Rethinking Power

Marxist theory and practice all over the world have tended to privilege economically motivated class struggle and have paid relatively little attention to the ideological dimensions of culture. Particularly in Cold War China studies, culture was left to intellectual (as well as art and literary) historians. Whether they inclined to the left (Wakeman 1973), right (Metzger 1977), or center (Levenson 1969), they operated with no explicitly articulated framework for understanding the constitution of social life. The abdication of Marxist historians of China from the study of culture reduplicated in the field the crippling theoretical split between base and superstructure, and between meaningful and material life, that has so vexed European Marxist historiography for years. If the "superstructural" dimension of an era or topic was taken up, it was dismissed as "ideological," in the narrow sense of "mystifying."

The writers in this volume wish to recoup a critical sense of culture as indeed ideologically motivated. But we read ideology as itself constitutive of the social forms and material practices under consideration, not merely as their distortion. Because we claim a positive role for signifying practices, Marxism provides us a with an indispensable critical vocabulary for understanding the articulation of social life within such practices. No one here uses "discourse" to confine the problem of social analysis to merely language or meaning. But we do emphasize that it is only through language and discourse more broadly conceived as signifying practices that we can grasp a problem at all (Spivak 1987; Williams 1977).

One fundamental insight of critical Marxist social theory after 1945 lies in thinking about power as intrinsic to the process of social reproduction. Power, rather than being seen as a stick with which rulers routinely beat the ruled, is instead envisioned as itself created along with the production of people, things, and modes of social communication. Newer formulations of the problem of power in social production push well beyond the comforting limits of the dialectics of economic reproduction, to account for culture as well as economy. Some anthropologists, for instance, have energetically sought as much to account for the production of meaning as for the "means of production." Terence Turner (1984), Nancy Munn (1986), Pierre Bourdieu (1977), Jean Comaroff (1985), and others have developed theories about "value," both social and economic, that locate power at the heart of the production of everyday life and the self.[8] The anthropology of work, a bastion of classic economistic theorizing on production, has recently been revitalized by explicit investigations of its cultural dimensions in producing selves as well as commodities (Calagione, Francis, and Nugent 1992).

Approaches to social life that emphasize its constructed nature open a field upon which people do more than contend for already available resources, symbolic or material. Instead they simultaneously create what they appropriate. In his famous formulation of power and knowledge, Foucault has redefined their relationship. Analysts must now confront their own role as historical actors shaping the very formations they "study." In our terms, we must confront our own common sense if we ever wish to fathom the common sense of others.

For Foucault, the matter is not so much knowledge *of* power. His interest lies in the fact that when people create knowledge they do it within conditions of existing power investments. He writes (Morris and Patton 1979): "Between each point of a social body, between a man and woman, in a family, between a teacher and pupil, between the one who knows and the one who doesn't, there pass relations of power which are not the pure and simple projection of a greater sovereign power over individuals."

Once society itself is understood as the never finished outcome of constant discursive negotiation and historical determination, analysts can glimpse power-as-relation. Many of the chapters here detail conflicts over categorizing, classifying, conceptualizing, and ordering within Chinese societies. These relations structure and effect the commonsense orderliness that writers in this volume seek to uncover and analyze as systematic relations of domination.

Various powers of ordering are taken up: for example, the power of classification itself. Ann Anagnost discusses the "power of naming": how the binary classification by the state of peasants as members, or not, of "law-abiding households" seeks to fix them in certain subject positions. In his analysis of the *koutou* (English "kowtow," a form of kneeling and bowing) in contemporary Shandong, Andrew Kipnis shows that the power to decide who will or will not *koutou* has become important in the contest between state discourses against feudal practices and peasants' advancement of their own continuing identity

The essays describe how desires for dominant positions in the social hierarchy take on perceptible order. According to Angela Zito in "Silk and Skin: Significant Boundaries," the emperor incarnated hegemonic powers not only by advancing the imperium's authoritative claims to reenact the relations of the sociocosmic whole, but also by kindling a desire for emulation of his yang subject/body in the pious families of the realm. In "The Classic 'Beauty-Scholar' Romance and the Superiority of the Talented Woman," Keith McMahon examines the contradictions between women's desire to strategize their given ends, to take up positions of powerful yang agency (dressing as men to take the civil service exams or find a husband of their choosing), and men's desire for erotic pleasure, which requires the eventual reinscription of chaste female geniuses as (fertile) wives. He thus contextualizes seventeenth-century erotic life within the moral discourse of kin "role."

These examples of the importance of naming and ordering in our texts show that the writers in this volume have felt compelled to reexamine the power of common sense itself, our own and that of the people within Chinese social formations that we study. We do this not only because they may not share our definitions of the obvious, but also to uncover what relations of domination are obscured by the truth effects of power in specific Chinese discourses of medicine, painting, ritual, literature, gender, and sexuality. By extending the terms of the problem of power outlined here, we can presume that control of the terms and practices that produce various "subjectivities" is itself a source of social power.

Subjectivities and Bodies

Why are we linking subjectivities to bodies as areas for investigation? Under the influence of the nature versus culture paradigm, the familiar scholarly commonsense view holds that the natural body is biological while the cultural subject is abstracted as spirit, mind, soul, or role. Body and subject have been conventionally joined in various oppositional ways. A sociology of the body appearing after the Enlightenment has overturned the older conception of the soul (in the care of the church) as preeminent, or at least as an even match for the flesh (B. Turner 1984:61). That being the case, it is important to distinguish carefully what we mean when we substitute "subjectivity" and "subject positionality" for older words like mind, consciousness, or subject. These older usages carry the sense that the person is a fixed essence because personality is to human organism as culture is to nature. Subjectivity and subject positionality are part of a vocabulary of twentieth-century critical theory, the core of which is Marx's nineteenth-century insight that human beings are engaged in and produced through social life.[9]

When twentieth-century Marxists developed more sophisticated theories of specific modes of production, they radically historicized the study of social life. They have thus substantially modified Marx's own continuing reliance upon a utopian notion of an essential human nature (if only as a putative universal goal). We accept the fundamental Marxist tenet that what has passed for "human nature" has in fact been a historically specific European, class-based, bourgeois notion that is not in the least natural. Feminist Marxists have further chipped away at the illusion of a unified human nature by pointing to the difference between man as human being and man as one of two genders (Rapp Reiter 1975). Black intellectuals in the Marxist tradition like Stuart Hall (1985), Cornel West (1991), and bell hooks (1984) have further attacked the conception by drawing attention to issues of race and ethnicity (San Juan 1992, introduction).

The retheorization of selves as subject positionalities has been enabled by historical scholarship that has continued the Marxist work of dissolving the illusion of universal mankind. Much inquiry has gone toward uncovering in European historiography deeper accounts of social experiences that people today take as obvious, transhistorical, transcultural—in short, "normal." Shown as constantly changing, these practices and experiences are rescued from eternal, timeless applicability. Most obviously, one thinks of Michel Foucault's work on the history of language, labor, life science, sexuality, and madness.[10] Other historians worked before and alongside Foucault, however, providing genealogies to such seemingly rock-solid notions as sexuality, etiquette, family and childhood, death, private life, perception, and even subjectivity and representation itself.[11] Historians of the West began this task of narrating how our own verities came into social and discursive being about the time those certainties were rendered contingent by the changing postcolonial world and the self-doubts intrinsic to modernism. Freeing ourselves from the belief that Western life has been the slow and irreversible unfolding of rational individualism also frees us from extending this heretofore universalized set of values to others.

Having disestablished "human nature" as motive, various Marxist thinkers were nonetheless left with the vexing fact that people *do act* to produce their social forms. How can this agency be theorized in the absence of the old categories of "consciousness, mind, and individuality" (as Judith Farquhar names them in this volume)?

Marxist notions of agency have gone through many permutations. Among the most important for our purposes are those bearing on ideology. The Althusserian notion of "interpellation" argues that ideologies "call upon" or, in Stuart Hall's popularization, "hail" people to answer in specific ways, to speak up for themselves from a position that is partly localized in that process (Hall 1985). In this way people engage as social actors, become human, in the materiality of communication itself, a ceaseless process that begins at birth. For example, ideologies of fatherhood may empower the state to "subject" its populace to the necessity of patronyms. At another level these same ideologies may suggest that little boys go to baseball games in the company of older men. Or they may, quite significantly, dictate that children of both sexes be subjected to child-rearing practices that induce certain conflicting emotional identifications with mothers and fathers that are so identified within the ideology itself.

Because subjectifications are accomplished through the material forms of language and gesture, they are intimately connected to how bodies have been imagined and lived. And indeed it is here that "subjectification" takes us beyond "roles" that presume a unified, unchanging "self" behind and anchoring the masks of social role playing, once again staging the individual (one and indivisible) battle for authenticity against society.[12] Subjectification builds conflict, loss, and absence into the very constitution of the person, opening up possibilities for contradiction and thus resistance to overwhelming cultural pressures and beguilements (Smith 1988:31; Young 1990:124).

Focusing on subject positionalities instead of "individuals" takes into account that selves are processual and that they change over a lifetime of experiences; that one person can simultaneously occupy many "subject positions" (woman, female, mother, daughter, wife, reader, consumer);

and that these dynamics are constructed within an ensemble of social relations. Dynamic and not substantial, subjectivities are imposed, suggested, or pieced together; they are positioned within discursive fields (the term "subject position" indicates the relative stability of the locations). Subjectivity as a category enables scholars to grant human selves conditional, specific, historical unities rather than essential qualities that everywhere and in every epoch interact according to the same set of universal laws.

In the Chinese historical tradition within which we have been reading, one thing that stands out is the persistence of writing on *li,* or ritual (as *dianli,* ceremony, or *lijie,* etiquette), especially before the twentieth century.[13] In this writing we find a vast repository of information for the reproduction of subjects. Within the tangible forms of the language and gesture of *li,* subjectifications of people occur as they live and imagine their bodies. We are most interested in these bodies of *li* and the methodological question for us is how to describe them.

In "Theorizing Woman: *Funü, Guojia, Jiating,*" Tani Barlow understands behaviors—for instance, here *li*—through the notion of "protocols." A protocol is "neither a mere code, nor a map, nor a 'role.' It rests on a shifting foundation, the cosmic activity of yin/yang, yet it provides advice and counsel on achieving naturalized, normative, gendered relational subjects."

We find many protocols explored in this book. McMahon notes that women and men get to be that way through certain behaviors that strike him as counterintuitive. For instance, women successfully pass as men in spite of their bound feet. By enacting the protocols of masculinity, they produce a body of *li* that is marked as male. As McMahon points out, these subjectivities are marked by the familiar striations of gender inequity, imperial and familial hierarchy, and geographic imagination.

John Hay asks, Where is the body in Chinese painting? He does not find a body of *li,* he finds a body of *qi* (energy). His body of *qi* is hardly invisible but it is dispersed. Thus the question ultimately becomes how to represent *qi* in brushwork. Since this is accomplished with lines, clothing turns out to be more useful than flesh. Moreover, not just the human body is privileged as the living nexus of *qi.* So we are not surprised when he concludes that Chinese painters cherish rocks in the way that European painters prize nudes.

But Hay also notes that the *qi* patterning the organism of the body within the cosmos and the social scriptings of *li* are intimately connected as they configure the self: "The primary sense of self was given by the pattern of relationships that defined it within the ritual complex of society. . . . Without such connectedness there was no self, and the self might be seen as evolving in the relation between the organic microcosm of the body and the social macrocosm of humanity. The cyclical feedback continued in the relation between the social microcosm and universal macrocosm."

In "Multiplicity, Point of View, and Responsibility in Traditional Chinese Healing," Judith Farquhar finds in the "discursive practice of contemporary Chinese medicine . . . numerous subject positions, constant reminders that perceptions are contingent upon the point of view of the perceiver, and an organization of knowledge . . . as a specific and momentary *relation* unifying knower and known." She argues explicitly that the body of Chinese medicine today is not a discrete but a processual body. It offers a site of struggle against the claims of clinical "Western" epistemologies. Farquhar points up the complementarity of the protocols of relationship between teachers and pupils and the contingency of each doctor's diagnostic encounters.

The importance of time and timing in establishing subject positions through bodies of *li* in performance is also explored in many of the essays. For instance, Andrew Kipnis's contemporary ethnographic discussion of the *li* of bowing called *koutou* concentrates on how bowing creates subjects inside and against the socialist state. In Kipnis's formulation, "villagers act on [two interwoven processes of subject construction] when performing *koutou:* intimate and imagined." His intimate subjects form in concert with others to whom they are personally linked. Imagined subjects, on the other hand, are potential collaborations between persons of similar religion, class, and nationality.

Kipnis provides two examples of how timing works in the village. The case of "an old man (who) spends an hour talking with an old woman and then performs a full *koutou*" involves timing because it reconsolidates a personal relationship within the temporality of a community festival. In the second instance, "when members of the younger generation of an immediate family *koutou* to their elders, and the elders urge them to rise quickly," timing emerges as a means to artfully mend social relations.

James Hevia's "Sovereignty and Subject: Constituting Relations of Power in Qing Guest Ritual" presents views from both sides of the boundary differentiating China from others. All those connected to the 1793 British Macartney embassy to the Qianlong emperor's court proceeded with very different ideas of what bodies signified in public space. How do we know? The European agent who refused to *koutou* understood his body as a site of representation, a thing referring to an abstract principle outside itself. But Chinese "bodies do more than carry signs of inner qualities; they also seem capable, through their movements and the actions performed, of inscribing meaning in space, of physically configuring it. In so doing, they configure their own significance. Bodily action realizes broader social and political relations and accomplishes the asymmetries of an encompassing sovereignty."

As Barlow says, "protocols instruct": in this volume both post-Maoist campaigns for civility and imperially sponsored ritual handbooks prompt particular political subjectivities.

Anagnost makes clear how the protocol orientation works on people from the outside in. In her words, "rituals objectify subjects." She traces the accumulation of powers of subjectification in the hands of Communist Party deputies who decide which households shall be distinguish as meritorious. Anagnost argues that these powers are redeployed in propaganda campaigns aimed at accomplishing suturing—a process in which a subject recognizes self in a discourse of another—and legitimating party claims to correctly "represent" subjects.[14] The consequent "politicized body" is the subject of endless state narratives. Her chapter elaborates the construction of politicized subjects like party secretaries and the peasant Zhou Yixiang, who defends himself from complete discursive subsumption by the introduction of such vulgarities as accusing others of "only knowing how to fart." In the subsequent narrative attention paid to this intrusion of the vulgar body, Anagnost notes that the state's legitimacy and power are forced to depend upon what, in practice, it tries to reject.

Zito likewise notices what is in effect the suturing of a political subject in her discussion of the body of the Qianlong emperor in the eighteenth century. She employs the surface of imperial portraiture, calligraphic inscription, and the concept of "face" to support an argument that each plane opened a surface where organizing actions analogous to ritual sacrifice could be staged to produce order from chaos. She calls this process "centering." It produced, she argues, a subjectivity that she terms the yang subject position of the ruler and the father. These positions stand in a hierarchical relation to subject positions she terms yin, especially the ruled and sons. These pairs of yang/yin subjectivities incited imitation by encouraging everyone's desire to exemplify the yang.

What have we uncovered about "Chinese bodies" so far? For Hay and

Farquhar bodies were, and to some degree continue to be, constructed as shifting foci in multiple discourses that disperse the human within some wider domain, a context each scholar specifies concretely. The priority of inscription, subjections, and subjectivity occupies McMahon, Zito, and Anagnost. The importance of performance and temporal duration for the interpellation of subjects absorbs Hevia and Kipnis.

Shigehisa Kuriyama's chapter, "The Imagination of Winds and the Development of the Chinese Conception of the Body," hints at a more agonistic vision, which Tani Barlow and Lydia Liu further elaborate. He suggests that, at least in the earliest written records, the Chinese medicalized body was both present and fundamentally unstable. It acted as a site of contestation, making cosmic harmony palpable while also disrupting it. He demonstrates how *feng*—winds or breath—lay at the heart of classical Chinese analyses of embodiment. The same vital *feng* or breaths that blew through bodies, he points out, animated many other things: the weather, poetry, politics, education and power, space and time. Thus the body and the landscape prove indivisible, except that bodies were marked as sites of especially dangerous irregularity. Kuriyama is of course speaking of the Han body that first emerged in the dynasty (221 B.C.E to 220 C.E.) from which Chinese people derived their own cultural designation as the "Han people."

Han dynasty writers and artists provided a reservoir of models and metaphors out of which later Chinese social thinkers, critics, and historians reinvented and rejected elements of the past. Later intellectuals would eventually disavow this assemblage as "tradition" at a time when female bodies emerged as a particularly important staging ground of the colonial encounter (from the 1890s onward).

Barlow's chapter argues that in the late nineteenth and early twentieth centuries, the scientific understanding of human identity as essentialized, corporeal organism turned Chinese women into their anatomical and sexual bodies. Essential woman (*nuxing*) took western European femininity as its hidden referent and formed a center for a politics of personal liberation. Colonialist reformulations of gendered subjects, she argues, were eventually encompassed by the socialist state construct *funu*, a female subject in the ideological space of Chinese socialism.

Lydia Liu, in "The Female Body and Nationalist Discourse: Manchuria in Xiao Hong's *Field of Life and Death*," approaches the nationalist struggle from a different angle. As a literary critic reading the novelist Xiao Hong's text, she asks, "Has the notion of national identity ever been contested by alternative narratives of the self? If so, what historical possibilities arise as a result of their engagement and contention?" Liu answers her own question in the voices of Xiao Hong's women characters, who announce to male relatives, "We are not part of your nation. We have no home." By virtue of their bodiliness, the fact that they menstruate, bear babies, can be raped, and die of sexual disease, these women can turn against a masculinist national discourse.

In Conclusion

From Kuriyama's Han body as the surface through which the winds of change blow to Lydia Liu's exploration of Xiao Hong's sexed organic female body as the ambiguous, ambivalent, and embattled site of a war between feminism and nationalism, Chinese bodies that bear their own histories also bear histories of conflict and resistance. As for bodies, so for histories. By presenting so much temporal and situational diversity, the contributors to this volume have made it impossible to totalize China into a single, essential unity.

The essays thus contribute to an emerging picture of human selves as fractured multiplicities who nonetheless experience their competing, ideologically structured cultural worlds as *possibilities* and not merely necessities. This multiplicity opens possibilities for resistance in unlikely places: in a peasant's insistence on being included in the state's roster of meritorious households (Anagnost); in peasants' willingness to *koutou* (Kipnis); in the modern discourses of essential woman (*nüxing*) counterposed to state inscriptions of kin logic (Barlow); in cross-dressing eighteenth-century lovers (McMahon); in the collaboration between patient and doctor (Farquhar); in the yang body of power that gives the lie to an easy ideologically motivated symmetry of yin/yang (Zito).

These essays also reconfigure the objects of study. Driven by doubts caused by the gaps and difficulties we found in our documents and artifacts, we came to question our own common sense. We realized that we were seeing different subjects than we had expected to find. Eventually the contributors all came to question texts or categories received within naturalized genealogies of scholarship. The essays collected here contest views rooted in the specificity of European thought and material experience, in the Greco-Judeo-Christian tradition, in the powerful machinery of Cartesian rationality, in economies shaped by the processes of capitalism and the power of Western human sciences as a universal model through time and space. The different and specific history of the social formation now called the People's Republic of China leads us to conclude that fundamental questions of power, subjectivity, and bodiliness in Chinese contexts can and should be rethought. Undertaking this task also implies a critique of the universalizing, ideologizing function of "Western" social science, imposing against it explanation and retheorization of Chinese practices within their own historical genealogies.

A deeply rooted canonical verity of Western social science holds that representation is an eternal picture window for viewing nature. Once the habit of reading "representations" as signs of extradiscursive "objective realities" has been broken, anything from a medical or ritual text to a portrait of an emperor, clothing, erotic illustrations, or naturalistic descriptions of women's bodies can be taken as part of the repertoire by which Chinese people actively produce very particular social forms. Historians and anthropologists take up the metonymic traces of past activities. The metaphors we shape out of the traces of these forever-lost ventures look forward to the time when no historian of Europe or North America will again freely universalize "man" from uncontested ground.

Notes

The editors thank Donald Lowe, John Calagione, Judith Farquhar, and Ann Anagnost for their comments on various versions of this essay. Thanks also to Miriam Silverberg and to an anonymous reader for their fine editorial suggestions on the manuscript as a whole.

1. The common sense of those who modestly deny that they "are any good at all this theory stuff" is, as Catherine Belsey (1980) pointed out in regard to literary new criticism, itself an invisible theory. Antonio Gramsci (1977) held that the hegemonic formations that ensure smooth rule flourish on common sense. Hence the methodological and the political intersect at this most fundamental, and seemingly personal, level of thoughtful organization.

2. The best route into this critique lies through feminist writing, although the problem itself belongs as much to the realm of formal logic as to critical politics (Spivak 1987; Fuss 1989; Jardine 1985).

3. Editorial comments carried in the second volume of the *Bulletin* state that "part of the function of a radical medium is to dissolve some of the artificial distinctions which have fragmented our modern perception: distinctions between professional and universal concerns, history and the present, piety and politics" (Statement of Purpose, October 1969, 4).

4. In discussions of China, the interminable debates over the failures of capitalism—substitute individualism (Pye 1985) or feminism (Stacey 1983)—to

emerge in China as a kind of "natural" stage provide lush historiographic reminders of this fundamental problem. These debates have also had a reverse effect as some have rushed to assert that the Chinese *do* have X characteristic. For instance, Thomas Metzger (1977), contra Weber, produces anxiety-ridden neo-Confucian individuals; William T. DeBary (1983) has devoted decades to finding roots of liberal democracy in post-Sung Chinese philosophy; and Joseph Needham (1973) provided inspiration for innovative, even controversial, rereadings of many texts seeking Chinese science. While respecting the moral motivation of such scholarship, one can question a reading of the historical record that tends to reproduce the Chinese as resembling our own best selves.

5. Focusing on bodies is as ideologically motivated as any other research project. We note with concern that some recent work on the body privileges it as a ground of common sense from which to criticize theorizing in general. John O'Neill's *Five Bodies: The Human Shape of Modern Society* (1985) provides an example of how a romantic recuperation of physicality can lead to antifeminist stances as women are made to bear the brunt of a bodiliness seen as crucial to humanity (by a masculinist theorist).

6. In *Gender Trouble* (1990), Judith Butler provides a poststructuralist feminist investigation of the naturalizing common sense underlying much philosophical and psychoanalytical writing sexuality.

7. This is one of Michel Foucault's central insights into "modernity." See *The Birth of the Clinic* (1975), *Discipline and Punish* (1977), and *A History of Sexuality* (1978).

8. This approach has been applied most thoroughly on Chinese materials by the anthropologist P. Steven Sangren in his *History and Magical Power in a Chinese Community* (1987).

9. For a general discussion of the limitations and benefits of theories of subjectivity, see Smith 1988.

10. For a critical bibliography of Foucault, see Dreyfus and Rabinow 1982.

11. Thomas Laqueur, *Making Sex* (1990); Julia Epstein and Kristina Straub, *Bodyguards: The Cultural Politics of Gender Ambiguity* (1991); Norbert Elias, *The Civilizing Process*, vol. 1, *The History of Manners* (1978); Phillippe Ariès, *Centuries of Childhood: A Social History of Family Life* (1962), and his *Western Attitudes toward Death: From the Middle Ages to the Present* (1974); Philippe Ariès and Georges Duby, *A History of Private Life* (1987–91); Donald M. Lowe, *History of Bourgeois Perception* (1982); Dalia Judovitz, *Subjectivity and Representation in Descartes: The Origins of Modernity* (1988).

12. Thus subjectivity is not the same as individuality, although one of our Euro-American forms of subjectification is individualism (Smith 1988: 3–23). See also Dumont 1986.

13. By the 1920s the question of *li* is abstracted for critique as *lijiao,* or "ritual as theology."

14. A recent article (28 August 1992) in the English-language *China Daily* (often where new themes are sounded for the country's English-speaking intelligentsia) was headlined "Individuals Gain Importance in Drive toward Economic Reforms." But its discussion of the government's awarding bonuses and new cars to enterprising individuals indicates that the state still tries to reserve the right to recognize such merit. The article ends with, "It will be the government's responsibility to maintain a balanced relationship between the interests of individuals and communities so the country as a whole can remain both dynamic and stable."

References

Ariès, Philippe. 1962. *Centuries of childhood: A social history of family life*. New York: Vintage.

———. 1974. *Western Attitudes toward death: From the Middle Ages to the present*. Baltimore: Johns Hopkins University Press.

Ariès, Philippe, and Georges Duby, eds. 1987–91. *A history of private life*. 5 vols. Cambridge: Harvard University Press.

Baudrillard, Jean. 1989. *America*. London: Verso.

Belsey, Catherine. 1980. *Critical practice*. New York: Methuen.

Bourdieu, Pierre. 1977. *Outline of a theory of practice*. Cambridge: Cambridge University Press.

Bryson, Norman. 1983. *Vision and painting: The logic of the gaze*. New Haven: Yale University Press.

Butler, Judith. 1990. *Gender trouble: Feminism and the subversion of identity*. New York: Routledge.

Calagione, John, D. Francis, and N. Nugent, eds. 1992. *Workers' expressions: Beyond accommodation and resistance*. Albany: State University of New York Press.

Comaroff, Jean. 1985. *Body of power, spirit of resistance: The culture and history of a South African people*. Chicago: University of Chicago Press.

Coward, Rosalind. 1983. *Patriarchal precedents: Sexuality and social relations*. Boston: Routledge and Kegan Paul.

DeBary, W. T. 1983. *The liberal tradition in China*. New York: Columbia University Press.

Dreyfus, Hubert L., and Paul Rabinow. 1982. *Michel Foucault: Beyond structuralism and hermeneutics*. Chicago: University of Chicago Press.

Dumont, Louis. 1986. *Essays on individualism: Modern ideology in anthropological perspective*. Chicago: University of Chicago Press.

Elias, Norbert. 1978. *The civilizing process*. Vol. 1. *The history of manners*. New York: Urizen Books.

Epstein, Julia, and Kristina Straub. 1991. *Bodyguards: The cultural politics of gender ambiguity*. New York: Routledge.

Fairbank, John King, ed. 1968. *Chinese thought and institutions*. Phoenix ed. Chicago: University of Chicago Press.

Feher, Michel, ed. 1989. Introduction. In *Fragments for a history of the human body*. New York: Zone Books.

Foucault, Michel. 1975. *The birth of the clinic: An archaeology of medical perception.* New York: Vintage Books.

———. 1977. *Discipline and punish: The birth of the prison.* New York: Pantheon.

———. 1978. *A history of sexuality.* New York: Pantheon.

Fuss, Diane, 1989. *Essentially speaking: Feminism, nature and difference.* New York: Routledge.

Gramsci, Antonio. 1977. *Selections from political writings (1910–1920).* London: Lawrence and Wishart.

Hall, Stuart. 1985. Signification, representation, ideology: Althusser and the post-structuralist debates. *Critical Studies in Mass Communication* 2 (June).

———. 1990. *New times: The changing face of politics in the 1990s.* New York: Verso.

Harootunian, Harry. 1988. *Things seen and unseen: Discourse and ideology in Tokugawa nativism.* Chicago: University of Chicago Press.

hooks, bell. 1984. *From margin to center.* Boston: South End Press.

Jardine, Alice A. 1985. *Gynesis: Configurations of woman and modernity.* Ithaca: Cornell University Press.

Judovitz, Dalia. 1988. *Subjectivity and representation in Descartes: The origins of modernity.* Cambridge: Cambridge University Press.

Laqueur, Thomas. 1990. *Making sex: Body and gender from the Greeks to Freud.* Cambridge: Harvard University Press.

Levenson, Joseph. 1969. *Confucian China and its modern fate.* Berkeley and Los Angeles: University of California Press.

Levy, Marion J. 1968. *The family revolution in modern China.* New York: Atheneum. Originally published 1949.

Lowe, Donald M. 1982. *History of bourgeois perception.* Chicago: University of Chicago Press.

Macdonell, Diane. 1986. *Theories of discourse: An introduction.* Oxford: Basil Blackwell.

Metzger, Thomas. 1977. *Escape from predicament: Neo-Confucianism and China's evolving political culture.* New York: Columbia University Press.

Morris, Meaghan, and B. Patton, eds. 1979. *Michel Foucault: Power, truth and strategy.* Sydney: Feral Publications.

Munn, Nancy. 1986. *The fame of Gawa: A symbolic study of value transformation in a Massim (Papua New Guinea) society.* Cambridge: Cambridge University Press.

Needham, Joseph. 1973. *Chinese science and explorations of an ancient tradition.* Cambridge: MIT Press.

O'Neill, John. 1985. *Five bodies: The human shape of society.* Ithaca: Cornell University Press.

Pye, Lucian. 1985. *Asian power and politics.* Cambridge: Harvard University Press.

Rapp Reiter, Rayna, ed. 1975. *Toward an anthropology of women.* New York: Monthly Review Press.

Sangren, P. Steven. 1987. *History and magical power in a Chinese community.* Stanford: Stanford University Press.

San Juan, E., Jr. 1992. *Racial formations/critical transformations: Articulations of power in ethnic and racial studies in the United States.* London: Humanities Press.

Schram, Stuart. 1973. *Authority, participation and cultural change in China.* Cambridge: Cambridge University Press.

Smith, Arthur. 1894. *Chinese characteristics.* New York: Fleming H. Revell.

Smith, Paul. 1988. *Discerning the subject.* Saint Paul: University of Minnesota Press.

Spivak, Gayatri Chakravorty. 1987. *In other worlds: Essays in cultural politics.* New York: Methuen.

———. 1989. The political economy of women as seen by a literary critic. In *Coming to terms: Feminism, theory, politics,* ed. Elizabeth Weed. London: Routledge.

Stacey, Judith. 1983. *Patriarchy and socialist revolution in China.* Berkeley and Los Angeles: University of California Press

Stoller, Anne. 1992. Carnal knowledge and imperial power: Gender, race and morality in colonial Asia. In *Gender at the crossroads of knowledge,* ed. Micaela di Leonardo. Berkeley and Los Angeles: University of California Press.

Suleiman, Susan. 1986. *The female body in Western culture: Contemporary perspectives.* Cambridge: Harvard University Press.

Turner, Bryan S. 1984. *The body and society.* New York: Basil Blackwell.

Turner, Terence S. 1984. Dual opposition, hierarchy and value. In *Différences, valeur, hiérarchie: Textes offerts à Louis Dumont,* ed. Jean-Claude Galey. Paris: Ecole des Hautes Etudes en Sciences Sociales.

Wakeman, Frederic E. 1973. *History and will.* Berkeley and Los Angeles: University of California Press.

West, Cornel. 1991. *The ethical dimensions of Marxist thought.* New York: Monthly Review Press.

Williams, Raymond. 1977. *Marxism and literature.* Oxford: Oxford University Press.

Young, Robert. 1990. *White mythologies: Writing, history and the West.* New York: Routledge.

Dispersing
Bodies

1

The Imagination of Winds and the Development of the Chinese Conception of the Body

Shigehisa Kuriyama

There are few things in the world, the classics of Chinese medicine warn, more dangerous than wind. Winds cause chills and headaches, vomiting and cramps, dizziness and numbness, loss of speech. And that is just the beginning. "Wounded by wind" (*shangfeng*), one patient burns with fever; "struck by wind" (*zhongfeng*), another drops suddenly comatose. Winds cause madness. Winds kill. Although we today may not blame it for any illness, Chinese physicians saw wind's ravages in nearly all. "The hundred diseases," the *Huangdi neijing* declares, "arise from wind."

What should we make of this fear of wind? How did the Chinese imagine the breezes that drift *around* us wreaking violent, even fatal havoc deep *within* us? In short, what does wind consciousness in classical Chinese medicine mean? This is the puzzle I want to explore.[1]

There is an obvious answer: winds loomed large in the Chinese understanding of the body's afflictions because they loomed large in the Chinese understanding of the world. The imagination of winds reached beyond medicine and meteorology to encompass ideas of space and time, poetry and politics, geography and self But this answer only raises the further question, What exactly was the *relation* between the winds of the body and the winds of time, and poetry, and self?

My essay thus traces two developments: the evolution of the imagination of winds from Shang times (eighteenth through twelfth centuries B.C.E) up through the medical classics of the Han dynasty (206 B.C.E. to 220 C.E.), and the evolution of the Chinese conception of the body. My thesis is that these two processes were related. My aim is to elucidate how.

Wind and Sickness

Winds appear in the earliest inscriptions—the queries of Shang diviners. "Will the wind come from the east?" "Will the wind come the west?" "Will destructive winds arise?" "Will winds bring rain tomorrow?" Already in the thirteenth century B.C.E, the Chinese sought earnestly to know winds.

It is not hard to imagine why. Winds brought nourishing rains to crops or swept in bitter frost; they stirred up the storms that made hunting dangerous, or they stirred nothing and left sweltering drought. Weather ruled much of life in Shang China, and weather, then as now, was ultimately wind.

Yet examined more closely, Shang wind consciousness opens onto alien horizons. Winds were not mere movements of air, but were identified with divinities; sacrifices were performed to call them forth or seek their retreat. Furthermore, the direction from which they blew was crucial: wind blowing from the east came from the spirit Xi; southerly breezes derived from the spirit Yin; Yi raised the westerly gusts, and yet another spirit the fierce gales from the north. Neither abstract conventions imposed upon Euclidean space nor simply the compass defined by the sun's daily circuit, the cardinal directions represented radically individualized quarters of the cosmos, distinct spiritual abodes with distinct powers. Winds were the prime expression of a dynamic and divinely ordered space.[2]

Winds thus haunted the Shang imagination not as a vague meteorological phenomenon, but as east wind and south wind, west wind and north wind. The fascination of these winds, in turn, lay in their power to transform: the winds of the four quarters governed the myriad metamorphoses of the world. They shifted direction, and abundant game became sparse; shifted again, and deathly chill replaced warmth; shifted yet again, and a losing battle turned to victory. Sensitivity to this dynamic was critical to Shang kingship: "Should the king begin his tour in the south?" "Should the king hunt to the east?" Whether it was royal tours of the kingdom or the hunting of game, success in all enterprises required alignment with the dominant quarter of the moment. "Should the king begin his tour in the north?" "Will the king encounter great wind in the hunt today?" Hunting in the west when one should be hunting in the east was at best fruitless, at worst fatal.[3] On the other hand, of one king who presumably heeded the oracles we learn: "Today the king hunted in the east, and indeed captured three pigs."

To ponder winds, then, was to contemplate the mystery of change. This is the theme that runs throughout the history of the Chinese imagination of wind. Winds foreshadow change, cause change, exemplify change, are change. "Wind is movement" (*feng, dong ye*), says the *Guangya* dictionary. Winds presage the waxing and waning of imperial charisma (*Huainanzi, juan* 13) and warn of imminent wars and famines (Sima 1978, *juan* 27). When certain breezes blow insects begin to stir,[4] and horses and cows are seized by the urge to mate (*Zuozhuan*, Duke Xi year 4).

> When the spring wind arrives, tender rains fall, nurturing the myriad things. . . . Grasses and trees burst forth and flower, and birds and animals reproduce. All of this is accomplished, and yet we don't see the effort. Autumn wind brings frost, retreat, and decline. . . . The grasses and trees retrench to their roots, fish and turtles crowd back into the deep. All is reduced to formless desolation, and yet we don't see the effort. (*Huainanzi, juan* 1)

Invisible, yet ubiquitous in its influence, wind inspired profound wonder.

We can glimpse already the logic that will eventually link winds to medicine: on the one hand, the study of sickness is the study of altered states; on the other hand, "wind," as Han dynasty commentators would gloss it, "is alteration" (*feng, hua ye*). The often-repeated maxims of the *Huangdi neijing*—"Wind is the chief of the hundred diseases" (*Suwen, pian* 19, 42), and again, "Wind is the origin of the hundred diseases" (*Suwen, pian* 3, 60; *Lingshu, pian* 49)[5]—gave voice to the intuition that medicine's deepest secrets lay in the enigma of how one state of being became another.

But this is clearly just a start, for such broad thematic associations shed little light on the most intriguing aspect of wind consciousness in China, and that is its history. Wind was not always so intimately intertwined with medicine; it was only in late antiquity that it emerged as the preeminent cause of disease. We must do more, therefore, than gesture vaguely toward winds and sickness and the shared theme of change. We must explain how these notions became fused in classical medicine.

To some extent, Shang shamans already acknowledged wind's menace. They regularly performed sacrifices to appease the four winds, and one reason—though not the only or the main one—was that winds could make a person sick (Yan 1951:15). But the preponderance of Shang references to sickness identify it not with wind, but rather with the vengeance of unhappy ancestors (Miyashita 1959). Ancestral curse was the primary explanation for fevers, headaches, and other ailments. "Divining this tooth affliction. Should we hold a festival for Fuyi?" "Ringing in the ears. Should we sacrifice a hundred sheep to Ancestor Geng?" Shang diagnosis sought above all to identify the disgruntled ancestor—whether Fuyi, Ancestor Geng, or someone else; prevention and treatment centered on rituals to forestall or mollify ancestral dissatisfaction.

In the Spring and Autumn period, we encounter an alternative approach. In his exposition of the causes of disease, the physician Yi He (sixth century B.C.E.) makes no mention of ancestral curses. He speaks instead of six influences: the yin, the yang, wind, rain, obscurity, and brightness. These influences, he explains, are essential to the working of the world; but in excess, they make one sick. Excess yin results in cold diseases; excess yang, in fevers; excess wind produces diseases of the limbs; excess rain, abdominal diseases; excess darkness induces delusions; excess brightness, diseases of the mind (*Zuozhuan,* Duke Zhao year 1). Wind was thus one cause of disease—but only one of six, and not among the most important at that. Yi He's theory still leaves us far from the classical fixation on wind as "the origin of the hundred diseases."

Part of the explanation for the eventual marriage of wind and sickness, I shall argue, lies in a change in the conception of wind—a change in the imagination of change. Han dynasty physicians and Shang healers conceived of wind quite differently. But before we can appreciate the significance of this shift, we need to reflect upon another development critical to the rise of wind consciousness in classical etiology, and that is a shift in the conception of medicine itself.

Traditional formulations of the divide between archaic and classical healing have typically opposed Shang magic against Han rationality, primitive fears of supernatural spirits against the demystified analysis of natural forces. But I shall propose a less familiar contrast: classical medicine was, above all, a science of the body; archaic medicine was not.

In order to diagnose and treat fevers and toothaches, Shang healers had to know how to recognize and negotiate with spiteful ancestors. This was the knowledge that mattered most. The peculiarities of a patient's somatic condition shed no more light on a fever or a toothache than they would on a storm that destroyed one's crops, for the ancestors' venting of their ire on the body was incidental. They could as easily have inflicted drought or floods. On other occasions, the vengeance of the dead took other forms.

Classical medicine, by contrast, made the study of illness and the study of the body virtually inseparable. Han dynasty physicians sought the roots of all sickness within the patient. While fully recognizing the destructive powers of pathogens like wind and cold, they nonetheless maintained that these pathogens could harm only individuals with predisposing weaknesses, bodies that were already in some way vulnerable. Accompanying this conviction was an intensive analysis of somatic detail. The trained physician had to distinguish the hollow organs from the solid organs and master their complex interrelations with each other and with the skin, sinews, and other parts. Essential too was a grasp of over a hundred sites of acupuncture and moxibustion, some separated by only millimeters, but each inducing specific changes. And then there was the study of the most exquisite fluctuations: the nuances separating, say, a tense pulse and a hard pulse could spell the difference between recovery and death; the feel of the pulse when one pressed down with a light touch meant something totally separate from the pulse discerned when one pressed slightly harder. Such fine distinctions formed the core of the physician's science.

Our inclination today, I think, is to view the classical approach as the natural one. While our own conception of the body certainly differs from that advanced in the *Huangdi neijing*—while, indeed, the Chinese conception of the body strikes us as quite strange—still, we too identify medicine as a science of the body. But Shang healing reminds us that this equation is neither obvious nor necessary. At different times, in different societies, medicine concentrated on other things—on unhappy ancestors, for instance.

There are less exotic alternatives as well. Consider the influential Hippocratic treatise *Airs, Waters, Places*. It lists, as the first two subjects the Greek physicians should master, "the effect of each of the seasons of the year," and "the warm and cold winds, both those that are common to every country and those peculiar to a particular locality." Here knowledge of environmental and dietary influences mattered far more than insight into internal structures. Human dissection, in fact, and the notion of anatomy as the indispensable foundation of medicine, developed only after Hippocrates, in the Hellenistic period; and even then the idea was blasted by some who argued that anatomy had no practical relevance (Edelstein 1935).

This question thus seems basic: How and why did knowing medicine come to mean first and above all knowing the body? By what process did Chinese physicians come to seek the secrets of sickness in the fine-grained articulation of the body and its changes? That great dangers were associated with wind in classical etiology makes it clear that the process was more complex than a mere transfer of focus, from external menaces to internal disruptions. But it also suggests that we cannot understand this emergence of body consciousness without exploring the history of the imagination of wind.

Wind and Change

From Huang Ding's *Guankui jiyao* in Qing times back through Mao Yuanyi's *Wubei zhi* (*juan* 165) in the Ming dynasty, Zeng Gongliang's *Wujing zongyao houji* (*juan* 17) in the Song, and Li Chunfeng's *Yisi zhan* (*juan* 10) in the Tang, we can trace a long tradition of texts that teach how to divine winds (Sakade 1991:53). The first extant treatise on the subject appears in Yu Jicai's *Lingtai miyuan*, a Six Dynasties collection; but wind prognostication (*fengzhan*) was ancient. Wang Chong (C.E. 27: 100) describes how the direction and timing of winds were used in his day to predict individual prosperity and famine and the shifting moods of the people (Wang 1983, 1:650–51); and He Xiu, the great Han dynasty authority on the *Spring and Autumn Annals*, composed a commentary on a *fengzhan* treatise (Sakade 1991:102–3). Already in the sixth century B.C.E., the diviner Zi Shen observed an explosive gale and successfully foretold a great conflagration (*Zuozhuan*, Duke Zhao year 18). And well before Zi Shen, of course, there were the Shang wind oracles.

Scrutiny of winds was thus old and enduring; but the nature of this scrutiny changed decisively in late antiquity. Sima Qian (145–90 B.C.E.) reports that Han rulers prepared for the year ahead by having diviners observe the winds at the dawn of the new year:

> If wind comes from the south, there will be great drought. If it comes from the southwest, a minor drought. If it comes from the west, there will be military uprisings. If it comes from the north- west, the soybeans will ripen well, rains will be few, and armies will move. If it comes from the north, the harvest will be average. If comes from the northeast, there will an exceptional harvest. If it comes from the east, there will be floods. If it comes from the southeast, there will be epidemics among the people, and the har- vest will be bad. (Sima 1978, *juan* 27)

When we compare these predictions with Shang queries about wind, we immediately notice a shift in the aims of divination. Shang oracles asked *whether* winds would blow, and what might be done to call them forth or restrain them. But in Han prognostication the key question con- cerns the *meaning* of the winds that are already blowing.

A second shift is subtler. We saw before that a keen sense of direction framed Shang interest in wind. "Will wind blow from the east?" diviners asked. "Will wind blow from the west?" Sima Qian's account tells us that orientation remained paramount in Han wind consciousness. But there is a refinement: the diviner now distinguishes eight directions instead of just four. This is, it turns out, a broad and significant trend. From late antiquity onward, Chinese discourse on winds would almost always invoke eight winds, *bafeng*—those of the cardinal directions and the winds of the northeast, southeast, southwest, and northwest.

Texts begin to speak explicitly and often of eight winds, and to distinguish them with individual names, only near the end of the Warring States period. Even in Qin and early Han times, this nomenclature is still in flux (Major 1979). The *Zuozhuan* does, to be sure, speak of *bafeng* much earlier. But there the phrase has a musical, rather than a meteorological sense: it designates not eight winds but eight tunes or airs.[6] It is during the course of the Han dynasty that the eight wind names become fixed and the eightfold partition of directions emerges as the standard framework for divining wind's influence. Ming and Qing wind prognostication would still draw largely on the divinatory system established in the Han (Sakade 1991:69–72).

I emphasize the transition from four to eight winds because it entailed more than just a refinement in the divisions of space. The eight winds of the Han behaved differently than the four winds of the Shang. The cardinal winds spirits of the Shang served an almighty divinity, the heavenly emperor (*di*), whose whims determined all. "Will *di* send wind on this day?" "Should we sacrifice three dogs so that *di* will order forth wind?" Winds arose, changed directions, and died erratically, unpredictably, much like the feelings of a moody person. But when, in the late Warring States and Han periods, winds developed the new identity of *bafeng*, they also assumed a new role: they became the guardians of temporal order.

The eightfold partition of space anchored an eightfold division of time: eight forty-five-day segments made up the year, and each was governed by one of the eight winds. Beginning with the easterly breezes, which brought spring, winds made their way clockwise around the circle of directions—from east to southeast, to south, and so on to northeast, and finally back to east; and it was the orderliness of this succession that ensured the regularity of seasonal change. Recall the *Huainanzi* passage cited earlier: "When the spring wind arrives, tender rains fall, nurturing the myriad things. . . . Grasses and trees burst forth and flower, and birds and animals reproduce. . . . Autumn wind brings frost, retreat, and decline. . . . The grasses and trees retrench to their roots, fish and turtles crowd back into the deep." Effortlessly and irresistibly, each wind inspired distinctive transfigurations. The phrase "the eight winds and four seasons" (*bafeng sishi*) thus became a recurring formula in the writings of physicians and natural philosophers of late antiquity, summarizing the vision of a world changing rhythmically in cadence with the winds of the eight directions.[7]

One expression of this new vision was the divination technique of "the nine palaces and eight winds" (*jiugong bafeng*). The eight winds were the winds of the eight directions; the eight directions and the center formed the nine abodes of the deity Taiyi—the "nine palaces." Although the details of the technique need not concern us, we should note that a leading practitioner of nine-palace divination, the Han dynasty expert Zhao Da, derided those diviners who patiently tracked winds outside, even in harsh weather (Yamada 1980:206), for he himself derived his prognostications mostly in the comfort of his home. In 1977 archaeological excavations unearthed divining boards of the sort used by Zhao's school, and these boards help explain his condescension: rather than observing and interpreting each wind that happened to blow, Zhao's technique relied primarily on mathematical calculations (Yan 1978; Yin 1978). It presupposed a systematic, albeit complex, regularity in the timing and direction of winds.

Philosophers pounded hard on the human implications of cosmic regularity. Social and political life, they insisted, had to synchronize with the rhythm of the eight winds and four seasons. For each wind there were certain robes to be worn, particular foods to be eaten, fixed rituals to be performed, specific activities to be pursued. To the eight winds (*bafeng*) corresponded eight modes of government (*bazheng*). When the east wind blew, marking the onset of spring, those imprisoned for minor crimes were to be released. When the wind subsequently shifted to the southeast, messengers bearing gifts of silk cloth were to be sent to the various feudal lords (*Huainanzi, juan* 3). And what held true for social and political life naturally held all the more for individual welfare. In medicine, the doctrine of temporal alignment became the foundation of hygiene. The second chapter of the *Suwen,* "the great treatise on regulating the spirit in the four seasons," thus advised: "[In spring] the myriad things flourish, engendered by heaven and earth together. Going to sleep at nightfall, one should get up early and stride leisurely in the garden. Letting one's hair down and putting oneself at ease, one should give rise to one's ambitions. Engender and do not kill. Give and do not take away. Reward and do not punish. That is what is appropriate to the spirit of spring." For each season, actions and feelings in line with the spirit of cosmic change—this was the key to cultivating life.

What has all this to do with the turn toward the body in classical Chinese medicine? At first there may appear to be little connection. If anything, one might expect belief in the eight winds and four seasons to have hindered rather than promoted the formation of a distinct body consciousness. After all, the theory spotlighted sweeping cosmic transformations; it embedded human lives within universal change. And this embeddedness is what most scholars of Chinese medicine have hitherto emphasized. The founding insight of traditional Chinese medicine, we are always told, is the unity of human microcosm and heavenly macrocosm.

I do not dispute the importance of this idea. But this seamless unity expressed only an ideal—it did not correspond to actual experience. This much is obvious: if all lives were snugly synchronized with the seasonal spirit, and if the pace of cosmic transformation were unerringly steady, there would be no sickness. The very commonness of sickness made plain the unrealistic character of the premise. Somehow, cosmic time commonly went awry. The implications of this disparity between the real and the ideal, though less obvious, are absolutely crucial: the most significant consequence of the new sense of cosmic regularity expressed by "the eight winds and four seasons," I suggest, was a heightened awareness of irregularity. The more comprehensive and detailed the vision of cosmic harmony became, the more sharply disharmonies were cast in relief.

When the body emerged as the central concern of Chinese medicine, it did so as the locus of habitual irregularity, as an all too easily forming pocket of private rhythms. Human beings required elaborate instructions on what to do and feel at each time of year, precisely because what they did and felt easily diverged from, and even ran counter to, the spirit of the seasonal wind. Individuals emerged as individuals in their propensity to slip into idiosyncratic cadences. Bodies became the focus of medical attention in China as sites of temporal disjunction, ruptures in cosmic time.

Therefore classical medicine defined sickness and its degrees of severity not least by the fact and the degree of seasonal dislocation. To diagnose a patient, one had to situate the individual with respect to cosmic time. A winterlike pulse in spring was pathological; the same pulse in summer might indicate the approach of death. Similarly, anatomy too was framed by seasonal affiliations: the liver was the organ that should be most active in the spring, the lungs the most active in the fall. The same held as well for pathology: the southerly winds of summer normally attacked the heart; winter's northern blasts struck the kidneys (*Suwen, pian* 4). The articulations of the body articulated the possible loci of temporal rift.

In the last part of the chapter I shall return to this idea of temporal rift and relate it to what is perhaps the most distinctive characteristic of the Chinese conception of the body—the intense concern with the pores and (acupuncture) points at the surface of the skin. But we need now to look more carefully into the relation between winds and human life.

Wind and Self

When I speak of wind, I am translating the Chinese term *feng*. But *feng* had other senses as well. The earliest references to "the eight *feng*," as I noted above, use the term to speak of music. There are thus the "five notes, six pitch pipes, seven tones, eight airs [*bafeng*], and nine songs" (*Zuozhuan*, Duke Zhao year 20); and ritual dance is regulated by the eight tones and eight airs (*Zuozhuan*, Duke Yin year 5).[8] The opening section of the *Classic of Odes* (*Shijing*), the most ancient and often-cited collection of Chinese poetry, bears the title *Guofeng* (Airs of the states). *Feng,* wind, in other words, was also *feng,* song.

According to the Great Preface of the *Odes,* the link is again the theme of transformation. "By airs [*feng*] superiors transform their inferiors, and by airs inferiors satirize their superiors. The principal thing lies in their style, and reproof is cunningly insinuated. They can be spoken without giving offense, and yet hearing them suffices to make people circumspect in their behavior. This is why they are called *feng*."[9]

Songs are *feng* because they alter feelings and comportment. Indeed, the Preface goes on to explain, the *Guofeng* was first compiled because "the kingly way had declined, propriety and righteousness had been abandoned." Appropriate airs could save a state by influencing the attitudes and the behavior of its people.[10] Songs could transform mores.

But poetry did not just move the people; it also expressed their feelings and aspirations. According to legend, kings in ancient China periodically collected the songs of the various states in order to assess the people's reactions to the rule exercised by local princes. It was from this practice that the *Classic of Odes* supposedly arose.

We may have doubts, of course, about whether such song polling ever really occurred; but belief in the revelations of local airs was certainly widespread. The *Zuozhuan* recounts, for instance, how in 554 B.C.E. the musician Shi Kuang of Jin predicted this about the imminent attack from the southerly kingdom of Chu: "There is no danger. I sang a northern air [*beifeng*] and a southern air [*nanfeng*]. and the southern air was weaker, and gave the notes of many deaths. Chu will certainly fail" (*Zuozhuan*, Duke Xiang year 18). Similarly, when Prince Jizha of Wu visited Sun Muzi, he asked the latter's singers to perform songs from each of various states and interpreted what each song implied about the state. Whereas he found the songs of Zheng too refined and predicted that Zheng would be the first state to perish, he judged the songs of Qi to be "great airs" (*dafeng*) expressing a state with unfathomable possibilities (*Zuozhuan*, Duke Xiang year 29).[11] Jizha presumably diagnosed in the airs of the various states the feelings and disposition of the people who sang them. The *Lüshi chunqiu* would summarize, "One hears the songs [of a state] and knows its mood [*feng*]."[12]

We could also translate, "One hears the songs of a state and knows its customs [*feng*]."[13] The term *feng* encompassed not only the songs people sang, but also their mores. Airs, mood. and customs all expressed the dynamics of a locality. They were all aspects of local wind. The *fengsu* of a region designated the customs and life-style of its people; but the term bespoke the intuition that local psychology was inspired, quite literally, by the air the people breathed (*Hanshu, juan* 28).[14] The geography and environment of a region, its *fengtu* (literally, "wind and earth"), referred also to regional mores.

The point I am leading to is the commonality of the outer and inner realms—of nature and human nature. Against the traditional emphasis on cosmic harmony and unity, my interpretation of the development of Chinese medicine highlights the decisive role of disharmony and individuation. But I also want to stress that individuation in classical China had no ontological basis. The nature of the self that slipped out of phase was ultimately the same as that of the environment it emerged from: the self was itself windlike.

The philosopher Zhuangzi (fourth century B.C.E.) offers an eloquent expression of this blending of wind, breath, music, and self:

> The Great Clod [the earth] belches out breath and its name is wind. So long as it doesn't come forth, nothing happens. But when it does, then ten thousand hollows begin crying wildly. Can't you hear them, long drawn out? In the mountain forests that lash and sway, there are huge trees a thousand spans around with hollows and openings like noses, like mouths, like ears, like jugs, like cups, like rifts, like ruts. They roar like waves, whistle

like arrows, screech, gasp, cry, wail, moan, and howl, and those in the lead calling out yeee!, and those behind calling out yuuu! In a gentle breeze they answer faintly, but in a full gale the chorus is gigantic. And when the fierce wind has passed on, then all the hollows are empty again.

This symphony of wind rushing through the hollows Zhuangzi calls the "music of the earth"; but this music of the earth echoes "the music of heaven," which is nothing less than the music of the pneumatic self:

> Pleasure and anger, sorrow and joy, anxiety and regret, fickleness and fear, impulsiveness and extravagance, indulgence and lewdness, come to us like music from the hollows or like mushrooms from damp. Day and night they alternate within us but we don't know where they come from. . . .
>
> Without them [the feelings mentioned above] there would not be I. And without me who will experience them? They are right near by. But we don't know who causes them. (Watson 1968:36–37)

There is, Zhuangzi assumes, an I, a self. But it is a self in which thoughts and feelings mysteriously arise, of themselves, like the winds of the earth. Anchored in neither reason nor volition, the self is the site of moods and impulses whose origins are unfathomable. Individuals, in this view, are not distinct essences—Orphic souls, say, cast into the darkness of matter—or immaterial minds set against material bodies. Rather, individuation simply mirrors the plurality and unpredictability of winds. Different localities have different airs, individuals have personal breaths, and—we shall learn shortly—individualized orifices on the body's surface mediate the confluence of cosmic, local, and personal winds.

Wind and *Qi*

I have not spoken yet of *qi* (energy, vital breath, pneuma) and its expressions in yin and yang and the five phases (*wuxing*)—the central concepts in most accounts of Chinese medical theory. If my previous discussion of cosmic rhythms seemed somewhat unfamiliar, it is no doubt because I concentrated on the eight winds rather than on the well-known dialectic of yin and yang *qi*. But as numerous scholars have pointed out, the notion of wind was the conceptual ancestor of *qi* (Hiraoka 1968:48; Akatsuka 1977:442). Thus late Warring States and Han texts frequently still spoke of *feng* and *qi* interchangeably. Wang Chong in fact glosses wind as *qi* (Wang 1983, 1:220);[15] and conversely, the *Lingshu* explains, "What is meant by proper *qi* [*zhengqi*] is proper wind [*zhengfeng*]" (*Lingshu, pian* 75).[16]

Nonetheless, differences remained. Despite their genetic connection and semantic overlap, wind and *qi* never became identical. Although the classical medical texts spoke far more frequently of *qi* than of wind, and spoke of *qi* in many contexts where earlier texts had spoken of winds, and though phrases such as spring *qi* and autumn *qi* gradually dispatched talk of spring winds and autumn winds, *qi* never entirely replaced wind.

This brings us to the heart of the matter: if *qi*, as wind's avatar, subsumed so much of wind's meaning, why did winds persist? And why did the *Huangdi neijing* cite wind, not *qi*, as "the chief of all diseases"?

I suggest that the answer lies in an ambivalence in the classical conception of wind. On the one hand, we have noted how winds came to embody the regularity of nature. Blowing one after another, the winds of the eight directions drove the year through the four seasons. But the classical analysis of illness also introduced some new concepts: we now hear of "proper winds" (*zhengfeng*) and "evil winds" (*xiefeng*), "full winds" (*shifeng*) and "empty winds" (*xufeng*). The distinctions here turned not on qualities of air, but on the timing and direction of the winds. Proper or full winds blew from the proper direction at the proper time; for example, easterly winds in spring. They blew, in other words, from the "palace" (recall the theory of the "nine palaces and eight winds") made full by the presence of the divinity Taiyi. Evil or empty winds—cold northerly blasts in summer, for instance—arose inopportunely, from a palace where Taiyi was absent.[17] Proper winds could, if they became excessively violent, make one sick; but the illnesses they induced were usually minor, and people recovered quickly, often even without treatment (*Lingshu, pian* 66). It was especially the "evil winds"—the winds that disrupted the regularity of the cosmos—that ravaged the body and destroyed the mind.

Although the timely, "proper" winds ordering the four seasons were gradually subsumed into the notion of *qi*, the notion of wind survived and flourished in classical medicine especially in the form of disorderly, "empty" winds. I am speaking, of course, of trends and not neat dichotomies. Winds could still represent regular change (e.g., "the eight winds and four seasons"), and physicians could speak of evil *qi* (*xieqi*) as well an evil wind. But understood *as* a trend, this analysis captures two characteristic features of classical medicine: on the one hand, the general drift in Han discourse from wind to *qi* mirrored the ascendency of the vision of cosmic regularity; on the other hand, the persistence of winds in discourse on disease reflected the acute awareness that this regularity was just an ideal.

The theory of *qi*, articulated through the schemes of yin and yang and the five phases, presented nature as a system of predictable transformations. But instead of committing Chinese physicians to a universe of inexorable regularity, this ideal of orderly change allowed them to probe the ever-present edge of chaos. This was the fascination of winds: they embodied contingency and chance, the obstinate halo of uncertainty that made all science only approximate.[18] Evil winds arose unexpectedly, spontaneously, irregularly; they made abrupt, harsh shifts. Whence the association of winds with the most dramatic illnesses—stroke, epilepsy, madness. More generally, it was wind's protean volatility, its lack of regularity (*wuchang*), that led physicians to conclude, "Wind is the chief of all diseases."

I argued earlier that the notion of the body crystallized in Chinese medicine as a site of independent rhythms: the ideal of a universe changing at a regular pace sharpened the consciousness of irregular selves. I am now making a parallel argument for the winds of classical medicine: they represented the fringe of disorder brought into relief by the orderliness of yin and yang *qi*. The winds that lay at "the origin of all diseases" were the empty winds that blew at the wrong time, from the wrong direction—the warm southerly breeze in winter, say, luring flowers into premature blossoming.

Recognizing this split between proper and evil winds allows us to clarify a peculiar ambivalence in classical notions of hygiene. For alongside the rhetoric of harmonization, which taught that health consisted in blending oneself smoothly into the flow of cosmic transformation, the medical classics also evince a contrary and equally marked tendency toward somatic isolation. We can now see why. For insofar as one conceived the world as orderly and harmonious—insofar, that is, as one focused on the eight winds and four seasons—then the tendency of the self toward temporal uncoupling represented a vulnerability, a propensity toward sickness. But if one considered the menace of untimely winds, the wild disorder that could suddenly invade a person, then the relative independence of the body became an advantage to be nurtured rather than an obstacle to be overcome.

We must understand the utter seriousness with which Chinese physicians monitored the body's orifices in light of this ambiguity. For the skin divided inner breaths from outer winds. It was the skin that the hundred diseases first attacked, and it was through its pores that they penetrated the body (*Suwen, pian* 56, 63; *Lingshu, pian* 66). One had to be especially careful, therefore, to avoid winds after exertion, when sweat was pouring out and the pores were wide open. This was how so many catastrophic diseases arose—from winds streaming in through loose, unguarded pores (*Suwen, pian* 35). Conversely, if the flesh and sinews were firm and the pores were tight, then even great gales could do little harm (*Suwen, pian* 3). Tight pores at once signified and guaranteed vitality, demarcating and safeguarding the inner self from outer chaos (*Suwen, pian* 3, 26; *Lingshu, pian* 46, 50, 79).

Of the myriad orifices puncturing the skin—medieval texts would count 84,000 pores—none were more intensely investigated than the points of acupuncture. These were known as *xue* (literally, "holes" or "caverns"), a term that seems strange until one remembers the myths tracing the origins of winds to the earth's hollows and openings.[19] According to one Chinese legend, winds arose when the *feng* bird emerged from the wind cavern (*fengxue*) in which it lived and subsided when it returned to the cavern (*Huainanzi, juan* 6). In another version, the four directions were staked out by four caverns from which blew the four cardinal winds.[20] Underlying the term *xue*, in other words, was a conception of the body in which winds streamed in and out of strategic orifices in the skin, just as winds streamed in and out of the hollows and caverns of the earth.[21] And from this followed their pivotal importance for the body and its afflictions. As the passageways of wind, these *xue* mediated between personal breath and cosmic breath. They represented the microstructure of the human connection to universal time. More than any other feature of Chinese medicine, the extraordinary attention devoted to the skin and its orifices mirrored the interdependence between the Chinese conception of the body and the imagination of winds.[22]

The decisive development in classical medicine, therefore, was not so much a shift in emphasis from external demons and other pathogens to internal imbalances and depletions as the crystallization of this very opposition of outer and inner, the emergence of a distinct consciousness of a body related to, but separate from, the world around it. There is a temptation, when we identify wind with change and time, to treat wind as simply a poetic trope. But the earnest vigilance with which Chinese physicians monitored the skin and pores reminds us that more was involved. The imagination of wind sprang from a concrete *experience* of oriented space and local place, a directly felt sense of seasonal drift and human moods. It bespoke an embodied apprehension of an ever shifting self in an ever changing universe. Personal breath could harmonize with cosmic breath, and habitually the two might be reasonably in phase. But the character of all winds, inner or outer, was that they always retained some chaotic contingency, the possibility of suddenly blowing in new and unexpected directions.

Notes

1. For insightful analyses of the relation between ideas of wind and the formation of the *Huangdi neijing,* see Yamada 1980 and Unschuld 1982. In his survey of the pathology of winds, Ishida (1991) extends the discussion beyond the classical period.

2. It was Hu Houxuan (1944) who initially drew attention to ancient Chinese wind names and the wind spirits governing the four directions. Since then, the nature of Shang wind conceptions, has been elucidated by such scholars as Yan Yiping (1957), Ding Shan (1988), Kaizuka Shigeki (1971), and Akatsuka Kiyoshi (1977).

3. For inscriptional references to winds and hunting, see Akatsuka (1977: 425–27).

4. The Han dynasty dictionary *Shuowen* suggests that the insect radical in the character for wind derives from the fact that insects stir when the wind blows.

5. The claim is hyperbolic; traditional Chinese medicine recognized many sources of disease. Still, wind occupied a unique and privileged place in classical etiology; no other pathogen had wind's power or scope. Moreover, the understanding of how one succumbed to wind became the paradigm for understanding how one succumbed to disease in general.

6. For more on the connection between wind and music, see below.

7. For early attempts to relate the eight directions and the eight partitions of the year, see the *Huainanzi, juan* 3 and 4.

8. See also *Zuozhuan,* Duke Xiang year 29: "The five sounds are harmonized, and the eight airs equally [blended]."

9. The association of winds, politics, and the power of indirect persuasion also appears in the Confucian *Analects* 12.19: Ji Kang asked Confucius about government, saying, 'What would you think if, in order to move closer to those who possess the Way, I were to kill those who did not follow the Way?' Confucius answered, 'In administering your government, what need is there for you to kill? Just desire good yourself and the common people will be good. The gentleman's virtue is like the wind; the virtue of the common people is like grass. The wind sweeps over the grass, and the grass is sure to bend.'"

10. The Lesser Preface thus observes, "Airs [*feng*] originate as the means by which the empire is transformed [*feng*] and the relations between husband and wife are regulated.

11. Confucius also objected to the lewd songs of Zheng and worried about its pernicious effects on people elsewhere (*Analects* 15.10).

12. Lin, *Lüshi chunqiu, juan* 6, *pian* 3. The passage continues: "By examining this *feng* one knows the will [*zhi*] [of the people], and by scrutinizing this will, one knows their virtue—whether it is rising or declining, whether [the people are] wise or foolish, sage or petty. All of these manifest themselves in music and cannot be hidden."

13. Sir John Davis thus translates *Guofeng* as "Manners of the different states" (cited in Legge 1985, 4:2).

14. *Pian* 12 of the *Suwen* also discusses the impact of local geography on health. We are not far from Hippocrates' *Airs, Waters, Places,* or for that matter, from the environmentalism of a Jean Bodin or a Montesquieu. For a survey of Western thinking on nature and human nature, see Glacken 1967.

15. See also the *Huainanzi, juan* 7: "Blood and *qi* are rain and wind."

16. Similarly, in his commentary on the *Taisu*, Yang Shangshan (1983:549) explains that "Wind and *qi* are one. When it is slow and relaxed we call it *qi;* when it is rapid and swift we call it wind."

17. For details of the theory of the nine palaces and eight winds as it applied to medicine, see Ishida 1991.

18. The relation between wind's radical unpredictability and the limits of medical knowledge is expressed in an interesting way by Plato: "As for what is known as the art of medicine, it also is, of course, a form of defense against the ravages committed on the living organism by the seasons with their untimely cold and heat and the like. But none of their devices can bestow reputation for the truest wisdom; they are at sea on an ocean of fanciful conjecture, without reduction to rule. We may also give the name of defender to sea captains and their crews, but I would have no one encourage our hopes by the proclamation that any of them is wise. None of them can *know* of the fury or kindness of the winds, and that is the knowledge coveted by every navigator" (*Epinomis* 976a–b).

Just as the sea captain attempts to defend his ship against shifting winds, so the doctor seeks to defend the body against the ravages of untimely climate. The analogy is not random. In the *Statesman* (299b), Plato again refers to seamanship and medicine together, equating the former with inquiry into nautical practice and the latter with inquiry into "winds and temperatures." The first concern of the physician, in other words, is with weather and climate; but weather and climate hinge on inscrutable winds. This dependence on winds, common to both physicians and seafarers, results in a shared consequence: it establishes an irreducible core of contingency in medicine and navigation. It prevents both from becoming true sciences. For winds cannot be truly known.

19. This association of wind and *xue* underlies Zhuangzi's earlier cited remarks on the "music of the earth." Other texts that touch on this connection include the *Huainanzi* (*juan* 6) and Zhang Hua's *Bowu zhi* (*juan* 8).

20. Other myths link winds to strategically situated "gates," whence the numerous acupuncture points with the character *men* (gate) attached to them.

21. This suggests a close connection between the science of medicine, with its focus on the dynamics of points on the body, and the Chinese science of geomancy, with its focus on the dynamics of sites on the earth. For geomancy was *feng shui* (literally, the science of "wind and water"), and geomantic sites, like acupuncture points, were called *xue*.

22. I should stress that I present this as a partial account of how acupuncture points were conceptualized, not as an explanation for the *origins* of acupuncture. For that, I think, we must look into the histories of bloodletting and moxibustion. For some initial steps toward a theory of origins, see Epler 1980 and Yamada 1985.

References

Primary Sources

Hanshu. 1981. 5 vols. Taipei: Dingwen Shuju.
Huainanzi. 1976. Taipei: Zhonghua Shuju.
Legge, James. 1985. *The Chinese classics*. Vol. 4. *The She king, or The book of poetry*. Taipei: Southern Materials Center.
Lingshu jing. 1977. Taipei: Zhonghua Shuju.
Lin Pinshi. 1990. *Lushi chunqiu jinzhu jinshi*. 2 vols. Taipei: Shangwu Inshuguan.
Sima Qian. 1978. *Shiji*. Hong Kong: Zhonghua Shuju.
Suwen [*Suwen Wang Bing zhu*]. 1976. 2 vols. Taipei: Zhonghua Shuju.
Wang Chong. 1983. *Lunheng jiaoshi*. 2 vols. Taipei: Taiwan Shangwu Inshuguan.
Watson, Burton, trans. 1968. *The complete works of Chuang Tzu*. New York: Columbia University Press.
Yang Shangshan. 1983. *Huangdi neijing Taisu*. Beijing: Renmin Weisheng Chubanshe.
Zhuangzi. 1979. Taipei: Zhonghua Shuju.
Zuozhuan [*Chunqiu zuozhuan zhengyi*]. 1979. 4 vols. Taipei: Zhonghua Shuju.

Secondary Sources

Akatsuka Kiyoshi. 1977. Kaze to miko. In *Chûgoku kodai no shûkyô to bunka*, 415–42. Tokyo: Kadokawa Shoten.
Ding Shan. 1988. Sifang zhi shen yu fengshen. In *Zhongguo gudai zongjiao yu shenhua kao*, 78–95. Shanghai Wenyi Chubanshe.
Edelstein, Ludwig. 1935. The development of Greek anatomy. *Bulletin of the History of Medicine* 3:235–48.

Epler, D. C. 1980. Bloodletting in early Chinese medicine and its relation to the origin of acupuncture. *Bulletin of the History of Medicine* 54: 337–67.

Glacken, Clarence. 1967. *Traces on the Rhodian shore: Nature and culture in Western thought from ancient times to the end of the eighteenth century*. Berkeley and Los Angeles: University of California Press.

Hiraoka Teikichi. 1968. *Enanji ni arawareta ki no kenkyû*. Tokyo: Risôsha.

Hu Houxuan. 1944. Jiaguwen sifang fengming kaozheng. In his *Jiaguxue Shangshi luncong*, 2: 1–6. Chengdu: Chilu University.

Ishida Hidemi. 1991. Kaze no byôinron to chûgoku dentô igaku shisô no keisei. *Shisô* 799: 105–24.

Kaizuka Shigeki. 1971. Kaze no kami no hakken. In *Chûgoku no shinwa*, 76–109. Tokyo: Chikuma Shobô.

Major, John. 1979. Notes on the nomenclature of winds and directions. *T'oung Pao* 65: 66–80.

Miyashita Saburô. 1959. Chûgoku kodai no shippeikan to ryôhô. *Tôhô Gakuhô* 30: 227–52.

Sakade Yoshinobu. 1991. Kaze no kannen to kaze uranai. In *Chûgoku kodai no sempô: Gijutsu to jujutsu no shûhen*, 45: 127. Tokyo: Kembun Shuppan.

Unschuld, Paul. 1982. Der Wind als Ursache des Krankseins: Einige Gedanken zu Yamada Keijis Analyse der *Shao-shih* Texte des *Huang-ti nei-ching*. *T'oung-Pao* 68: 91–131.

Yamada Keiji. 1980. Kyûkyû happû setsu to shôshiha no tachiba. *Tôhô Gakuhô* 52: 199–: 242.

———. 1985. Shinkyû to tôeki no kigen. In *Shin hakken chûgoku kagakushi shiryô no kenkyû: Ronkô hen*, ed. Yamada Keiji, 3–122. Kyoto: Kyoto Daigaku Jimbun Kagaku Kenkyûsho.

Yan Dunjie. 1978. Guanyu Xihan chuqide shipan he zhanpan. *Kaogu*, 334–37.

Yan Yiping. 1951. Zhongguo yixue zhi qiyuan kaolue. *Dalu Zazhi* 2, no. 8: 20–22; 2, no. 9: 14–17

———. 1957. Puci sifang shinyi. *Dalu Zazhi* 15: 1–7.

Yin Tiaofei. 1978. Xihan Ruinhou mu chutude zhanpan he tianwen yiqi. *Kaogu*, 338–43.

2

The Body Invisible in Chinese Art?

John Hay

Throughout the first millennium of Chinese pictorial art, figural painting and sculpture were dominant. Even to the present such subject matter
has maintained a lively if erratic importance, and the models and methods
of the first millennium have remained visibly alive within later praxis.

From the life-size terra-cotta army found in the mausoleum of the first
emperor of Qin (d. 210 B.C.) to the luxuriatingly beautiful court ladies of
ninth-century painting in the Tang dynasty, human figures were indeed
the commonest subject matter of painters and sculptors. In the tenth century the subject matter of *shanshui,* "mountains-and-waters," began to
dominate. Not only are most surviving examples of representational art
from the Tang and earlier closely connected with human figures, but most
art criticism of that same period assumes such figuration as its principal
field. Even the normative explanations in the catalog of the art collection
of the emperor Huizong (r. 1101–26) rank "Daoist and Buddhist" subjects first, "figure [*renwu*]" subjects second, architecture third, "barbarian
tribes" fourth, "dragons and fishes" fifth, and *shanshui* sixth out of ten
(animals, flowers and birds, ink bamboo, vegetables and fruit remaining).[1]

Since there are no people or animals without bodies, representations
of them must deal with this in some way. What do we mean by "bodies"?
In the Western cultural sphere in the twentieth century—the place of almost all the writing of art history—the human body seems inseparable
from the phenomenon of the nude. The nude seems to be the neutral
starting point for our bodily perceptions, explicitly in the artist's studio and
more confusedly but no less essentially outside it. In East Asia, however,
there are very few examples and no obvious tradition of representing the
nude. What does this mean? Why does the body seem to be almost invisible in a figurative tradition that flourished for over two thousand years?

Chinese painters from the Tang dynasty onward often employed techniques of traditional *bimo,* "brush and ink," that gave tangible substance

to shape and surface. In the seventeenth century, influenced by Western art, portraitists modeled the face in particular with effects of falling light and cast shadows.[2] But no Chinese painter ever produced a "nude" in the sense of that cluster of culturally defined anatomical shapes and surfaces so prominent in Western art. However much one enlarges the field, this remains essentially true throughout the history of Chinese art. Some potential exceptions will be mentioned below, but I may safely state that the reasons lay outside the art itself. To summarize and generalize rather broadly, such bodies were not represented in art because they did not exist in the culture. And to extend the terminology in keeping with present fashion, the culture itself did not so represent its own body.

This very notion of the lack of the nude, however, locates the question itself entirely within the Western tradition. In China and Japan the question does not even exist until imported from beyond their borders. It is true that it was introduced in some form by the art of Buddhism, especially between the seventh and ninth centuries A.D. As cultural history, this passage is extremely hard to delineate, partly because it had already lost most of its meaning—whatever that may have been—by the Song dynasty. The issue did not really materialize in its aggressively disguised form, that is, as a question about *Asian* cultures, until the nineteenth century, as part of the Occident's creation of an "Oriental" other. Beyond even the special case of "the nude," a comparison between the pictorial arts of East Asia and the West might suggest a more general absence of the body. But here again we need to place "body" in quotation marks, as the absence of a particular kind of body. The missing body is objectified and "solid": the nude body that reveals itself through the garments and in accordance with the laws of physics, if the artist is both technically and conceptually competent. The comparison, indeed, has often been made in terms of "competence."

There is something peculiarly Western about the current obsession in Western cultural studies with "the body." Beyond those agendas set essentially by the power structure of Western intellectual inquiry, would one find this as the topic of so many conferences and studies in so many fields? I very much doubt it. Even the enterprise in which this essay so happily participates, with its wish to reveal more of the structures of Japanese and Chinese cultural history, is a peculiarly Western enterprise, an effort to remove the obscuring clothes of culturalized perception and misperception, thereby revealing the Chinese and Japanese bodies in some more realistically denuded state.

The criteria of visibility and clarity, however, are also at issue here. Seeing as a mode of knowledge and understanding has been predominantly formulated within the science of optics, and the clarity long associated with it implies particular notions of objectivity. Chinese art was produced and seen within a very different set of frames. Within this art, the human body was far from invisible. It was dispersed through metaphors locating it in the natural world by transformational resonance and brushwork that embodied the cosmic-human reality of *qi,* or energy.

The "representation" of the body is a process of construction, not mimesis. There was no more a lack of naked bodies in China than there was a public parading of them in Western cultures. It seems likely that the male nude *entered* Western art through Greek social practice. But this was not the case for the female nude. Unlike men, women did not appear naked in public, and except for the depiction of prostitutes in archaic vase painting, the female nude does not appear even in Greek art until the late fourth century B.C. Subsequent to this instance, social practice does not seem to have been the direct source of nude representation for either male or female. The body as it existed in a cultural sense was a different body. As Anne Hollander has perceptively remarked, even the Western tradition of the nude cannot, in fact, exist as though beyond clothes: "Above all, Western representational art had to invent a nudity that allowed for a sense of *clothes*" (Hollander 1975:84). Nudity is a form of clothing, and conversely, "Clothes have the same relation to the body that language has to truth or pure thought. That is they are somehow a necessary form that bodily truth must take in order to be told and understood at all" (447).

When trying to understand the human figure in Chinese art in contrast to the nude in Western art, we must also bear in mind the naked body's complex and inextricable dialectic with clothing. Although there was no nude in China, there was certainly nakedness. Common to both Western and Chinese traditions, and perhaps all others, is the notion that social identity and even individual qualities of person could not be manifested without clothes. Nakedness, it could be said, obscures rather than reveals; and garments define rather than hide. Hence, in any figurative art that has a social function we tend to find an overiding importance of dress in the art of both traditions. But what happens to the Chinese body in this circumstance? Does the absence of the nude lose its significance even as a spur for inquiry? This relates not only to contrasting social customs, different through these may have been, but more generally to the ontology of a dispersed rather than an objective body.

1

We may accept as a set of multiple frames for our questions the common ground of physical human presence and function, experienced from within both ourselves and others, defined by our own perceptions and incorporating the mirror of the other's eyes, in both solitary and collective contexts. These phenomenological frames must be activated, given meaning, through cultural construction. The self-reflexive definition in a material medium of these framed perceptions is the arena of "the body." By self-reflexive, I mean that the modes of sensory perception are themselves incorporated by necessity into the definition. Self-awareness is always present at some level. It is fair to call this process "representation," since it often is. There is a sensed but entirely unarticulated presence. The accompanying articulation into meaning is a re-presentation in the cultural domain, whereby the individual acquires social substance and identity.

Such representation is always executed in a particular way. It has a style. Whenever human presences and functions are the subject matter of figurative art, the representation is doubled. At one level style is substance, the cultural construction in which the art participates or to which it refers. At another level the work of art (from dance to architecture and beyond) remakes the representation, reiterates it, and maybe comments on it. The style of this redoubled representation may simply participate in that of its context/referent, or it may significantly differ—and it may choose to use that difference as a comment.

The "body," to use that term now as a shorthand reference to a system of framed experiences, is of particular interest in the domain of artistic practice, and vice versa, because it has been a necessary site in all varieties of this practice. Hence questions of definition tend to inevitable circularity; particular artistic practice will inevitably involve a culturally specific perception of "body."

The presence or absence of the body, in art as in other cultural practices, has been most generally seen as a matter of objective knowledge and representation. But as we now acknowledge, the body is a site of multiple discourses, a veritable fleshly tower of Babel. Even the most conservative modern studies admit sexuality, for example, as an inseparable factor, thus opening the way for the inclusion of medical, moral, and aesthetic discursive influence upon the body.[3] To the Western eye Chinese art has often seemed almost empty of the sexual charge that has activated so much Western art. A sinologist has remarked, "Chinese pictures of the human body, clothed or semi-clothed (in a furtive pornography [of specifically erotic pictures]), are—to Western eyes—meager, schematic and inadequate" (Elvin 1989:267). But the allure exercised by female beauty upon the male and the construction of women in that light is no less prominent a theme in Chinese literature than it is in most other literatures. In a comparison where it is difficult to find the required symmetries, I will use this aspect of sexuality as a node in the argument.

Desire between the sexes, generally as viewed by the male, is functionally a theme and formally a group of genres with a long history in Chinese literature. In light of the strongly literary affiliations of Chinese pictorial art, it would be very surprising if this theme did not enter the latter. I will turn to two texts as intersections of problems of body, sexuality, and representation. Each was written in a period when this set of issues was becoming especially lively; each came to be seen as a locus classicus; and each was illustrated soon after being written. The first, written in A.D. 222 by the highly regarded poet Cao Zhi (A.D. 129–232), is a romantic poetic narrative about a refined gentleman returning home from a visit to the capital. In this *Luoshen fu,* "The Nymph of the Luo River," a gentleman and his party, after the long and tiring first day of travel, are making camp by the Luo River when he suddenly sees a woman. He asks:

> Who could she be, so fair a lady in so desolate a place? "They say," said his charioteer, "that there is a goddess of this river whose name is the Lady Fu. Perhaps it is she whom my lord sees. But tell me first what face and form are hers, and I will tell you if she is the goddess or no." Then I said, "She moves lightly as a bird on the wing; delicately as the rain-elves at their play; she is more radiant than the sun flowers of autumn, more verdurous than the pine-woods of the spring. Dimly I see her, like a light cloud that lies across the moon; fitfully as swirls a snow-wreath in the straying wind. Now far away, she glimmers like sunshine peeping through the morning mist. Now near, she glistens like a young lotus, a bud new-risen above the waters of the lake. . . . Her shoulders are as chiselled statuary; her waist is like a bundle of silk. Her body is anointed not with perfumes, nor is her face dabbed with powder. The coils of her hair are like cloud-heaps stacked in the air. Her long eyebrows join their slim curves." . . . I was enamoured of her beauty; my heart was shaking and would not rest. There was no matchmaker to lead us to our joy; so to the little waves of the stream I gave a message for her ear. . . . [and] took pendant from my girdle and cast it to her. . . . She sighed accep-

tance of my vows, of my gift and my fair words. With jasper she requited me and with the milk-white Stone of Truth; she pointed into the river depths in token that there she would meet me.[4]

This passage is both deeply and broadly representative. In Cao Zhi's account the gentleman, after this vision of loveliness and moment of desire, suddenly gets cold feet at the prospect of being lured into everlasting separation from reality. The Lady Fu swirls off in a huff (fig. 1), and the gentleman exchanges everlasting bliss for a meditative night of regret.

The language employed in the poet's description of the Lady Fu's charms has ancient precedents. For example, a poem that has been attributed to the eighth century B.C. reads:

Hands soft like rush-down,
Skin smooth like lard.
Neck long and white like a tree grub,
Teeth like melon seeds
Cicada's head and moth's eyebrows.
Smiling a charming smile,
Her beautiful eyes have the black and white clearly marked.[5]

FIG. 1. *The Nymph of the Luo River* (detail), twelfth to thirteenth century, traditionally attributed to Gu Kaizhi (ca. 344 to ca. 406). Hand scroll. Courtesy of the Freer Gallery of Art, Smithsonian Institution, Washington, D.C.

The poem probably praises a royal mate. Both here and with "The Nymph of the Luo River," there is no mistaking within these conventions that the attraction is sexual. One point of Cao's poem, indeed, seems to lie precisely in that fact, although there may be an ultimately metaphorical purpose. The beauty of the goddess and her attraction to the gentleman are both physical. Conventions are exploited to make this clear, but to the Western ear, the nearer they get to the physical point, the more elusive and allusive they become. Her shoulders are almost promising—"as chiselled statuary"—but when we get to her waist the incipient flesh at once becomes "a bundle of silk." An incipience of the physical point, however, is a matter of expectancy; and such expectations are more cultural than physiological.

All this indirection might be partly understood as a not unusual example of customary delicacy in a culture often seen as being aligned with the Victorians in its avoidance of direct physical reference. Such prudery had its place in Chinese culture also, but this view may be very misleading. Sexuality is not in doubt here. We are faced, rather, with questions about the body itself.

For an extreme, but nevertheless still classic, illustration of this circumstance, we may turn to a famous novel of the early seventeenth century, the one translated by Clement Egerton under the title *Golden Lotus*.[6] The novel mainly narrates the degeneration of a certain Ximen Qing as he pursues his own power and pleasure with a nearly complete lack of scruples. His pleasures are extensively sexual, and the author describes them with a scrupulousness of attention that complements the unscrupulousness of his main character. The novel opens with a poem, whose last stanza reads:

> Beautiful is this maiden; her tender form gives promise of sweet
>   womanhood,
> But a two-edged sword lurks between her thighs, whereby
>   destruction comes to foolish men.
> No head falls to that sword; its work is done in secret,
> Yet it drains the very marrow from men's bones.
>   (Egerton 1972 : 1.1)

Pan Jinlian, "Golden-Lotus Pan," the principal female character in the novel, embodies this "two-edged sword." Ximen Qing meets her by accident, when she drops a bamboo pole on his head as he is passing in the street. Turning to curse her, he suddenly beheld an incredibly pretty woman. Her hair was black as a raven's plumage; her eyebrows mobile as the kingfisher and as curved as the new moon. Her almond eyes were clear and cool, and her cherry lips most inviting. Her nose was noble and exquisitely modelled, and her dainty cheeks beautifully powdered. Her face had the delicate roundness of a silver bowl. As for her body, it was light as a flower, and her fingers as slender as the tender shoots of a young onion. Her waist was as narrow as the willow, and her white belly yielding and plump. Her feet were small and tapering; her breasts soft and luscious. One other thing there was, black-fringed, grasping, dainty, and fresh, but the name of that I may not tell. Words fail to describe the charm of so beauteous a vision. . . . Her luxuriant coal-black hair was as thick as the clouds. . . . Two peach flowers adorned her willow-leaf eyebrows. The jade pendants she wore were remarkable, but the glory of her uncovered bosom was that of jade beyond all price. (Egerton 1972:1.42–43)

This passage still retains some of the conventions of the poems of millennia earlier. Noticeably more adventurous, however, it includes belly, breasts and "the name of that I may not tell."

Ximen Qing pursues the cooperative Pan Jinlian with dedicated zeal and has the impediment of her husband removed by murder. On the way to acquiring the two-edged sword for his own household, he has his first assignation with her. When the moment comes, "Without giving her time to object, he carried her to old woman Wang's bed, took off his clothes and, after unloosing her girdle, lay down with her. Their happiness reached its culmination" (Egerton 1972:1.67). A poetic elaboration follows in which "the silken hose are raised on high/And two new moons [her bound feet] appear above his shoulders." Within a couple of pages they are at it again. On this occasion we are introduced promptly to what one might call the principal parts in the plots:

Ximen Qing's desire could no longer be restrained; he disclosed the treasure which sprang from his loins, and made the woman touch it with her delicate fingers. . . . Upstanding it was, and flushed with pride, the black hair strong and bristling. A mighty warrior in very truth. . . . Then Golden-lotus took off her clothes. Ximen Qing fondled the fragrant blossom. No down concealed it; it had all the fragrance and tenderness of fresh-made pastry, the softness and appearance of a new-made pie. (Egerton 1972: 1.71)

Several interesting points can be made here. First, prudery is no impediment. Looking back on the culture of late imperial China, both through the prism of contemporary custom and through literature of that time, there is an impression of a characteristically uninhibited acceptance of bodily functions.[7]

Concurrent with such openness, however, there was a highly developed hierarchy of propriety. What might be perfectly acceptable in one situation would be unthinkable in another. Such distinctions, coextensive with the structure of society itself, were probably both well articulated and also mutually compatible. That is, different modes of communication and expression were not psychologically incompatible but were acceptable or even required as aspects of the same person as she or he adjusted appropriately to different social contexts and functions. There was a distinction both broad and deep between the public and private spheres. But the structure was much more complex than that simple dichotomy, and I do not think that a self-righteous Erewhonian model of hypocrisy is appropriate here. Such a model implies choice, but when social interaction is so radically and complexly governed by context, the factor of choice is defined by the same pattern. The absence of body imagery in one particular context certainly says something about the social articulation of the body, but it should not be taken as a statement about the body in general. Any such generalized statement is, ipso facto, beyond social possibility when various contexts so deeply inform the body/self.

Turning to the specific context of *Golden Lotus*, we are at once confronted, within a few moments of our introduction to Pan Jinlian, by the fullest and frankest description of her physical charms. It comes within a sentence or two after her bamboo pole strikes Ximen Qing on the head, while she is still fully clothed and he is standing in the street. The novel immediately presents the reader with an exemplary inventory of her resources. When Ximen Qing's subsequent seduction achieves its unobstructed end, there is no revelation of her body as seen or not seen by her seducer. Pan Jinlian's genitalia are isolated and served up as a gastronomic delicacy upon the table of the text.[8] The vocabulary of the descriptions, remarkably consistent from the eighth century B.C. to the seventeenth A.D., with its plethora of natural similes, has a very distinctive style. One might take this simply as a distinctive style of erotica, and as such it is traceable over centuries. Aspects of this enduring style—for example, hair, eyebrows, and from the Ming onward, an obsession with bound feet ("golden lotus" also signifies "bound feet")—may strike the non-Chinese sensibility as exotic, thus obscuring its substance and its mundaneness.[9] But the "style" must be understood as representing a much broader context, in which what is represented is not the body so much as its cultural ontology.

The absence of a visible body, either female or male, characterizes the innumerable and exceedingly varied conjugations throughout this very long novel. Descriptions frequently specify functions of the body and specific details of sexual anatomy, but there is no body of the sort that Western readers might expect, especially where the pornographic drive is so overwhelming. There is no image of a body as a whole object, least of all as a solid and well-shaped entity whose shapeliness is supported by the structure of a skeleton and defined in the exteriority of swelling muscle and enclosing flesh.

2

This latter avoirdupois image tends to dominate the visions offered by Western art. From the sculpture of Praxiteles to the centerfolds of *Playboy*, from divine ideal to pornographic exploitation, the nude in this sense has played an extraordinarily prominent and persistent role. Extremes can readily inhabit the same body, as in the still far from banished awfulnesses of Hiram Powers (1805–73), whose slick and pearly sculptures of nude young women represented the ideal of classical civilization in many an American courtyard. That they can coexist in a civilization committed to the creed of the excluded middle term (Gernet 1980) indicates some extraordinary degree of resistance within the image itself. The libidinal drive within even the most transcendental images has perhaps only recently begun to receive due attention, and the nature of this cultural artifact may now be deconstructed in myriad different ways. Helena Michie writes, "Full representation of the body is necessarily impossible in a language that depends for meaning on absence and difference, and literal representation is impossible in a language that is itself a metaphor for thought."[10] Synecdoche is perhaps never absent, and Michie points out that modern pornography "has produced an inversion of the Victorian representational tropes, where the historically unnameable parts of the female body come to stand for the rest of it."[11] Nevertheless, in our comparative frame, the image appears in its own existential right. It has had, in Western civilization, a persistent and highly distinctive autonomy.

The same propulsion of desire was no less relevant in China. Cao Zhi's gentleman survives because, while sensitive to sexuality, he resists with the

claims of society; Ximen Qing comes to grief because he indulges it without restraint in an entirely unsocialized manner. But the body image con-
noted by "nude" rather than "naked" never materialized. I would also
suggest, if only hesitantly, that distinctions between female and male
bodies have been much less strictly drawn in Chinese culture. That each
sexual polarity contains the irreducible germ of the complementary opposite was, of course, a cosmological fact. Such a condition is more suit-
ably embodied in a morphological analogy, rather than objectified in a
mimetic representation.[12] As in some other contexts, one has a sense, in
the Western case, of a solid, objective reality, against which deconstructive
criticism has often been turned; in the Chinese case, in contrast, it is of
a dispersed reality, in the face of which a reconstructive need has often
struggled.

There were illustrations of Cao Zhi's "Nymph of the Luo River." Several versions have been attributed to a sequence going back to the emperor
Mingdi of the Jin (r. 322–25).[13] The one in the Freer Gallery of Art in
Washington may be an eleventh-century example of this development.
Both style and image may be called exemplary, even classical. Not only
were many qualities of the (hypothetical) original rather closely preserved,
but the representational style itself survived both in recognition and in
actual practice until the present era.

The first representation in the Freer Gallery scroll (fig. 1), which lacks
the beginning of the composition, shows Lady Fu just after the gentleman's social intellect has triumphed over his senses. Even though the
image has passed through several copies, it is both attractive and expres-
sive, in a distinctively Chinese convention. One obvious embodiment of
humanity is in the face, which is relatively large and dominant in the figure
as a whole. In painting of this tradition, intense interpersonal interaction
embodied in finely specified eye contact was a crucial function.[14] In this
example, the precision of Lady Fu's incipient reaction to the gentleman's
rejection has been blurred by the process of transmission. Knowledge of
other examples could enable one to read such quality back into this
example.

The image retains a general mode. Even the newcomer to Chinese art
is likely to suspect that the prominent attention paid to the Lady Fu's
clothes and to the billowing complexity of their ribbons is typical of a
tradition. Yet the generality of tradition, even when intensified by copying,
does not exclude particularity. The lively rhythms of the ribbons and drap-

ery folds embody both the physical and the psychological movements of
the Lady Fu. The specific narrative situation is seen both in the turning
attitude and in the agitated confusion overcoming this lively concert of
rhythms at ribbons' end.

These configurations also represent the sensuous charms to which the
poet refers. Even the sexual promise may be indirectly discerned. There is
what one might call an aerial vocabulary both in the poet's words, with
"the coils of her hair like cloud-heaps stacked in the air," and in the floating drapery. One of the commonest terms for sexual union was the "play
of clouds and rain." The persistence of cloud imagery in descriptions of
women's hair is very evocative in this connection. The swirling motions of
seemingly wind-borne garments may also be linked intimately with the
contextual significance of the clouds-and-rain imagery.

The eroticism of clothes in response to the body within is at one level
universal, but at others it is more specifically cultural. A glimpse of a classic
instance of body/clothing transmutation in Western art may demonstrate
both the similarities and the differences. Of Bernini's sculptural master-
piece *The Ecstasy of Saint Theresa*, executed in 1645–52 (fig. 2), Mario
Perniola has written, "It makes no sense to seek anything beneath the
fabric: 'Theresa lives essentially in her tunic.'"[15] But here we are clearly
outside the world of the Chinese body. The body Bernini revisualizes in
Saint Theresa's ecstatic robe is, equally clearly, still a Western body.

In the case of *Golden Lotus*, when we go from the text to imagery, we
find a very consistent state of affairs. This particular novel was illustrated
early in its history.[16] There was already a well-developed tradition of erotic
prints that had developed in the flourishing urbanity of the sixteenth and
seventeenth centuries. The earlier work, which has almost all been lost,
represented a very distinguished achievement of the woodblock printer's
art, sometimes using several color blocks.[17] The *Golden Lotus* illustrations
are only partly related to such prints, which had a more specific function
within the world of prostitution. The pictures for the novel, more hum-
drum and in black ink alone, lie within the broader tradition of literary
illustration. They are, however, respectable examples of illustrative practice
and technique. Compared with prints that were more exclusively intended
to titillate sexually, the figures are smaller. Nevertheless, the differences are
only in degree and do not affect our very generalized comparisons.

In the *Golden Lotus* illustrations, there is no compunction about representing sexual and even scatological activity, but the ambience does not

Fɪɢ. 2. Gianlorenzo Bernini (1598–1680), *The Ecstasy of Saint Theresa*, 1645–52. Marble. Cornaro Chapel, Santa Maria della Vittoria, Rome.

FIG. 3. *Burning the Husband's Spirit Tablet, the Monks Overhear Lewd Noises*. Anonymous woodblock illustration to chapter 8 of *The Golden Lotus*. From *Xinke Jin Ping Mei cihua*, vol. 1. Illustrations from the Chongzhen edition (Beijing: Guyi Xiaoshuo Kanxinghui, 1933). University of California, Berkeley, East Asiatic Library, Rare Books Collection.

in any way dramatize the nature of such events (fig. 3). Seeing at first glance an everyday interior or garden scene, if one peers more carefully at the small details of figures one may well be startled to discover a triple-X performance. In the compositional formula of a pictorial paragraph—the single illustration, that is—only a sentence or two needs to be changed to create each specific instance. More than this, of course, there are no bodies in the sense of a nude figure. Although a sexual act may be the point of the plot at this moment, that becomes significant in relation to its social context, not as an act of individual bodies. Sometimes a few clothes need to be rearranged in order to reveal some narratively essential detail, such as male or female genitals. Sometimes all clothes are removed, but even then it is matter of nakedness and not of a nude, a nakedness that is somehow, nonchalantly, absorbed into the surroundings. Conceptually, there is no more revelation of an anatomical body to the viewer than there apparently was to Ximen Qing in the bedroom.

The initial description of Pan Jinlian, which the novel shares with the reader, is not the literary representation of a revealed body that a later draftsman failed to pick up. To begin with, in the literary text most of the fleshly qualities described are redistributed, even dissolved into various other categories: kingfishers, silver bowls, and onions, for instance. Bowls and onions do have shapes, but there is no shape to this body. Pan Jinlian's breasts are "soft and luscious" but shapeless. This technique of dispersing the body's attributes continues throughout the novel.[18] Even these fleshly attributes are organized not as a coherent description of a body-object, but as items in the woman's native dowry.[19]

We may return to the illustration of the Nymph–Lady Fu at this point (fig. 1), since its visualization of clothing presents a more productive set of questions about the body. Her floating ribbons are obviously related to her literally wind-borne motion. In Chinese as in Western images, such features, more generally, tend to invoke a supernatural state. In addition, in China they are more closely associated with female than with male subjects. There may be a reflection both ways, of divine allure on female desire and vice versa, and indeed there is a distinctively feminine cast to some Chinese conceptions of divinity.

§

There is, no doubt, an inherently yielding gracefulness in these flowing garments that partakes of a very widespread convention of feminine imagery. Another famous painting, attributed also to the fourth-century painter Gu Kaizhi, shows the subtleties possible. This work, titled *Admonitions of the Palace Instructress,* illustrates another third-century text that, on the surface at least, describes the norms of attitude and behavior proper to a female member of royal household. In one section a consort meekly reposes in her proper place and attitude (fig. 4). Her garments gently rise and softly subside in a configuration that is fetchingly beautiful, whatever one might think of its sociological transmutation. In another and contrasting psychological category, a woman presumes on the continuing favors of her lord and is inevitably rebuffed (fig. 5). In a configuration that is

FIG. 4. *Admonitions of the Palace Instructress.* Tang copy after Gu Kaizhi? (ca. 344 to 406). Hand scroll. Section 7: "Observe how the tiny stars were made free and content and learn your lesson." British Museum, London.

partly comparable to that of the presumptuous nymph, her garments stream out with improper directness, only to be turned back by the emperor's reproof.[20] Needless to say, such material and visual conformations can be as readily transmuted into sexual modes as into social ones.

An aspect of eroticism in Western imagery becomes relevant to our general inquiry here. Mario Perniola's essay, cited above, locates eroticism in the possibility of transit between two states, the clothed and the naked, hiddenness and uncovering (Perniola 1989:243). Of Bernini's *Saint Theresa* he also writes, "Transit has completely engulfed the form of her body and transformed it into fabric" (255). When an image shifts to either of two extremes, to a Judaic "metaphysics of clothing" or the Greek "metaphysic of nudity," eroticism is not possible (239). Eroticism in Chinese imagery does not usually seem to be framed in this way.

Some of the exceptions, however, are substantial. The mid-Tang is one of these. The subject matter of court ladies that flourished in painting of this period served several purposes. The erotic must have been one of them, even though it has been obscured by subsequent tradition. One of the best-known artists specializing in the painting of court ladies was

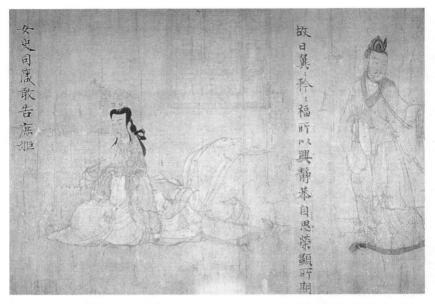

Fig. 5. *Admonitions of the Palace Instructress,* Tang copy after Gu Kaizhi? (ca. 344 to ca. 406). Hand scroll. Section 6: "Favor must not be abused, and love must not be exclusive." British Museum, London.

Zhou Fang (ca. 730 to ca. 800). Perhaps the best among a fine, if heterogeneous, body of attributions is a scroll of palace ladies with elaborate flowered headdresses, strolling in a garden with domesticated animals (fig. 6).[21] This painting is remarkable for its sensuousness. The effect is concentrated in the exquisite rendering of silk robes, especially transparent gauzes, but it appears in several other places, such as the hands, faces, and hair. In this painting, more than most others, the possibility of transit seems to be offered.

Another view of eroticism in figurative art sheds more interesting light on this example. For Anne Hollander, an erotic awareness of the body contains an awareness of clothing and always requires a reference to fashionable norms. Further, direct influence of fashion in images of the nude can be detected "only during those centuries of Western society when true fashion actually existed"—from the fourteenth century onward in Europe. "If fashion in dress means constant perceptible fluctuations of visual design, created out of the combined forms of tailored dress and body, then . . . much of the eastern hemisphere [has] not experienced 'fashion' as we know it" (Hollander 1975:88–90). Hollander picks up Kenneth

FIG. 6. Zhou Fang (ca. 730 to ca. 800). *Ladies with Flowers in Their Hair.* Hand scroll. Palace Museum, Beijing.

Clark's radical distinction between the "drapery" of classical dress and the tailored garb of the European tradition. Her argument is both problematic and helpful. Although one can usefully make distinctions between "draped" and "tailored" garments in China, the meanings involved are often different. As I am suggesting, there are also other forms of the erotic. Nevertheless, for the mid-Tang her argument is very suggestive. There is considerable evidence that society at this time was obsessed not only with taste but also with fashion.[22] This had a great deal to do with the extraordinary flux of Tang metropolitan culture. The exotic often is closely associated with the erotic. It is at exactly this time that Chinese art most explicitly incorporates nakedness, even though it is still restricted, generally to foreign bodies in a Buddhist context.[23] Chinese pictorial art also makes its closest approach to linear perspective at this time. In regard to many of these phenomena, Perniola's notion of "transit" is suggestive.

§

Before and after the Tang, except for occasional transgressions, Chinese figurative imagery does *not* invite us into such transitory play, just as it does not present us with concrete constructions.[24] Earlier, it is possible that the original "Nymph of the Luo River" played on the possibility of such a threat. In general, however, the transformational dynamics are a reassuring norm rather than a threat.

If one searched the evidence more carefully, one might come up with a more specific interpretation. In medical theory of this time, for instance, "wind" is an exterior state of physiological energy (*qi*) that affects the interior transformational balance. Paul Unschuld sees this development as moving from a "demon" to a "wind etiology" and reaches the conclusion that "in addition to the concept of wind as a pathogenic agent, a more general and comprehensive concept was introduced, namely, of environmental influences that affect the organism from outside but are present within the organism as well."[25] It is possible, for instance, that a degree of asymmetry and instability in Lady Fu's garments may implicate the threat of indulgence and transgression against which the gentleman reacts. Only a sufficiently articulated spectrum of instances would enable one to judge this. But we can already see, first, that clothes are a great deal more than assemblages of fabric, more than even symbolic assemblages; second, that a body is implicated but not the body of the Western tradition; third, that the worlds within and outside the clothes are not insulated and in some ways not even divided from each other; and fourth, that there is a process of continuous transformation at work between states such as the somatic, the psychic, and the social.

§

Leaving aside the issue of eroticism, however fascinating it becomes here, broader issues of body image immediately confront us. The phenomenology of "transit" depends on exclusive alternatives and the consequent precariousness, even danger, of intermediate states. This frame can be endlessly remapped—onto the "mind/body" and "spirit/matter" dichotomies, for instance. Such conceptual dichotomy was not dominant in the Chinese tradition, where a transformational coexistence of alternatives was generally the norm. Neither extreme, of objectification or of transcendence, was eventually sustained as a possibility.[26]

All representations of the body, of course, are transmutations of one sort or another, in various simultaneous directions. The transmutation from flesh and mind (themselves cultural artifacts) into clothing was much broader and deeper than a mere pictorial convention. We may test this by returning to *Golden Lotus*. The introductory description of Pan Jinlian herself, quoted earlier, continues:

> She wore a blue gown bound with a long silk-embroidered sash, and in her cuff a tiny satchel of perfumes. Beneath her delicate chin, a many-buttoned corsage concealed her throat. Her feet were graced by tiny shoes made like the mountain-crow, with tips embroidered to look like claws. Their high heels were of white silk, so that she always seemed to walk upon a fragrant dust. Her scarlet silken trousers were decorated with birds and flowers and, as she sat or when she rose, the wind would puff out her skirts and flowing undergarments. From her mouth there came a perfume as delicious as that of orchids and musk, while her cherry lips and beautiful cheeks had the glory of a flower. One glimpse of this vision, and the souls of young men would flutter away and die. (Egerton 1972:1.143)

Of the many points here that tie directly back into our account of the earlier material, let me simply note the length and elaboration of the description. Clearly, the physical and psychological qualities of Jinlian are being directly conveyed, not simply some decorative superfluity. Both specific passage and cultural context show that these garments are not just transparent symbols. We are not expected to see straight through them to some somatic reality, even that whose "name I may not tell." It is not that naming the woman's genitals is not acceptable, for an example of graphic description was given earlier. To treat this description as symbolic would be, inappropriately, to drop the symbol once the reality had been grasped.[27] This set of sensual, material images is not disposable. In a universe of correlative resonance, different phases of the transformations maintain their material presence, constantly expanding and enriching the images. The qualities of Jinlian's body are actually embodied in and not just invested in her garments, and beyond her garments in the environment at large. This, in greatly varying degrees of economy and control, was the cultural norm. In this case, one might say, the profligate pleasures of Jinlian's body are dispersed with appropriate generosity. Remembering Helena Michie's remark about metaphor, I might suggest that, in the Chinese sphere, when the entire ontology was metaphoric, then individual "metaphors" were simply realistic.

In relation to the body, the evidence for this is inevitably more circumstantial than explicit. It is circumstantial, for example, in the overwhelming tendency of pictorial art to represent figural subjects primarily in terms of clothing and environment, and in the extensive use of such descriptions in literature.[28] In a negative, but very powerful way, it is more explicit in the complete absence of the nude as a motif and still more as a genre from the pictorial arts.

3

I shall suggest some areas that the consistency of the body in the Chinese tradition derives its meaning from, areas that may be incorporated in attempts to understand the body in Chinese art. To begin with, the body, even the body as sexual object in *Golden Lotus,* is unmistakably social. It is questionable whether the unsocialized body could even have been an object of contemplation. Its elaboration through ornament and clothing, so extensively described in *Golden Lotus,* locates and defines the body in a social context. One might try to hypothesize the completely unadorned body as the untutored innocent, the farm-fresh wench of nineteenth-century English imagination. But this conception, a perversion both of Eve and of the Noble Savage, so far as I know did not exist in China either in the original or in its perverted forms. They depended upon the notion of original sin and a prelapsarian society, which could be elevated to a romantic ideal or could degenerate into the droit du seigneur and beyond. These conditions did not exist in China, where there was no external and supreme deity to act as either creator or model.[29]

It is true that in Confucian and to some extent in Daoist texts a distinction is drawn between "substance," *zhi,* and "accomplishment," *wen.*[30] This distinction is at least analogous to that between body and clothing. At any stage there may even be an overlap. The body, to have social meaning, needed to be socially articulated by some code of ornament. Early Daoist texts, concerned with substance rather than society, tend to refer to the body in a physiological and evolutionary way. In the *Zhuangzi,* for instance, we find: "The bright and shining is born out of deep darkness; the ordered is born out of formlessness; pure spirit is born out of the Way. The body is born originally from this purity [or seminal fluid], and the ten thousand things give bodily form to one another through the process of birth" (Watson 1968:22.238). But early Confucian texts, in the period when the structures of both society and the state were first being explicitly articulated (eleventh to third century B.C.), seem to draw a basic distinction between simple ornament and dress-and-ornament, referring to the wearing of clothes in opposition to the tattooing of skin as a marker between the civilization of the Chinese and the noncivilization of barbarians.[31] The very notion of civilization, which lay at the core of the self-image of China itself, was understood partly as the process of ornamentation in a semiotic sense, the articulating of pattern in the substance of humanity. Since the idea of "China" was fundamentally cultural rather than ethnic, one might suspect that the completely uncoded body would have been felt to be not human, and the naked body not, or not yet, Chinese.

§

This distinction, however, is not articulated in geometric terms or, strictly speaking, as a "natural/unnatural" contrast. The difficulty in mapping its conceptual structure is comparable to the difficulty we find in another important distinction, that of "inner/outer," *nei/wai*, which also is not geometric. Both *zhi/wen* and *nei/wai* are more distinctions between two different states of being, expressed in the need for a dynamic balance. There is an evaluative leaning toward the *zhi* and *nei* polarity, but this is balanced by the realization that human culture materializes in the *wen-wai* process. History was written into this discourse, as applied to politics, literature, and calligraphy.[32] In the magnificent synthesizing of Song neo-Confucian thought, of course, the notion of *ti,* "embodying," in natural philosophy reaches one of its most sophisticated achievements. It is no accident that in the same period the representation of natural embodiment in mountains-and-waters also achieved its apogee. It is within this larger context of embodiment that we return to the issue of human bodies.

The body, in the very act of being acknowledged, was a social body and must have varied according to social norms and structure. Any serious attempt at disentangling Chinese representation of the body would have to proceed along these lines for at least part of the way. Thus, in the developed tradition, the hierarchic, Confucian structure of imperial, official, and family society, with its powerful sense of a responsible head, most surely had its corporeal analogy. This set of relationships is powerfully exemplified in imperial portraits. In contrast, what Kristofer Schipper has called the "Daoist body" was just as complex an image, one of change rather than of stability. It was an especially potent case of the macro/microcosmic relationship, so prevalent in China, in which Laozi, the mythical founder of the Daoist church, was understood as incorporating the universe in his own body, a relationship that could be reflected back upon the universe itself. The leader of a Daoist community, embodying this situation at a more local and temporal level, was able to affect both the universe and therefore his community in concert, by acting internally upon his own physical, microcosmic body. Laozi was also seen as his own mother in a cyclical exchange of functions, another classic instance of bi-polar simultaneity. The Daoist body, as a whole, appears to have incorporated a primarily female semiotics that symbolized yin.[33] This, of course, was within a yin/yang polarity. Confucian conceptions were also largely contained by this same polarity, although a weighting on the yang side is apparent from the Han dynasty onward. Analyzing the male-yang semiotics of the Confucian construction may, however, be more difficult.

This irreducibly social body was also intimately correlated with topography. This correlation, as it appears in Schipper's discussion of the Daoist body, was not anthropomorphic in our usual sense. It was part of this general nexus, but it presents an environmental category of activity rather than of social class. In the texts of *shanshui hua* (landscape painting) in the Northern Song (A.D. 960–1126) we find descriptions of the mountains-and-waters in physiological terms. Guo Xi (active third quarter of the eleventh century) notes casually that "a mountain has water as blood, foliage as hair, haze and clouds as its spirit and character" (Bush and Shih 1985:167). This is clearly a long-established formulation. Almost certainly by this period mountain ridges were already termed *qimo,* "energy artery pulses." This opens up the large question of *shanshui* terminology and conceptualization that is most specifically articulated in the topological practices of *dili,* "earth patterning."[34]

It is significant that the core of this terminology was applied, in a well-known instance in the first century B.C., to the "body economic." Huan Kuan, in his account of the "Debates on Salt and Iron," compares the technique of applying pressure in the distribution of wealth to the doctors' reading of the artery pulse.[35] This returns us to a more central point, the body in medicine.[36]

The body also existed as an organ in its own right, at a much more significant level than that of an object of contemplation and one from which the categories above drew much of their meaning. The socialization, however, worked as much inward as outward. It is abundantly clear that the functional and structural organization of the body was persistently seen in a sociological mode. This sociology, certainly a dominant Chinese trait, was detailed in medical texts but appears in a great many other contexts. For example, the function called *xin,* usually translated "heart-mind," was that of "sovereign rulers." That of the *fei* (lungs) was "prime minister." The body was systematic in this sense, comprehensively and coherently organized as was the political body of the empire. Both were hierarchic and highly centralized, but with a highly effective system of power distributed and contributed. The effectiveness of this image was doubtless intensified by the social nature of the self.[37] Recent scholarship has paid increasing attention to the profound differences between the norms of self-definition in Western and Chinese culture (see Munro 1985). There was a definite, indeed a powerful, role for a sense of individuality and creativity in traditional China, but the primary sense of self was given by the pattern of relationships that defined it within the ritual complex of society. Whereas most of us today would probably consider our connections with society to be an external system that our selves must somehow come to terms with, in the traditional Chinese norm they were felt as the structuring of the self itself. Without such connectedness there was no self, and the self might be seen as evolving in the relation between the organic microcosm of the body and the social macrocosm of humanity. The cyclical feedback continued in the relation between the social microcosm and universal macrocosm.

To return to the organic microcosm of the body, once we observe the mediating concept of "function" between the organs of government and those of the body, we may realize that this is more than a metaphor. It is an extremely adaptable and powerful model. The most powerful application of this model is in the *mo*, or "energy artery pulses," both structuring and distributing the particular states of energy associated with each of the *zangxiang*, or visceral functions (such as the *fei*, "lungs"). This "artery pulse" system was widely adaptable, into spheres such as the body of mountains-and-waters. One may describe this function/structure physiology as one of pattern mapped onto process. In looking back at the examples of figurative art introduced earlier, we may find ourselves seeing them in this way. As exemplifications, manifestations, embodiments, and constructions of cultural meaning, we may see in them varying balances of *zhi* and *wen*, of stasis and movement, while questions of representation and realism become increasingly elusive.

The consistent articulation and development of this systematic correlation of systems over more than two millennia was possible, at one level, because it was very effective in applied practice; at another, because it developed out of, and continued in turn to validate, a very comprehensive and stable worldview. In some ways, of course, this broadest context is the most important for the themes of this multilateral inquiry. But in practical ways it is barely possible and perhaps not even desirable to do more than invoke it. I will rashly suggest the following very generalized set of defining cosmogonic factors, treated with the same historical latitude that characterizes the rest of this chapter:

1. The ultimate constituent of all matter, both physical and psychological, is *qi*, for which the best and simplest general-purpose translation is "energy."[38]

2. Phenomena materialize through a process of transformation, *bianhua*, in which *qi* passes into and out of hierarchically differentiated and structured states. These transitions are described in functional and qualitative terms.

3. Differentiating and structuring are activities of reactive resonance, *yun*, in the plenum of *qi*. This resonance occurs within a system of polarities. The primary polarity is the yin/yang resonance, and from this comes *shengqi*, "vital energy," or "generative energy."

4. The resulting relationships are synchronic and inductive rather than linear and causal (Porkert 1974 : 1–8).

5 The universe is conceived and projected not primarily in a geometric mode, as was that of the West, but in evolving patterns of hierarchic and resonating categories.

6. Primary values cluster around interiority.

7. There are no absolutes, and there is no external creator. Creation is its own agency (Mote 1971 : 17–20, 28).

There are many ways that some sense of these horizons of thinking and seeing may clarify some of the problems of body imagery introduced earlier. The centralized coherence of Chinese elite culture and the correlational nature of Chinese epistemology and ontology mean that analogous modes of description and explanation underlie phenomena that we might think very heterogeneous, such as medicine and calligraphy. Phenomena at all levels, not only the cosmic, tended to be understood as concentrations and conformations of *qi* rather than as geometric objects demarcated by solid planes and edges. Solids and voids were not exclusive opposites, but polar extremes of structure. Surfaces were not impenetrable faces of geometric solids, but palpable interfaces through which the structural values of interiority interacted with the environment. Thus not only body organs, but bodies themselves were such phenomena. The body was the environment of the viscera and was itself within an environment at a higher level. Bodies were inseparable from psychologies. The fascination with texture rather than shape, as in the case of female breasts with heterosexuality (and equivalently of buttocks in homosexuality), is entirely consistent with this environment.

Such fleshly textures were not, however, an interest of painters. The traditional technique of the Chinese painter, with calligraphic brush and ink, might not seem suited to them. But as I stated earlier, the representational possibilities of techniques are usually wider than one might expect. In fact, the texture of flesh was simply not within the normative subject matter of painting. At the same time there was an almost obsessive concern with texture in subjects such as landscape. Texture was, indeed, a cultural concern, as the cosmology would lead one to expect. But the texture of tree bark or rock face was a relevant category for painters, whereas that of flesh was not.[39]

The most persistently dominant concern in painting, clearly revealed in its often reasserted relation to calligraphy, was linearity. It is probably at this level that we can find a clarification—one can hardly call it an explanation—of the fundamental tendency to represent people through their garments. Apart from the level of social significance, the physical substratum of linearly evolving patterns so important to physiology found its most effective analogue in the patterns of drapery folds. One cannot say that the patterns of drapery represent directly those of the artery pulses, but one might say that they provided the most convincing way of embodying the kind of structures that gave the body both its existence and its life. These relationships between imagery and technique are central for the painters of, for example, "The Nymph of the Luo River" and the *Admonitions of the Palace Instructress*. The process of linearity is there quite consciously embodied in the brush. For the illustrator of *Golden Lotus*, however, in cutting a woodblock print the linearity is rendered almost static in the technique and materializes more strongly in the overall pattern.

Linearity itself lies somewhere rather close to a core definition of life, as the phenomenon of the energy artery pulse indicates. For the same reason, calligraphy lies closer than painting to the core of art and to the definition of art. Calligraphy, among other things, may be said to constitute a body in linearity. And the critical assessment of calligraphy is in some ways comparable to diagnosis of the body. One reads the quality of energy through the pulses. The critical and conceptual languages of calligraphy are indeed far more corporeal—in a physiological rather than an anatomical mode, of course—than are those of painting (see Hay 1983b:74–102, 1983c:70–84).

The essential coextensiveness of personality can readily be incorporated into body as linear pattern. This is seen in the crucial prominence and elusiveness of a term that unites the psychological, spiritual, philosophical, and material worlds, namely *shen*.[40] It is often translated "spirit." In the context of medical terminology, Porkert describes the "heart-mind" (*xin*) as "'sovereign': seat of the configurative force (*shen*), conditions the character and cohesion of the personality" (Porkert 1974:164). Seen in a universe of self-generating pattern, therefore, the *shen* labels the negentropic force that directs the materialization of all phenomena to their specific existence and, by definition, inheres within each phenomenon. The structural function of *shen* is equally essential to physical and psychological phenomena. The physical and psychological aspects of the body are therefore inseparable, so long as it is a *person* that is in question. A *shen* is equally necessary, also, for a person, a passage of calligraphy, a painter, a painting, a representation in a painting, and a rock. At the same time, *shen* is used attributively of all these phenomena, if they are *sufficiently good*. I add a rock for a particular reason (Hay 1985). Sculpture of the nude body has been extraordinarily prominent in Western society for millennia. In China, not only has the nude in this social sense been entirely absent, but so has sculpture. The place of sculpture has largely been taken by the natural rock. More than that, the typical Chinese rock, with its convoluted, foraminate, complexly textured form, might well stand as a culturally quintessential Chinese body. The classical image of the Western tradition is the Apollo or the Venus. The classical image of the Chinese tradition is the rock (fig. 7).

In conclusion, we may note a peculiar relevance of the notion of "image." The generic Chinese term for a visceral system, such as that of the "heart-mind" or "lungs," is *zangxiang,* as given earlier. *Zang* by itself is "viscera," but in a systematic context it requires the suffix *xiang,* which may be roughly translated as "image." Portraits are *xiang*. Both the term and certain concepts behind it are central to the *Yijing,* the *Book of Change* that remains, so infuriatingly to some, a Chinese cosmological key. In the ontology that developed into the *Yijing* in the second half of the first millennium. B.C., these concepts appear to have incorporated a perception that the universe is a process of self-imaging.

All phenomena are images generated by an autonomous process out of potentiality.[41] As an ontological foundation, this must have profoundly affected the account of man's world at both general and specific levels. Consciousness, in this world, is a process of participation rather than of objectively seeing. In this context, the notion of "the representation of the

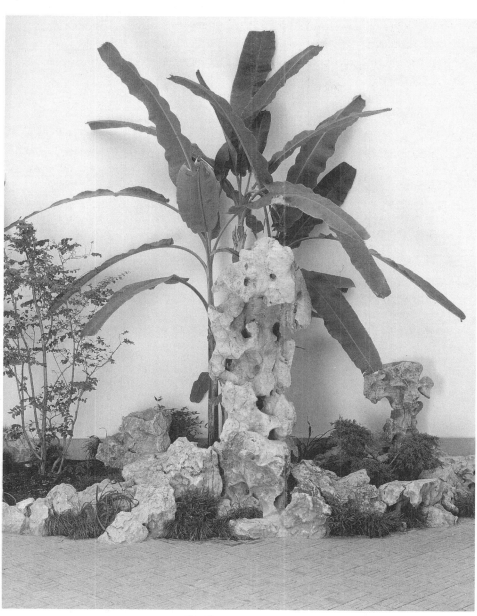

FIG. 7. Lake Tai rock. Astor Garden Court, Metropolitan Museum of Art, New York.

body" may be descriptive rather than analytical. It *was* "a representation" rather than an "object," but a representation given in the very genes of the universe itself, and hence as objective as one might ever hope to get.

Notes

1. See Bush and Shih (1985:1035–5). This volume of translation and commentary is an invaluable resource for material from the earliest texts down to the fourteenth century. Reading through its first hundred pages will immediately provide the principal substance of this history. See also Ledderose (1973:69–83).

2. See Cahill 1983, especially the discussions of Zhang Hong and Zeng Jing. For a somewhat different account of the relation between brush technique and shape and surface, see Hay (1983a:72–111, 1984:102–36).

3. See Kenneth Clark 1956. Despite the shifts in intellectual interest, this study remains very valuable. For another comprehensive study that elaborates the context much more fully, in part as a critique of Clark, see the excellent book by Hollander (1975), especially chapter 2, "Nudity." See also Barkan 1975. Since that time, the questions have become too dispersed to allow so broad an approach. For example, see *Fragments for a History of the Human Body,* especially the invaluable article by Mark Elvin (1989).

4. Translation by Arthur Waley, in *An Introduction to the Study of Chinese Painting* (1974:60–62), quoted by Thomas Lawton (1973) in his excellent study on the scroll in the Freer Gallery of Art. This catalog of Chinese figure paintings in the Freer Gallery is full of expert scholarship, besides being the only thematic study of this subject matter.

5. Translated with comments by Robert Van Gulik in his *Sexual Life in Ancient China* (1974:18–19). This excellent study, though well known, is not as widely utilized as it should be.

6. The Chinese title is *Jinping mei* (Plum of the golden vase), a complicated reference to the novel's content that includes the leading female character Pan Jinlian, "Golden-Lotus Pan." The novel's beginning actually dates from the late sixteenth century. For a recent study and summary of scholarship, see Plaks (1987:55–182).

7. This is not to deny substantial historical shifts owing to various factors. Toward the end of imperial China, for example, under Manchu rule (1644–1911) this openness was significantly restricted. In another kind of shift, the southern cultures of today are more forthright than the northern, a difference that probably has a long precedent. But consistent tendencies can nevertheless be seen.

8. The gastronomic transformation is obviously a theme of some importance. Later, for example, Ximen Qing strings up Pan Jinlian's ankles and tosses iced plums into this same "pie." Elvin notes, with agreement, a view "that the Chinese

seem to have relatively strong consciousness of their oral and digestive systems, and a relatively weak consciousness of their genital systems" (Elvin 1989:285). The transformation between eating and sex is not uncommon in an erotic context, and some specifically historical manifestations have been studied semiotically. See Helena Michie (1987:23–28). Michie notes that in Victorian novels women do not eat in public, just as their bodies remain absent from the texts. In the case of novels by female authors, "women's hunger, associated not only with the orality of eroticism or eating, is also linked in the novel to speech and writing" (28). Part of Michie's argument revolves around a more general but distinctively feminist view of the "body." Although this developing genre of scholarship has much to offer, even cross-culturally, in many cases, as here, the premises of the discourses under study are quite different. Whereas there must be some element of universality in phenomena such as orality and sexuality, and perhaps even in the relation between them, the cultural articulations of the body in which they occur are specifically different. The body is a cultural construction. Sexuality and orality, of course, are also constructions in at least three ways: ontogenetically, as articulated in language, and as part of an explanatory theory. The distinction between universal and cultural construct (nature and nurture) is always relative to context and pragmatic distinctions between background, foreground, and motif.

9. I am not proposing these three examples as systematic, but they illustrate two aspects of exoticism. Hair is widely linked with sexuality; compare the "Tale of Genji" illustrations from Heian Japan and the pre-Raphaelite women of Victorian England (Hollander 1975:72–73; Michie 1987:99–102). The motif is common, and an exotic quality arises from differing visual style seen across cultures. Bound feet, seen from outside their own culture, are exotic as an isolated motif. They may also suggest an exotic style of sexuality. Eyebrows lie in between, as a shift of a familiar motif toward an exotic fringe. The practice of foot-binding deserves serious semiological study (n.b. Levy and Van Gulik). I think it is characteristic of the Chinese tradition that it produced such a move on its own ground. In an early nineteenth-century novel, *The Destinies of the Flowers in the Mirror,* male travelers find themselves in a culture where men are coded as women and vice versa (to describe it simply as theatrical "role reversal" seems inadequate, and any attempt to explain the text in these terms becomes impossibly convoluted; it is an exercise in semiology). One of the men has her feet bound. "When the [female] King came upstairs to take a look in person . . . he [i.e., she] gazed with attentive pleasure at the golden-lotus feet, smelled him all over his head and body, and fondled him in every possible way" (see the translation and discussion in Elvin (1989:825–89).

10. Michie (1987–149). I am using the Western material to provoke questions rather than as a comparative study. But we should note two qualifications. First, an objectifying visual epistemology has been characteristic of the West, and it is precisely the predominance of a visual image that counts. The literary mode

of description has typically been more fragmentary, but it has generally assumed the coherent visual entity as a reference point. To put it another way, in most cases one has to read literary descriptions in the context of a visual mode. This leads to the second qualification, which is that most modern scholarship on the Western body is primarily *concerned about* fragmentation, especially of the female body. It assumes, frequently unselfconsciously, that the coherent entity is the norm and that its fragmentation is a strategy of dominance. A golden rule of cross-cultural studies should be that contrasting, alternative cultural strategies should never be seen as exclusive. Thus there is a positive deconstructive view in the West, and in China an objectifying epistemology was far from entirely absent. But priorities were reversed. My purpose in this essay is to describe a dominant cultural mode. This is not to deny that a strategy of sexual dominance could not simultaneously be identified in a text such as *Golden Lotus*. I leave the question open.

11. Michie (1987:141), part of an extended discussion of synecdoche and description of the female body.

12. The style of visualization involved in, for example, the hexagrams of the *Yijing* and ubiquitous yin/yang symbol (the earliest instance of which I do not know) is a problem that should be studied.

13. All the attributions are speculative. The painting was attributed to Gu Kaizhi (ca. 344 to ca. 406) in the thirteenth century. See the careful analysis by Lawton (1973:23–29).

14. The notion that psychological interaction between people is a central aspect of the personality of an individual, and that such interactions should be represented by painters through the motif of the eyes, was made explicit in a text attributed to Gu Kaizhi (ca. 345 to ca. 406), to whom the "Nymph of the Luo River" has also traditionally been attributed (Bush and Shih 1985:33).

15. Perniola (1989:255). His quotation is from R. Kuhn. A comparison between two paintings would be more respectable, but the *Saint Theresa* is a locus classicus for this condition, and the degree of translatability between sculpture and painting in this period is very high.

16. Possibly in the fourth and fifth decades of the seventeenth century. See Plaks's summation of the extensive arguments over the dating of various editions (1987:66).

17. Some discussion in Van Gulik 1974 but extensively published in the original *Erotic Colour Prints of the Ming Period, with an Essay on Chinese Sex Life from the Han to the Ch'ing Dynasty, B.C. 206–1644* (a very limited private printing in 1951).

18. For this and the following observation, as well as much of the rest of my limited knowledge of *Golden Lotus*, I am much indebted to the generosity of Peter Rushton, University of California, Santa Cruz, in sharing some of his unpublished doctoral research on the novel. See Rushton 1986.

19. It is often suggested that the absence of a solid and three-dimensional

body is due to the peculiarities of a medium, specifically within woodblock printing or even more generally within Chinese brush painting. But the limitations in effect that can be achieved in particular media, such as woodblock printing and brush painting, are never as strict as the limitations of the associated technology, such as the relationship between carving, block, and printing or between brush, ink, and paper. That is, the material availability of the medium may often be an inflexible condition—Chinese artists could not have suddenly summoned up oil paints or pencils had they become frustrated by mineral pigments and fox-hair brushes. But material properties are often amazingly flexible. Western etching can reproduce the shading of light, and Chinese woodblock printing can reproduce the hair marks of a calligrapher's brush. In fact, Chinese artists characteristically delighted in media trompe l'oeil, such as lacquer "metalware" in the Tang, and embroidered "paintings" in the Ming and Qing. A complete technological practice, however, represents a complex set of cultural choices. The suspicion doubtless remains that, had these illustrations been painted by a painter instead of carved by an engraver, they could have been much more substantially embodied. Undoubtedly this would have been *possible*.

20. For a discussion of this painting, now in the British Museum, and its text, see Shih Hsio-yen (1976:12). I first discussed these same attributions and problems in Hay (1983a:90–96).

21. The scroll, in ink and color in silk, is in the Liaoning Provincial Museum. It is reproduced in *Zhongguo lidai huihua*, pls. 38–43. A later but complete copy is in the Yale University Art Gallery. The painting obviously has some specific reference. For information about Zhou Fang, see the entry on another fine attribution in the Nelson-Atkins Museum in *Eight Dynasties* (1982:8–10).

22. "Taste" and "fashion" are obviously related but not identical. Taste does not necessarily imply the constant visual developments involved in fashion. Another obvious area to test Hollander's observations would be in Heian Japan (and also Edo). The taste/fashion distinction (mine, not Hollander's) is much at issue there.

23. Note, however, the association of nakedness with non-Chinese ethnicity. See comments on this below.

24. One might suggest the seventeenth and nineteenth centuries as periods when there was a powerful tendency to exception. The painting of "denizens of the street and market" done in 1516 by Zhou Chen is an unusually interesting earlier example. Originally an album, these paintings have been divided and remounted as two scrolls, one in the Cleveland Museum and one in the Honolulu Academy of Arts. See *Eight Dynasties* (1982:194–96).The catalog entry is informative, but its concluding suggestion that this painting should be seen as "the private, personal expression of a painter with a social conscience" is not articulate in terms of social history.

25. In Unschuld (1985:73) see the section titled "The Concepts of Wind and Ch'i" (67–73).

26. The dialogue with Buddhism was the principal arena in which this argument was conducted.

27. One might take Zhuang Zhou's "fish basket" as a theory of symbolism, but I think one would be wrong.

28. Compare the extraordinary sophistication of this technique in another seventeenth-century novel, the *Honglou meng,* beautifully translated by David Hawkes (1973). Elaborate descriptions seem, to the Western reader, to bring the narrative to a halt and to disperse it to the extent that the narrative thrust is lost. The activity of description, problematic in a Western context, is crucial in the Chinese case. Another strong tradition, very influential in painting, sees the character of person distributed in a landscape. This can be inverted, not surprisingly, so that the landscape is found within the person. See the excellent essay by Shou-chien Shih, "The Mind Landscape of Hsieh Yu-yu by Chao Meng-fu" (1984:238–54). The painting by Chao Meng-fu (1254–1322) is in the Elliott Collection. The painter Gu Kaizhi said that Hsieh Yu-yu (Kun, 280–322) should be portrayed "among hills and streams." Chao did this. Meanwhile, in the twelfth century, the scholar-gentry had begun to develop the idea that such "hills and valleys" could form spontaneously in the mind. See Bush (1971:45).

The development of "personality studies," as in the *Renwu zhi* by Liu Shao (third century A.D.), and of portraiture in the same period, is an especially important area for studying these issues. See Shyrock 1937; and for a sociological study, Spiro 1990.

29. The Daoist notion of an ideal, unregulated society was, I think, political rather than religious or evolutionary. This is not to deny that peasant women were in some contexts seen as more available or even as physically more potent. Note also a long-established imperial practice of choosing sexual mates from the farming class (Van Gulik 1974:17), explicable in terms of Daoist conceptualization. No idea of a more perfect body was involved.

30. *Analects* 6.16: "Where the solid qualities (*zhi*) are in excess of accomplishments (*wen*), we have rusticity; where the accomplishments are in excess of the solid qualities, we have the manners of a clerk" (Legge 1983:190).

31. In the *Wangzhi* section of the *Zhouli,* referring to the "disheveled hair, patterned body, engraved forehead, and twisted feet" of the Southern Man. Confucius's *Analects,* laconic though they are, pay close attention to clothes. Book 10, chapter 6, begins by stating, "The superior man did not use deep purple, or a puce colour, in the ornament of his dress. Even in undress, he did not wear anything of a red or reddish colour." It continues through a number of sartorial conditions (Legge, *Confucian Analects* [1983:230]). The remarkable life-size figurines in the first emperor of Qin's mausoleum may also be seen in this light. The driving force behind their representational style seems to have been a need to detail every feature of dress (including hair) that marked the status and function of each figure. So unused are we to such obsessive detailing that we react to it as "realism." Although

in this case it must be related to the legalist notion of *fa,* the specifications of rules governing identity, at a more generic level it is comparable to the sartorial conventions of Confucius's "superior man."

32. For a very helpful discussion of *zhi* and *wen* in the Tang, see McMullen (1973:307–44). I have discussed it very briefly in relation to calligraphy and rocks in Hay (1987:5–22).

33. See Schipper 1982, one of the very few specific studies in this area so far. Chapter 2 is devoted to the "interior landscape."

34. For the best introduction to this subject, see Bennett (1978:1–26).

35. Huan Kuan, *Yantielun, Sibu beiyao* ed., 3:3a–b. In relation to *shanshui* discussed briefly in Hay (1984:110–11).

36. See Porkert (1974:110–62). The two most useful authors are Porkert and Unschuld (1985). Porkert's work is a very highly systematized explanation; Unschuld's specifically criticizes it for taking systematization to a misleading extreme but deals with many of the same issues in a not necessarily incompatible way.

37. This high degree of systematization was probably related to the practice of medicine as a profession, one that fitted into a Confucian structure. There is a substantial body of texts from this tradition, but there were doubtless physiological representations that were less systematic, or even anarchic, and that were associated with different social categories.

38. This disguises a problem of enormous importance in sinology. A specific analysis of the problem may be found in Porkert (1974:166–76); a lengthier approach is to read Needham 1956. Some think the term *qi* should not be translated (cf. Schwartz 1989), whereas others think that Porkert's account of "energetics" is far too systematic (cf. Unschuld 1985:72). In my own view, "energy" is an extremely useful guide so long as one remembers it is an analogy and not an equivalent, and this is perhaps justified by the understanding among many scientists that the concept of "energy" in science is itself an invaluable working device, despite or even because of the great problems in defining it.

39. There is a distinct linking between the texture of skin and jade, and jade was a peculiar phenomenon of substance. The connection is probably worth investigating.

40. Confusingly, this is not the *shen* in the title of Mark Elvin's essay. "Tales of *Shen* and *Xin.*" Elvin translates that *shen* as "body-person," pointing to the aspect of physicality with a particular life span (275). As Elvin's discussion makes clear, even this physical *shen*-body is contextually defined in both space and time.

41. Even novels may read this way, as suggested above.

References

Barkan, Leonard. 1975. *Nature's work of art: The human body as image of the world.* New Haven: Yale University Press.

Bennett, Stephen. 1978. Patterns of the sky and earth: A Chinese science of applied cosmology. *Chinese Science* 3.15–27.

Bush, Susan. 1971. *The Chinese literati on painting: Su Shih (1037–1101) to Tung Ch'i-ch'ang (1555–1636)*. Cambridge: Harvard-Yenching Institute.

Bush, Susan, and Hsio-yen Shih. 1985. *Early Chinese texts on painting*. Cambridge: Harvard University Press.

Cahill, James. 1983. *The compelling image: Nature and style in seventeenth century Chinese painting*. Cambridge: Harvard University Press.

Clark, Kenneth. 1956. *The nude: A study in ideal form*. New York: Anchor Doubleday.

Egerton, Clement, trans. 1972. *Golden Lotus*. London: Routledge and Kegan Paul.

Eight dynasties of Chinese painting. 1982. Cleveland, Ohio: Cleveland Museum of Art.

Elvin, Mark. 1989. Tales of *Shen* and *Xin:* Body-person and heart-mind in China during the last 150 years. In *Fragments for a history of the human body*, ed. Michel Feher, pt. 4. New York: Zone Books.

Fragments for a history of the human body. 1989. Ed. Michel Feher. New York: Zone Books.

Gernet, Jacques. 1980. Chinese and Christian visions of the world in the seventeenth century. *Chinese Science* 4 (September).

Hay, John. 1983a. Values and history in Chinese painting. Part 1, Hsieh Ho revisited. *Res* 6 (Autumn): 72–112.

———. 1983b. The human body as a microcosmic source of macrocosmic values in calligraphy. In *Theories of the arts in China*, ed. Susan Bush and Christian Murch. Princeton: Princeton University Press.

———. 1983c. Arterial art. *Stone Lion Review* 11:70–84.

———. 1984. Values and history in Chinese painting. Part. 2, The hierarchic evolution of structure. *Res* 7–8 (Spring and Autumn): 102–136.

———. 1985. *Kernels of energy, bones of earth: The rock in Chinese art*. Catalog of an exhibition prepared for the Chinese Institute in America, October 1985–January 1986. New York: Eastern Press.

———. 1987. Structure and aesthetic criteria in Chinese rocks and art. *Res* 13 (Spring): 5:22.

Hollander, Anne. 1975. *Seeing through clothes*. New York: Viking Penguin.

Honglou meng. 1973. Trans. David Hawkes as *The story of the stone*. London: Penguin Classics.

Lawton, Thomas. 1973. *Chinese figure painting*. Washington, D.C.: Freer Gallery of Art.

Ledderose, Lothar. 1973. Subject-matter in Chinese painting. *Oriental Art,* n.s., 19, no. 1:69–83.

Legge, James, trans. 1983. *The Confucian Analects*. In *Chinese classics*, vol. 1. South Pasadena, Calif.: Oriental Bookstore.

Loehr, Max. 1973. Changing themes and content in Chinese painting. In *Proceedings of the International Symposium on Chinese Painting*. Taipei: Taiwan National Palace Museum.

McMullen, David. 1973. Historical and literary theory in the mid-eighth century.

In *Perspectives on the Tang,* ed. Arthur F Wright and Denis Twitchett. New Haven: Yale University Press.

Michie, Helena. 1987. *The flesh made word: Female figures and women's bodies.* Oxford: Oxford University Press.

Mote, F. W. 1971. *The intellectual foundations of China.* New York: Knopf.

Munro, Donald, 1985. *Individualism and holism: Studies in Confucian and Taoist values.* Ann Arbor: University of Michigan Press.

Needham, Joseph. 1956. *Science and civilization in China.* Vol. 2, *History of scientific thought.* Cambridge: Cambridge University Press.

Perniola, Mario. 1989. Between clothing and nudity. Trans. Roger Friedman. In *Fragments for a history of the body,* pt. 2, ed. Michel Feher. New York: Zone Books.

Plaks, Andrew H. 1987. *The four masterworks of the Ming novel.* Princeton: Princeton University Press.

Porkert, Manfred. 1974. *The theoretical foundations of Chinese medicine: Systems of correspondence.* Cambridge: MIT Press.

Rushton, Peter. 1986. The Daoist's mirror Reflections on the neo-Confucian reader and the rhetoric of *Jin Ping Mei. Chinese Literature: Essays, Articles, Reviews* 8:63–81.

Schipper, Kristofer. 1982. *Le corps taoiste.* Paris: Fayard.

Schwartz, Benjamin. 1989. *The world of thought in ancient China.* Cambridge: Harvard University Press.

Shih, Hsio-yen. 1976. Poetry illustration and the works of Ku K'ai-chih. *Renditions* 6:23–39.

Shih, Shou-chien. 1984. The mind landscape of Hsieh Yu-yu by Chao Meng-fu. In *Images of the mind: Selections from the Edward L. Elliott Family and John B. Elliott collections of Chinese calligraphy and painting at the Art Museum, Princeton, University,* ed. Wen C. Fong et al. Princeton: Princeton University Press.

Shyrock, John K. 1937. *The study of human abilities: The "Jen Wu Chih" of Liu Shao.* New Haven, Conn.: American Oriental Society.

Spiro, Audrey. 1990. *Contemplating the ancients: Aesthetic and social issues in early Chinese portraiture.* Berkeley and Los Angeles: University of California Press.

Unschuld, Paul U. 1985. *Medicine in China. A history of ideas.* Berkeley and Los Angeles: University of California Press.

Van Gulik, Robert. 1974. *Sexual life in ancient China.* Leiden: E. J. Bill.

Waley, Arthur. 1974. *An introduction to the study of Chinese painting.* New York: AMS Press.

Watson, Burton, trans. 1968. *The complete works of Chuang Tzu.* New York: Columbia University Press.

Zhongguo lidai huihua. 1979. vol. 1. Beijing: Palace Museum.

3

Multiplicity, Point of View, and Responsibility in Traditional Chinese Healing

Judith Farquhar

This essay is about the historical and practical contingency of bodies.[1] Though it was planned as part of a group of essays on body, subject, and power in China, I have sought to temporarily replace this vast triad with humbler terms that I can more easily relate to the discourse and practice of contemporary Chinese medicine: multiplicity, point of view, and responsibility. I argue that the Chinese medical body is a multiplicity, that many subject positions are acknowledged in medical emphasis on specified points of view, and that despite these multiplicities and relativities (or perhaps because of them), responsibility for correct action is a serious issue. This three-part structure governs the discussion presented here. But in reflecting on the body that emerges from this material, a simpler point can be made: that the body is contingent not only on vicissitudes of the natural environment but also on occasions of analysis and the purposes for which analyses are made. Practices produce structures, both normal and pathological. This being the case, certain conclusions can be drawn about the nature of subjectivity and healing power.

Introduction

In Chinese medicine illness is just as stubborn as it can be in our own medical experience. There are plenty of nasty smells and messy fluids, and doctors touch and manipulate vulnerable people in familiar ways.[2] Still, whatever it is that doctors of traditional Chinese medicine work on, it cannot properly be called "*the* body." I will try to show how thoroughly multiple are the bodies that emerge from even the most superficial study of Chinese medicine.

Similarly, the word "subjectivity" conjures up something quite fascinating within Euro-American history and experience, the conceptual heir to consciousness, mind, and individuality (cf. Smith 1988). Yet as analytic object, subjectivity proves elusive in Chinese materials. What I find instead in the discursive practice of contemporary Chinese medicine are numerous subject positions, constant reminders that perceptions are contingent upon the point of view of the perceiver, and an organization of knowledge (of disease, of medical tradition) as a specific and momentary *relation* unifying knower and known.

Further, though it would be foolish to deny that there is such a thing as power in the social life of Chinese medicine, I have found that the models of power relations provided by Western medical sociology and anthropology have not helped much as we try to understand what goes on in Chinese clinics and hospitals. One could provide a long string of negatives: doctors are not gods walking the earth, Chinese herbal medicines are not a magic bullet, patients are not "dehumanized" (whatever that really means), and so on. Instead of addressing classic problems of power, I want to focus on responsibility, which is not unrelated. Specifically, what is the distribution of responsibilities in medical practice? How do doctors, sufferers, and families decide on an efficacious course of action? How can a responsible path be negotiated among the multiplicities and relativities of Chinese medical bodies?

Problems of Comparison

This investigation, I should say immediately, is unavoidably comparative. The background to my appreciation of certain basic characteristics of the knowledge and practice of Chinese medicine is a Western medical history, one in which the dissected body, the constitution of a unified observer point of view, a master narrative of authoritative knowledge, and the abstract norm have played a tremendous role (Foucault 1975; Canguilhem 1978). Modern medicine's foundations in anatomy and functional physiology, along with its cultural context of powerful ideals of beauty, cleanliness, and respectability (Stallybrass and White 1986), have begun to crumble; in both the basic science laboratory (Latour and Woolgar 1986) and the modern clinic (Saunders 1988), "the body" is decentered, fragmented, and dispersed. Still, we have a commonsense or "textbook" knowledge of medicine in Europe and North America, in which we cling to the discreteness, mechanism, and anatomical architecture of the body; this bodily self-image is reinforced by an individualism run amok in the steroid-smooth bodies of athletes and the surgically improved bodies of Hollywood stars, anxiously forefronted by the sexual obsessiveness of our popular culture (Baudrillard 1976; Kroker and Kroker 1987).

Yet as Bryan S. Turner has pointed out, the body has been noticeably absent from our social scientific, historical, and philosophical discourses (Turner 1984). In addition, it has been tremendously problematized in biology and the medical sciences, thoroughly deconstructed in knowledge that replaces gross anatomy with cells and signal systems (Haraway 1991). I would argue, however, that a unitary, discrete, and mechanical body continues to fulfill an important (if often tacit) function in knowledge ranging from public health to political science: a body composed of structures, having predictable functions, and caught up in an economy of needs is borrowed in much social science from a certain ideal moment of classical biology. Its architecture and mechanics function as the natural given of the human, a known point of reference for human nature that is immune to determination by politics, culture, and history. The body is reified at the assumptive level of these discourses, contributing to the coherence of arguments on topics as different as birth control for teenage mothers and the efficacy of traditional healing in Africa. It is this essentialist body, elusive and unreliable as it is, against which I want to critically juxtapose the bodiliness that can be discerned in the literature and practices of traditional Chinese medicine in the contemporary People's Republic of China (PRC).

I will draw upon Chinese medical texts that are widely available in the PRC: introductory college textbooks, published case histories, and biographical sketches of Chinese doctors.[3] These sources are apposite partly because, like this essay, they are intrinsically comparative. Chinese health care has been officially dualistic since the 1950s, and discussions of the relative merits of *zhongyi* (Chinese medicine) and *xiyi* (Western medicine) are easy to elicit from almost any Chinese city dweller.[4] In fact, the modern practice of Chinese medicine could be developed as an object lesson in the powers, pitfalls, and bitterly acknowledged consequentiality of cross-cultural comparison.

In the PRC today no general treatment of "traditional Chinese medicine" can neglect the task of asserting Chinese medicine's systematicness, scientificness, and healing efficacy. This assertion is always made in explicit or implicit comparison with "Western medicine" and is often clearly framed as resistance to the hegemonic force of Western science in twentieth-century Chinese society. As with any comparison, certain capitulations are made to the metaphysics and ontology of the more hegemonic position: some basic Euro-American categories are accepted as correct, and pieces of Chinese medical knowledge that could previously claim only distant relationships are accumulated and integrated to fill them.[5] One of these categories (informed, no doubt, by the rise of "Chinese humanism," "individualism," and Maoist dialectics) is the body.

Let me provide an example that will resonate with points to be made in the rest of this chapter. In the opening pages of 1977 national textbook called *Foundations of Chinese Medicine*, an attempt is made to define Chinese medicine and to characterize the Chinese medical body within it:

> With respect to knowledge of the physiological functioning and pathological changes of the human body and with respect to the diagnosis and treatment of disease, Chinese medicine has many special characteristics. For example, it regards the body as an organic whole that takes the visceral systems of function and the circulation tracts as its internal interconnections, and it considers that between man and the natural world there is an intimate connection. It acknowledges the significance of such factors as the "six excesses" and "the seven emotions" in the occurrence of disease, and though it does not rule out the influence of the outside world in disease-inducing factors, it strongly emphasizes the function of internal factors of the organism. With regard to the diagnosis of diseases, it has formed a syndrome differentiation theory that takes the "four examinations" as its method, the "eight rubrics" as its differentiating categories, and "visceral systems syndrome differentiation" as its basic content. With regard to the avoidance of disease, it emphasizes prevention, particularly advocating "curing the illness that has not yet happened"; in addition, it has advanced a set of therapeutic principles such as "when curing illness seek the root" and the notion that one should deploy treatments according to [specific characteristics of] the person, the place, and the time. (Beijing College of Traditional Chinese Medicine 1978:4)

The strongly additive quality of this complex piece of text is typical of much contemporary writing in Chinese medicine. Pithy reductionist definitions are not aimed at, and "special characteristics" must be gathered from many quarters to assemble a single discipline called Chinese medicine that can be compared with Western medicine. Anatomy is missing entirely, and considerable tension can be found with regard to the body: "[Chinese medicine] regards the body as an organic whole that takes the visceral systems of function and the circulation tracts as its internal interconnections." It is interesting that the body should need to be defined at all. Clearly it is not an extramedical given, especially when we consider the dynamic and transformative character of the "internal interconnections" that constitute it. Implicit in this careful definition of the body is a strong contrast with anatomy. Theorists of Chinese medicine such as those on the committee that wrote this textbook view anatomy as a parceling out of the body into discrete viscera with relatively little direct interconnection; in emphasizing the "organic holism" of Chinese medicine, they refer to the spatial and temporal fluidity of the physiological effects they can describe. Such fluidity is conceptually impossible, they feel, in a conventional anatomy of mechanically interacting masses. Having rejected anatomy, then, are they asserting a different kind of foundational role for this body? I think not.

They assert in this definition of the Chinese medical body that the visceral systems and the circulation tracts are the sole "internal interconnections" of the body—a fairly radical statement. As I will briefly discuss below, such an assertion refuses fixity and discreteness; the visceral systems and the circulation tracts are uncentered and interpenetrating subsystems of concrete physiological and pathological activity. Like any activity, they must be continually maintained in optimal order or they will, almost of themselves, disintegrate. If Freudian psychodynamics has shown us that being of one mind is no more than a fragile and contingent result of psychic activity, Chinese medicine has analogous ways of problematizing the stability and taken-for-grantedness of bodies.

The Multiplicity of Chinese Medical Bodies

The only Chinese medical specialty in which bodies are routinely represented in a form nonspecialists find familiar is acupuncture. Textbooks contain numerous line drawings in the style of biomedical illustrations (fig. 1). They show the routes of the circulation tracts marked by solid lines on the surface of (almost always) a male body; these lines continue inward with dotted lines to connect with sketchily depicted but "anatomically correct" internal organs.[6] There are also, of course, the ubiquitous statuettes on which the twelve cardinal tracts can be traced and most of the acupuncture loci on them shown. This imaging tradition, in its current form not very old but nevertheless important, can be compared with anatomical drawings in European medical history. It is multiple in the sense that no one rendering can diagram the whole body in cardinal and reticular tracts, but the systematicness and internal consistency of acupuncture knowledge is made quite clear by these elegant drawings. Of course no biomedical illustrator ever attempted to capture "the body" in one picture,

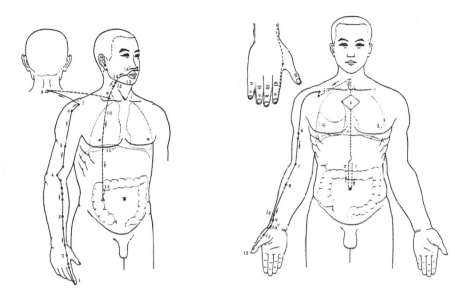

FIG. 1. Illustrations of circulation tracts from an acupuncture textbook. On the left, the Hand Yang Brightness Large Intestine Tract. On the right, the Hand Major Yin Lung Tract.

either; systematic anatomy too had its points of view, its partial images, its microcosms and homunculi.

In parallel with what Manfred Porkert has argued—that the tracts are not held to "exist" per se but are better thought of as schematic or mnemonic lines along which the "real" effective points can be properly located[7]—I suggest that these pictures are not representations at all. In other words, they are not images in the mirror of art of some founding reality called the body; rather, they are guides for the clinician, of indifferent (or at best contested) ontological significance but irreplaceable as a teaching tool.

Acupuncture texts attest to the practical emphasis of this subdiscipline; moreover, they insist on the partiality of the acupuncture version of the body. In one such text, acupuncture therapeutics are characterized as follows: "Acupuncture is a constitutive part of our fatherland's medicine. Prescription in acupuncture is decided upon through the syndrome differentiation methods of the eight rubrics, visceral systems, etc., according to characteristics of the sufferer's personal qualities, the illness state, and the season, and with reference to the function of the loci on the circulation tracts and the action of acupuncture" (Li and He 1982:305). This statement shows that the practices of acupuncture are intelligible only in relation to a wider arsenal of diagnostic and descriptive techniques that relate to each other in an enabling and supplementary way. The list could be lengthened quite easily without producing any sense that a proper division of labor or referral protocol needs to be organized. Even when every mode of describing and working on disorders is listed (and long lists are very characteristic of modern Chinese medical writing), a summary image of a hierarchically structured unity densely woven with circulation tracts—that is, something that could be called the acupunctural body—is eschewed. Put another way, it appears that the systematizers of modern Chinese medicine concentrate more on relating subdisciplines and techniques to each other than on assembling internally consistent accounts of the physical body (cf. Office of the 1977 Physicians of Western Medicine Class in Chinese Medicine 1977:164–65).

Perhaps it is inappropriate, however, to look for the Chinese medical body in acupuncture, a subfield that is much more strongly therapeutic than diagnostic. Surely diagnosis must rely on a sense of the whole body as a normal unity; a description without cross-purposes or contradictions must underlie any true account of a malfunction. Even in contemporary Chinese medicine, however, despite its often-asserted "holism," no such description can be found. Instead we find many modes of diagnosis, not all of which seem to require any (even implicit) version of "normal physiology."

One method (rarely applied alone) is illness factors (*bingyin*) analysis. It focuses almost exclusively on the war between heteropathic and orthopathic *qi*,[8] the relations between climatic or other environmental excesses (e.g., of heat, damp, wind) and physiological heat, damp, or sluggishness. More comprehensive than illness factors analysis is eight rubrics (*bagang*) analysis, a strongly reductionist method that classifies effects according to heat and cold, interiority and exteriority, repletion and depletion, and yin and yang. Eight rubrics analysis ultimately enables a yin/yang dynamic to be perceived. In effect this method classifies symptoms so as to reveal the state of yin/yang play at any moment of the illness's progress. Since it is only a specific, though simplified, classification of symptoms, however, it has few pretensions to comprehensiveness in terms of physiology.

Turning to "visceral systems imagery" (*zangxiang*), however, we are presented with something that is much more tempting, as beautiful as the

Table 1: The Five Visceral Systems of Function

Acts on	Stores	Unfolds in	Affiliated with
Heart system			
Blood	*Shen* (vitality)	Vessels Manifests in face Vents at tongue	Small intestine
Lung system			
Qi Breathing Clears away, carries downward		Skin and body hair Regulates the "watercourse" Vents at nose	Large intestine
Spleen system			
Transmission and transformation; elevates clear fluids; in charge of blood flow		Flesh Four limbs Vents at mouth Manifests in lips	Stomach
Liver system			
Dispersion upward and outward	Blood	Sinews Vents at eyes Manifests in nails	Gallbladder
Kidney system			
Fluids Marrow Accepts *qi*	*Jing* (semen)	Bones Manifests in hair Vents at ear, genitals, anus	Urinary bladder

abstractly channeled body of acupuncture but far more challenging to the systematizer. Table 1 summarizes the five visceral systems of function; similar tables can be found in Chinese medical college textbooks. I want to draw attention first to the interpenetration of the five systems. Each system has a sphere of influence extending from head to toe, yet functionally they are rather well differentiated from each other. For example, the liver system effects upward and outward dispersion (of *qi*, generally speaking); but because it includes the sinews of the limbs, it has a certain responsibility even as low as the feet.

Perhaps more important, no one system is more determinative of healthful functioning than the others. No hegemony of the central nervous system here! As a frequently encountered proverb has it, "Each looks after its own domain," but these domains interpenetrate both spatially and temporally.[9]

Also note the verbs into which I have inadequately translated the functions of the five visceral systems: the most frequently used verb is *zhu*, which is usually translated as "rule" or "control." In this table most of the "acts on" relationships are a *zhu* form of "control," as are those relationships in the "unfolds in" column that do not incorporate another verb such as "vents at" (*kaiqiao*) or "manifests in" (*hua*).[10] If a case is to be made for the discreteness (and therefore the very systematicness) of these five "systems," much hinges upon the meaning of these verbs. What, for example, is the difference between the "dispersion" (*shuxie*) accomplished by the liver system and the "transmission and transformation" (*yunhua*) managed by the spleen system? Are the lips as a "manifestation" of the spleen system separate from the mouth at which the liver system "vents"? As the classic "problem" of the *sanjiao* makes clear, the materiality of the visceral systems is not in their structural massiveness, not a matter of adding together the liver, the eyes, the sinews, and some blood to arrive at the "hepatic orb."[11] Rather, the reality of the five visceral systems lies in their production of physiological effects, their patterns of generating (concrete, observable) bodily phenomena in time and as experienced.

Thus visceral systems imagery provides us with no body that is in any way parallel to the one we tend to take for granted. This is not because the systems are abstract or ideal, but because they are concrete in quite a different way; of course your anatomical liver and palpable sinews are components of your liver system, but they are manifestations of its healthy activity just as are the twinkle in your eye and the luster of your nails.[12]

Subject Positions, Points of View in Clinical Work

I have emphasized the impossibility of organizing the physiological knowledge of traditional Chinese medicine with reference to a modern anatomical body, and I hope I have demonstrated that the field in which Chinese medicine intervenes is a profoundly temporal and functional physiology and pathology. I have named a few of the methods that guide Chinese doctors as they deal with illnesses, acupuncture and visceral systems imagery being the two most important. They are important partly because each gives a rather comprehensive account of physiology and pathology, and the armamentarium of either can be deployed against many of the same complaints. Theoretically congruent with neither of these, and yet usually deployed in tandem with them, are the less totalizing methods of illness factors and eight rubrics analysis. In addition, there is an unsystematized but nevertheless pervasive concern with substance flow and transformation, discussed in textbooks under such headings as "*Qi*, Blood, *Jing*, and Dispersed Body Fluids" (Sivin 1987; Liu 1988). And for acute exogenous illnesses, there are two competing analytic and therapeutic sys-

tems, one using the "six warps" as analytic categories and the other focusing on "defensive *qi,* active *qi,* constructive *qi,* and Blood."[13] How can one
image, one internally consistent and replicable account of an illness, be put
together from this forest of discursive possibilities? In the absence of a
localized and technologically visible organic lesion or growth, in the complex weave of systemic responsibilities for each normal or pathological
effect, how can a doctor see any specific disorder, any clear malfunction on
which to act? This question is answerable, but let me move on to a further
problem of multiplicity and relativism.

Not only are many modes of grasping the features of a disorder available to the clinician, none of them reducible to any of the others (in the
way we like to think anatomy is reducible to cell biology, for example),
but the major ones posit a close interdependence among their entities.
Thus in acupuncture the twelve cardinal tracts link up at their ends, each
connecting to the next in line, so that local excesses or insufficiencies of *qi*
can be transmitted to neighboring systems and also induce pathology
there. As for the visceral systems of function, each system produces needed
substances for some while relying on the productions of others; each exists
in relations of conditioning and being conditioned by the four other main
complexes.[14] These systems have no ultimate boundaries, no edges or
bounding membranes that physically and conceptually confine a disorder
to a given subsystem. Yet they are distinguished from each other, "each
looks after its own domain," and clinicians can think of the speed or fa-
cility of transmission along a sequence of systems.[15]

The multiplicity and interdependence of diagnostic choices means
that much depends on point of view. Therapy relies on an analysis, and all
analysis simplifies, reduces, and highlights some features while obscuring
others. The discursive practice of specifying from what point of view a
statement is being made, so widespread in modern Chinese speech, is
much more than a casual affectation. The discussions attached to published case histories almost invariably show how therapy relies upon the
selection of a point of view on complex illnesses. For example, from a case
of Dr. Zhuong Jianhua's published in 1977, titled simply "Stomachache,"
comes the following summation:

> Stomachache is also called stomach cavity pain. Quite a few classic
> works of Chinese medicine also called it "heart pain," linking it to
> the illness syndromes that frequently have stomach cavity pain as
> a main feature. The most common causes are the emotions of
> longing, worry, rage, and irritation, loss of regulation in the liver

visceral system, horizontal backwash attacking the stomach, or lack of vigor of the spleen and stomach system, with concomitant loss of orderly descension functions. It can also be brought about by fire stagnation or Blood stagnation of long duration transforming into heat and giving signs of collateral channel damage. To treat it it was necessary to enliven Blood and transform stasis to stop the aching, regulating Blood to aid *qi*. Although Blood was being treated, the movement encouraged was that of *qi,* which was assisted with *yuanming* powder to flow downward. Hence this therapy incorporates a courageous insight. (Yu and Gao 1983 : 198, 200)

This therapy "incorporates a courageous insight" partly because the patient had already been diagnosed by a doctor of Western medicine as having a duodenal ulcer. Dr. Zhong's therapy neither denies the pertinence of the ulcer nor treats it directly; rather, it focuses on altering long-standing pathologies of Blood and *qi* movement. Undoubtedly Dr. Zhong felt that these underlying pathologies had produced the ulcer in the first place. In a move typical of modern Chinese medical practice, to be taken up again below, the organic lesion is turned into a symptom, and the doctor works on its dynamic causes.

More important to my immediate point, however, Dr. Zhong's discussion foregrounds his own choice of a point of view on the illness he has characterized as so complex, a point of view that immediately entails a therapeutic strategy. The commentary discusses several diagnostic possibilities, all of them relating to a condition of Blood stasis. Rather than choosing among these "traditional" classifications, Dr. Zhong's strategy is to emphasize the intimate relationship between *qi* motion and Blood flow; he improves *qi* dynamics in order to disperse pathological static accumulations of Blood. This is, then, another aspect of his "courageous insight." A medicine that goes beyond the classificatory to the analytic is advocated, and a decision to motivate whole-body *qi* is chosen to the exclusion of other therapeutic options.

This situated analysis does not produce an account of the illness that has the authority of absolute truth. Nor is it certain to be replicated either by a different clinician or by Dr. Zhong the next time he is faced with a case of stomach pain. Truth claims of the kind Euro-American epistemology has exercised itself about cannot be made in a medicine that assumes no single topography called the body, which is then seen as external to discourse; where one of many possible points of view must be accepted before phenomena can be clearly perceived and acted upon, there is neither one account of "what's going on" nor one objectively describable reality against which to test competing accounts.

Responsibility

These insights about Chinese medicine—that its objects are many and that within the resulting relativism there are varying points of view—are admittedly clichéd; they do not go far beyond Chinese Philosophy 101. Where our book learning about Chinese worldviews fails us, however, is in the realm of action. Two problems recur in the attempts of my students and friends to grasp the nature of action in a field like Chinese medicine. The first is a certain ethnocentrism: we are Weberians through and through; we assume that action is based on knowledge. The two moments, knowing and doing, must be kept separate and in their proper sequence; knowledge is action's foundation, not vice versa. As students struggling with anthropological theory keep demonstrating to me, in our tradition to relativize knowledge is to (seem to) disempower. Most students feel that science (a collective undertaking) provides true knowledge and that action (a matter of individual choice) cannot be responsible without this sound foundation. These assumptions render both the knowledge and the activity of non-Western peoples problematic; hardest to imagine for many students is how people who are burdened with "culture" can ever be free.

The second problem we encounter in trying to study action in Chinese medicine has to do with certain features of discourse in Chinese: Chinese textual traditions (even modern ones) incorporate a different relation of the said and the unsaid within them—different, that is, from the patterns of erasure and supplementarity that students of literature have recently been examining in Euro-American texts. There are many genres of text in Chinese medicine, but there is one reticence that all seem to share: a certain silence on the issue of how choices are made by doctors, how cautious and effective courses of action are determined. Dr. Zhong's case discussion of stomachache quoted above is no exception. This is not to say that doctors do not explain their reasoning in discussions of cases, because they do; but in my experience these explanations only begin to address the complexity of the physiological and pathological state of affairs. They focus on a few threads, a couple of points of view, and cannot show us how vast amounts of possibly relevant material were eliminated from consideration.

This taciturnity should not be read simply as secretiveness or elitism, however. It can more productively be seen as a mode of positioning the individual doctor in the medical field and its history; that is, in relation to sources. When these case discussions are read closely, they give many clues to the genesis of the actions in question. Many, if not most, of these clues lead to social relations, especially with teachers and mentors. It is very rare to find any text associated with the biography or practice of a "senior Chinese doctor" that pays no homage to its subject's teachers or fails to identify his or her orientation to a school of thought.

Accompanying these references to apprenticeship (broadly conceived) is a pervasive concern with "experience" (*jingyan*). This is evident even (or perhaps especially) in the titles of published cases and biographical sketches, which are often phrased as follows: "Senior Chinese Doctor Gu Zhaonong's Experience with the Clinical Use of the Method of Opening up with Warmth" or "Senior Chinese Doctor Wang Shaohua's Experience with Using Rhubarb to Treat Blood Syndromes" (Xi 1987; Wang 1987). These texts are not simply accounts of one doctor's treatment of one disease. They should rather be read as characterizations of that doctor's significance (as teacher, I think) *through* an examination of his lifelong tendency to use certain methods or interpretations to organize much of his practice. In other words, these essays are assertions of the reliable efficacy of a particular point of view. They demonstrate how symptoms can be understood with reference to this bias on physiology and pathology, how prescriptions can be more imaginatively designed and customized— in short, how healing can be more powerfully and safely accomplished. They do not tell us how Dr. Gu or Dr. Wang arrived at his characteristic bias, or how he makes the fine discriminations that are required to act in different situations (the silence holds in these crucial areas). But by citing the filial relation of teacher and student and by centering the notion of experience, such texts show us that practical medicine, the humane art of healing, is inseparable from history and the social.

This discursive tendency gives us, I think, a clue about Chinese medical forms of power. In keeping with John Hay's insightful discussions of artery (*mo*) forms in genres as remote from each other as medicine, calligraphy, and kinship, we could see the many Chinese medical traditions as long historical lines of relationship. Teacher-student relations are actively perpetuated, both broadened and extended according to the logic of relationship (*guanxi*) and filiation. If we take seriously what case histories and biographies are only too happy to tell us—that healing power comes from the specificities of lineage knowledge and the refinements of personal ex-

perience—we can see clinical work as something like an enfolding of the
patient's illness process in a deeper and more wholesome history, a broad-
ening and application of the continuity of generations of healers.

Contrary to the expectations of American undergraduates, then, we
find when we read Chinese medical texts (attending both to the said and
to the unsaid) that knowledge is individual—it must be accumulated in a
long process of embodiment as a doctor practices—and action is collective, that is, impossible outside of relations with teachers and experience
with former patients. Responsibility has little to do with correct deployment of an impersonal science; rather, it relies on knowledge, skills, and
sensitivities that are slowly developed in practice—in a complex field of
social relations.[16]

I have argued that senior Chinese doctors offer little overt explanation
of their most central decision-making processes. The mainstream discourse
of contemporary Chinese medicine does, however, have an overarching
policy about action, a sort of banner flying over practice in the form of a
quotation from the *Plain Questions:* "In treating illness it is necessary to
seek to the root [*zhi bing bi qiu yu ben*]." Whatever role this principle may
have played in earlier centuries (and I suspect it has been far from obscure), it could be argued that "the root" today does battle with the notion
of cause perceived to be so fundamental to Western medicine. Again and
again we find clinical moves like that of Dr. Zhong above; where a doctor
of biomedicine would locate the "cause" of "symptoms" in an anatomical
lesion (the ulcer), a Chinese doctor finds a "deeper" root. Unlike cause,
which is one event in a law-governed sequence, "root" can be thought of
as developmental in a more openly historical sense; that is, an idea of
natural law is not really required to trace a present manifestation back to
its specific historical sources, but a refined technology of symptom correlation is very useful.

In addition to differentiating itself from Western medical readings,
every clinical decision positions itself vis-à-vis the multiple possibilities for
Chinese medical interpretation as well. Where some other Chinese doctors
might have seen the central problem as one of spleen-stomach system inadequacy (i.e., an interpretation according to visceral systems imagery),
Dr. Zhong chose to focus on treating *qi* flow, speaking within a framework of vital substances dynamics.[17] When he argues that Blood stasis is
the fundamental and long-standing problem, he reorganizes the body
away from Western anatomical unity *and* away from many other possible
images in Chinese medicine. He makes strong claims that the root he has

sought is the best organization of bodily phenomena, and of course the proof that he was right consists entirely in the effectiveness of his treatment. The root is ultimately a practical, not an epistemological thing.

History, Anatomy, and Materialism

As it stands, this discussion is not fully historical. By insisting on a nonanatomical logic and practice-based standards of value for Chinese medicine, I do not directly address the extent to which a Western medical body has entered and altered Chinese medical discourse. This is a problem because Chinese medical writers, teachers, and scientists have often added the vocabulary of anatomy to what they already know, locating Chinese physiological processes that are already spatially conceived with a structural language of organs and lesions. There is a standard logic to this appropriation, that of historical materialism; the anatomical body is often posited as the "material foundation" for a superstructure of Chinese medical effects. This move serves to partly reorganize older forms of Chinese medical knowledge such that anatomically unlikely physiological activities (e.g., the "transmission and transformation" of the spleen visceral system) seem externally determined, abstract, and ideal, while bodily structures, authorized by "science," are ahistorical and inert, safe from any revision or challenge from Chinese medicine. But this "scientization" is far from successful or complete in the contemporary discourse of Chinese medicine. For some of the reasons I have indicated above, older medical knowledge and practice have their own rigorous materialism and offer their own solutions to contemporary problems of healing.

In this essay, in order to say something about the challenging differences that Chinese medical knowledge and practice present to those of us who read the literature, I have idealized aspects of such knowledges into something typically "Chinese medical." This is a problem only if we naturalize our own creation, only if we insist that the "typical" or "coherent" body of knowledge we have delimited is more "real" than the syncretic, fortuitous, and oppositional, more true than the diverse facts that help Chinese doctors in their practice. This amounts to privileging "truth" over effectiveness, something that doctors of Chinese medicine resist with much of their work and their lives.

Conclusion

I want to return briefly to that North American (crypto-Weberian) model of knowledge and action that I discussed above. Of course this structure is still alive and well in our academies, and not only for under-graduates, as can be seen in the charges of "relativism" that are constantly leveled against poststructuralist social theory and postmodernist aesthet-ics. The problem of relativism is not something that can simply be con-demned away, however, either in today's academy or in today's world. The materials I have presented here suggest that Chinese medicine has been working relativistically for a long time: doctors must act, and they must have an ethics and a politics. But they must intervene in illness while knowing that there is no one world, no single objective standpoint, no absolute truth. One key to their efficacy lies in their willingness to accept teaching from the past and from elsewhere, their understanding that slowly embodied virtuosity cannot be finally verbalized, and their politics that can function in a world of multiple biases and bodies.

Let me close by bringing together some of the diffuse themes of this discussion in a more direct consideration of body, subject, and power. By arguing that the body of Chinese medicine is thoroughly multiple and perspective dependent, I have not sought to deny or reduce its materiality. Chinese medical notions do, however, somewhat recast materiality itself. Taking the duodenal ulcer of Dr. Zhong's case history as a figure, we can see that physical organs and painful lesions are cast more as products than as substrates. The material bodiliness that we tend to think of as stable and given (especially if we are young and healthy) is therefore in these Chinese discourses quite the opposite: the body is historical and constructed, ever vulnerable to disorganization and in need of continued reinvention in the form of proper hygiene of eating, washing, sleeping, sexual practice, and feeling. Medicine as a technology of the temporal and contingent joins with the forms of wholesome daily life to orchestrate what Nathan Sivin has called the "ensemble of processes" that is the body (Sivin 1987:91).

The necessity of taking an analytic point of view on this temporally fluid ensemble has been discussed above. But a point of view is an abstract epistemological object; its importance could be argued for any form of medicine. What relationship might be posited between point of view and an embodied "subjectivity" enduring through time—between "analysis" and "experience"? Recent use of the term "subject position" in the human sciences has tended to conflate the logical problem of perspective with the messier historical concerns of thinking and acting. An increased commit-ment to delineating the perspectives available in discourses has left us ag-nostic about the stubborn positive features of subjects and agents. Thus "Dr. Zhong" as a subject position is quite fictional, both in the original published case history and in my consideration of it here. His virtue (here understandable perhaps as publishability) lies in his ability to select an effective strategy from among many offered within the logic of Chinese medicine, a strategic negotiation of a subject position.

·   This "Dr. Zhong's" sole personal characteristic is "courage." We are reminded, then, in the last sentence of the case summary, that healing is not an intellectual game in which any point of view is as good as all the others. Courage is required as doctors reduce the multitude of possible bodies to one salient interpretation, one treatment strategy that might yield relief of symptoms. They must take responsibility for a sound analysis before any outcome; no action can be taken on a ground of infinite possibility. One suspects, then, that whatever the historical doctor Zhong Jianhua may have been like, he had every reason to assemble a coherent and consistent medical "experience," a stable set of biases on bodiliness and therapy that could restrict the logical openness of the Chinese medical field. As they accumulate clinical experience, doctors rely on redundancies and analogies to increase the predictability of their practice and decrease the need for "courageous insights."

For patients, too, the multiple body involves a certain subjectivity: much of what has been observed in Chinese clinics can be better understood when we grasp the consciousness of vulnerability and the attitude of activism encouraged by this more dynamic understanding of materiality. Medical care for many Chinese patients is continuous with their own individual and family strategies for maintaining health. This continuity of activity, this carefully extended artery of selfhood and embodiment, articulates with many other continuities in Chinese medical practice: examples are the knowledge lineages discussed above, commonalities between food and drugs, and the social networks that bring patients to specific doctors and enable long-term relationships with them.

Such patients surrender little power to their doctors as individuals (cf. Kleinman 1980:60); the authority accorded to senior Chinese doctors appears to be organized quite differently from the subtle claims and pressures we Westerners allow our doctors. I have shown above that Chinese doctors tend to claim authority by forging a specific relationship to history, both locating themselves in a long line of skillful forebears and asserting the specificity and efficacy of their own clinical experience. It is harder to say what power is actually accorded to doctors by patients, but anecdotal evidence suggests that pedagogical lineages and rich clinical experience are also important to them. In addition, patients and their families continually reassess the practical value of medical interventions in the context of their own wider strategies. In short, not only the power to heal but also the complex power of knowledge in medical social life are derived from a collaboration between doctors and patients. This is not a submission of a sick body, a little piece of extradiscursive nature, to the power/knowledge of a medical master of nature; rather, it is an interlacing of two profoundly social specificities, in which the doctor's medical powers to embody and make history are brought to bear on the sufferer's contingent and active embodiment.

Notes

1. With respect to my most recent thinking about characteristics of Chinese medical knowledge, I wish to acknowledge very great debts to the following scholars: Nathan Sivin, John Hay, Shigehisa Kuriyama, James Hevia, Angela Zito, and Charlotte Furth. Donna Haraway, Barry Saunders, and Deborah Gordon have provided a fascinating comparative background on "Western medicine." Jean Comaroff made many valuable suggestions as I was revising this chapter. Support for the field research on which the chapter is based was provided by the Committee on Scholarly Communication with the People's Republic of China of the United States National Academy of Sciences.

2. "Chinese medicine" herein refers to the institutionalized practices of traditional Chinese medicine (*zhongyi*) that currently are officially recognized in the People's Republic of China (PRC). I address neither the world of biomedicine in China nor premodern Chinese medical institutions and practices.

3. Most college textbooks are nationally published in the PRC. Sivin (1987) has translated much of an introductory text (originally published in Chinese in 1972), and Liu (1988) has published in English a two-volume version of the national "foundations of Chinese medicine" course that was offered throughout the 1980s. Texts of this genre, used in "foundations" courses, make a particularly nice comparison with introductions to medicine in American medical schools; arguably the knowledge in these texts stands in an equally problematic relation to more advanced understandings and practices as gross anatomy (the first-year medical school staple) does to biophysics, cell biology, and immunology.

Case histories and biographical sketches of senior Chinese doctors are published in traditional medicine journals and also in collections that are sold in the rapidly expanding traditional medicine departments of science and technology bookstores.

Just as I am not acknowledging here the sophisticated elaborations and postmodern imagery of Western laboratory science and the baroque horrors of modern hospital practice, I will also have to ignore the work of those clinicians and scientists in China who are exploring the conceptual and practical margins of traditional Chinese medicine in important and fascinating ways.

4. Partly following Chinese usage, I will use the terms Western medicine and biomedicine more or less interchangeably.

5. This process of mixing old wine to put in new bottles has hardly gone unnoticed by thoughtful Chinese doctors and scholars, of course. I do not wish to demean the work of the textbook committees, policymakers, and theorists who have carefully structured their characterizations of Chinese medicine as a discipline and a profession in this way. What they have done may be more than strategically necessary; it may represent their deep conviction that Chinese medicine has long needed some "grounding" in "objective" observable material structures such as anatomy. Moreover, this radical rewriting of Chinese medical knowledge is not unprecedented; the seventeenth-century revisions of the Warm Illnesses school arguably cut just as deeply into received categories and the "normal science" practices of the time.

6. "Circulation tract" is Sivin's translation for *jingluo*. See Sivin 1987 for most of the other translations of Chinese medical terminology used here.

7. Porkert (1974:198). He is not the only authority on this issue, though the point has its proponents in the contemporary professional literature of Chinese medicine. Much research has been done in the PRC in recent years on the "material foundation" of acupuncture effects. It was of course quickly noted that the circulation tracts have no direct parallel in gross anatomy, so this material foundation is usually conceptualized in rather subtle functional terms.

8. For discussions of the term *qi* (*ch'i*), see Porkert 1974, Sivin 1987, and Kaptchuk 1983. Porkert glosses the term as "configurative force"; its chief significance for this discussion is as the bodily substance that drives blood.

9. Western residents at Chinese colleges have noted the way soccer games, basketball games, and baseball games often play "through" each other on playing fields. Outfielders can be standing in the midst of a soccer game, and volleyball players are interrupted by clutches of basketball players ducking under their net. This is an image that goes beyond permeable boundaries to interpenetration: of course all players must keep track of their own game and play it with a very refined spatial sense; but no pair of teams can lay exclusive claim to a territory.

10. The challenging translation "unfolds in" is taken from Hay (1983b). In Hay's important comparison of classical medical writings with calligraphy, a picture is developed of multiple dense centers that disperse outward, from source to manifestation as it were. He shows that the logic of such dense centers and dispersed peripheries cuts across various fields in China. The implications for the reference of the word *zhu* and consequently for our understanding of power, rulership, and social relations in China are very great. David Hall and Roger Ames (1987) have developed a similar imagery at great length. Also see articles on rulership by Hevia and Zito in this volume for suggestive arguments.

11. See Porkert 1974, Sivin 1987, and Kaptchuk 1983 for discussions of the *sanjiao,* or "triple burner," "triple processing locus." The problem arises because this is a visceral system of functions (Porkert prefers to call them "orbs") that is not affiliated with any one anatomical organ

12. Internal organs need not be privileged as foundation in a medical materialism that is thoroughly functional and temporal. This is not to say they have not been privileged in just this way; Manfred Porkert calls the organs the material substrate of the "orbs," and many contemporary scholars in China prefer to think of anatomy as a kind of foundation of the functions for which Chinese medicine has such a sensitive vocabulary. I base my antifoundationalist reading more on the logic of practice and the continuing force of ancient texts (in which anatomy hardly figured) in contemporary discourse.

13. "Blood" is capitalized here to indicate that the substance being referred to differs markedly in its semantic range from that of the English word "blood."

14. One prominent scholar in the PRC has argued that the relations of interdependence of the five visceral systems take the form of five phases production and control relations (Deng 1981).

15. I have elsewhere interpreted the elaborate diagnostic and therapeutic systems organized around the "six warps" (*liu jing*) and "defensive *qi,* active *qi,* constructive *qi,* and Blood sectors" (*wei qi ying xue*) as precisely this: a mode of specifying the speed of transmission of pathological effects through the various physiological systems of function (Farquhar 1986). Interestingly, however, these two systems posit analytical entities separate from the five visceral systems of function and the twelve cardinal circulation tracts in order to accomplish this spatiotemporal analysis. Another multiplication of the body.

16. This is arguably true of all healing including "Western allopathic medicine." But in our clinical settings therapeutic action based on practical experience tends to be devalued—"empirical" treatment is a last resort after "scientific" diagnosis has produced no results.

17. Dr. Zhong's commentary does not mention it, but analysis of the prescriptions used in this case reveals a strong specificity for the liver system. So his root has a subroot, as it were; since he needs to enliven Blood, and the liver system both stores Blood (and thus is in danger of promoting stagnation) and governs "dispersion," it can be a good locus for reenlivening Blood. But the point made here still holds; many clinicians would prefer to intervene in the functioning of the spleen-stomach or even the heart systems, and would phrase their explanation much more strongly in the language of visceral systems imagery.

References

Baudrillard, Jean. 1976. *L'échange symbolique et le mort.* Paris: Gallimard. Unpublished translation by Barry Saunders.

Beijing College of Traditional Chinese Medicine, eds. 1978. *Zhongyixue jichu* (Foundations of Chinese medicine). Shanghai: Shanghai Science and Technology Press.

Canguilhem, Georges. 1978. *On the normal and the pathological.* Trans. Carolyn R. Fawcett. Dordrecht: Reidel.

Deng Tietao. 1981. [Dialectical factors in Chinese medicine's five phases theory] and [A reconsideration of dialectical factors in Chinese medicine's five phases theory] (in Chinese). In *Xueshuo tantao yu linzheng* (Theoretical inquiries and clinical encounters). Guangzhou: Guangdong Science and Technology Press.

Farquhar, Judith. 1986. Knowledge and practice in Chinese medicine. Ph.D. diss., University of Chicago.

————. 1992. Rewriting traditional medicine in post-Maoist China. Paper presented at the Conference on Epistemology and the Scholarly Medical Traditions, Montreal, 13–16 May.

Foucault, Michel. 1973. *The birth of the clinic: An archaeology of medical perception.* Trans. A. M. Sheridan Smith. New York: Pantheon.

Hall, David L., and Roger T. Ames. 1987. *Thinking through Confucius.* Albany: State University of New York Press.

Haraway, Donna. 1991. The biopolitics of postmodern bodies: Determinations of self in immune system discourse. In *Simians, cyborgs, and women: The reinvention of nature.* New York: Routledge.

Hay, John. 1983a. Arterial art. *Stone Lion Review* 11:70–84.

————. 1983b. The human body as a microcosmic source of macrocosmic values in calligraphy. In *Theories of the arts in China,* ed. Susan Bush and Christian Murck. Princeton: Princeton University Press.

Kaptchuk, Ted J. 1983. *The web that has no weaver: Understanding Chinese medicine.* New York: Congdon and Weed.

Kleinman, Arthur. 1980. *Patients and healers in the context of culture.* Berkeley and Los Angeles: University of California Press.

Kroker, Arthur, and Marilouise Kroker. 1987. Panic sex in America. In *Body invaders: Panic sex in America,* ed. Arthur Kroker and Marilouise Kroker. New York: St. Martin's Press.

Latour, Bruno, and Steve Woolgar. 1986. *Laboratory life: The construction of scientific facts.* Princeton: Princeton University Press.

Li Wenrui and He Baoyi. 1982. *Shiyong zhenjiuxue* (Practical acupuncture and moxibustion). Beijing: People's Health Press.

Liu, Yanchi. 1988. *The essential book of traditional Chinese medicine.* Trans. Fang Tingyu and Chen Laidi. New York: Columbia University Press.

Office of the 1977 Physicians of Western Medicine Class in Chinese Medicine, Guangdong College of Traditional Chinese Medicine. 1977. [Relations among several kinds of diagnostics] (in Chinese). In *Zhongyi jichuxue* (Chinese medical foundations) app. to chap. 5. Guangzhou: Guangdong College of Traditional Chinese Medicine.

Porkert, Manfred. 1974. *The theoretical foundations of Chinese medicine: Systems of correspondence.* Cambridge: MIT Press.

Saunders, Barry. 1988. The undeath of the clinic: A pathology of medical conception. Paper presented at the meeting of the Society for Health and Human Values, April.

Sivin, Nathan. 1987. *Traditional medicine in contemporary China*. Science, Medicine, and Technology in East Asia series, vol. 2. Ann Arbor, Mich.: Center for Chinese Studies.

Smith, Paul. 1988. *Discerning the subject*. Minneapolis: University of Minnesota Press.

Stallybrass, Peter, and Allon White. 1986. *The politics and poetics of transgression*. Ithaca: Cornell University Press.

Turner, Bryan S. 1984. *The body in society*. Oxford: Basil Blackwell.

Wang Weizhong. 1987. [Senior Chinese doctor Wang Shaohua's experience with using rhubarb to treat blood syndromes] (in Chinese). *Xin Zhongyi* (New journal of traditional Chinese medicine) 5:4.

Xi Zengye. 1987. [Senior Chinese doctor Gu Zhaonong's experience with the clinical use of the opening up with warmth method] (in Chinese).

Xin Zhongyi (New journal of traditional Chinese medicine) 1:3.

Yu Yingao and Gao Yimu. 1983. *Xiandai ming zhongyi leianxuan* (Selected classified cases of famous contemporary Chinese doctors). Beijing: People's Health Press.

Inscribing
Bodies

4

Silk and Skin: Significant Boundaries

Angela Zito

In a famous portrait, the Qianlong emperor (who reigned from 1735 to 1794) sits on a low divan, backed by a free-standing screen on which a landscape is painted (fig. 1).[1] Another portrait of the emperor hangs upon and partially covers this bit of framed nature. The emperor on the divan and the emperor in the hanging portrait turn toward each other. Both are encompassed by the inscription in Qianlong's hand whose first line titles the picture: *Is It One or Two?* The emperor signs himself "Cave of Narayana," a three-faced Buddhist deity, and so draws attention to the writing self that faces this painting of him posed before his own portrait. It is an arresting and famous image, one well suited to focus investigation of the relationship of signification and subjectivity in eighteenth-century China.

In eighteenth-century China successful intervention in cosmic process, or correct *li*, depended upon the peculiarly human ability to provide the site for ordered pattern to emerge from chaos.[2] Discourses on painting, medicine, and ritual converge in emphasizing the site of this emergent pattern as an ever-shifting boundary or surface, which is then accessible as various forms of knowledge.

In this chapter I will explore the sites of centering, the surfaces and boundaries that produced certain subjectivities and bodies as sources of signification and the texts that constructed those subjectivities and provided them with historicity. After situating the analysis against previous work on body and subject, I will return to *Is It One or Two?* to discuss the display of the emperor in painting and then as the site of signification and centering in sacrifice. These insights about surfaces will then be examined in light of traditional concepts of "face," or *mianzi*. Finally, I will briefly explore the implications of a politics of boundary and surface.

Fig. 1. *Is It One or Two?* From *Qingdai dihou xiang.*

Boundaries, Bodies, and Subjectivities

Many modern philosophers have interpreted *li* in the context of something they call "Confucian humanism."[3] They see Confucius's writings as marking a turn from the supernatural toward the ethical in a classificatory move that rests on an analogy made between Confucianism's immanental anthropocentrism and European Renaissance humanism. Furthermore, these philosophers have often translated *li* as propriety, emphasizing its abstract quality as a rational standard of value for individuals.[4] In doing so they have opposed Confucianism to Daoism as the cultural and ethically obsessed opposes the natural and innocent.

The creation of these dual categories bases itself in yet another analogy with European experience, a Cartesian framework that posits an internally consistent, psychological subject who exists in tension with external society and then opposes the social order to the natural.[5] A more socially oriented alternative to this individualist reading comes from within the Chinese Marxist tradition, where *li* is seen as the ideology of the aristocratic classes. The influence of European modernist rationalism creeps in here as well, however, as a "progressive" break is posited between "ethical" Confucianism and the "superstitious" past.[6]

These philosophers share a tendency to neglect or de-emphasize the ceremonial practices associated with *li* in favor of a "meaning-centered" approach based upon readings of Chinese interpretive texts. In unconscious collusion with the philosophic texts they study, they make the performing body disappear, along with its material circumstances and limitations. In the past decade, as part of a growing group of cultural, social, and intellectual historians in the United States, I have drawn attention to the ceremonial aspect of Chinese *li*. I have used handbooks and illustrative catalogs of artifacts and clothing, as well as visits to surviving architectural spaces. As a cultural historian, I have turned to cultural anthropological methods, which I believe supplement social and intellectual history in specific and needed ways. This critical move repeats one made in anthropology itself: the cultural critique of social anthropology. American anthropologists like David Schneider (1968, 1980), Clifford Geertz (1973), Sylvia Yanagisako (1987), and Ronald Inden (1990) have criticized work done in the British social/functionalist tradition for taking Anglo-American commonsense categories, themselves culturally constructed (e.g., family, gender, politics), as the basis of universal human experience.[7]

Imperial sacrifice bridged material and thoughtful life by enacting on its altars certain philosophic propositions about humanity and its cosmos; the emperor and his imperium produced through their practices meaning and value that ramified into every corner of Chinese life. In turn, monarchy drew its power from its participation in categories significant in everyday life, embodying such morally charged imperatives as filiality through use of a shared repertoire of gesture, architecture, and language.

"Centering" is what I have termed the generation within imperial sacrifice of boundaries that create difference and bring it under control. Often traces of this power were displayed upon surfaces. The Chinese word *zhong* (center) does not mean "inside." That idea is conveyed by *nei*, whose antonym is *wai* (outside); *zhong* has no proper opposite term. As a noun it mean "middle," but an empty one, found between the inner and outer, where the upper and lower meet and where there is no movement in the four directions. As a verb, *zhong* means to hit the center. "Centering" thus constantly creates itself through the correct separation of upper and lower, the correct bounding of inner and outer. Conceived of in this manner, it is the mediate third that makes meaningful difference possible. When people "make the triad with heaven and earth" they *zhong*, providing their meaningful connection.[8]

I have previously explored "centering" or *zhong* as it was embodied in the bodies and vessels of imperial ritual (Zito 1990). When translated as "etiquette" or "ritual," *li* seems to imply the imposition of transcendent apolitical rules upon an asocial, "natural" body. But eighteenth-century ritualists constituted and displayed bodies of shifting boundaries and interfaces that interpenetrated other significant surfaces in the material world. The subject positions created in this social universe were brought into being unequally; this essay explores the concrete logic of yin/yang encompassment.

This metaphysics of resonant transformation underlay the simultaneous production of self and world in constant interaction. Far from being an abstract and transcendent standard of behavior imposed upon all people equally, *li* were finely differentiated practices that created a network of relationships within which situated subjectivities came into being.[9]

These subject positions (ruler, subject, father, mother, son, daughter, friend of higher status, friend of lower status, elder, younger)[10] were practically embodied in a variety of ways that produced reciprocal hierarchical relations in a circulation of powers. The primary constructive metaphor for bodies in imperial ritual practice was the vessel: the positions of embodied power it constructed were ruler/subject, father/son (positions usually, *but not always* occupied by biological males;[11] positions endowed with the yang power of initiation rather than the yin power of completion).

Chinese ritualists imagined both vessels and bodies differently than we do. For them, the vessel's nature as a "container" was secondary. On the contrary, its function as boundary between interior and exterior and as sign-bearing surface resonated with the body. The body as vessel was a body contextualized within an ontology of process, in an immanental cosmos devoid of God the singular, within a thoroughly transformative metaphysics (Hall and Ames 1987:15–16; Farquhar, n.d.).

By the eighteenth century in China, ritualists, painters, and medical practitioners found surfaces and boundaries to be significant ways of coping with the final era of the Chinese metaphysics of interpenetrating and constantly transforming being-in-process. People who did not "center" faced exclusion from the twin authority of both writing and ritual. Those interpolated into the positions of mother, daughter, younger (often, *but not always,* the biologically female) were obviously disadvantaged under inscriptions that privileged the yang body of boundary making and encompassment.[12] We must suppose that rituals for producing other subject positions would operate through other materialized metaphors, lest we

universalize one body throughout Chinese sociality (and mistake the ideology of emperorship for the wider sociality it sought to control). Thus
the bodies/selves under investigation here are the specific ones of rulers/
subjects and fathers/sons who write and perform sacrifices.[13] The question
we must ask is how these bodies of power were produced, and to what
effect.

As historians we have tended to ask, What do texts record? As critical
social theorists we must also ask, How do texts leave traces at all, and why?
In the Chinese case, we must notice that ritual and writing were practices
that produced specific and powerful embodied subjectivities by creating
charged sites for their coming into being.

The distance of an eighteenth-century Chinese metaphysics of transformation from the post-Cartesian framework of positivist science points
up the inadequacy of a "symbolic analysis" grounded in the positivist faith
in the really real and its mimesis in representation. But if texts do not
record or imitate, what do they do? I am suggesting that the function of
representation is only one axis of the text's work (but the one privileged
in most historiography). In fact, texts are not merely innocent and mute
metaphors of something else. They are also metonymic traces of "signification as the process of making sense." To continue Henriques et al.
(1984:97): "Signification does not represent anything at all, rather it is a
production." Let us turn to the materialization of the Qianlong emperor
through painting.

Silken Painting

Is It One or Two? differs in important ways from a post-Renaissance
European realist portrait, a self objectified and represented. It has little
in common with that modern consciousness of the self as interior, separate from a world constituted as exterior and objective. The emperor
did not paint it, yet he participated in its production by the supplement
of his calligraphy. Thus we have a writing self, a self posed, and a self
portrayed: the memorialization of the appreciation of a representation.
The work is perfectly emblematic of a century when scholars were scrutinizing older epistemological traditions in order to question past forms of
representation.

Portraiture in general enjoyed a revival in the seventeenth century
after an eclipse by landscape that James Cahill connects to the Song pre-
occupation with pattern underlying all cosmic phenomena. Song artists
thought these patterns were best expressed through extrahuman motifs of

FIG. 2. Portrait of the Qianlong emperor (1736–95) in the style of Giuseppe Castiglione. From *Qingdai dihou xiang*. From the collection of the C.V. Starr Library at Columbia University.

landscape (Cahill 1982:106). By the eighteenth century, the few profound studies of faces that rely upon the face's physical expression to convey the inner being of the subject were influenced by visiting European painters such as Castiglione (fig. 2).[14] The sense they convey of a body/person isolated in empty space only highlights the difference of portraiture within the social formation we are examining here.

As Steven Goldberg (n.d., 9) has shown, from the pre-Han period, Chinese painters portrayed human beings within specific topoi that provided them with an identity. This identity, however, is shifting and contextual, denoting a relative point of convergence among culturally and historically specific sets of determinant relations. Goldberg discusses the contextual topoi of gardens, palaces, hermitages, and trees and rocks beside rivers. Thus, instead of the portrayed body itself bearing the burden of representation of singular identity, it is the relationship of a figure to its context that constructs it as something occurring between them. The figure is often surrounded by objects that suggest an inner life (Cahill 1982:115).[15] Qianlong sits among the accoutrements of an artist and man of letters, a *wenren:* painting and screen, scrolls and albums, brushes and inkstone. In an amusing reversal of the usual portrait convention of the person sitting under a tree, we see trees beneath the man; miniaturized pine and *Prunus* indicate Qianlong's love of microcosmic reproduction.[16]

In other words, the things pictured in a portrait signal inward traits, brought to visibility and displayed upon the surface of the painting. The interior of the emperor's self is not a space marked off sharply from an exterior, a private sanctum for secret thoughts appropriate to that space. It is instead the origin for readable, external signs. In this portrait, those signs may be personal and not particularly important. In ritual, however, the king's body becomes source and site of cosmically key representations.[17] I will return to *Is It One or Two?* but should pause to note how this way of depicting the relations of body interior and exterior in painting resonates with the body constructed by traditional medicine in China.

Correlative Contexts

The discourses of art, medicine, and ritual shared a founding moment in the Han (206 B.C.E. to 220 C.E.), with the rise of yin/yang theory and correlative thinking. At that time the cosmos was conceived as a vast plane of systematically resonating sets of perceptible correlations. Most scholars agree that these theories reached a height of systematization with Dong Zhongshu and his theories of *ganying,* or resonance.[18]

Some basic forms of correlative thought included correspondence between heavenly and imperial order, between cosmic changes and human life, and those based upon the Five Phases (Henderson 1984:1–22). In their continuous transformation, the Five Phases of water, fire, wood, metal, and earth provided a model of order for diverse natural and human phenomena. Ted Kaptchuk calls them "five kinds of processes" and says they comprise a system of "correspondences and patterns that subsume events and things, especially in relationship to their dynamics. More specifically, each Phase is an emblem that denotes a category of related functions and qualities" (1983:343, 344–57).

Joseph Needham charts a selection of twenty-nine sets of correlations including the seasons, cardinal directions, tastes, smells, numbers, musical notes, stars, the weather, colors, and instruments. Also included are the five senses (*wuguan*—eyes, tongue, mouth, nose and ears), as well as the human psychophysical functions (*wushi*—demeanor, vision, thought, speech, hearing), parts of the body, affective states, and the viscera.[19] Thus humans were thought to be subject to the same transformations as other elements of the world.

I suspect this innovation in cosmology overtook and subsumed the older imaginings of self and world we find in the writings of Confucius, particularly a notion of the body/self as a focused field with a dense center that ideally could interpenetrate with other selves.[20] In the Han, the attributes of the things and people of the world were serialized, scrutinized, and compared. The links between them were locally articulated, without reference to a transcendent unifying principle. In constant transformation, the cosmos brought itself into being with the aid of human beings who could design properly resonant ritual action. As they edited ritual handbooks, eighteenth-century ritualists painstakingly retrieved Han and pre-Han ritual institutions through evidential investigations.[21]

This metaphysics of resonance and transformation underlay theorizing about the human body in Chinese medicine.[22] Bodies were (and are) thought of as a complex network of energized matter known as *qi*. Observable manifestations are organized into an integrated set of functions that coexist as a multiplicity (Kaptchuk 1983:52, Farquhar, this volume). These bodies' energetics have little in common with the substantialized bodies of Western anatomy with their discrete organs that exist in mechanically articulated relation to one another, separated from the outside world. For the Chinese medical body, boundaries between interior and exterior are conceived dynamically as the point or interface where internal and external processes engage, and this changes according to point of view or function.

For instance, the whole system of acupuncture meridians depends on the patterns of energy deep in the body's interior being palpable at its surface (Hay 1983b:89). These points happen to coincide with the skin. In contrast, there is a kind of *qi* called *feng* that circulates between the microcosmic body and the macrocosm, providing an interface beyond the barrier of the skin (Hay 1983b:92).[23] Thus body and world interpenetrate one another in a shifting relationship. What I wish to emphasize here is that the interface of interior and exterior, the surface formed as the site of their interaction, is also the privileged site of signification in the overlapping discourses of art, medicine, and ritual.

In this system, the human is dissolved into related processes and correlated with the nonhuman world. Rather than acting merely as observer, stimulated by external signs, the participating ritualist himself—his faculties, senses, responses, clothing, and actions—is systematically included in that very set of signs called forth by the ritual. The portrait convention that turns the emperor inside out through the objects arrayed beside him provides an eighteenth-century example of the "planar," surface-oriented signification that assumes no fixed boundaries between the internal self and the external world. Instead, self and world are contextualized in a web of interconnection, leading to a fascination with texture and text.

Within this cosmos of transforming resonances, it remained vital for people not so much to "join" nature, which implies a separation, as to display that there was not and never had been a gap. But it was possible to signify the absence of an absence only with a presence, and this was perforce accomplished through the *materia* of signs, substantial artifacts, sounds, and movements.[24]

To return to the artifact at hand, the dynamic and relative relationship between inner and outer is also portrayed through the two portraits themselves. They are a temporal series; in his mind's eye is not the first, hanging portrait farthest from the emperor? Yet as we look at the painting and imagine the emperor inscribing it, paradoxically, it is the hanging portrait that is most encompassed. In this case the innermost portrait exists as a portion of the whole, not just as its complement but as its microcosm. It contains the exterior as the exterior encompasses it (it is a portrait, after all, of the man holding its "frame" painting). More important, the first painting was a necessary element in the design of the second. As a metaphor for interiority, it does not assert itself against the world but participates in its creation.

Another portrait convention we notice in *Is It One or Two?* is the invisibility of the corporeal body behind its folds of clothing. Although Chinese painters do not display the body's flesh in form, they leave constant traces of their own bodies' efforts in the brushstrokes that animate the silk (Bryson 1983:89, 92).[25] John Hay has persuasively argued that the aesthetic vocabulary that anthropomorphizes calligraphy into possessing bones, flesh, sinews, blood, veins, and breath derives from traditional medicine (Hay 1983b:78, 1983a). These usages are not only metaphorical. Calligraphy is, in Hay's words, "a line of energy materializing through the brush into the ink trace" (Hay 1983b:88). In fact it is a vein, *mo,* of ink that pulses in the rhythm of the painter's own "arteries" (also *mo*), an extension of the painter's real body. The emperor's calligraphy metonymizes the metaphors of similitude that are the two portraits. All the brushstrokes call attention to the various heart-minds—embodied consciousness—that have produced the painting.

In his calligraphic entitlement, the emperor names himself but does not describe himself. His writing is fundamentally an act, not a portrayal, and this distinction would stand even if we were dealing with a realistic self-portrait. But can we so easily separate calligraphic "act" and painterly "representation"? It is just this performative quality of the Chinese notion of the written word that led me to propose that ritual, especially Grand Sacrifice, be thought of as text/performance, communicative activity as a continuum composed of objects, writing, gestures, and oral presentation.

The sage-king in the *Liji* presents a precise ritual analogue to the duality of the emperor in this portrait, simultaneously producer and product of signification. A sage-king, whether creating writing, the trigrams of the *Yijing,* or music, discovered an already present dynamic order in the cosmos and devised a pattern for extending and resonating with it (Cheng 1982; DeWoskin 1982). It is not quite correct to say that in the traditional Chinese cosmology humankind "occupied" the center of the world. Rather, people "centered" it through rituals. They facilitated the signification of cosmic order by giving it voice through music, pattern through writing, and social order through *li,* or ritual. Like a membrane or tympanum, people mediated through total participation, an *im*mediate boundary. This role was both active and passive. People actively facilitated ritual, which was the perfect model of resonance with the cosmos, and simultaneously submitted to their own dissolution as part of its system of signs (*Liji Zhengyi* 2:1423–24).

A question also suggests itself: which heart-mind is indicated—the emperor's own or the original painter's?[26] It seems that poor men like him have had the honor of elision in the service of the imperial ego. Now, this single painting may seem a petty example. But in fact, even while making a wishful and whimsical joke (the inscription is in fact a little satire on the inability to distinguish representational difference; its answer to its own question, "Is it one or two?" can be summed up as "It doesn't matter!"), the emperor cannot escape the conventions of monarchy, although his irony is a perfectly mid-Qing response. His subsumption of the painter's work under his own inscription not only was royal prerogative, it was fundamental to the creation of the monarchical form whose king was also a sage, who summarized as the One Man the voices of the realm before heaven.

In fact, a third and final convention of portraiture will allow us to further expand this point. Qing literati enjoyed picturing themselves as famous people of the past. *Is It One or Two?* was painted after a number of earlier versions. Art historians generally point to the self-portrait of Ni Zan (Yuan dynasty, 1279–1368) as the model: the Qianlong emperor has replaced the landscape artist on the couch and has dressed himself the same way. But there is an even earlier Song version of a painter on a divan that is quite similar. Thus Qianlong was also imitating Ni Zan's *own* gesture to the past.[27] We might think of this as the topoi of historical time spatialized.

Thus three painters have been displaced from the portrait: the emperor is pictured *as a painter* (something he was not) *of* a self-portrait (that he did not paint) *in* a painting he did not make. His act of entitlement, that calligraphic trace (as a king whose brush carried the power of life and death), gathers meaning for himself as a writer accompanying a representation of himself as the ultimate writer-artist of the kingdom, present and past.

The portrait constitutes a plane that carries the patterns of *wen* and brings them to visibility. It is the place where inner and outer take physical form (following Hay 1985). We can now move from the surface of a painting that displays the emperor to sacrifice, where the emperor's body displays and motivates a surface of signs.

The Yang Body Between

In the eighteenth century rituals, or *li,* were considered visible extensions of the *dao* in the world of humanity and thus both moral/political and extrahuman/cosmological. The hyper-development of devotion to *wen,* or "cosmic text pattern," during the eighteenth century once more drew together the discourses on ritual, medicine, art, and music. The goal was the embodiment of the eternal and ever changing *dao* in material signs.

The four Grand Sacrifices were elaborate events. They constituted the emperor as cosmic mediator (Sacrifice to Heaven and Sacrifice to Earth); most filial son (Sacrifice to Ancestors); and center of his imperium of literati officials (Sacrifice to Land and Grain).[28] In my own work I call Grand Sacrifice "text/performance" because, certainly by the eighteenth century and probably before, the ritual began with acts of editing and classifying the ritual canon to ensure the proper embodiment of sagely history in the present reign. The ceremonial action that followed was a resplendent version of ancestral veneration carried out in lineage halls and homes.

The power of the throne thus lay in its ability to ritually constitute and display the intersection of two very powerful discourses: textuality and filiality (*wen* and *xiao*). The fetishizing of writing and the nurturing of sons provided venues for the production of persons and of meanings.

Elsewhere I have called its ritual process "centering." In centering, contrasting categories were encompassed and hierarchized as parts of a totality. The bounding of difference brought difference into being, mediated it, and most important, allowed for its control.[29] Thus boundaries and interfaces were highly charged, highly significant, and uniquely human creations. These interfaces were always dynamic: they were enacted and controlled in transgression and transit.

Grand Sacrifice also allowed the throne to display and control contradictions of the reproduction of its own power: Should power be inherited by filial sons or by knowledgeable scholars? Grand Sacrifice produced the emperor, who was of course both son of heaven and sage-king. Although this "solution" was performed into being through the body of the emperor, the generalizability of ancestor veneration into all households and the ideal of classical literacy for all males allowed its infiltration into everyday life.

The four Grand Sacrifices shared an identical ceremonial order. During five days of preparation, participants were secluded, animals were killed, and finally the carefully prepared vessels and spirit thrones were placed in prescribed fashion upon altars and participants' places were marked. On the day of the ceremony, the emperor moved in procession toward the appropriate altar and himself offered each of the Three Presentations (*sanxian*) of jade, silk, and cups of wine. His movements were accompanied by music and dance, interspersed with the chanting of hymns.[30]

The yearly Sacrifice to Heaven was performed outdoors at the winter solstice on a great three-tiered and balustraded white marble altar, in an area called the *jiao*. Usually translated "suburban," *jiao* in fact means "boundary." Thus we note that the site of the sacrifice was between the city and the countryside, since its sacrificial action mediated between heaven above and earth below.[31]

The white marble altar was empty except for ritual occasions when the carpets were unrolled, torches fired, and tents, spirit tablets, and vessels of food offerings laid out. The vast open space of the northern China sky bearing down on the cold altar must have dwarfed the objects themselves. By far the most impressive sight on that altar was the emperor with his officialdom, in their dragon robes and fur-trimmed, jewel-topped hats (fig. 3).

Court dress, or *chaofu*, was prescribed for all ceremonial occasions, and men who passed the palace examination in the Qing were presented with a complete set by the emperor. Court dress was made of silk, its motifs either woven in as tapestry or embroidered.[32] *Chaofu* shared the same decorative motifs with the more commonly produced dragon robes. Both are covered with cosmic signs. Earth, sea, and sky are represented: the hem is water, and at the four axes of the robe (the four cardinal directions) mountains jut upward into a cloud-filled sky where dragons fly and other symbols associated with king and cosmos float (Cammann 1952:81). When the robe was worn and the head emerged above the clouds on the collar, the observer was presented with a mobile microcosm of the eighteenth-century Chinese universe. All members of the imperium wore dragon robes.

The emperor's clothing, however, added to this overall structure the ancient Twelve Symbols (*shi er zhang*). Included were the sun, moon and stars, mountains, small dragons, birds, *fu* symbols denoting his civil power to adjudicate and an ax denoting his power to punish, sacrificial cups, water weeds, and fire and grain (Cammann 1952:87–88).

The Twelve Symbols had always been closely associated with sacrifice. By the eighteenth century they were thought to refer not only to the extrahuman cosmos (the four principal sacrifices, animate nature, the Five Phases) but also to the qualities of a model sovereign. (These included enlightenment, protectiveness, adaptability, filiality, purity, and so on; Cammann 1952:90–91.) Their double reference to the larger cosmos and the inner man marks their wearer, the emperor, as the chief centerer in these rituals.

But although the emperor was differentiated by certain colors and by

FIG. 3. Portrait of the Qianlong emperor Ch'ien Lung (1736–95) as a young man, wearing his dragon robes and cap. Unidentified artist, colors on silk. The Metropolitan Museum of Art, Rogers Fund, 1942 (42.141.8).

the Twelve Symbols, in fact his clothing rather tended to blend in with that of his courtiers—a fitting reminder that the son of heaven was above all a model: of sageness, of filiality, of human perfection.

Indeed, the period of *bei*, "perfecting" or "preparation," before the day of sacrifice, included all participants, not only the emperor. At that time people went into seclusion, animals were fattened, washed, and slaughtered, vessels were filled with food, and prayers were composed. Participants, victims, and vessels were inspected and manipulated to prepare them as boundaries between an inner and an outer field.

A logic of resemblance through imitation (*fa, xiang*), contiguity (*chen*), and correspondence (*ying*) underlay these elaborate homologies. From the intricate textual discussions and precise provisions for foods, clothing, and vessels and their treatment, the abstraction of the yin/yang bipolarity of inner and outer materialized in things. In other words, to enable "centering," a division was first created. Vessels were divided into outer forms and inner contents, people into inner heart-minds and outer costumed roles. But with victims' transformation into pure boundary, drained of blood inside and shaved of fur outside, we understand that the point of this division was to provide occasion for the display of a hierarchically organized unity that preserved difference through the arrangement of sacrificial objects, including people.

The altars of Grand Sacrifice were concentric zones of boundary walls and levels of platforms. Ritual manuals highlight action at the points of transition: gates between inner and outer, stairs between upper and lower. Ritualists' bodies moved together through this inscribed space, centering it in ceremonial action (Zito 1989:271–324).

Each participant's own body was not a closed container-thing but rather, like the altar spaces, a complex concatenation of ever more intimate boundaries. The body was an ensemble of focused fields whose shifting edges and surfaces provided the sites for articulation between inner and outer. If the self could contain and develop an interiority, it was because it could differentiate and bind. What we interpret in philosophical texts as the privileging of interiority, an inner self, can be better understood as valuable proof of boundary creation and control. Thus the "centering" action of the self through the body paradoxically takes place at its edges, on its surfaces and through its senses, which act as gates to the outside world. Concentrating upon the body as boundary maker focuses us firmly in the realm of culturally constructive practices like dress and gesture. We overcome the metaphysical discourses of secret, hidden interiority when the "inside" is exposed as created in relation to the "outside" by the boundary itself.³³ There is no boundary unless there is the possibility of its transgression; for "centering" to occur, boundaries must be reestablished and reproduced.

The members of the imperium knelt and prostrated themselves behind the rows of vessels arranged before the Spirit Tablets of Heaven. Their jeweled hats even looked like vessel lids (fig. 4). The human body as vessel was clothed in a tissue of silk whose symbolic web marked the participant as a "centerer," the site of transformation between inner emotion (*qing*) and outer cosmos. Through eating the perfect boundary stuff, the sacrificial meat of victims, the celebrants encompassed the wholes articulated by that boundary. Identity is not the issue here; inner and outer are not so much rendered similar as brought into coincidence. "Boundary" creates and then may stand for this necessary contiguity of separate domains. Thus by extension sacrifice manifested other ideally articulated social

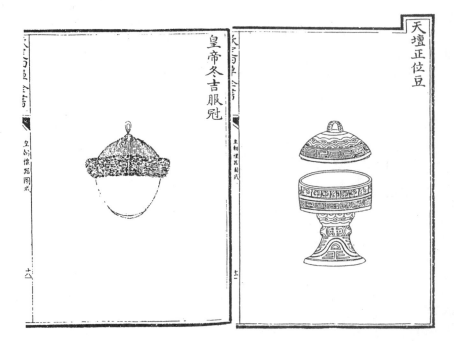

Fig. 4. Ceremonial hat and vessel. From *Huangchao liqi tushi,* 1.11a and 4.16a.

wholes such as the relations between fathers and sons or between lords and their servants.

On the Surface of Face

This construction of the body as interfacing membrane, taking up its life "in between," as it were, had (and has) an analogue in everyday life: the concept of "face." Face is the boundary that articulates the self in social life. Hu Hsien Chin points out that there are two words for face in Mandarin: *lian,* which refers to physiognomy, and *mianzi* (Hu 1944)— the "social skin," as Terence Turner might put it (1980). According to this dichotomy, *lian* is the more fundamental layer; it is that claim to dignity that all human beings share. Thus to "tear one's face" (*polian*) is very serious and results in shame. *Mianzi,* on the other hand, is additional, accruing upon one's *lian* as one grows in social influence and power.[34] Both layers of interfacing self depend for their construction upon interaction with others. In other words, in creating "face" a surface meets a gaze.

These gazes are hierarchizing because, while everyone ideally possesses the same *lian,* how far one's *mianzi* extends is a matter of the importance attached to one's social role. The perfection with which one fulfills these roles, primary among them that of the filial son or daughter, dictates how "big" one's *mianzi* is. One can *mian* others—that is, "face" them—but equality is not necessarily implied in this way of describing a relationship. Here *mianzi* is a site from which communication is possible.

A nice example of the intricacies of *mianzi* is found in the eighteenth-century satire *Rulin waishi* (The Scholars) (Wu 1981). The greasy, obnoxious village head Hsia tries to impress a group of townsmen with his invitation to dine with Bailiff Huang, a man described as someone who can "face" (*mian*) the magistrate. Here *mianzi* hardly implies equal status but rather functions as a site from which hierarchical communication is possible. Furthermore, when someone in the group reminds Hsia that Bailiff Huang is out of town, Hsia explains impatiently, not at all embarrassed, that in fact Constable Li is acting as host and borrowing Bailiff Huang's house. Thus Huang's *mianzi,* enlarged by its contact with the magistrate, is borrowed by Constable Li to shelter his pretensions for "hosting" the village head, who in turn proudly displays this whole nest of hierarchical interfaces to the villagers. Huang's house is the literal container for this mutual construction of positioned identity and prestige.[35]

Chung-yin Cheng defines face as "the presentation by means of which a person stages his social existence and communicates its meaningfulness" (1986:330). I agree that perfection of the interior does control the extension of exterior social power. But even more important is the fundamental process made possible by the connection of inner and outer: in the gaze of the community, the mediating "layer" called *mianzi* that is positioned between the inner *lian* and the outer world is the site of the social construction of the self, simultaneously articulated with interior and exterior.

The Politics of Boundary

In conclusion, I shall explore briefly the implications of surface and boundary-making in the eighteenth century. The various discourses of painting, ritual, and medicine in China shared this construction of an underlying "principle of thirdness," a site of emergent knowledge as an ever shifting, humanly created boundary. Metaphors for this site were two-dimensional—those of the surface (*mian,* in its social sense of "face"), the woven web (*jing,* the classics), the network (*mo,* arteries and veins of calligraphy and body energetics), and the vessel (*qi,* center of sacrifice).

The subject constructed within such discourses has little in common with our modern Western idea of the disembodied Cartesian subject, a unitary consciousness that has found social expression in the ideology of possessive individualism. Instead, in eighteenth-century China human consciousness as agent constantly performed itself into being through actions of (social) significance, the set of practices called *wen*. These signifying practices produce both bodies and texts simultaneously. Let us first take this process at the level of the embodied subjectivities of father/son and ruler/subject.

The vessel-body that writes and edits also displays inscriptions upon its surface. It exists at the nexus of metaphor and metonymy, privileging neither but acting as the transformative agent between them. The power is produced at this "boundary": the bounding of women in courtyard and foot bandages, and the insistence that they remain cut off from literate production of meaning, ideally reduced them to the "metaphorical" axis of the "inscribed upon."

In ceremony, the two-dimensional orders of signification in text were embodied by three-dimensional bodies; textual knowledge was transformed into bodily action; perimeters of self were extended as boundaries were pierced and the inner/outer and high/low centered. When the subject who centered was the king himself, a general production of self and society within the ritualist metaphysics produced instead a particular order: the imperium. I have already mentioned that imperial Grand Sacrifice concerned itself with the production of filial sons (embodied subjectivities in the position of "son"—often women took up this role) and the circulation of meaning as *wen* (controlling literacy and its rewards).

At the more encompassing level of normalizing discourse, imperial Grand Sacrifice, as text/performance, also articulated a specific relation of hegemony between the gentry/literati and the common people within itself (like a hinge). For the literati, the imperium consecrated the claim of successful examination candidates to be *the* inscribers of culture in general as they wrote the emperor's rites. The cultural categories they inscribed were reenacted in every home performance of sacrificial rituals of ancestor worship. In performance, the emperor's altars displayed the categories of social arrangement on a microlevel—the inner/outer, the high/low, and the "center" are ways that Chinese still arrange their social terrain. Thus the imperial center can be seen as one factor enabling this hegemony—the mediating third party that made it possible—rather than simply as wielder of the direct power of force, either military or economic.[36]

The word used in modern Chinese for "subjective" is the binomial *zhuguan*, composed of *zhu* (ruling or main) and *guan* (to observe). The binomial for "subject" is *zhuti* (ruling and body). In Chinese medicine, *zhu* designates the central point of the internal energy spheres of energy that make up the body. These are not organs, but rather points of centrality that organize radiating and shifting fields around themselves.[37] In ritual, the *zhuren* is the main sacrificer in ancestor worship, or the banquet host. The emperor himself, surrounded by his imperium of qualified sacrificers, was the most perfect *zhuren* and provided a sort of dense center of "centering" in the so-called Middle Kingdom. Thus in the body politic there was a kind of radiating dispersal of ritual power that reached into every family's home through the father. In the Qing conceptual universe, the body personal and the body political were available for discursive modeling of social relations in terms associated with activity, rather than merely through metaphors of resemblance.

The Chinese politics of surface and boundary remains to be written, but it will surely look different from our politics of subject/object. It will perhaps be a calculation of an algebra of position rather than a geometry of solids. Clearly, however, to posit the embodied subjectivities of ruler/subject and father/son as "the body" in the Chinese case is to mistake a body of ideology that sought to generate desire of imitation for the whole of social life. For the analyst, it is to fall victim to the imperium's own vision of itself. The emperor's power lay in the distance of longing his imperium could create between this yang body of power and the bodies of everyday life. We do know that imitation itself was considered a form of profoundly meaningful participation; the imperium provided a modeling of modeling.

However, we still do not know much about its rules of exclusion, its negativities, and the ways it coerced people in their everyday life. Certainly women were coerced and excluded in particular ways. In Grand Sacrifice we see clearly that the throne sought control over both the production of meaning and the production of persons: discourses of *wen* and filiality. Women were doubly negated: ideally never literate, they could only approximate the fulfillment of duty due to ancestors. Yet they were necessary to this particular discursive production in dauntingly material ways. They wove the silk upon which men wrote and bore the sons who venerated their husbands.

Postscript

The formation of boundary/surface that I have described culminated in the eighteenth century with its hyperdevotion to discourses of *wen*. The proliferation of surface decoration on porcelain, furniture, walls, and clothing reached an apogee of excess under Qianlong. Women were ever more closely bound to the interior of the house, both architecturally and by the yards of fabric binding their feet. Chinese surfaces/boundaries, the sites of transformation from this to that, were not easily recoverable unless they were covered. But by the mid-nineteenth century, things changed.

The painter of the self-portrait in figure 5 was Ren Xiong, who died in 1857 at age thirty-five. The portrait is life-size and seems even larger. The extraordinarily realistic torso is painted in flesh tones; the cloak is blue, the pants are white. But we are struck mostly by the stark contrast between the luscious flesh and the clothing, mainly a network of energetic, heavy black ink lines that are clearly done by the same brush as the inscription. Indeed, as James Cahill has said, the clothing mediates between the organic body and the "entirely conventional signs of the inscription" (1989:9). But the body seems to find no comfort in the cloth and to motivate it in no way. Instead, Ren seems to be sloughing off the dense net of brush writing. He inscribed his self-portrait, giving us a document that converts the body personal into the body political.

FIG. 5. Self-portrait by Ren Xiong (1820–57). Palace Museum, Beijing.

A marginal man in every way, Ren was born poor. He studied painting but was not a scholar. He was interested in the martial arts and excelled at wrestling, archery, and riding. An art historian of the People's Republic claims that Ren joined the army to fight against the Taiping rebels but later quit out of revolutionary sympathy. Ren's inscription complains that heroic men are usually left out of the record, and finally he asks, "But who are the ignorant ones and who are the sages? In the end, I have no idea. All I can see is a boundless void."

What we see is not only the anger of a common man, forced to deal from the margins of poverty with rich literati and merchants; we see also a man who can no longer make the distinctions of virtue and class that count in social life. He finds them meaningless and their record useless. He catches himself in the very act of emerging naked from the tangle of markings and traces that make the boundaries of Qing life.

Notes

1. From *Qingdai dihou xiang* (Beijing, n.d.). I thank the members of the original panel discussion and the other contributors to the volume, whose patience and hard work made this book possible. Funding for research into imperial ritual was provided by the Committee for Scholarly Exchange with the People's Republic of China and the Social Science Research Council.

2. This essay appears in expanded form in a forthcoming book on the relation between writing and ritual in eighteenth-century China.

3. Herbert Fingarette (1972:2) has also criticized this tendency among philosophers who study China.

4. One of the most influential American texts is Wing-tsit Chan's *Sourcebook in Chinese Philosophy* (1963:14–15). See also Chan, "Introduction: The Humanistic Chinese Mind," in Moore (1969:1–10), and Jochim (1986:34). In China, Yulan Feng has maintained a similar stand. See *A History of Chinese Philosophy* (1959:337–39) for discussion of *li* as external constraint. Benjamin Schwartz (1985:72–75) also takes thoughtful issue with the criticism raised by Fingarette.

5. For excellent recent analyses of the production of Cartesian subjectivity and its consequences for subsequent philosophical and social scientific discourse, see Judovitz 1988. See also Reiss 1982. For a discussion of the inadequacy of "humanism" in bridging the great divide between individual and society, and its concomitant failure to theorize a liberating modern psychology, see Henriques et al. (1984:15–18).

6. A sophisticated recent example is Li Zehou (1985:8–15).

7. These culturalists have themselves been criticized for reifying meaning

structures by more dialectically inclined anthropologists. I not only would criticize culturalist reification on grounds of unsound methodology but also (turning their own mode of critique upon them) would accuse them of providing a symptom of the (historically specific) objectivist epistemology I criticize in this chapter.

8. The quotation is from *Liji* (Li transforms), *Liji Zhengyi*, 2: 1422.

9. An excellent introduction to the development of "subjectivity" as an analytic concept is provided by Henriques et al., *Changing the Subject* (1984). The authors, clinical and theoretical psychologists, propose that "subjectivity" allows us to overcome the deeply entrenched theoretical split of individual and society toward understanding how selves exist as the site of intersection of multiple demands, desires, and rules of normalization. Their commitment to criticizing the institution of psychology gives their work a convincing historical context.

10. Theorizing about social life within discourses of *li* constantly emphasized the five bonds of ruler/subject, father/son, husband/wife, elder/younger sibling and friend/friend.

11. I owe this phrasing to Tani E. Barlow's project on the deployment of strategies of gendering and sexing in the twentieth-century transition, which has enormously enriched and challenged my thinking on ritual practice. See her chapter in this volume for a discussion on how the relationality of subject positions renders impossible "woman" as a foundational and essential category in imperial China. On kinship positionality see Barlow (1989: 12–15).

12. For explication of yang as "encompassment," see Zito 1984.

13. I include both halves of the bonded dyads because "rulers" and "fathers" do not exclusively occupy positions of power. Sons and subjects are clearly empowered in these relationships because they are crucially invested in their creation. I examine this issue through the concept of "hegemony" in Zito 1987.

14. *Qindai dihou xiang* (1934–35).

15. In this essay Cahill does not mention a possible influence through Buddhist iconographic traditions of depicting a deity's attributes. Later these attributes come to stand for the deity.

16. I am thinking of Jehol, where the realm was reproduced in miniature, including a small Potala palace patterned after Lhasa's.

17. Francis Barker's extraordinary essay contrasting Jacobean conventions of representation and the body with the "disembodied Cartesian body" becomes directly relevant when he discusses the Jacobean king: "The figure of the king guarantees, as locus and source of power and as master signifier, a network of subsidiary relations which constitute the real practice and intelligibility of the lives of subjects. . . . The body of the king is the body that encompasses all mundane bodies within its build. . . . the social plenum *is* the body of the king, and membership in this plenum is the deep structural form in the secular realm. . . . this sovereignty achieves its domination . . . across an articulated but single ground" (Barker 1984: 31).

18. Dong Zhongshu has been described as the heir to the fusion of the theories of the yin/yang, Five Phases school, with Mencian thought. The greatest New Text scholar of his day, he interpreted the classics in light of these theories of correlation. Zheng Xuan incorporated much of Dong's work in his own sweeping commentary (Fan Wenlan 1979:307).

19. See Joseph Needham (1978, 1:154–55) for a table of selected correlations. For an explanation of Five Phases theory, see his *Science and Civilization in China*, 2:243–68. See also Porkert (1974:43–54).

20. Hall and Ames 1987 describes this organization of embodied selves in some detail.

21. I have proposed that eighteenth-century devotion to Han texts hinged upon a true interest in the precision and bodiliness of Han ritual practice (as opposed to Song *theorizing* about ritual). How evidential ritual scholars coped with the curious fact that those bodily articulations were retrievable only in the form of texts tells us much about the relationship between body, text and rite (Zito 1989).

22. For an important discussion of how Chinese medicine bases itself within a "transformative metaphysics" that contrasts with "our own essentialist natural science tradition," see Farquhar (n.d., 15–35).

23. In this volume, Shigehisa Kuriyama discusses *feng* or "winds" in detail, pointing out that their circulation was crucial to health. In the Han, both acupuncture and geomantic "dynamic sites" were called *xue*, or "caves." According to Kuriyama, it was during the Han that "the decisive pivot of health was seen concentrated *on the body's surface*" (my emphasis). See "The Imagination of Winds and the Development of the Chinese Conception of the Body."

24. The referent for artistic signs becomes problematic if the things of the world are so systematically inclined in the unified and correlated realm brought into being by such production. Where is the "outside" of a natural or real world opposed to culture? See DeWoskin (1982:167).

25. Bryson uses Chinese ink painting as the generalized "other" as he provides an excellent summary of the emergence in European painting of the "optical theorization of the body," which reduces and simplifies the material, muscular body, continuous with physical reality. "This [new] body of perception is monocular, a single eye removed from the rest of the body and suspended in diagrammatic space" (Bryson 1983:94). At the risk of reversing Bryson's simplification of the Chinese painting body, this "Cartesian self" is of course the contrast to the construction of subject and sign I am proposing for eighteenth-century China.

26. This raises the interesting problem of the relative authoritativeness of painting versus calligraphy. (I intend to confine speculation upon this complex problem firmly to notes.) Of course, it depends on who writes/paints. But putting that paramount issue aside, a movement in the Song period (960–1279) bestowed enormous prestige upon *xieyi* or *wenren hua* (literati painting), a black-ink style

closely allied with calligraphic expression. So even within "painting" calligraphic brushwork has pride of place.

27. The Ni Zan painting is reproduced in *Zhongguo zongdai minghua ji* (1965:220). It also appears in Cahill (1983:117). According to its seals, this painting was held by the Qianlong emperor. I saw reproduced in the Cornell Knight Slide Collection an anonymous Song painting held in the Taipei Palace Museum Collection. See also a very early variation, minus the screen, by Qiu Ying in *Lidai renwa hua xuanji* (1959, no. 52).

28. The temporal details of Grand Sacrifice were culled from the *Da Qing tongli* (Comprehensive rites of the Qing), chief compiler Lai Bao; commissioned in Qianlong 1, 1736, completed in 1756, 50 *juan*. This edition is collected in the *Siku quanshu*, reprinted in the *Siku quanshu zhenben*, ser. 8, vols. 125–29. A second edition was commissioned in 1819, chief compiler Mukodengo. It gained four *juan*, one in "Auspicious Rites" and three in "Felicitous Rites," and was completed in 1824. I also use an 1883 woodblock reprint of the 1824 reediting. Illustrations are found in *Huangchao liqi tushi*, a Qianlong woodblock book reprinted in the *Siku quanshu zhenben*, ser. 6, vols. 122–29.

29. In his thorough critique of the "tribute system" model, James Hevia (1989) shows that lordship in the Asian context operated through encompassment that preserved difference as a form of power and completeness, rather than through exclusion as did European monarchies cum nation-states.

30. In Zito (1989:271–450) I narrate and comment upon an entire Sacrifice to Heaven. See part 4, "Performance: The Ritual Body Inscribes."

31. Under the Qing, the situation was more complex: Peking had two walls; the emperor lived in the inner city, the peasants outside the walls of the outer city. The altar was between the two areas, within the walls of the outer city where Chinese members of the imperium and merchants lived.

32. In passing I should note that silk was the preferred surface for painting and calligraphy. But even more pertinent for our purposes is the plethora of metaphors in editing that contrast webs and networks of knowledge to the single connecting thread of analysis.

33. One locus classicus for work on boundary making is Douglas 1989. Judith Butler has recently applied her thinking to gender (1990), emphasizing in a manner analogous to my own the liberating possibilities of moving from metaphysics of gender essence to the cultural construction of gender as performance.

34. This double layer of face once again is uncannily described by Barker, speaking within the Jacobean context: "The world achieves its depth not in the figure of interiority by which the concealed inside is of another quality from what is external, but by a *doubling of the surface.* . . . It functions to extend time rather than to excavate a hidden level of reality" (italics in text; Barker 1984:28–29).

35. Which, we must note, takes its ultimate efficacy from its articulation with

the throne's local representative, the district magistrate, whom Hsia refers to as "Laoye" or "grandfather" (Wu 1981:16).

36. See the suggestive essay by S. J. Tambiah (1985) on the "galactic polity" and Ronald Inden's (1990) concept of "imperial formation" for alternative designations for premodern, non-Western empires that take into account the difference between these forms of government and the modern nation-state. Such new imaginings are crucial to understanding questions of the formation of "popular" versus "elite" sensibilities and their mutual implications as forms of social consciousness.

37. In her work on medicine, Judith Farquhar follows John Hay's translation of *zhu* as "unfolds in," explaining that this usage widens our understanding of "logics of dense centers and dispersed peripheries" (Farquhar, n.d., and Hay 1983b).

References

Barker, Francis. 1984. *The tremulous private body.* New York: Methuen.

Barlow, Tani E. 1989. *I, myself, am a woman.* Boston: Beacon.

Bryson, Norman. 1983. *Vision and painting: The logic of the gaze.* New Haven: Yale University Press.

Butler, Judith. 1990. *Gender trouble, feminism and the subversion of identity.* New York: Routledge.

Cahill, James. 1982. *The compelling image: Nature and style in the late Ming dynasty, 1570–1644.* History of Later Chinese Painting Series, vol. 3. Salem, Mass.: Weatherhill.

———. 1989. Jen Hsiung and his portrait. Paper delivered at the Symposium on Chinese Painting of the Ming and Qing Dynasties, Cleveland Museum of Art, 6–7 May.

Cammann, Schuyler. 1952. *China's dragon robes.* New York: Ronald Press.

Chan, Wing-tsit. 1963. *A sourcebook in Chinese philosophy.* Princeton: Princeton University Press.

Cheng, Chung-yin. 1986. The concept of face and its Confucian roots. *Journal of Chinese Philosophy* 13 (September).

Cheng, François. 1982. *Chinese poetic writing.* Trans. D. Riggs. Bloomington: Indiana University Press.

Da Qing tongli. 1756/1824. (Comprehensive rites of the Qing).

DeWoskin, Kenneth. 1982. *A song for one or two: Music and the concept of art in early China.* Michigan Papers in Chinese Studies, no. 42. Ann Arbor: University of Michigan Press.

Douglas, Mary. 1984. *Purity and danger: An analysis of the concepts of pollution and taboo.* New York: Ark Paperbacks. Originally published 1966.

Fan Wenlan. 1979. Jingxue jiangyen lu (Lectures in classical Chinese). In *Fan Wenlan lishi lunwen xuanji* (Collection of essays on history by Fan Wenlan). Peking: Zhongguo Shehui Kexue Chubanshe.

Farquhar, Judith. n.d. *Knowing practice: The clinical encounter of Chinese medicine.* Boulder, Colo.: Westview Press, forthcoming.

Feng, Yulan. 1959. *A history of Chinese philosophy.* Trans. Derk Bodde. Princeton: Princeton University Press.

Fingarette, Herbert. 1972. *Confucius: The secular as sacred.* New York: Harper Torchbooks.

Geertz, Clifford. 1973. *The interpretation of cultures.* New York: Basic Books.

Goldberg, Stephen. n.d. Figures of identity: Topoi and the gendered subject in Chinese art. Unpublished manuscript.

Hall, David L., and Roger T. Ames. 1987. *Thinking through Confucius.* Albany: State University of New York Press.

Hay, John. 1983a. Arterial art. *Stone Lion Review* 11:70–84.

———. 1983b. The human body as microcosmic source for macrocosmic values in calligraphy. In *Theories of the arts in China,* ed. Susan Bush and Christian Murck. Princeton: Princeton University Press.

———. 1985. Poetic space: Ch'ian Hsuan and the association of painting and poetry. Paper delivered at the symposium Words and Images: Chinese Poetry, Calligraphy and Painting, May.

Henderson, John. 1984. *The development and decline of Chinese cosmology.* New York: Columbia University Press.

Henriques, Julian, et al. 1984. *Changing the subject: Psychology, social regulation and subjectivity.* New York: Methuen.

Hevia, James. 1989. A multitude of lords: Qing court ritual and the Macartney embassy of 1793. *Late Imperial China* 10 (December): 72–105.

Hu, Hsien Chin. 1944. The Chinese concept of face. *American Anthropologist* 46:45–64.

Huangchao liqi tushi. n.d. (Illustrations of the ritual paraphernalia of the dynasty). Siku quanshu zhenben, ser. 6, vols. 122–29. Beijing: Chonghua Shuju, 1963, reprint 1983.

Inden, Ronald. 1990. *Imagining India.* London: Basil Blackwell.

Jochim, Christian. 1986. *Chinese religion.* Englewood Cliffs, N.J.: Prentice-Hall.

Judovitz, Dalia. 1988. *Subjectivity and representation in Descartes: The origins of modernity.* Cambridge: Cambridge University Press.

Kaptchuk, Ted J. 1983. *The web that has no weaver: Understanding Chinese medicine.* New York: Congden and Weed.

Li Zehou. 1985. *Zhongguo gudai sixiang shilun* (Discussion of the history of ancient Chinese thought). Beijing: Renmin Chubanshe.

Lidai renwu hua xuanji. 1959. (A selection of portraits through the ages). Shanghai: Xinhua Shudian.

Liji zhengyi. 1980. (Verification of meanings in the Record of Rites). In *Shisanjing zhushu* (Notes and commentaries on the thirteen classics), vol. 2, ed. Ruan Yuan. Conjoined 1816 edition with collation notes; reprint Beijing: Zhonghua Shuju.

Moore, Charles V. 1969. *The Chinese mind.* Honolulu: East-West Center Press.

Needham, Joseph. 1956. *Science and civilization in China.* Vol. 2, *History of scientific thought.* Cambridge: Cambridge University Press.

————. 1978. *The shorter science and civilization*. Cambridge: Cambridge University Press.

Porkert, Manfred. 1974. *The theoretical foundations of Chinese medicine: Systems of correspondence*. Cambridge: MIT Press.

Qingdai dihou xiang. 1934–35. (Portraits of emperors and empresses in the Qing). Beijing.

Reiss, Timothy. 1982. *The discourse of modernism*. Ithaca: Cornell University Press.

Schneider, David. 1980. *American kinship: A cultural account*. 2d ed. Chicago: University of Chicago Press.

Schwartz, Benjamin. 1985. *The world of thought in ancient China*. Cambridge: Harvard University Press.

Tambiah, S. J. 1985. *Culture, thought and social action: An anthropological perspective*. Cambridge: Cambridge University Press.

Turner, Terence. 1980. The social skin. In *Not work alone: A cross-cultural view of activities superfluous to survival,* ed. Jeremy Cherfas and Roger Lewin. Beverly Hills, Calif.: Sage.

Wu Jingzi. 1981. *Rulin waishi* (The scholars). Beijing: Renmin Wenhua Chubanshe.

Yanagisako, Sylvia Junko, and Jane Fishburne Collier, eds. 1987. *Gender and kinship: Essays toward a unified analysis*. Stanford: Stanford University Press.

Zhongguo zongdai minghua ji. 1965. (A collection of famous paintings of various dynasties). Beijing: Renmin Meishu Chubanshe.

Zito, Angela. 1984. Re-presenting sacrifice: Cosmology and the editing of texts. *Ch'ing-shih Wen-t'i* 5 (December): 47–78.

————. 1987. City, gods, filiality, and hegemony in late imperial China. *Modern China* 13 (July): 333–371.

————. 1989. Grand Sacrifice as text/performance: Ritual and writing in eighteenth-century China. Ph.D. diss., University of Chicago.

————. 1990. The body as vessel: Centering in Grand Sacrifice. Paper presented at the American Ethnological Society meeting, Atlanta, April.

5

The Politicized Body

Ann Anagnost

The Chinese film *Red Sorghum* (*Hong gaoliang*, directed by Zhang Yimou, 1987) is striking for its imagery of the body. Through its revalorization of the tribal aspects of peasant culture and its festive excess, the film aims to recoup the image of a prepoliticized body still "intact" from the onslaught of political rituals of the socialist party/state. These images of the body might at first glance be dismissed as a mythification of a pre-socialist peasant society, a dream of lost plenitude when the body was not yet alienated from the "spontaneous" pleasures of the lower bodily stratum. However, the film constructs this grotesque body as a deliberate displacement of a politicized body inscribed within the civilizing rituals of the party/state.[1]

In this essay I explore the discourse of the body that the film's imagery is working against. Therefore my starting point is the question of how individuals become stitched into subject positions within the state's own ritual forms and how far these positionings have the power to structure people's lived reality—to define their social being and even their inner sense of themselves. I push my argument further, however, to explore how the production of docile political subjects in these ritualized ways undergirds a projection of the party/state as a subject writ large, as the unified voice of the "people as one"—a projection that conceals the internal fragmentation and diversity not only of "the people," but also within the party organization itself.

This essay therefore deals with the issue of subjectivity at two levels: at the level of individual bodies and at the level of the body politic. My intent is to demonstrate that politicizing the body is not merely a manipulative project of the state to ensure social control and ideological domination but is essential to the party/state's own self-identity, its creation of a self-referential reality that is in itself an ideological effect.[2] Finally, I explore how these processes of subject making, while they may resemble in certain respects the mechanisms of Foucault's disciplinary state, are also quite different from Western disciplinary technologies, both in the degree of individuation of the political subject and in terms of Foucault's distinction between the visible and invisible modalities of power. In other words, I wish to explore the ways the operations of power may be specific to the contemporary Chinese socialist state.

The Power to Name and the Power of Naming

I shall begin with a story, reported as true, from the *Nongmin Ribao* (Peasant daily) that will provide the ground for the discussion that follows.

Exchanging His Huqin for a Plaque

In Xingfu village, Maoping township, Lianyuan city, Hunan Province, everyone is talking with great approval of how Zhou Yixiang won his plaque.

This year Xingfu village had a competition to designate "law-abiding households [*zunji shoufahu;* an honorific designation]" Zhou Yixiang was the first to be affected. He resolutely put down the *huqin* [the horsehead fiddle used by diviners] that had accompanied him from village to village as he defrauded people of their money by telling horoscopes [*bazi*]. He had resolved to change his heterodox ways for rectitude. He worked from dawn to dusk, competing to become a "law-abiding household." At the end of June, the village party secretary and the village committee appraised the entire village to select the "law-abiding households." Zhou Yixiang was passed over without mention. He saw the brightly painted red-and-gold plaques on the doorframes of others and felt cut to the heart. The next day, the more he thought about it, the more agitated he became. He ran over to the party secretary and asked him flat out, "Why didn't I get a plaque?"

Liang Lunyu, the party secretary, recalled Zhou's past practice of feudal superstition and the money he had fraudulently obtained in this way and felt this was not up to the standard of a "law-abiding household." Old Zhou saw immediately what was in the party secretary's mind and argued his case: "If it was because I used to read horoscopes, I have washed my hands of it ever since you announced the 'law-abiding household' competition, and I promise to do it no longer." One of his neighbors tugged at a corner of Zhou's clothes: "Brother Yixiang, don't argue until you are red in the face and your ears scarlet. Anyway, there is no monetary reward. It doesn't matter whether you have a plaque or not." When old Zhou heard this, he became even angrier. He rushed at this fellow villager, saying, "You only know how to fart [*ni xiaode gepi*]. If there had been an award of ten or so yuan, then I wouldn't have said anything. It would have reflected badly on the issue of my reputation. But if it is simply a matter of qualifying for this status, then I must contend for it!"

Secretary Liang was very moved by what old Zhou had said. That same night he called a meeting of the village cadres, where Zhou Yixiang's request was earnestly discussed. In response to Zhou's application and based on his promise to engage no longer in feudal superstition, the party secretary and the village committee decided that they would designate his family as a "law-abiding household."

At dawn the next day, just as Zhou Yixiang rose from his bed, he heard a great clamor of gongs and drums at his door. It was Secretary Liang leading the village committee to deliver his "law-abiding household" plaque. (*Nongmin Ribao* 1987, 8.7:2)

This story is very like many others I have collected from newspapers of this period. And yet, despite its typicality, it is also arresting in certain of its narrative features that allow it to capture a very revealing moment in the everyday negotiation of power relations in the post-Maoist state. However, the nature of the story as a narrative demands that it be examined from two perspectives: first, from the perspective of its representation of the real—that is, the operations it describes as actually taking place on the ground—and second, from the perspective of the text as a text and the ideological effects it produces as an artifact to be read. From this latter perspective, it is clear that the very strategies the state must now depend on to make the narrative work as intended also point to where the limits of power can be drawn.

We may begin then with a discussion of the story as a representation of a ritual. The competition for model household status described above is one of a number of similar "ceremonies of objectification" that distribute subjects onto a bureaucratic grid for the purpose of specification and judgment. But even more important than the ability of these ceremonies to subject everyone to the panoptic gaze of power is their ability to position subjects in a ritual display of a transcendent reality. The bestowal of status honors, through the issuing of ritual markers and public processions, demonstrates the power of the state to define discursive positions in political culture through its classificatory strategies—its power to name and to sort persons into the hierarchically arranged categories of a moral order. I assert that though this power to name does not go unchallenged (e.g., by competing discourses of family, kinship, social relations, or ritual hierarchies), it does exert a powerful force in defining the subject in contemporary Chinese political culture. In the post-Mao period, however, this power of state ritual to determine the subject confronts even more potent challenge—a popular distrust of the ideological, a legacy of the excesses of the Cultural Revolution. And yet, despite the party's present emphasis on liberalizing the economy (and perhaps even because of this), its ideological project remains critical to its self-definition.

The question then arises of what it means, in the post-Mao period, to be inscribed within the symbolic order of the state through rituals such as the one just described. The neighbor who reminds Zhou Yixiang about the monetary worthlessness of the award may in fact be indicating an even more general disregard for what it signifies at the symbolic level.[3] Before dismissing such ritual markers as meaningless, however, we should perhaps consider the implications of not receiving one. What does it mean for the party to create a category that is inscribed within a totalizing symbolic system, and to sort people into it or its negatively defined other? This categorical exclusion of individuals from the social body isolates them in a state of extreme moral, as well as political, ambiguity.[4] The "law-abiding household" plaque, as a material item of display, is a binary code that encompasses all through its very presence or absence. At one level, these designations are signs that connote a subliminal message about submission to the power of the state. To aspire to inclusion within the connotations of this sign is to announce, in Havel's words, that "I know what I must do. I behave in the manner expected of me. I can be depended upon and am beyond reproach. I am obedient and therefore I have the right to be left in peace" (1986:42). Conformity with the model appears to originate from a "disinterested conviction" about the moral values it represents. Zhou Yixiang presents his claim for this status as if his only concern were a regard for official propriety and not fear of the various forms of political harassment that his negative classification might make him subject to. In this sense his seeking to be reinscribed within the model is, as Havel suggests, a dignified cover for his own subjection. But this subjection is one that is shared by all those who suffer themselves to be evaluated and who subsequently display the markers that identify them with the party's moral leadership. Individuals thereby actively comply with the forces that make them subject to the symbolic order of the state. They allow themselves to be absorbed into the "panorama of everyday life," which is composed of signs, such as "law-abiding household" plaques, that maintain the play of appearances and give substance to the claims by the party/state to be a highly visible arbiter of everyday practice.

And yet what becomes inscribed through these designations is a propriety not solely defined by the state but one that is also heavily imbricated with popular notions of respectability. The quality of law-abidingness defines a value not entirely alien to a sense of local propriety, although the behaviors that constitute this value in terms of local sensibilities may differ significantly and even contest those of a centralized authority.[5] At the same time, we cannot assume that the state's definition of propriety has completely failed to influence popular notions of correct practice. Zhou's failure to receive a plaque thus marks him with a lack of propriety that spills over into a position not just of political ambiguity, but social and moral ambiguity as well. This lack is therefore something that may not be easily deflected from one's inner sense of worth but must be construed as a very real attack on one's social respectability, one's "face" (*mianzi*).

The power to name, in this instance, is the power to discriminate between those who fulfill the requirements of the model and those who do not; and it is a power that the party reserves for itself, as a "universal" and "transcendent" authority (Yang 1988:414–15). As shown by our story, this authority is exercised in practice by the local party secretary, albeit supported by committees of local worthies. What I suggest is that, with the diminution of party control over economic practice in the post-Mao period, the reformation of everyday practice has become a heightened locus for concern by a party anxious to exert its ideological authority and leadership at the local level. In making such a suggestion, I am contesting the accepted wisdom that the post-Mao period has seen an end to ideology and a return to a more "rational" pragmatism in the political and economic spheres. Those everyday activities in which local party officials continue to exercise their powers of discrimination are precisely where we see a restoration of the arbitrary power of local officials to determine the distinction between what is and is not—a power that in some important respects has not diminished in the post-Mao period of reform. Moreover, although there is much about this exercise of power that is specific to its socialist context, it appears to be continuous with certain practices of the imperial state. Indeed, one is tempted to invoke the notion of the "rectification of names" as something eternal to any construction of power that is quintessentially "Chinese."

> Classical Chinese philosophers focus on names (distinction mak-
> ing) and desires rather than beliefs and desires. To be able to ac-
> quire a shared naming convention a human must have or acquire
> the ability to make a distinction—a *shih* (this), *fei* (not this).
> Along with this ability comes a socially appropriate attitude to-
> ward the things distinguished in this way and a set of dispositions
> (desires) involving them. Chinese philosophers fasten on these
> acquired discrimination abilities and the attitudes (desires) which
> accompany them rather than on the creation and modification of
> beliefs. Our "raw impulses" are tuned when we internalize ways
> of classifying and categorizing things. Thus, language shapes be-
> havior. (Hansen 1985 : 366)

This process of naming has a distinctly ideological function, however: certain people get to name, others are relegated to acting accordingly (Zito
1993). In the classic distinction we make between orthopraxy and ortho-
doxy as somehow capturing the difference between East and West, this
dimension that is specific to a particular modality of power gets displaced
onto something called Chineseness.[6]

Confucianists conceptualized government as guiding this process of
discrimination and setting up models for the moral edification of the
masses. In the late imperial period these models were promulgated by
the local gentry, in whom Confucian values were deeply inculcated. In the
socialist period, the local party organizations have replaced the gentry as
the responsible agents for guiding the design of models for local emulation. Throughout the socialist period the local party secretary, especially,
has been the critical link between the universal discourse of the state and
the particulars of local practice. His motivations and willingness for playing this role reveal the complexity of his political subjectivity, composed
of a mix of both conviction and will to power, and not always easily reduced to one or the other.[7] But however complex his motivations might
be, his power to judge between what is and is not is a powerful mechanism
for control, and we would be mistaken if we attributed this process of
rectifying names to its deep cultural roots. Oppositional pairs have a
deeply ideological function in all systems of meaning, and this is especially
true in totalizing systems of meaning where alternative coding is repressed
or where the intent is to obliterate prior coding through a revolutionary
transformation of values.[8]

In Chinese political culture the opposition between *shi* and *fei* often
takes on more than merely discursive form. It is inscribed onto bodily

dispositions—one's carriage and positioning in the rituals of power. This was more overtly observable in the struggle sessions of the past, with all their attendant techniques of the body—the submissive stance with bowed head, the wearing of dunce caps and placards—all means through which one's "face" (*mianzi*), the measure of one's social respectibility, was destroyed. Post-Mao literary re-creations of that earlier period have powerfully detailed the violence of an ascriptive system that reduced one's moral status to one's class background and thereby determined one's inclusion among "the people" or among their enemies. In the successive political campaigns of the 1960s, however, as more and more categories of persons were named as class enemies and excluded from the social body (Billeter 1985), its arbitrary nature was also made more visible. This was especially true as the authority to draw the line defining class enemies became disseminated and contested among rival political factions.

But despite this erosion of the power of class background to ascribe one's position in the status hierarchies of Chinese socialist political culture, I suggest that the distinction between *shi* and *fei* remains a potent oppositional coding of the post-Mao period, although the terms in which it is configured and the degree to which the authority to name may be concentrated in a unified party identity may differ through time. At the same time, despite their reduced salience in political culture, the categories of class remain a subterranean code, one that can be applied to mask other, more real, contradictions in Chinese society in periods when political conflict sharpens, as it did in the spring of 1989. For instance, attempts by the central leadership to redefine the massive popular demonstrations for democratic reform as "counterrevolutionary activity" incited by a "small minority of people" (*jishaoshuren*) were intended to offset the public expression of alternative characterizations, for example, as a "patriotic democratic movement."[9]

Although the distinction between *shi* and *fei* remains and continues to be coded in terms reminiscent of the Maoist period, it takes on the less confrontational mode used to deal with "contradictions among the people."[10] The aim of these distinctions is therefore no longer to exclude a pariah group, but to absorb as many subjects as possible into the embrace of a state-defined standard through the reformation of behavior. *Shi* and *fei* now marks the old Maoist distinction between "backward" (*houjin fenzi*) and "advanced" (*xianyin fenzi*) in radically new ways that reflect the modernization ideology of the Dengist state. It is the transformation of these elements from backward to advanced status that now becomes the

primary means through which these activities produce their results. Therefore, although the overt rituals of humiliation and the use of physical violence have been abandoned, the objectification of targets is still no less
important, since they are now the vehicles for the circulation of signs in a
play of representations that makes power visible.

Returning to the story of Zhou Yixiang, we see an opposition based
not on antagonistic class positions between individuals, but defined by
contrasting states of being in a single individual—from benightedness to
enlightenment, from feudal superstition to socialist propriety. In his transformation, we see reinvented a classic structuring figure of socialist realism
that marks the difference between spontaneity and consciousness (Clark
1985). Once again we see the antithetical positioning of the politicized
body, whose bodily dispositions are guided by consciousness—"party
mindedness"—against a prepoliticized past, in which the inchoate pleasures of the spontaneous body disrupt the social and political order, but
for quite different political effects. It is perhaps no accident that many of
the pleasures of the lower bodily stratum, celebrated by Bakhtin, define
these domains of practice that are the targets of the party's civilizing zeal.
And they are targets precisely because, as figures of excess—large-scale
banqueting, gambling, ritualized reciprocity, and sexual reproduction—
they offend the technological rationality through which the party seeks to
reform society.[11]

Yet, the assignment of these categories is not merely a discursive act.
It is a call to action. Households and individuals that are marked as "backward" are subjected to unremitting pressure from the entire spread of
party organizations—the local party branch, the youth league, the wom-
en's association. New organizations are also called into being expressly for
this purpose, variously titled "social ethics appraisal committees" (*shehui
daode pingyi hui*), "village people's educational activities groups" (*cunmin
jiaoyu huodongzu*), "councils on weddings and funerals" (*hongbai xishi lishihui;* to discourage ostentatious family rituals), or "civilization committees" (*wenming zu*). These groups are generally composed of a mix of
party personnel and persons of communally recognized high moral standing, selected under the direction of the local party organizations.[12] "Backward elements" become the target of all these diverse groups in a great
mobilization of concerted attention. They are cajoled, publicly shamed,
and generally pestered into conformity with model behavior. This attention leads to tearful renunciations of former behavior that are not offered
as a literal submission to the powerful pressures exerted on them, but en-

acted in a public recognition of the tremendous concern and trouble that the party has expressed through these very activities. The target, positioned in a state of extreme moral insufficiency, is described as overwhelmed by this public display of concern on his or her behalf. To fail to respond to these efforts would be, in effect, a refusal to reciprocate this lavish demonstration of "human feeling" (*renqing*), a violation of propriety itself.

The tearful denouements of these humble dramas are essential to their operation as signs of the party's own efficacy, its successful operations on the social body.[13] Backward elements thereby provide the raw material to be worked on by the machinery of the party organization; they become the stimulus to reanimate a deadened party apparatus during a period of increasing alienation from and deteriorating prestige among the people. And indeed, images of the body cluster thickly in communicating this possibility. These organizational innovations to mobilize the sleeping potential of the local party apparatus are described as "resensitizing the deadened nerve tissue" in, may I suggest, the extremities of the body politic.[14]

We would therefore be in error if we attempted to understand these rituals of objectification solely in terms of their specified ends—the reformation of behavior. They are also rituals of subjection, of subject making; they produce docile bodies and transform these bodies into signifiers that figure in a master narrative of progress toward a socialist modernity. These rituals objectify subjects in a way that does not individuate them but causes them to be subsumed within a mass identity, the "people as one," for whom the party becomes the sole authorized voice. If, as Michel de Certeau (1984) has suggested, "every power is toponymical and initiates its order of places by naming them," then the power to name, in this sense, is a negation of otherness that appropriates what is other into the self. To be named is to be heteronomous; it means to be absorbed into another's reality, to be subject to the rule of the other.

As I have noted above, the power to make these distinctions is essentially a discursive one; it is a speech act, an act of naming. But just as the power to name, in a sense, illustrates how things can be done with words, the power of that doing, as Bourdieu (1977) has suggested, issues not from the speech act itself but from its empowering institutional structure. The local cadre has the power to name because he himself is inscribed within a larger social vision that organizes the subjectivity of the state—as a subject writ large, as it imagines itself as a palpable force in society. But a great part of that imaginary subjectivity of the state is its presumption to speak as the voice of the people. This presumption is one that results from a confusion of identities that must be constantly reproduced. The party clearly has the power to delineate the models, but it is continually rediscovering them anew as creations of the people. It appears in a state of perpetual surprise at this creative energy. The masses lead, and the party propagates and promotes the best effects of these popular impulses. And yet the model is always part of a larger, more universal signifying system. Therefore the delineation of the model is by no means purely local, despite the fiction of press accounts reporting on local areas that the specific models are the novel creations of the people that must, in the best tradition of the mass line, be gathered up by central authorities to propagate their good effects more widely.[15]

This is a subtle point but one that can help us focus on the mysterious process of how the party as a subject writ large constitutes itself as a self-referential reality. If "suturing" occurs when the subject recognizes himself or herself in the discourse of the other so that an identification is formed, then the process I am describing here is a curious inversion of this.[16] The party continually sees its own reflection in these models, and it misrecognizes itself as the other, in that the models are identified with the creativity of the people. This misrecognition allows the party to take up these models as representing the will of the masses; it underpins the party's assumption that the popular will has been delegated to it. The party authorizes itself to "represent," in the sense of "speaking for," the people as a unitary social body. Any dissent from the party's will must therefore come from "outside the people" (Lefort 1986). In this circular progression of the subject, we have what Michel Pêcheux (1982 : 108) calls the "Munchausen effect," in honor of the legendary baron "who lifted himself into the air by pulling on his own hair," in which the subject is caught within a network of signifiers so that he or she—in this case the state—results as a "cause of itself." This circular relationship in the sphere of politics has been sketched by Bourdieu:

> It is because the representative exists, because he *represents* (symbolic action), that the represented or symbolised group exists and then in return brings into existence its representative as representative of a group. We see in this circular relation the roots of the illusion which makes the representative appear even to himself as the causa sui since he is the cause of that which produces his power and also because he thinks that the group would not ex-

ist—or not fully exist—if he were not there to embody it. (Bourdieu 1984–85:56–57; emphasis in original)

If we substitute the party for Bourdieu's representative, we can then begin to address what he calls "political fetishism," in which the act of delegation authorizes the party to speak for the masses. But once that authority is made self-evident, it becomes the principle of political alienation in which the party is now the sole source of social agency, thereby rendering the masses an "inanimate object" (Pêcheux 1978). Again returning to Bourdieu:

> Someone speaks in the name of something which is made to exist through this very discourse. A whole series of symbolic effects in everyday politics rests on this sort of usurping ventriloquism, they consist in speaking and yet making it appear that it is someone else who speaks, speaking for those who give one the right to speak, who in fact authorise one to speak. Usually when a politician says "the people, the masses" he invokes the oracle-effect. This is the act which consists in producing the message and deciphering it at the same time, in making others believe that "I am the other," that the spokesperson is a simple substitute for the people, is truly the people in the sense that what he says is the truth and life of the people. The usurpation which resides in the fact of affirming oneself as capable of speaking *in the name of* is what authorises the movement from indicative to the *imperative*. (Bourdieu 1984–85:63; emphasis in original) [17]

This self-referentiality of the party as a subject writ large is an ideological effect; it is what gives the system its inner coherence, without which, as Havel suggests, it would "collapse in upon itself . . . in a kind of material implosion." And because ideology is ultimately subordinated "to the interests of the structure . . . it has a natural tendency to disengage from reality, to create a world of appearances, to become ritual. . . . It becomes reality itself, albeit a reality altogether self-contained, one that on certain levels (chiefly inside the power structure) may have greater weight than reality as such" (Havel 1986:46–47).

Who Is Spoken Here?

Although this subheading may seem ungrammatical, it is asking what subject position the story of Zhou Yixiang is reinscribing. At first glance, it appears to register the transformation of Zhou Yixiang himself, whose subject position traverses a fundamental anthithesis in the discourse of the party—from backward to advanced element. But this text works doubly as a tale of transformation, and the subject that is reinscribed is not really Zhou Yixiang, whose transformation is described but not truly effected by the text, but perhaps the party secretary himself. To demonstrate how the story does this, we can show that it works in a readerly way, in which the reader is assumed to be a passive consumer of meanings fixed in the text, stitched into a position that works to constitute the larger subjectivity of the state. In other words, this reading of the socialist realist text can make visible the mechanisms within it that contribute to its ideological effect, its construction of a self-referential reality.[18]

We can start by noting the proper names that define character and place and the attributes that cluster around these proper names. The story centers on three protagonists, only two of whom have proper names: the diviner Zhou Yixiang; the party secretary Liang Lunyu; and an unnamed bystander. Connecting the three is a dual axis of power. The relationship between Zhou and the party secretary is clearly vertical, while Zhou's relationship with the bystander is horizontally inscribed. The implications of this triangulation of relationships will be made evident later.

The attributes that define character cluster most thickly about Zhou himself; and these are incorporated into a larger conceptual scheme of what it means to be "backward"—that is, feudal, self-interested, untrustworthy, uncivilized, and so forth—as opposed to "advanced" or "law-abiding"—the antithesis of all that is backward. What is intriguing about this story in particular is that all the attributes that inscribe both backward and advanced statuses cluster about the diviner from the very beginning. He has undergone the transformation from one status to the other, but this transformation has gone unrecognized in the eyes of power. The dramatic tension of his being caught "between" demonstrates all the more clearly that these semic markers are not neutral but are "ideologically symptomatic"; they inscribe the text with power relations (Silverman 1983:255). They make possible "strategies for understanding persons and places which are really ways of signifying and controlling those persons and places" (254).

In contrast, the coding of the party secretary is somewhat less defined—we know his proper name and we know that he is powerful—but the values attributed to him are not clear from the start of the narrative; and indeed, they become clearer only in the unfolding of the text. The attributes of the bystander are the least well defined. We do not even know for sure if he himself attained model status, which might have determined some status distinction in his relationship with the diviner, a relationship that is otherwise horizontally inscribed between two relatively powerless people. At the same time, Zhou is given the opportunity to demonstrate his moral superiority over the bystander by rejecting his insinuation that money is the universal standard of value. The bystander performs the narratological function of a "helper" who allows Zhou to achieve his goal and lets the narrative function as intended. He also provides Zhou with the pretext for switching codes from the infantilizing discourse of the slave, in which he begs for recognition, to the uncensored speech of the spontaneous body, which releases his anger in a direction away from a direct confrontation with power.

Next we may chart the sequence of events that seems to unfold in a predictable order. This is most apparent in "fixed generic forms," such as the socialist realist tale of transformation, in which there is a high degree of "previsibility" (Silverman 1983:263). This predictability confers on the reader a sense of having been there before—the textual equivalent of déjà vu (déjà lu?). Indeed, the formulaic nature of socialist realist literature is invariably pointed out in attempts to define its essential character. However, this story was particularly arresting because it does not follow the typical chain of events. More typically, competition for model status locates and identifies backward elements upon which the party apparatus can work. The tale of transformation details the coming to consciousness of the backward individual and charts his progress toward model status. This transformation frequently takes the form of moving from a state of passivity or even paralysis to one of activism and vigor. In Zhou Yixiang's case, however, this transformation was already accomplished at the beginning of the story, and instead we have an account of his struggle for recognition.

The narrative unfolds in the following order. An omniscient and invisible narrator specifies time and place and the history of the events that precede the moment when the narrative shifts into direct speech. In the exchange between Zhou and the party secretary, only the direct speech of the diviner is represented, while the omniscient narrator summarizes what is going through the party secretary's mind. The party secretary is silent, yet we are allowed to follow his inner thoughts. Zhou responds to this silence by an apparently clairvoyant understanding of the party secretary's reflections. He is, after all, a diviner who knows how to read signs cor-

rectly. He counters the party secretary's silence with a sincere disavowal of
his former practice. This vertical exchange is then displaced by the inter-
ference of a third party, who enables Zhou to authenticate his sincerity
through an unleashing of emotion. This displacement is highly significant.
Throughout this second exchange, the party secretary silently listens at a
slight remove, like a voyeur, to an exchange not ostensibly intended for his
ears. Zhou's uncensored speech is authenticated by its horizontal trajectory, by the exhibition of his anger, and by its discursive marking by vulgar
speech. The reference to farting is certainly not "civilized" (*wenming*), but
it imbues the atmosphere of Zhou's speech with a sense of the spontaneity
of the lower bodily stratum; it instills a certain "cachet" of peasant earthi-
ness that knows no pretence. It disrupts the text with an officially disvalued
discourse for calculated effect. Again the party secretary remains silent
while the omniscient narrator, whom we must recognize as the authoritative voice of the party itself, informs us that he has been moved by Zhou's
speech.

In this sequence of events, we see power being reinscribed in the ellip-
tical moment. The party secretary is apparently convinced more by Zhou's
second exchange with the bystander than by Zhou's more direct submission to power. If it is now generally assumed that all exchanges on the
vertical axis must give rise to the lie, a mere surface effect, then the second
exchange becomes necessary to instill a stronger effect of the "true." If the
first exchange must be understood as a performance on Zhou's part, then
the implication is that when he speaks to his neighbor, he is no longer
"performing" but is speaking the uncensored language of truth. Both exchanges are most likely performances, and the second exemplifies the
Bakhtinian idea of the dialogical angle in which speech operates at multiple levels of meaning and is directed to more than just its ostensible
interlocutor. In his "spontaneous" and "uncensored" speech to his neighbor, Zhou may still be performing an "inauthentic" self, but this one has
a stronger effect of the "true." And yet in the story Zhou's uncensored
speech cannot be allowed this power. The party secretary refuses to reveal
that he is swayed by the power of Zhou's uncensored speech in such a
public way. Instead he silently withdraws; he submits Zhou's application
to model status for reevaluation by the bureaucracy of power and then
"surprises" him the next morning with a clamorous procession that reaf-
firms the power not of Zhou's performance, but of the party's paternal
authority. In the narrative structure of the story, the panopticism of the
party is preserved. It hears what is not intended for its ears; but even

more important, it controls the conditions under which it offers itself to view.

In the realist text, the hermeneutic development of the narrative moves the reader toward the disclosure of something hidden. This disclosure is not just the revelation of the "truth," however, but is also a closure—a fixing down of meaning, the closing off of other interpretations. The hermeneutic code projects "a stable subject about whom things can be ultimately discovered." But in the structure of the socialist realist text, this process of discovery is not strictly parallel, for reasons to be explored in the concluding section of this chapter. Briefly, the process of discovery here does not probe under the surface into the psyche of the subject; it is not a process of understanding the subject more deeply, revealing something hidden that is peculiar to the individual; what it reveals instead is the hidden agency of the party's appeal to a universal ethical standard. In this sense the hermeneutic code in the socialist realist text does parallel its operation in the realist text to the extent that it reinscribes "a culturally determined position or group of positions to which the reader is expected to conform" (Silverman 1983:262).

Within the brief confines of our story, there is not much room for a sustained suspension of the central enigma. The question whether Zhou Yixiang had indeed been "misclassified" as backward is briefly equivocated in his neighbor's attributing to him a desire for financial gain. But his sincerity apparently convinces the party secretary, who is taken by surprise by Zhou's vehemence; this is the moment of revelation when the ideological practices of the party show themselves to be working effectively. This element of surprise is perhaps the central clue to understanding the text as being "about" the party secretary himself and not about Zhou Yixiang at all. After all, the probable readers of the *Peasant Daily* are rural cadres and not ordinary peasants. The reader will therefore recognize the party secretary's surprise as his own surprise in "discovering" that these sorts of emulation campaigns truly have the power to effect the dramatic transformation of everyday practice.

The symbolic structure of this narrative is closely tied to the figure of antithesis, what Barthes (1974) refers to as the most ideological of oppositions, setting two categories or states of being "ritually face to face like two fully armed warriors." Antithesis "admits of no mediation between its terms. They are represented as eternal and 'inexpiable.' Any attempt to reconcile them is seen as 'transgressive'" (Silverman 1983:270). These binary oppositions are therefore "central to the organization of the cultural order." They define the normal, the moral, the orthodox, and the good by a principle of exclusion that denies or denigrates alternative modes of being. They fix the subject into a stable meaning that, even in the process of transformation from one term to the other, is no more than a movement between fixed positions that does not challenge the symbolic economy of the opposition itself. To be defined as a backward element allows for "the power of legal substitution" in which "backwardness" quite automatically and "naturally" signifies a wealth of other values. This "order of just equivalence" (Barthes 1974:216) is the anchor of the readerly text in which meaning is stable and signs do not circulate beyond a fixed universe of connotations. The power of this order is demonstrated in the story when Zhou Yixiang's neighbor attributes to him a material self-interest in his wish to change his status. Practitioners of feudal superstition are characterized in the discourse of the state as the purveyors of a "false commodity" for personal gain. This attribution to him of a hope for material gain threatens to force Zhou Yixiang back into the negative category from which he aspires to free himself. To traverse the distance between opposed terms, Zhou must rearticulate his being from a love of material gain to a regard for his moral character—what in the Chinese idiom translates as "face" (*mianzi*).

Zhou Yixiang's vehemence and the party secretary's surprise, however, point toward yet another transformation that the text itself is working to effect—a restoration of faith in the party and in the efficacy of its social engineering. In this context, this opposition, which is less visibly articulated than the other, regulates the distinction between negative and positive visions of the party bureaucracy—between party functionaries who are apathetic, unimaginative, and pro forma in the exercise of their duties and activist social agents who judge on the basis of "facts" and not by the routine application of set categories. The rural cadre who reads this text undergoes an experience of "anagnorisis," a recognition of his own truer self, a coming to know himself anew as a committed party member endowed with a sense of his own political agency. The party secretary's surprise at Zhou's vehemence is recognized as the reader's own surprise, and he finds himself "hailed" by the text and thereby reinscribed with a renewal of faith in the party's ability to effect real social change. At least this is the way the text is supposed to work. Its weak point lies in one's reading of Zhou's vehemence—whether the reader is convinced by the "effect" of Zhou's spontaneous outburst, apparently outside the rationality of control. This vehemence, if it is read as "true," presents itself as a lesson to be learned by the party and its agents that comes from "the people", here represented in the lowly person of Zhou Yixiang. It attests to the power of the party's categories in defining social respectability, and thereby it becomes the means through which the party renews its self-image as a spiritual vanguard. The motivation of the retired diviner to jump into his new role as an advanced element does not go entirely unquestioned, hence the equivocation about his possible interest in a material reward. But it is not problematized in any way that would challenge the moral coloration of any alternatives to the party's definition of "the good"—of what it means to be "civilized."

The symbolic antitheses that are set up in this short narrative are fundamental to the maintenance of the cultural code, which is here that of socialist realism. As a cultural code, socialist realism transcends its usual characterization as a mere protocol for art and literature and itself becomes a part of lived reality. The representation of society as it is desired to be, rather than as it really is, becomes a means to magically affect one's sense of reality. It invites one to participate in the play of appearances, which for the moment becomes the reality. It is the transience of this effect that demands that this reality be constantly reinscribed, however. Therefore the revelatory transformation of the party secretary in our little story is one that has been experienced before in endless textual repetition. Each return offers an opportunity to realize the model, to redeem oneself and in the process redeem the authority of the party, which rests on this demonstrated efficacy of its social technologies. Indeed, it is through the cumulative effect of these small *récits* that the party attempts to build its surface effects of substance.

If the "reading effect" of this text is to reaffirm the party's leadership in a period when that role has been increasingly challenged and brought into question, then the "who" that is spoken here is neither Zhou Yixiang nor perhaps even the party secretary, but the party itself, once again asserting its agency as a unified subject. The important question now becomes, To what extent is this effect limited to those who are already caught within the embrace of this ideological system as its representatives? Are we seeing, in this text, the party merely gesturing to itself? And to what extent does the urgency of this self-affirmation betray a lack of decision or conflict within the party about its role? Even before the events of spring 1989, it was quite evident that the party was going through a period of intense self-reflection in response to its deteriorating relation with the masses. I suspect that today the problem of *dangqun guanxi* (the relation between party and masses) is an even more critical issue for many party members, who were scandalized by the slaughter of early June and who had genuinely hoped that the possibility for dialogue might have opened new avenues of communication between the party and the masses it claimed to represent. The repression of the democracy movement was an' all too effective reminder of the illusory quality of those pseudodemocratic reforms of the 1980s that might have supported the hope that the structure of power relations had changed.[19] And finally, we must also ask to what extent this self-referential reality retains the power to pull the participation of others from outside the party into its ritual performances, because these performances should never be underestimated as displays of empty formalism. They are the very enactment of subject making and political subjection within an ideological system that aims to structure people's lived reality by making them, themselves, become the signs that construct a socialist reality.

In determining the reading "effect" of our story, we must also consider whether stories like this can be read only as readerly texts where meaning is fixed and alternative interpretations are foreclosed. But even the most readerly text opens onto a world that exceeds it and that lends to it the possibility of a plurality of scandalous readings that threaten to disrupt all the mechanisms that work internally to fix its meaning. A more cynical interpretation of Zhou Yixiang's transformation would read it as a tale of imposture, the specific genre of which could here be called "the apparently reformed individual." Such a reading would acknowledge all those forces of political intimidation that compel Zhou to jump into the play of appearances, while at the same time recognizing that his participation must be accompanied by the consciousness of playing a role in a larger fiction, a consciousness of an inauthenticity of being. This awareness of one's own duplicitous participation in the play of appearances is in itself a passive recognition of the truth. Zhou is offered no dignified alternative to participating in the party's socialist realist fictions about its role as the true representative of the popular will.

But must we assume, as Havel suggests, that Zhou Yixiang's supposed consciousness of his complicity in the construction of this dual reality can be construed only as a measure of his degradation? Is this not granting the state too much power? The text lends itself to perhaps yet another interpretation of the play of power relations represented there. Zhou Yixiang's very insistence that he be reclassified might also be read as a subtle form of resistance to the powerful discourses of the state. The diviner's meta-phorically tapping the official on the shoulder may also be read as a moment of active resistance. The subject is setting for himself the limits on how far he is willing to allow the discourses of the state the power to redefine his person. Zhou Yixiang is essentially saying to the party secretary, "I have played your game up to this point. Recognize me now or forever lose this opportunity to use me to make visible your power." For if the party were to ignore this subtle reminder of the limits to its power, it would risk a negation of its very basis.[20] The alienation of the players from the game may result in their quiet refusal to play. Their willingness to subject themselves to the symbolic order of the party is the necessary precondition for any sustained production of a socialist reality. Nor does this refusal necessarily take the form of direct political opposition. Rather, it may occur in the arena of what Havel has termed the "prepolitical," which encompasses the sometimes infinitesimal resistances of everyday life. In Zhou Yixiang's case, perhaps his only alternative would be to refuse to allow his exclusion from a state-defined morality to redefine his inner sense of moral worth, to exercise his freedom to choose to be excluded.[21]

Power and Visibility

This brings me to a concluding point. My analysis based on methods of reading the realist text assumes that one can apply the same methods to the socialist realist text. This is a big assumption unless one takes into account the significant differences between these two very different cultural productions. Barthes's semiotic codes, for instance, were aimed primarily at reading the realist text that is the specific product of a socio-historical moment—the rise of the European bourgeoisie.[22] The difference that must be accounted for is perhaps in the ways these two genres create specific kinds of reality. The realist novel instills an effect of the real within a fictional space, and it does this through the individuation of its characters based on the kinds of knowledge of the human psyche that are produced by the disciplinary technologies of Western capitalist society—the silent and invisible modes of knowledge that are coextensive with a particular economy of power—what Foucault calls biopower that constructs an interiority. The socialist realist text, it seems to me, operates according to a quite different principle. It projects a utopian fiction onto the space of lived reality, and it does this not through the individuation of its characters, but through a different operation. It classifies its characters into coded positions, representations that are moral exemplars, clusters of signs that must be made visible in order to circulate throughout the social body and thereby produce the effects of power by making the party, in its turn, also supremely visible in a dazzling display of presence.

In China we see many technologies of power that at first appear to be fully disciplinary in Foucault's sense of this term—placing persons on a grid that makes even intimate areas of practice visible to a panoptic gaze. Exposed to that gaze are the gaps between actual practice and the model; the meticulous rituals of criticism and self-criticism, which on the surface appear so analogous to the individuating rituals of the confessional mode, and the dossiers that record each person's political history, resembling at least superficially the scriptural economy of the disciplinary state. I suggest, however, that the knowledge these technologies produce is quite differently constructed. Subjects are not so much constituted as objects of knowledge in a science of the individual as classified into a system of signs that locates them as factors in a historical drama, a master narrative about the consciously directed progression toward socialist modernity. The location of actors in this narrative becomes a mode of inquiry into a discourse that represents itself as more truly "scientific" than any claims to knowledge of the bourgeois social science. In the discourse of historical materialism as spoken by the post-Maoist state, history itself becomes the fetishized object.

What we are observing here is perhaps not altogether a disciplinary technology in Foucault's sense, but rather something that resembles more closely what he called a semiotechnique that, in order to work, must make its subjects visible—not just to the panoptic gaze of an invisible and anonymous power, but with a visibility that is produced at large by the circulation of signs throughout the social body. Signs play on the surface of subjects, reordering their outward practice rather than their inner psyches. It is not that these techniques fail to affect one's sense of self, but they affect it more in terms of a submersion of the self into a moral category, a state of selflessness that merges into the collectivity, than by elaborating the self in all its particularity. The goal is not so much the orthopedic refashioning of the individual, so that deviance is made to conform to a norm presumed to be present in the social body, as it is the radical re-formation of that very social body, in which old practices are displaced by new in the teleological movement toward a modernity that calls itself socialist.

Finally, although the spatial metaphor of the panopticon may still apply as an adequate figure of the operation of power in the Chinese socialist state, it must be amended to suggest that its working is contingent on the hypervisibility of the apparatus of power and its operations on the social body. The tower at the center is not just a darkened space inhabited by an invisible gaze; it may be an illuminated stage from which the party calls, "Look at me! I make myself visible to you. Your return gaze completes me and real-izes my power." To recapitulate the opening line of our story, "Everyone is talking with great approval of how Zhou Yixiang won his plaque."

Notes

I thank Elena Feder, Akhil Gupta, Bill Kelleher, Gail Kligman, Carolyn Wakeman, and Angela Zito for their comments on earlier versions of this chapter, as well as the two anonymous manuscript reviewers. I also thank the University of Illinois Campus Research Board, the University of Illinois Hewlett Summer Awards for International Research, and the Stanford Humanities Center for research support.

1. This reading of the film is indebted to an essay by Yingjin Zhang (1990) in the *East-West Film Journal*.

2. In part, my object here is to redress what I feel to be a lack of attention to the issue of ideology in Western social science research on the post-Mao period. I attribute this lack of attention to the undertheorization of ideology in the study of Chinese politics. The tendency is to see it as a manipulative tool of the state rather than as something that suffuses all of society—that structures what Havel 1986 calls "the panorama of everyday life"—and within which the leaders are themselves enveloped.

3. Indeed, in this highly stylized account, his comment may be the only "authentic" voice in the story. My thanks to Carolyn Wakeman for this insight. The irony is that including such authentic elements both constructs and deconstructs the versimilitude of the story. While it may heighten the drama of Zhou's struggle for recognition, it also interrupts the text with the possibility of a counterdiscourse, outside the party, about the lack of power of these ritual markers to signify anything of value.

4. I write elsewhere of how these categories operate in the post-Mao moral discourse on wealth and in the context of the one-child family policy (Anagnost 1988, 1989). In both, not only is the household opened to the panoptic gaze of the state, but the deployment of economic and other sanctions is made possible through the process of specification and judgment to induce a reformation of social practices.

5. The criteria for assigning the status of "law-abiding household" may vary from place to place, but it assumes compliance not only with state law but also

with locally drafted regulations. In the post-Mao period, these latter often take the form of "village regulations" (*xianggui minyue*) that address local concerns of social order and interpersonal conflicts. For an ethnographic account of the drawing up of a local charter and its implementation by the local party apparatus, see Huang 1989. A common complaint by higher authorities is that these local charters often contradict national law or the policy concerns of the central government.

6. It is perhaps one of the ironies of history that this concern with correct practice became manifested in Maoism as a concern with how ideology is situated in practice, a basic premise underlying the concept of cultural revolution, which in turn has had a rather significant impact on Western Marxisms since Althusser and that now contributes to critical attempts to understand the society Mao helped to create. Therefore this articulation between ideology and practice now has a global trajectory.

7. This issue of his (rarely her) political subjectivity is one that could easily become a lengthy discussion in itself. As an agent of the party/state, he represents its interests in the local community; but as a member of that small community, his social being is to a certain extent defined by a network of relations of obligation and influence that structure social life. The current wisdom that structures our understanding of the interests and motivations of the local official is that, whereas in the early years of the socialist state his commitment to the party and its ideals and projects for the most part outweighed his social obligations within the community—that is, he identified himself more as an agent of the party than as a member of the village—increasingly in the past couple of decades he has taken a more defensive posture to protect local interests from the arbitrary demands of a state that did not take sufficient account of local needs or circumstances. At the level of ideology, this shift is understood as moving from a relatively idealistic early period of Chinese socialism to a more pragmatic, cynical worldview that presumes an end to ideology. We should not assume this split within the local official between his official and social selves to be a clean one, however. To do this would oversimplify a conception of the subject. Rather, I suggest that the local-level official is a fragmented subject, a complex assemblage of opportunistic self-interest, conviction, social vision, and desire for power. Furthermore, I suggest that this cynical disavowal of ideology expressed privately, if not publicly, is not necessarily a total rejection of socialist ideas for self-interested goals, but rather a kind of despair. Detailed portraits of local party leaders by both Madsen 1984 and Huang 1989 communicate some of the complexities of their political subjectivity.

8. Yang (1988:415) attributes the necessity for these oppositions to the party's self-definition as a universal and transcendent authority. She contrasts this totalizing tendency to the more subterranean influence of a relational ethics based on personal ties of kinship, reciprocity, or common identity.

9. Although counterrevolutionaries are not, strictly speaking, a specific class in the Marxist sense, they do compose one of the categories in the class/status system of the Maoist era that falls on the side of "class enemies" (Billeter 1985).

10. This distinction between "contradictions among the people" and the contradictions of class was made by Mao in his classic essay "On Contradiction."

11. And yet here is precisely where power most deconstructs itself, since these are the very activities that mark the power of the corrupt official, who has always existed as "the other within" the party subject to its own disciplinary rituals but has increasingly become the popular image of power rather than the hagiographic representations of model party secretaries.

12. Fengcheng County in Liaoning Province instituted at the village level the "village people's socialist ethics appraisal committees" (*cunmin jiaoyu huodongzu*) mentioned above (*Nongcun gongzuo tongxun* 1988, 7:42–43). These committees are composed of three to five members who take units of ten households each as the object of their educational activities. The group members are elected by the people at large or are selected by the party branch in consultation with the masses. They tend to fall into six categories of persons: party members, youth league members, retired village cadres, people of high moral character, women "heads of household" (*nüdangjia*) and individuals of known ability (*nengren*). These small groups are to carry out propaganda and educational tasks, mobilize the masses for public works, resolve conflicts, transmit information, provide mediation services, and serve other functions. Their primary means are supposed to be persuasion and exertion of personal influence. The *shehui daode pingyi hui* is found in Wei County, Hebei Province (*Nongmin ribao* [Peasant daily] 1987, 7.15); The *hongbai xishi lishihui* was reported in the *Nongmin ribao* (1987, 7.15:2), and the *wenming zu* in *Renmin ribao* (1986, 5.27:5).

13. The language used to elicit such an emotionally charged response would be interesting to examine. Unfortunately, the published examples of this "heart talk" (*tanxin*) are too fragmentary to really explore the subtleties of its operation. One can imagine a parallel in José Arguedas's *Deep Rivers,* where the Catholic priest subdues an Indian revolt by addressing the rioters as wayward children who are humbled by the highly emotional expression of concern for them. There is no alternative for them but to occupy a disempowered and debased position within this discourse that "hails" them as children or beasts of the field. The emotive power of these rituals must necessarily draw our attention to the symbolic power relations embedded within discourse. As Bourdieu (1977:648) suggests: "Competence [eloquence, the power to move one's auditors] implies the power to impose reception." In this sense the language of *tanxin* is both a part of everyday discourse and also alien to it as something imposed from above.

14. In Fengcheng County, Liaoning Province, these sorts of organizational innovations were praised for their efficacy in "resensitizing the deadened nerve

endings" (*mamude "shenjing moshao" you lingminie*) of the social body and restoring avenues of communication between party organizations and the masses. (Can we assume between the head and the body? [*Nongcun gongzuo tongxun* 1988:7].

15. For example, a lengthy discussion of the goals and methods for building spiritual civilization in the countryside states: "The great mass of peasants have created [*chuangzaole*] in practice a number of excellent forms for the construction of spiritual civilization in the countryside based on the special characteristics of rural social life" (Fan et al. 1987:6).

16. I am adapting here a "specular logic" borrowed from feminist film theory, specifically from Kaja Silverman's discussion of suture in *The Subject of Semiotics* (1983).

17. This discussion resembles in some respects Lefort's discussions of the Egocrat (1986).

18. In reading the text this way, I will be using the schema of Barthes's five semiotic codes: semic, proairetic, hermeneutic, symbolic, and cultural. I will be working through all five codes in that order. I have also been guided by Kaja Silverman's *Subject of Semiotics* and Seymour Chatman's *Story and Discourse,* along with discussions with Elena Feder on the narratological dimensions of the story.

19. The "law-abiding household" competition is itself a part of this quasi-democratic discourse. I deal with this in my forthcoming book on imagining the state.

20. We could point in the recent literature to at least one example where this limit to power went unrecognized. Party Secretary Ye, in Shu-min Huang's recent book *The Spiral Road,* describes his alienation from the party bureaucracy and his own struggle to maintain socialist ideals in the face of the pressure to decollectivize. In 1984 a delegation from above came to his village to promote the construction of "socialist spiritual civilization." They did nothing but criticize local conditions: the unpaved roads, the poultry running loose, the uncovered sewage ditches and stinky latrines. "I was furious. Who did they think we were? A bunch of rich overseas Chinese building a retirement compound in the countryside? . . . After they ate our good food and smoked our special cigarettes, they slapped our faces for being filthy peasants" (Huang 1989:168–69). The next day he called a meeting to organize the division of the brigade.

21. See Mbembe 1992 for a powerful argument of how we need to transcend the crude binary between domination and resistance; the two are so intimately intertwined that it is impossible to prise them apart. He suggests the simultaneity of both as constant struggle over where to set the limits of power. Moreover, I believe Foucault said as much, though perhaps not as clearly and certainly not in the specific context of colonialism and postcoloniality.

22. One could also argue, however, that narratological theory was founded on Propp's structural analysis of the folktale, which claims a more universal appli-

cation. See Clark 1985 for her adaptation of the structural analysis of narrative to Soviet socialist realist literature.

References

Anagnost, Ann. 1988. Family violence and magical violence: The "woman-as-victim" in China's one-child family policy. *Women and Language* 1, no. 2: 16–22.

———. 1989. Prosperity and counter-prosperity: The moral discourse on wealth in post-Mao China. In *Marxism and the Chinese experience: Issues of socialism in a Third World socialist society,* ed. Arif Dirlik and Maurice Meisner. Armonk, N.Y.: Sharpe.

Arguedas, José. 1978. *Deep rivers*. Trans. Frances Horning Barraclough. Austin: University of Texas Press.

Barthes, Roland. 1974. *S/Z*. Trans. Richard Miller. New York: Hill and Wang.

Billeter, Jean-François. 1985. The system of "class-status." In *The scope of state power in China,* ed. Stuart R. Schram. London: SOAS.

Bourdieu, Pierre. 1977. The economics of linguistic exchanges. *Social Science Information* 16:645–68.

———. 1984–85. Delegation and political fetishism. *Thesis Eleven,* nos. 10–11: 56–70.

Certeau, Michel de. 1984. *The practice of everyday life*. Berkeley and Los Angeles: University of California Press.

Chatman, Seymour. 1978. *Story and discourse: Narrative structure in fiction and film*. Ithaca: Cornell University Press.

Clark, Katerina. 1985. *The Soviet novel: History as ritual*. Chicago: University of Chicago Press.

Fan Zuogang et al., comps. 1987. *Nongcun jingshen wenming jianshe xintan* (New explorations into building rural spiritual civilization). Beijing: Nongye Chubanshe.

Foucault, Michel. 1979. *Discipline and punish: The birth of the prison*. New York: Vintage Books.

Hansen, Chad. 1985. Punishment and dignity in China. In *Individualism and holism: Studies in Confucian and Taoist values,* ed. Donald Munro. Ann Arbor: University of Michigan Press.

Havel, Václav. 1986. The power of the powerless. In *Václav Havel, or Living in truth,* ed. Jan Vladislav. London: Faber and Faber.

Huang, Shu-min. 1989. *The spiral road: Change in a Chinese village through the eyes of a Communist Party leader*. Boulder, Colo.: Westview Press.

Lefort, Claude. 1986. The image of the body and totalitarianism. In his *The political forms of modern society,* ed. John B. Thompson. Cambridge: MIT Press.

Madsen, Richard. 1984. *Power and morality in a Chinese village*. Berkeley and Los Angeles: University of California Press.

Mbembe, Achille. 1992. Prosaics of servitude and authoritarian civilities. *Public Culture* 5 (Fall): 123:45.

Nongcun gongzuo tongxun. 1988, 7:42–43.

Pêcheux, Michel. 1978. Are the masses an inanimate object? In *Linguistic variation: Models and methods,* ed. David Sankoff. New York: Academic Press.

———. 1982. *Language, semantics and ideology.* New York: St. Martin's Press.

Renmin ribao. 1986, 5.27:5.

Silverman, Kaja. 1983. *The subject of semiotics.* New York: Oxford University Press.

Yang, Mayfair Mei-hui. 1988. The modernity of power in the Chinese socialist order. *Cultural anthropology* 3 (November): 408–27.

Zhang, Yingjin. 1990. Ideology of the body in *Red Sorghum:* National allegory, national roots, and third cinema. *East-West Film Journal* 4 (June): 38–53.

Zito, Angela. 1993. Ritualizing *Li:* Implications for studying power and gender. *Positions: east asia cultures critique* (in press).

6

The Female Body and Nationalist Discourse: Manchuria in Xiao Hong's *Field of Life and Death*

Lydia H. Liu

In a short essay written at the outbreak of the war in 1937, titled "Shimian zhi ye" (The night of insomnia), Xiao Hong, a novelist from Machuria, described her ambivalent feelings toward the patriotism that her lover Xiao Jun embraced. She questioned his notion of home, in particular, when Xiao Jun expressed the wish to take her back to his parents' village after Manchuria was liberated from the Japanese. The question she raised on this occasion was, "But what about me? Would your family treat an outsider such as *xifu* [daughter-in-law] equally well?" (Xiao Hong 1987b:59; translation mine). In her view a woman was condemned to permanent exile by the stigma of her gender, and it would be difficult for her to identify a place as home: "As far as I am concerned, it always comes down to the same thing: either riding a donkey and journeying to an alien place, or staying put in other people's homes. I am never keen on the idea of homeland. Whenever people talk about home I cannot help but be moved, although I know perfectly well that I had become 'homeless' even before the Japanese set foot on that land [Manchuria]" (ibid; translation mine). What does Xiao Hong's ambivalence tell us about the ideas of homeland, nation, gender, and identity? Benedict Anderson's familiar notion of imagined political community has often been used by poststructuralist critics to deconstruct established notions of national identity (Anderson 1991). But having understood that national identity is a historical construct rather than the manifestation of some unchanging essence, what else do we know about this problem? For instance, has the notion of national identity ever been contested by alternative narratives of the self? If so, what historical possibilities arise as a result of their engagement and contention?

In this chapter I will situate the problem of national identity in the intersecting area between the female body and nationalist discourse and focus primarily on the question of literary representation. The text I will be using here is Xiao Hong's novel *The Field of Life and Death*. This novel is important because it engages a significant moment in Chinese history where nationalist discourse constitutes the female body as a privileged signifier and various struggles are waged over the meaning and ownership of that body. Those struggles open up an important avenue toward understanding the problem of nationalism itself.

Gender and National Literature

Xiao Hong (1911–42) lived in a time of national crisis and wrote novels, stories, and essays in response to contending discourses that were fought out on the symbolic terrain of the female body. Because of her ambivalent relationship with nationalism, her "canonical" status in modern (read "national") Chinese literature has been extremely controversial. My reading of her work, however, does not aim to improve her status in the canon so much as to question the practice of nation-oriented and male-centered literary criticism. In that sense I will be dealing with two levels of discursive practice surrounding her text: production and reception. The former involves Xiao Hong's engagement with nationalist discourse within the space of her novel and the latter a body of criticism that seeks to recuperate her text in the name of national literature. In so doing, I hope to help reframe the questions of nation, gender, and literary practice as first posed by postcolonial, poststructuralist, and feminist theory.

The reception of Xiao Hong's novel in China has been dominated by nationalist discourse since its publication in 1935. Like Ye Zi's *Harvest* and Xiao Jun's *Village in August* (two other works in the Slave Society Series that Lu Xun, the most influential leftist writer of the time, helped put in print), Xiao Hong's novel has been evaluated primarily on the basis of nationalism from the very beginning (Beifang Luncong Bianji Bu 1983). Most critics celebrate the work as a "national allegory," a quintessential anti-imperialist novel imbued with patriotic spirit—so much so that one can hardly read Xiao Hong today without being aware of the existence of a highly developed, institutionalized, male-centered critical tradition that has tried to frame and determine the meaning of her work. In fact the gendered politics in the practice of literary criticism in China has largely escaped the notice of well-intentioned scholars in the West, who are themselves entrapped in a similar situation at home, and thus greatly complicates the way Orientalized knowledge is produced or perceived.

Fredric Jameson's controversial article "Third-World Literature in the

Era of Multinational Capitalism" (1986) is a good example. The essay begins with an interesting preamble about non-Western intellectuals and their obsession with the nation. The author apparently assumes that those intellectuals represent the "Third World" to the West and that their representation is transparent and unproblematic. This assumption enables him to arrive at the much-disputed hypothesis of the essay—that Third World literature is characterized by national allegory. In light of the author's unreflexive relationship with the non-Western intellectual, his hypothesis becomes meaningful and revealing, rather than simply false, because it plays right into what I would call the nation-oriented and male-centered practice of literary criticism within some of the non-Western countries. It never occurs to him that this kind of critical practice, rather than Third World literature, is the stuff that the non-Western (male) intellectual represents so "authentically" to the West.[1] Jameson's attempt to establish Third World literature as national allegory elides the agency of literary criticism in the production of canons and texts within the national context. For instance, his choice and reading of Lu Xun is to a large extent predetermined by established readings that surround Lu Xun's text in the modern Chinese literary canon. So rather than just another instance of Orientalism or "rhetoric of otherness," as his critics often suggest, I see in his essay an eloquent example of the coauthorship of nationalist discourse by Marxian intellectuals of the First World and Third World.[2]

The allegorical readings of Xiao Hong's novel were initially framed by the views of Hu Feng and Lu Xun, who contributed an epilogue and a preface, respectively, to the first edition. As editor of the Slave Society Series, Hu Feng wrote his epilogue to praise the anti-Japanese spirit of the book and the awakening of the Chinese peasants to nationalism. "These antlike, ignorant men and women, sad but resolute, stood on the front line of the sacred war of nationalism," he says. "Once they were like ants, living in order to die. Now they were titans, dying in order to live" (Hu Feng 1935:3).[3] Lu Xun does not force the epithet of nationalism onto the novel in his much quoted preface, but he too obscures the fact that Xiao Hong's novel is more about the lives of rural women than about "the tenacity of the people of northern China in their struggle for survival and resistance to death" (Lu Xun 1935:1; my translation). The field of *sheng* (birth, life) and *si* (death), as my analysis will show, primarily represents the experience of the female body; specifically, the two areas of rural experience relating to peasant women: childbearing and death from suicide, sickness, or abuse. Lu Xun's own national agenda, which comes out clearly in his allusion to the rumor of war in Shanghai's Zhabei District and to places such as Harbin, or the British and French Concessions, is responsible for the blind spot in his reading.

It is not surprising that nationalist interpretation of this novel is the rule rather than the exception in Xiao Hong scholarship.[4] In his preface to Xiao's later novel, *Tales of Hulan River,* Mao Dun, a leading critic of the time, also judges the author on her commitment to the national cause, although his opinion runs counter to that of Hu Feng. In short, Xiao Hong is criticized for *not* participating in the national struggle this time. Reminiscing about the last moment of her life in Hong Kong, Mao says:

> It is hard to understand how a woman with her high ideals, who had struggled against reaction, could "hibernate" in such stirring times as the years just before and after 1940. A friend of hers, trying to explain her frustration and apathy, ascribed them to a series of emotional shocks that confined this poet, richer in feeling than intellect, within the small circle of her private life. (Although she condemned that circle, some inertia kept her from breaking boldly with it.) She was cut off completely from the tremendous *life* and *death* struggle being waged outside. As a result, although her high principles made her frown on the activities of the intellectuals of her class and regard them as futile talk, she would not plunge into the laboring masses of workers and peasants or change her life radically. Inevitably, then, she was frustrated and lonely. (Mao Dun [1946] 1984:10–11; Goldblatt, 289–90; italics mine)

It is ironic that Mao Dun evokes "life" and "death" here—words that are reminiscent of the title of Xiao Hong's first novel—to criticize her abstention from nationalist movements. His notion of "life" and "death," which is largely a gender-neutral reading of her earlier text, prevents him from looking at her struggle from a different perspective. The perspective I suggest below does not oblige Xiao Hong to share Mao Dun's view of private and collective experience or, for that matter, male-centered notions of society, nation, and war. If, to the author of *The Field of Life and Death* and *Tales of Hulan River,* the meaning of "life" and "death" resides in the individual body, particularly the female body, more than in the rise and fall of a nation, then her lack of commitment to nationalism should by no means be construed as some kind of failure. Not that Xiao Hong did not wish to resist Japanese aggression or feel attracted to the national cause.

Her dilemma was that she had to face two enemies rather than one: imperialism and the patriarchy. The latter tended to reinvent itself in multifarious forms, and national revolution was no exception. Xiao Jun's first novel, *Village in August,* provides a very good example. The novel is worth mentioning not only because the author had a romantic relationship with Xiao Hong for some years, but because the two authors published under strikingly similar conditions and yet their views on gender and nationalism contrast so sharply.

Xiao Jun's novel epitomizes the ways nationalist discourse deploys gender during the war. It contains a story about a peasant widow named Li Qisao, who suffers the horrible fate of losing her husband, lover, and child to the war and, on top of all her bereavements, is raped by a Japanese soldier. As a sign of symbolic exchange, the raped woman often serves as a powerful trope in anti-Japanese propaganda. Her victimization is used to represent—or more precisely, to eroticize—China's own plight. In such a signifying practice, the female body is ultimately displaced by nationalism, whose discourse denies the specificity of female experience by giving larger symbolic meanings to the signifier of rape: namely, China itself is being violated by the Japanese rapist.[5] Since the nation itself is at stake, the crime of rape does not acquire meaning until it is committed by foreign intruders. Li Qisao's tragedy is supposed to inspire average Chinese men and women to follow the path of revolution. But what exactly does the revolution mean in terms of women's liberation? As one of the guerrilla soldiers in this novel puts it in a conversation:

> Revolution? It means exterminating all those parasites who have lorded it over us since our ancestors' days. It means driving away all the Japanese soldiers who are now occupying Manchuria so that we would have our own land to farm. We wouldn't have to pay the excise tax to feed those bloodsucking parasites. You understand? Let me give you an example. Before the revolution, one rich guy alone has three, five, eight, or even ten wives. whereas you, in your thirties, cannot even afford a single one. *After the revolution, you could get a wife without having to pay a penny!* (Xiao Jun 1954 : 129; translation and italics mine)

The prospect is certainly rosy enough to those lower-class bachelors. But what about women? Are they given any subject position at all? The picture is particularly poignant in light of the fact that this guerrilla soldier has learned his revolutionary theory from Anna, the only intellectual woman in the troop. One wonders if revolutionary women such as Anna will escape the fate of being a mere wife after the success of the revolution to which she has contributed so much.[6]

The Field of Life and Death

Xiao Hong's novel *The Field of Life and Death* radically subverts the trope of the raped woman in nationalist discourse. As if in deliberate parody of Xiao Jun's novel, the rape that occurs in Xiao Hong's work, which is also set on the eve of the Anti-Japanese War, turns out to be committed by a Chinese man rather than by a Japanese soldier. The appropriation of the female body by nationalist discourse is contested relentlessly throughout. The remarkable thing about this novel is that the mise-en-scène of nationalist myths is narrated in stark contrast to the uncertain status of peasant women as national subjects, which raises poignant questions about what it means to be Chinese/peasant/woman. Gender, class, and national identities clash rather than conjoin, resulting in woman's loss of one identity or another and in her fractured subjectivity with regard to the nation.

In analyzing Xiao Hong's novel, I will be concentrating on the body of the peasant woman as an important site of contestatory meanings. As a matter of fact, such a reading is partially suggested by the controversy over the cover design of the novel the author herself made in 1935 (fig. 1). Needless to say, critics have a hard time trying to pin down the exact meaning of the drawing. Some say that the black shadow suggests an old fortress while the deep crimson in the background represents the blood of the people of Manchuria who died during the war of resistance. Others hold that the black area actually represents the map of Japanese-occupied Manchuria (Liu 1983:209–10). In an interesting article on Xiao Hong as an artist, Liu Fuchen points out that the black shadow is the profile of a woman's head while the diagonal line across the cover symbolizes the divided territory of China. He reads the uplifted face of the peasant woman as well as the firm lines of her neck and mouth as representing the anger and strength of the people of Manchuria in their struggle against the Japanese (1983:210). But Liu fails to explain why Xiao Hong uses a female head instead of a male head to represent the people of Manchuria. Having hinted at a possible reading from a gendered point of view, he immediately displaces it with nationalist discourse. If one takes the black shadow as representing a female head coinciding with (and parodying) the map of Manchuria, the diagonal line across the page may very well be interpreted

FIG. 1. Cover design for Xiao Hong's novel *The Field of Life and Death* made by the author in 1935.

as a symbol of the split national subject as well as the divided territory of China. As for the conjecture that the deep crimson may signify the blood shed by the people of Manchuria, there is also strong evidence within the text that it refers to women's blood specifically, because the female body in this novel is always linked with bleeding, injury, deformation, or death, be it from childbirth, beating, sickness, or suicide. The omnipresence of the female body casts an ominous shadow on nationalist discourse and insists on assigning its idiosyncratic meanings to the life-and-death strug-gle in rural Manchuria. Of course one need not accept any of these read-ings, but it is worth noting that the controversy surrounding the cover design calls into question the authority of a single nationalist interpretation that has heretofore prevailed in Xiao Hong scholarship and thus opens up space for alternative reading.

What does the female body have to do with nationalism? Critics have often wondered why Xiao Hong's anti-Japanese novel is filled with details about women's lives in the villages and does not begin to deal with the Japanese invasion until the last few chapters. Two Chinese women critics, Meng Yue and Dai Jinhua, have suggested in their book *Fuchu lishi dibiao* (Emerging from the horizon of history) that the meaning of *sheng* (birth, life) and *si* (death) should be perceived in terms of the experience of the female body, although their reading does not directly engage nationalist discourse (Meng and Dai 1989). In what follows, I intend to push their reading further by showing that the female body actually provides the critical angle for viewing the rise and fall of the nation rather than the other way around.

The boundary of the female body in this novel is chiefly defined by rural women's experience of childbirth, disease, sexuality, aging, and death. Despite the apparent allusion to the Buddhist concept of samsara in *sheng* and *si,* the novel does not espouse the Buddhist faith of some of its characters; on the contrary, it stresses the plight of the female body, locating the meaning of its suffering in the immediate socioeconomic context of this world rather than in a world of karma. Death, for example, is the horrible disintegration of the body rather than the ultimate escape from the distress of life. Poverty, ignorance, class exploitation, imperialism, and the patriarchy all conspire to reduce the rural people, especially, women, to animal existence.

As Howard Goldblatt points out (1976:xxi), animal imagery is one of the most striking features of Xiao Hong's language. The mere fact that animals are part of any rural scene can hardly account for the eerie power of those images in this novel. What is emphasized is the sheer physicality of the animal existence, stubbornly mute and intransigent, which parallels the condition of human existence in the rural community. The body of the animal, which exists, decays, and falls apart, often stands as a metaphor for the degradation of the human body. Xiao Hong's language becomes particularly powerful when metonymy as well as metaphor is used to evoke animals and humans contiguously so that the two species are joined in the homogeneous space of the body. In chapter 3, for example, Mother Wang is ordered by her master to sell the old mare to the slaughterhouse. The narrator describes her trip as follows: "A falling leaf landed on Mother Wang's head. It lay there silently. She drove her old mare ahead, wearing a yellow leaf on her head; the old horse, the old woman, the old leaf—they were walking down the road that led into the city" (Xiao Hong [1935] 1953:140; Goldblatt, 30). The dying animal, the old woman, and the fallen leaf are coordinated in a single syntactic sequence—reminiscent of classical Chinese song-poetry—that emphasizes the process of aging involving all three. The presence of the old mare evokes the oldness of Mother Wang metonymically, since the two have grown old together serving the same master and have both loved and suffered as mothers. The metonymy furthermore transforms itself into a metaphor when Mother Wang arrives at the slaughterhouse: "It was a short street, at the end of which a double black door stood open. As she drew nearer, she could see bloodstains splattered all over the door. The old lady was frightened by the bloodstains and felt as if she herself were entered an execution ground" (40; Goldblatt, 32). The hideous sight of coils of steaming intestines, the stench, the dismembered legbones, horse hooves, and animal hides, bring home the most somatic aspect of death that connects the aging animal to the old woman.

The intimate experience of the body shared by female animals and women alike is presented metonymically in chapter 6, which contains several shocking scenes of childbirth.

> On the haystack behind the house a bitch was giving birth. Its limbs trembled, and its whole body shook. After a long period of time the puppies were born. In the warm of the season the entire village was occupied with the birth of its young. Big sows were leading their litters of piglets squealing and running, while the bellies of others were still big, nearly scraping the ground, their many teats virtually overflowing.
>
> It was evening. Fifth Sister's elder sister could delay no longer. She went inside and spoke to her mother-in-law. "Get one of the old women. I really don't feel well." . . .
>
> Her mother-in-law gathered up the straw, stirring up clouds of dust. The naked woman squirmed on the *k'ang* like a fish. (69–70; Goldblatt, 52)

The bitch, the sows, and the woman whose naked body resembled a fish give birth in the same season, inhabit the same ritualistic space, and evoke one another contiguously. In their experience of the body, female animals and women have more in common than women and men do. The agony of having one's flesh torn apart, bones cracked, and life endangered generates a kind of knowledge impermeable to the male sex. What is worse for a woman like Fifth Sister's elder sister is that not only does her husband refuse to empathize with her pain, but he hates her: "Feign death, will you? Let's see if you still want to feign death now." In a drunken state, he flings his tobacco pouch at his wife whose body is soaked in blood and who already has the look of a corpse. The woman "dared not move a single muscle, for like the child in front of a patriarch, she lived in dread of her man" (71; Goldblatt, 53). In the end she is delivered of a dead infant, whose body joins birth and death in an uncanny moment.

Titled "Days of Punishment," chapter 6 casts an extremely negative light on the fertility of life. The excess of life certainly aggravates poverty in this rural village; more important, in the act of bringing forth new life the female body is severely punished. As the narrator describes this uniquely female world, her language is punctuated alternately by compassion for the agonized body of the mother and bitter mockery of the self-inflicted disaster driven by man's instinct to continue the species. Her compassion shines forth in the following description: "The naked woman could no longer even crawl; she was unable to muster the final burst of effort in this moment of *sheng* and *si* (70; Goldblatt, 53).[7] Besides Fifth Sister's elder sister, three more village women give birth in this crowded chapter. Golden Bough's labor is rendered difficult because her husband demanded sex the night before her labor. With the help of Mother Wang she gives birth to a baby daughter, who is dashed to the ground by her own father a month later. Second Aunt Li has a miscarriage that nearly costs her own life. Even the foolish wife of Two-and-a-Half Li struggles in labor. The birth of her baby is followed by someone's sow giving birth outside the window at the foot of the wall. The narrator's insistence on drawing the parallel between animals and humans in sexuality and childbirth sometimes verges on sarcasm:

> Cows and horses in their ignorance plant the seeds of their own suffering. At night as the people sat in the cool breeze, they could hear odd noises coming from the stable or cowshed. A bull that was probably battling for its mate crashed out of the shed, breaking the fence. . . .
> In the village, folks and beasts busied themselves at *sheng* and *si*. (74; Goldblatt, 56)

If life and childbirth are horrible realities for women, death is hardly a desirable alternative. Innumerable deaths from infanticide, fatal disease, war, and epidemic occur in the space of this short novel. Although men also die, females seem to succumb to death more often, and in most of those cases the narrator individualizes the female victim for us. Among those victims are, for instance, Mother Wang's three-year-old daughter and her grown-up daughter, the Feng girl; Golden Bough's little daughter who is murdered by her own father; an old woman from North Village who hangs herself with her granddaughter; the beautiful Yueying who dies of paralysis and neglect; and finally, Two-and-a-Half-Li's wife and her child who die during the war. The deaths of the few men are meaningful only inasmuch as they affect the lives of the women. When Golden Bough becomes a widow and is forced to make her own living, we are not told when, where, why, or how her husband died, whereas the manner of women's deaths, such as Mother Wang's suicide, receives extended treatment. Two women attempt suicide in this novel, Mother Wang before the Japanese occupation and the old woman from North Village after that. The reason is the same; namely, the loss of their beloved sons. Instead of elaborating on Mother Wang's inner sorrow when she hears the news of her son's execution by the government, the narrator plunges directly into the physical aspect of her suicide and the deformation of her body, giving details such as the froth gathered on her black lips, her distended stomach and chest, her terrifying howling, and the ghostly stare of her eyes. Mother Wang's suicide attempt is presented neither as a heroic act nor as social protest. It is the horrifying deformation of the body that is emphasized.

Since rural women live most intensely with their bodies, the transformation of the body in sickness is no less shocking than its deformation in death. Yueying was once a beauty. After she comes down with paralysis, her husband begins to lose patience and decides to give her up completely. He refuses to give her water, and to torture her further, he places a pile of bricks on her bed as a prop for her weak body. When village women come to offer their help, they discover that the poor woman is so neglected that the lower part of her body is soaked with excrement and that the former beauty is reduced to a horrible freak:

> The whites of her eyes had turned greenish, and so had her straight front teeth. Her frizzled hair stuck close to her scalp. She looked like a sick cat, abandoned and without hope. . . . With her legs like two white bamboo poles stretched out before her, her skeleton formed a right angle with the *k'ang*. It was a human shape composed of nothing but threads. Only the head was broader; it sat on the torso like a lantern atop a pole (51–52; Goldblatt, 40)

Yueying's bottom is so rotten that it has turned into caves for maggots. Little white crawling creatures drop on Mother Wang's arms as she tries to wipe the sick woman's buttocks. Yueying dies in the end, but not until after witnessing the horrible decomposition of her own body in the mirror.

Finally, the precariousness of the female body in this novel lies in rural women's experience of sexuality, which is always interconnected with pregnancy. Compared with the male body, the female body signifies a woman's lack of control over her destiny, not so much because sexual desire is an animal instinct as because patriarchy determines the meaning of desire and chastity so that it serves the interests of men. Golden Bough finds herself in deep trouble when she becomes pregnant before marriage, so she begins to fear and loathe her body:

> Golden Bough was in torment. Her stomach had become a hideous monstrosity. She felt a hard object inside, which, when she pressed hard on it, became even more apparent. After she was certain that she was pregnant, her heart shuddered as though it were retching. She was seized with terror. When two butterflies wondrously alighted one on top of the other on her knees, she only stared at the two copulating insects and did not brush them off. Golden Bough seemed to have become a scarecrow in a rice field. (30; Goldblatt, 25)

It is common for a woman to perceive literal alterations of the boundaries of her body such as violence, disease, and maiming as extreme threats to selfhood. Pregnancy, however, occupies a rather ambiguous domain of signification where meaning must be decided according to the social codes that govern a woman's behavior through regulating her body. In this instance Golden Bough experiences her premarital pregnancy as the body's deformation (monstrosity) and her illegal fetus as an alien intruder. The free copulation of the butterflies brings out, by contrast, the impasse a woman like herself faces in human society: the patriarchy desires her body, demands her chastity, and punishes her for her transgressive acts. Like a scarecrow, her body is emptied of its contents and reduced to a signifier of predetermined functions. This gendered knowledge is transmitted to the daughter through the mother who forbids Golden Bough to go near the edge of the river, where men seduce women: "'The wife of Fufa, didn't she come to ruin at the edge of the river? Even the children in the village were talking about it. Ai! . . . What kind of woman is that? Afterwards she couldn't find any man who would have her. Being pregnant, she had to marry Fufa. Her mother suffered such terrible shame that she couldn't hold her head up among the villagers anymore'" (25; Goldblatt, 21). It turns out that not only does Golden Bough tread the path of the wife of Fufa, but she is seduced by none other than Fufa's nephew Chengye. Like Fufa before him, Chengye does not care much for the woman he seduces. Whenever the lovers meet, he simply puts her down onto the ground and pounces on her body. He neither kisses her nor says words of love but is driven by a basic desire. Their marriage, arranged by Golden Bough's mother, who wants to cover up the daughter's shame, repeats the ancient story of conjugal hostility in the patriarchal Chinese family. The husband curses the wife—"You lazy wife, what were you doing during the day"—whereas it does not take long for the wife to learn how to curse a husband and feel that "men are heartless human beings, a feeling shared by the rest of the village women" (73; Goldblatt, 55).

Among the rural women treated in this novel, Mother Wang deserves special attention. She commands the respect of the village women and to some extent that of her own husband for possessing unusual wisdom, verbal power, courage, and an independent mind. In her youth she left the home of her first husband permanently in protest against his physical abuse. Her present husband, Zhao San, is the third she marries. The village women often gather in her home and absorb her stories. Mother Wang's profound knowledge about *sheng* and *si* comes from her personal experience of love, loss, poverty, and sorrow. When she tells stories, she speaks as an authority on woman's "history," and her audience, all women, is awestruck by her manner and her voice. Since Chinese women are denied subject positions in male history, storytelling or gossip becomes the only means of transmitting women's unique knowledge about life and death among themselves. One of the stories Mother Wang tells in the novel concerns the fatal fall of her three-year-old daughter. As she speaks, a streak of lightning appears in the sky, and the speaker is suddenly transformed into a disembodied voice:

> Ah . . . I threw her in the haystack, with blood flowing all over the hay. Her little hand was trembling and blood was trickling from her nostrils and her mouth. It was like her throat had been cut. I could still hear a rumbling in her stomach. It was like a puppy run over by a cart. I've seen that happen with my own eyes. I've seen everything. . . .
>
> My child's name was Xiao Zhong. For several nights I suf-

> fered. I couldn't sleep. What was all that wheat worth? From
> then on, grains of wheat didn't matter much to me. Even now,
> nothing matters to me. I was only twenty then. (11–12; Gold-
> blatt, 11–12)

From her intimate experience of death, which is so vividly filled with
bleeding nostrils, mouth, throat, hands, and stomach, Mother Wang
learns about the precariousness of the human body. It is this knowledge
that gives her a strong character and a compassionate heart as she goes
about assisting the village women in childbirth, nursing sick women such
as Yueying, or even walking the old mare to the slaughterhouse. But
Mother Wang's plight as a woman in the patriarchal society is also the
cause of her ultimate rejection of female identity. After her suicide attempt
fails, she sets out to teach her daughter to be a woman warrior in order to
avenge the death of her son. On the arrival of the Japanese in Manchuria,
Mother Wang joins men in their struggle for the nation's survival. It is no
surprise that, from then on till the end of the novel, her authority dwindles
in proportion to the significant rise of the village males as nationalist
fighters.

This brings us to Xiao Hong's position on nationalism, which Hu
Feng emphasizes so much in his epilogue. If we compare her treatment of
the rural life before the Japanese invasion with that of Xiao Jun in *Village
in August,* the ambivalence of her attitude immediately comes into focus.
For Xiao Jun, the rural world before the occupation does not in the least
resemble the sordid life Xiao Hong depicts. *Village in August* contains the
following description: "He [Little Red Face] recalled the peaceful days in
his past. Would he once again feel free to enjoy his plow and his pipe as
before? How soon would all this happen? When that wonderful day came
about, was it true that everyone of those who had bullied him and every
Japanese who had taken his land would have been shot and killed?" (Xiao
Jun [1935] 1954:4; translation mine). The discrepancy between the visions of the two authors is clearly attributable to the role that gender plays
in each novel. Xiao Jun's work concentrates on the soldiers' life and on
their skirmishes against the Japanese enemy, whereas Xiao Hong deals primarily with the life of women whose oppression makes it difficult to ide-
alize the patriarchal society before or after occupation. Whatever happens
to the nation, it is always the female body that suffers most. The final
chapters of her novel make it clear that national identity is largely a male
prerogative, which allows the village men to acquire national conscious-

ness and preach the new gospel to their women despite their own lowly status in society. Mother Wang's husband, Zhao San, for example, shows great enthusiasm for nationalist propaganda and particularly enjoys preaching to the widows:

> That night old Zhao San came home very late. He had been talking to everyone he met about the loss of the country, about saving the country, about volunteer armies and revolutionary armies . . . all these strange-sounding terms. . . .
>
> He roused his son from his slumber and, with pride, told him about the propaganda work he had been doing: how the widow in the east village had sent her children back to her mother's house so that she could join the volunteer army, and how the young men were gathering together. The old man was acting like an official in a magistrate's office, swaying from side to side as he spoke. His heart was also swaying, and his soul was taking giant strides. (Xiao Hong [1935] 1953:114–15; Goldblatt, 82–83)

Zhao San's propaganda work elevates his worth in his own eyes, for nationalism enables the poor village males to transcend their class status by giving them a new identity. This empowered identity, however, does not seem so different from that of the "official in a magistrate's office," because it reproduces the old patriarchal relation by putting men in the subject position of a new discourse of power. Interestingly enough, women joining the army—all widows—must reject their female identity in a suicidal manner to become Chinese and fight for the nation. With men it is a different matter. Not only does nationalism give them a new sense of identity, but it enhances their manhood at the same time. Li Qingshan's speech given during a solemn occasion when the village people pledge their loyalty to the nation shortly before taking off on an expeditionary journey indicates that nationalist discourse is unequivocally gendered: "Brothers, what day is today? Do you know? Today is the day we dare to die . . . it is decided . . . even if all our heads swing from the tops of the trees throughout the village, we shall not flinch, right? Isn't that right, brothers?" (120; Goldblatt, 87). When the widows respond to the call, they immediately lose their gender and join the ranks of the brothers. Ironically, they are the first to shout: "Yes, even if we are cut into a million pieces!" (120). One can hardly miss the familiar tone of the tragic Qiu Jin in their vows.

Chapter 13 represents the height of anti-Japanese sentiment in the novel. Instead of endorsing nationalism, it demonstrates how the national subject comes into being. Over the past years of his life, Zhao San was merely the head of a rural household like the rest of the rural men, and he was also a coward who dared not even defy his landlord. He "had not understood what a nation was. In prior days he could even have forgotten his own nationality" (119–20; Goldblatt, 86). It is through a discourse—nationalist discourse—that Zhao (re)constitutes himself as a national subject and is reborn. Speaking to the volunteer fighters, he pours out a torrent of nationalist emotions:

> The nation . . . the nation is lost! I . . . I am old, too. You are still young, you go and save the nation! My old bones are useless! I'm an old nationless slave, and I'll never see you rip up the Japanese flag with my own eyes. Wait until I'm buried . . . then plant the Chinese flag over my grave, for I am a Chinese! . . . I want a Chinese flag over my grave, for I am a Chinese! . . . I want a Chinese flag. I don't want to be a nationless slave. Alive I am Chinese, and when I'm dead, I'll be a Chinese ghost . . . not a nation . . . nationless slave. (121; Goldblatt, 87)

This is characteristic of all nationalist discourses in which the individual takes up a subject position ("I," "I am," etc.) in a homogeneous space ("Chinese," "nation") and thereby acquires a new identity and finds a new purpose in life ("save the nation"). Even Two-and-a-Half-Li, who cannot live without his goat, ends up joining in the revolution.

Unlike other men, Two-and-a-Half-Li is a cripple and is symbolically castrated from his own sex; moreover, his unusual attachment to the animal marks him out as someone closer to women in identity than to men. Just like Mother Wang, who caresses and talks to her mare, Two-and-a-Half-Li treats his goat like a family member. It is his "feminine" character that prevents him from jumping to join the national cause at the outset. After the assembly persuades him to offer his goat for the sacrificial ritual, he manages to find a rooster somewhere in order to save his beloved goat from the blade. "He was the only person who did not take the oath. He did not seem particularly distressed about the fate of the nation as he led the goat home. Everyone's eyes, especially old Zhao San's, angrily followed his departure. 'You crippled old thing. Don't you want to go on living?'" (121–22; Goldblatt, 88). After the death of his wife and child, however, his "masculine" character begins to assert itself, and the novel closes with Two-and-a-Half-Li leaving home in search of the People's Revolutionary Army. His transformation from a self-absorbed peasant into a national subject once again demonstrates that the stakes involved in becoming a national subject are very different for men and women. The patriarchy measures a man's power in terms of his possessions: wife, children, livelihood, if not in nobler forms of property. It is the loss of those possessions that turns Two-and-a-Half-Li against Japanese imperialism. Nationalist discourse enables this man to gain in manhood by giving him a new subject position. Compared with him, a woman who has lost her husband is left without many resources. The novel opens up two grim possibilities for a rural widow: she either rejects her female identity, joins the ranks of the "brothers" without the comfort of the elevated sense of manhood that real brothers enjoy, and gets herself killed like Mother Wang's daughter, or like Golden Bough, subjects herself to rape and exploitation in order to survive.

After the death of her brutal husband, Golden Bough decides to go to the city of Harbin to earn money as a seamstress. For fear of being caught by the Japanese, she smears her face with dust until she looks like an old, ugly beggar woman. On the road she encounters a troop of Japanese soldiers who order her to stop, but when the soldiers see her appearance they let her go unharmed. Having escaped from the Japanese, Golden Bough falls into the hands of a Chinese man in the city. As a seamstress she must visit the homes of her clients, and it is during one of those visits that she is raped. This experience gives her a new perspective on her life as a woman, so when Mother Wang discourses again on the atrocities of the Japanese soldiers, such as their slitting the bellies of pregnant women and killing innocent babies, "Golden Bough snorted: 'I used to hate men only; now I hate the Japanese instead.' She finally reached the nadir of personal grief: 'Perhaps I hate the Chinese as well? Then there is nothing else for me to hate.' It seemed that Mother Wang's knowledge was no longer the equal of Golden Bough" (140; Goldblatt, 100, slightly modified). Golden Bough's knowledge is earned at the expense of her body. To protect her body from men, she decides to leave the job in the city and become a nun. To her disappointment, the Buddhist temple in the village has long since been abandoned, and she is left with no hope for the future. The ending of the novel presents a sharp contrast between Golden Bough (in the penultimate chapter) and Two-and-a-Half-Li (in the final chapter). Despite her hatred for the Japanese, the woman never succeeds in becoming a national subject like the man. The experience of her body at the hands of her husband and the rapist contradicts the national identity that the presence of the Japanese imposes on her.

The female body in this novel is the field of life and death as well as the ultimate source from which the work derives its meaning. The author's refusal to sublimate or displace the female body leads to a gendered position that intervenes in a nationalist discourse the novel seemingly establishes but in actuality subverts. Nationalism comes across as a profoundly patriarchal ideology that grants subject positions to men who fight over territory, possession, and the right to dominate. The women in this novel, being themselves possessed by men, do not automatically share the male-centered sense of territory. "My home was dreary," says Xiao Hong's narrator in a refrain in a later novel, *Tales of Hulan River.* There are two temples in the narrator's home village, the Temple of the Patriarch and the Temple of the Immortal Matron, where even the immortals are subject to gender discrimination. The clay idols in the Temple of the Patriarch are given stern and imposing features, whereas those in the Temple of the Immortal Matron look benign and submissive. We are told that the people who cast those clay idols are all men:

> It is obvious that for a man to beat a woman is a Heaven-ordained right, which also holds true for gods and demons alike. No wonder the idols in the Temple of the Immortal Matron have such obedient looks about them—this comes from having been beaten so often. It becomes apparent that obedience is not the exceptionally fine natural trait it has been thought to be, but rather the result of being beaten, or perhaps an invitation to receive beatings. (1942:45; Goldblatt, 174)[8]

Indeed, the reason the author herself fled home at the age of twenty was that her father, who embodied the evils of the patriarchy in her eyes, tried to force her into an arranged marriage.[9] In "Chu dong" (Early winter), published along with the author's other familiar prose in the 1936 collection *Qiao* (Bridge), Xiao Hong's narrator expresses her firm resolution never to set foot in her father's house again: "I will never think of going back to a home like that. My father and I are adamantly opposed to each other, and I simply cannot live on his charity" (1987a:7; translation mine). This father figure haunted Xiao Hong throughout her short, stormy life as an exile in Qingdao, Shanghai, Tokyo, and many other places, terminating in Hong Kong in 1942.

Xiao Hong's life story illustrates a series of frustrated attempts to sort out the meaning of being a woman and Chinese. She had fled from her tyrannical father long before she and Xiao Jun escaped from Japanese-occupied Manchuria. In the subsequent years she spent with Xiao Jun in

Shanghai and elsewhere, she had the misfortune of being repeatedly abused and physically assaulted by him. When she could no longer bear his violence, she would often run away. Once she went so far as to leave China for Japan in order to stay away from Xiao Jun for a time. Given the deteriorating relationship between the two countries in 1936, the choice of Japan as her country of sojourn invites symptomatic reading. Whatever reasons might lie behind it, her choice indicates a strong desire to protect her body and mind from male domination even if it meant exile from her homeland and loneliness in the enemy country.

§

Until recently, the history of Xiao Hong's reception in mainland China has been trying to tell a different story, one given to eliding or condemning her ambivalence about nationalism and erasing her subversion of nationalist appropriation of the female body. Of course, this is not something that happens to Xiao Hong and her works alone. The subcategory of the woman writer in modern Chinese criticism itself has been created and legitimized in the name of "national" literature, which patronizes women's writing and subsumes it under the category of the nation in much the same way as the state deploys the category *funü* for political control. Such gendered practice of literary criticism, I want to emphasize, has been a major site for the production of nationalist discourse ever since China saw the introduction of the post-Enlightenment European notion that a nation cannot be a nation without a national literature.[10] Within this framework of knowledge, the long-standing practice of reading literary text, traditional or modern, within a nation-oriented and male-centered critical tradition is easily justified or simply could not be brought into question.[11] So rather than establishing *écriture féminine,* revisionary readings of women's works constitute an act of intervention into the hegemonic practice of modern literary criticism. It is a way of saying that national literature, nation-oriented literary criticism, discipline, and institution must be opened up, interrogated, and radically rethought.

Notes

A different version of this chapter is included in a volume edited by Caren Kaplan and Inderpal Grewal, *Postmodernism and Transnational Feminist Practices,* forthcoming from the University of Minnesota Press. I wish to thank Lisa Rofel,

Tani E. Barlow, Ellen Widmer, Inderpal Grewal, and Mayfair Yang for their valuable comments and criticisms of an earlier draft.

1. I will not take up his questionable use of the category "Third World" here. Aijaz Ahmad has addressed this issue in his "'Third World Literature' and the Nationalist Ideology" (1989).

2. See the exchange between Fredric Jameson and Aijaz Ahmad (Jameson 1986; Ahmad 1987) over the concept of national allegory.

3. Unless otherwise noted, the English translation used throughout this chapter is that by Howard Goldblatt and Ellen Yeung (1979).

4. Howard Goldblatt's study of Xiao Hong presents an interesting deviation from this critical tradition. In *Hsiao Hong,* he refuses to treat the novel as an anti-imperialist work (Goldblatt 1976). Recently two women critics in mainland China, Meng Yue and Dai Jinhua, have made a more radical break with the nationalist reading of Xiao Hong when they read her in light of the female experience as represented in the novel (Meng and Dai 1989:174–99).

5. This is not to deny the actual atrocities committed by Japanese troops against Chinese women during World War II. Here I am trying to suggest the complexities in women's experience of nationalism as borne out by the discursive practices of that period.

6. An understudied chapter of the history of the Chinese Communist Party is what happened to revolutionary women in military service after the victory was won in 1949. It appears that many of them were persuaded to retire to domestic life and take care of their husbands. Some were assigned inferior positions in the government.

7. I choose to leave *sheng* and *si* untranslated in order to retain the ambiguity of the first word, which Howard Goldblatt renders as "life." The rest of the quotation remains his translation.

8. The novel was completed in Hong Kong on 20 December 1940 and published posthumously.

9. In her memoir "Yongjiu de chongjing he zhuiqiu" (Perpetual dream and pursuit), the author describes her father as a man totally devoid of human compassion and decency. He was an influential scholar and a powerful landlord in Hulan who despised his daughter and would often beat her up. Xiao Hong's mother was also cruel to her. The only family member who loved her was her grandfather, but he was powerless and virtually an outcast in the family. See *Baogao* (Report) 1 (1937):164–70.

10. The circumstances surrounding nation building and literary practice in modern China are discussed in detail in my forthcoming book on translingual practice and literary modernity in China.

11. As I have noted elsewhere, women critics in mainland China use the concept of "female tradition" to reclaim women's works from male-centered criticism (Liu 1993).

References

Ahmad, Aijaz. 1987. Jameson's rhetoric of otherness and the "national allegory." *Social Text* 17: 3–25.

———. 1989. "Third World literature" and the nationalist ideology. *Journal of the Arts and Ideas* 17–18: 117–35.

Anderson, Benedict. 1991. *Imagined communities: Reflections on the origin and spread of nationalism*. Rev. ed. London: Verso.

Beifang Lucong Bianji Bu, ed. 1983. *Xiao Hong yanjiu* (Studies of Xiao Hong). Harbin: Harbin Shijan Daxue.

Goldblatt, Howard. 1976. *Hsiao Hong*. Boston: Twayne.

Hu Feng. 1935. Epilogue. In *Sheng si chang* (The field of life and death), by Xiao Hong. Shanghai: Rongguang Shuju.

Jameson, Fredric. 1986. Third-World literature in the era of multinational capitalism. *Social Text* 15: 65–88.

Liu Fuchen. 1983. Xiao Hong huihua soutan (Xiao Hong as an artist). In *Xiao Hong yanjiu* (Studies of Xiao Hong), ed. Beifang Luncong Bianji Bu. Harbin: Harbin Shifan Daxue.

Liu, Lydia H. 1993. Invention and intervention: The making of a female tradition in modern Chinese literature. In *From May Fourth to June Fourth: Fiction and film in twentieth century Chinese literature*, ed. Ellen Widmer and David Derwei Wang. Cambridge: Harvard University Press.

Lu Xun. 1935. Preface. In *Sheng si chang* (The field of life and death), by Xiao Hong. Shanghai: Rongguang Shuju.

Mao Dun. 1984. Lun Xiao Hong de *Hulan he zhuan* (On Xiao Hong's *Tales of Hulan River*. In *Huai nian Xiao Hong* (Reminiscences of Xiao Hong), ed. Wang Guanquan. Harbin: Heilong Jiang Renmin Chubanshe. Originally published 1946.

Meng Yue and Dai Jinhua. 1989. *Fuchu lishi dibiao* (Emerging from the horizon of history). Zhengzhou: Henoan renmin Chubanshe.

Xiao Hong. 1935. *Sheng si chang* (The field of life and death). Shanghai: Rongguang Shuju.

———. 1942. *Hulan he zhuan* (Tales of Hulan River). Guilin: N.p.

———. 1979. *"The field of life and death" and "Tales of Hulan River."* Trans. Howard Goldblatt and Ellen Young. Bloomington: Indiana University Press.

———. 1987a. Chu dong (Early winter). In *Xiao Hong diabiao* (Major works of Xiao Hong), ed. Xin Fujun. Zhengzhou: Huanghe Wenyi Chubanshe. Originally published 1936.

———. 1987b. Shimian zhi ye (Night of insomnia). In *Xiao Hong daibiao zuo* (Major works of Xiao Hong), ed. Zin Fujun. Zhengzhou: Huanghe Wenyi Chubanshe. Originally published 1937.

Xiao Jun. *Bayue de xiangcun* (Village in August). Beijing: Renmin Wenxue Chubanshe. Originally published 1935.

Ritualizing
Bodies

7

Sovereignty and Subject: Constituting Relations of Power in Qing Guest Ritual

James L. Hevia

In an article for the *New York Review of Books* that appeared in February 1988, John K. Fairbank wrote of Bernardo Bertolucci's *The Last Emperor:*

> Thanks to the help of the Chinese during the filming in 1986, the silk gowns, jewels, scarves, footwear, and headdresses of the hundreds of eunuchs, palace ladies, priests, and servants have a seemingly impeccable authenticity. When six hundred or more eunuchs and officials in long rows, each on his mat in the great courtyard, perform the three kneelings and nine prostrations of the *full kotow* at the strident command of an usher, the Forbidden City comes alive as a setting for *rituals of abject servitude*. Ever since 1912 the millions of tourist photographers who have responded to the architectural magnificence of the site have tried to imagine it peopled and in use. Bertolucci has done it on film. (1988 : 14; emphasis added)

Since Chinese filmmakers have for some time been producing impressive historical epics of the late empire, complete with authentic costume and ceremonial performances, Fairbank might have qualified these remarks by indicating that Bertolucci's *Last Emperor* was the first *Western-made* film to recreate the elaborate state rituals of imperial China. But this particular silence on Fairbank's—and for that matter, Bertolucci's—part is not what I really wish to draw attention to here. Rather, my concern is with the sentence that lies between the list of court costumes and the desires and imaginations of tourists, the one referring to the "full kotow" and "rituals of abject servitude."

Inscribed in this seemingly objective representation of the Chinese imperial state is a whole history of Western interpretations of that state, particularly those interpretations that were placed on state ritual and the *koutou*[1] by British and American diplomats, merchants, and historians.[2] We find similar references to subjection in the eighteenth- and nineteenth-century correspondence of British East India Company supercargoes in China and in the British records of the Macartney embassy to China in 1793. Quite often derogatory comments on the *koutou* buttress claims that the Qing state was "despotic."[3] In drawing attention to such representations of imperial China, my purpose is not to directly confront the issue of "despotism," which after all is a category generated from Europe's supposedly transcended past, but to shift the focus by comparing discourse on ceremony in eighteenth- and nineteenth-century Europe and China. At the end of the chapter I will discuss a view of ceremony that is more adequate for historical treatments of ritual in both contexts.

I will have more to say about the *koutou*'s becoming an object of struggle shortly. What interests me at this point is the extreme distaste for this act that one finds in the writings of Anglo-American historians.[4] In their works negative views of kneeling and prostrating might be seen as an enabling device that allows a phrase like "rituals of abject servitude" to make sense in the first place. More often than not, not only the act itself but also those who perform it are demeaned. Lord Macartney, for example, referred to ceremonial actions of Chinese officials as "tricks of behavior" (Cranmer-Byng 1962:222); later commentators have often used the term "calisthenics" (Fairbank 1942:132; 1969:160; Wills 1984:2) to refer to the *koutou,* giving the impression that it at least resides in a domain outside dignified behavior. The larger question is, Are Chinese notions of the body and its capacities akin to those of Europeans? And if not, what are the implications for a discussion of sovereignty and ritual?

Whatever the *koutou* was about, it does not seem to me very enlightening to transpose onto it the prejudices of eighteenth- and nineteenth-century Europeans or those of a nominally egalitarian modern age. For what these interpretations imply is that there are proper and in some sense natural relationships between states, and that the forms of relationship specific to the Qing imperial court were in some way a transgression of acceptable international norms. These transgressive forms are then accounted for by reference to Chinese isolationism, sinocentrism, or a Chinese sense of superiority, attributes that presumably stand in direct opposition to the open, cosmopolitan, and egalitarian West. Such oppositions constitute, in fact, what can be called textbook knowledge (represented most prominently in the term "tribute system") concerning the conflict between "China" and "the West" in the nineteenth century, and they are widely diffused across the sinological subdisciplines. Obscured by these dichotomies of open versus closed and hierarchical versus egalitarian, however, are issues that were of importance both to British actors in the eighteenth and nineteenth centuries and to Qing emperors and their officialdom. Central to these concerns, I argue, were competing and incompatible views of sovereignty.[5]

Eighteenth- and Nineteenth-Century British Views of Sovereignty

In the case of the British official and trading visitors to China in the late eighteenth and nineteenth centuries, sovereignty was based on a number of principles peculiar to the historical development of North Atlantic nation-states. From seventeenth-century absolutism, for example, came a notion of the irreducible unity of sovereignty. Sovereignty was conceived as something that could not be divided up—by definition it was a unitary whole epitomized in the seventeenth and eighteenth centuries in the actual person of the king.[6]

This irreducible whole was constructed according to an exclusionary principle that radically demarcated what was interior to any sovereignty, be it land, people, or practices, with direct reference to what was outside it (i.e., the process by which "otherness" is constitutive of "self"; cf. Foucault 1980; Ryan 1982; Fabian 1983; Young 1990). As nation-states emerged in Europe, the boundary so imagined enclosed the terrain of the state and, by so doing, established a claim to independence (cf. Anderson 1983). At the same time, no sovereignty—or I should say claim to sovereignty—existed in a vacuum; it existed physically juxtaposed to other sovereignties likewise constructed on principles of unity and exclusion. And it is here that we confront one of the great ironies of this European form of sovereignty.[7] In order for states to achieve any reality beyond their own assertion of unity and exclusivity, a recognition or acknowledgment was required from precisely what they had excluded in defining themselves—that is to say, from neighboring nations making parallel claims.

The forum for such recognition was court ceremonies that were common throughout Europe into the nineteenth century. Embassies from one court to another frequently began with mutual representations of the unity and exclusivity of each sovereignty. The mutual recognition of such representations operated chiefly through the actions of ambassadorial representatives, each seen to be an extension of the sovereign body of his king. The similarity in principle of bodily practices, what we sometimes call courtly decorum—that is, bowing at the waist, kneeling upon one knee, doffing a cap, kissing a hand—enabled such mutual recognition as a sign of equality of sovereignty, however unequal states might be in land, population, or wealth.

These practices were exchanged between participants based on their rank or importance, and considerable interpretive energy was spent grasping the subtle significances of every exchange. Even for an eighteenth-century American ambassador who argued that the "essence of things is lost in ceremony in every country of Europe" (Adams 1853, 8:259), the forms of ceremony were of concern. John Adams, whom I quote here, journeyed to England in 1785 to open diplomatic relations between the newly formed American republic and its former colonial ruler. Before leaving Paris for London, Adams gathered as much information as possible on ceremonies peculiar to the court of George III, including what sort of dress he should wear when being presented to the king. In May 1785 he was received by the king in a private audience, the details of which he meticulously described in correspondence to his government. Before and after this audience, Adams took pains to inquire of ministers from other European governments about whether he was being treated on the "same footing" as themselves. Moreover, he acknowledged the importance of the ceremonies in which he participated; other European nations could see that the United States was being treated as they themselves were by the British Crown (Adams 1853, 8:252–53, 266).

What these ceremonial bodily practices represented was an exchange of legitimacy and an assertion of the possibility of communicating across the boundaries each national entity claimed and imposed. This communication was called diplomacy. The point is that diplomacy was possible only when each state was willing to resort to a set of bodily representations whose efficacy was accepted by those alien to it. Mutual acknowledgment was in turn possible because by the latter part of the eighteenth century a number of domains of practice, including medicine, the arts and sciences, and political theory, emphasized the representational capacities of the body (Barker 1984; Stallybrass and White 1986). In many domains of knowledge and practice, the human body was becoming a set of objective, atemporal structures representing itself for the gaze of detached empirical observation (Foucault 1973).

These European developments lead one to suspect that it was precisely the Western view of the representational capacities of the body that produced one of the major foci of diplomatic conflict between the Qing empire and North Atlantic nation-states (a number of which were themselves

parts of empires) into the twentieth century. My reading of English and
Chinese diplomatic records indicates that this was the case. Let me mention a few representative incidents. There was the famous battle over chairs
in 1834, won by Lord Napier, who was able to shift the placement of
seating from a north-south to an east-west axis against the usual practices
of officials in Canton. There were also Thomas Wade's 1873 negotiations
with court officials over the form of imperial audience. In these Wade,
having scrutinized a variety of ritual texts and imperial ritual manuals,
repeatedly confronted court officials with his interpretation of their own
texts concerning ceremonial practices. There were the ongoing struggles
over audience sites extending into the 1890s in which Western diplomats
believed they were being inferiorized through the use of secondary or
"tributary" halls.[8] And finally, there was a nearly complete rewriting of
imperial audience in the Boxer Protocol of 1901, in which Western
nations succeeded in (1) formally eliminating various elements, including
the *koutou,* from audiences with the emperor and inserting European practices in their stead; and (2) reducing the emperor to only one among many
oriental princes (Hevia 1990). Each of these incidents speaks to the centrality of bodily practices as objects of struggle between the imperial
government and Western diplomats. Equally important, I believe, these
incidents demonstrate how the *koutou,* a practice the imperial court once
thought of as one among an ensemble of activities performed by those
who approached the emperor, was taken out of its context in broader
social and political practices, reified, and eventually transformed into an
essential feature of the "traditional Chinese world order."

    For its part, when confronted with the objections and resistance of
Euro-American diplomats, the Qing court seems itself to have narrowed
the focus from the broader field in which the act of *koutou* was implicated.
To note this is first to argue that we might better approach imperial ritual
or ceremony in terms of historical contingency rather than as transhistorical forms separated from political practices or as a cultural variable peculiar to the so-called world of tradition. Second, it is to suggest that objects
such as the *koutou* can be reconstituted in struggle, taking on new meaning
and significance.

    Once western and Chinese concerns with court ceremony are
grounded we can better understand why the forms of court audiences
between the Chinese emperor and European diplomats remained a bone
of contention until they were permanently and explicitly altered. In addition, when we consider culture-specific constructions of the significance of

certain bodily practices, it becomes easier to grasp why Western observers have so frequently found the very idea of the *koutou* so distasteful.

Manchu-Chinese Views of Sovereignty

The situation of the Manchu court was quite different from that of Great Britain. In Qing China the emperor's task was to include others (often quite alien others) in imperial sovereignty. Put another way, Manchu-Chinese imperial sovereignty was possible only through the successful encompassment of other centers of power, a kind of summation of the constitutive powers of an emperor, who could and must include the similar powers of other kings within his own kingship. This stands in contrast to the principles of exclusion and internal homogeneity discussed above in connection with North Atlantic imaginings of sovereignty. And imperial ritual was both the means and the arena of this encompassment.

Sovereignty, as it was fashioned in Qing ceremonial practice, manifested the generative powers of a superior to initiate and the capacities of inferiors, through their actions, to bring to completion the sequence of events set in motion by the emperor. In Chinese studies this is classically referred to as the power of the exemplar: the extension of imperial virtue into the world. Together superiors and inferiors constructed a historically specific and situation-contingent relationship between a supreme lord (*huangdi,* the emperor) and a lesser lord (*fanwang,* a lord of the periphery). The completing capacity of an inferior is crucial in the formation of such relationships, and it resonates throughout all audience rituals, including those that involve princes of the blood, the emperor's wives and concubines, and a variety of officials. Most important, the superior-inferior relationship thus produced corresponds with the relationship fashioned in the Sacrifice to Heaven, where the emperor performs the "full *koutou*" acting as the inferior to a superior heaven.

Seen in these terms, those of generative superiors and completing inferiors, Fairbank's characterization "rituals of abject servitude" seems out of place. It continues certain prejudices of the Western past about bodily management (cf. Stallybrass and White 1986 on the kneeling servant and the conflation of the low with the dirty) and reproduces a political history of East/West conflict in a way that cannot accommodate Qing imperial practices. At the very least, the description of completing inferiors as "abject" denigrates the agency of those who *koutou* and fails to recognize that without their participation as active contributors to the construction of the emperor's kingship, no imperial sovereignty is realizable.

But there is more here. Insofar as ceremonial presentation acknowledged the active power of inferiors, imperial sovereignty appears to have recognized national difference and interdomainal contention between the participants involved. Quite often (and especially in relations between the Manchu imperium and other kingdoms of Asia) there were competing, conflicting, or overlapping claims over land and populations, and there were differences in how rulership was conceptualized and relations of power were constructed. But these differences did not preclude ceremonial presentation or abort the processes by which imperial sovereignty and centrality were realized. Indeed, the Qianlong emperor's waiving of the *koutou* for Ambassador Macartney in 1793, coupled with the emperor's poetic observations on the extension of his ancestors' virtue throughout the world (i.e., Nurgaci and Hung Taiji, the first two Manchu emperors), his comparison of this encounter with previous embassies sent from Europe, his observations on the sincerity of the British king in wishing to be included in the emperor's kingship, and his critique of the gifts brought by the British embassy, provide excellent examples of the logic of encompassment and inclusion crucial to the formation of imperial sovereignty (Hevia 1989).

Recall that Lord Macartney did not wish to *koutou* for fear it would be understood by the court as submission of the English king to an Oriental despot. Unaware of how the British thought of the emperor, the Manchu court focused on the fact that this first British embassy to China indicated the extension of the imperium's virtue to the most distant kingdom in the world. Seen from the court's point of view, the Qianlong emperor's actions practically and discursively embedded the difference of the English within an encompassing imperial formation. In all this, bodily practice was of crucial significance; bowing, kneeling upon two knees, knocking one's head on the ground, moving through courtyards, taking up positions, and assorted other bodily actions, of which the "full *koutou*" is only one of many examples, were the stuff of which relationships were formed in diplomatic practice.

The question that arises after having said this is whether, as in the case of European actors, the ensemble of actions involved in imperial court audiences can be understood as *representational*. Prepared by late eighteenth- and nineteenth-century revolutionary state formation in the North Atlantic world and by the standardization of diplomatic practices achieved at the Congress of Vienna, we are used to thinking of diplomatic ceremony as merely representational or symbolic of an underlying realpolitik. And we have transposed that logic onto all other political orders.

A consideration of the disposition of persons in ritual space reminds us that bodies do not everywhere signify the same. As Judith Farquhar argues in this volume, the body that Chinese medicine worked on appears to have been quite different from the modern European body of discrete anatomical masses. John Hay (1983a, b), in comparing medicine to calligraphy theory, has emphasized that arteries (*mo*), which are both vessels (veins or conduits) and contents (blood, *qi,* pulse), are central bodily entities. In these works Hay discusses the language of body reference (words such as blood, bones, and hair) as organizing diverse domains of Chinese practice beyond those of medicine. This perception does not require that we privilege the body and medical knowledge as an a priori locus of reference for these terms. Put another way, the Chinese body should not be seen merely as a *source* of representations that can then be *transposed* into other discursive domains to give them meaning and order. If body discourse naturalizes relations of power in Chinese settings, we must consider the possibility that it does so in a way different from mechanisms that have been described for Western societies (on the latter see Scarry 1985).

One could digress here on the central position of the natural human body in eighteenth- to twentieth-century European philosophy, in which the body per se is unproblematic while the nature of being, from Cartesianism to phenomenology, becomes an issue. Indeed, following Dahlia Judowitz (1988) in her recent discussion of Cartesianism and modernity, we can see that the mind/body split crucial to the assertion of existence itself requires some form of representation. Western philosophers posited a dualistic mapping of the mental over the physical, or the symbolic over the real, as the ground upon which subject and object can be reunited through formal resemblance. Individual mind, conceived as an absolute principle that distinguishes human consciousness from a now objectified outer world (which curiously includes the human body as well), recaptures through representation the "real world" that has been set adrift and thus confirms its own being. This confirmation of being runs parallel to the process of unity and exclusion discussed above, constituting, as it were, a sovereign human subject.

The dualistic mapping of the mental over the phenomenal had an important consequence for relationships between human senses and mind, which in turn contributed to the triumph of representationalism. Privileged over other senses was the optic, the direct conduit for the human

mirroring of images from "reality." As a sensation, seeing—as opposed to touching, smelling, tasting, and hearing— was tied directly to the mental faculty of reason, while the other senses were devalued (Lowe 1982: 5–16). In this context, we might say then that seeing others and being seen oneself performing *koutou* was what actually constituted the act for a European subject.[9]

In China, by contrast, we find a dispersion of bodily and natural references, a concrete language of the physical in every specialty, none of which privileges a separate level of the real. Articulated through relativistic philosophies and ontologies in which becoming (specific developments and declines) is what merits attention, bodies embody a specific history unique to the individual embedded in social reality. Where the world is always becoming, the form of things, which includes the human body, is of much greater importance than their cause or essence. In such a universe, powerful processes of encompassment and inclusion work on large-scale forms of the social, what Ronald Inden (1990) has called, in another context, imperial formations.

Returning, then, to the constitution of imperial power, the emphasis to be found in ritual manuals on the spatial location of participants, the directions they face, and their reorienting movements during rites directs our attention to the crucial significance of the positions and actions (rather than the fixed structure) of the bodies of actors. David Hall and Roger Ames (1987:89) have made this point in their study of the *Analects of Confucius;* they argue that "the body is a changing configuration of processes," "a *variable* statement of meaning and value achieved in an effort to refine and enhance human life within the *changing* parameters of *particular* contexts" (emphasis added). Given the constitutive properties that appear in ritual texts to be encoded in the positional and gestural orientation of subjects, we may presume that ritually deployed bodies are indeed historically variable significations rather than functional elements enacting a static, timeless, and repetitious script.

One way such signification is accomplished is through the clothing worn by participants. As John Hay has recently argued in reference to Chinese figure painting and as Angela Zito explores in this volume concerning the continuity of silk and skin, clothing should be considered together with embodiment. Ritual manuals such as the *Da Qing tongli* (*Comprehensive Rites of the Great Qing;* 1756, *juan* 45) always specify the proper dress to be worn by the emperor and officials in each rite; and, in the case of guest ritual, the foreign ambassador and his retinue are supposed to wear the dress of their court in audience situations. The "silk gowns, jewels, scarves, footwear, and headdresses" with which Bertolucci awed Fairbank and which Lord Macartney saw as part of the pomp of Asian courts can be understood as among the means by which specific interdomainal relations were constituted in court ceremony. In such contexts clothing, rather than socially representing the person, is inseparable both from the person and from his or her collectivity. It is simultaneously an extension outward of inner qualities that are entirely continuous with flesh, breath, and bone, *and* a conventional form typical of a group. The orientation and directionality here is significantly worth repeating. Imperial ritual practice does not work toward inward contemplation, but rather involves the outward extension of inner virtue into the world, along with a specification of encompassed differences.

Movement through space is also important. Chapter 46 of the *Comprehensive Rites,* in a section concerning the management of embassies from a lesser lord, begins with host/guest relations between five ranks of imperial princes of the blood and five ranks of lesser lords. Particularly emphasized is the distance a host comes forward in the audience space to greet the guest and the various physical actions that are performed during their meeting. Cardinal directionality—high and low, near and far—and positions relative to various markers in halls and courtyards are all important.

In short, bodies do more than carry signs of inner qualities; they also seem capable, through their movements and the actions performed, of inscribing meaning in space, of physically configuring it. In so doing they configure their own significance. Bodily action realizes broader social and political relations and accomplishes the asymmetries of an encompassing sovereignty. Insofar as imperial audience worked on, constituted, and displayed specific states of political relations, the bodily disposition of ritual actors were far more than "merely ceremonial."

In the foregoing I have distinguished between two modes of sovereignty, one unitary and exclusive (the late eighteenth-century North Atlantic model) and the other hierarchical and encompassing (the Manchu/Chinese model). Arguing that ceremonial performance was crucial to the accomplishment of both, I have distinguished between a European emphasis on the representational (or symbolic) capacities of bodies (bodies refer to abstract principles or hard realities outside themselves) as opposed to a Chinese assumption that relationships are bodily constituted (ritual as a process of embodiment). Within this framework we can understand both the *koutou* itself and the sense of scandal that has pervaded the Western literature on it. In historical China the *koutou* was one among many ways asymmetrical and encompassing relations were forged; for British diplomats it was a barbaric transgression of "natural" human and European sovereign equality.

Beyond Symbolic Ritual

In her study of bodily practices in modern South Africa, Jean Comaroff (1985:551) notes that in the colonial context, practices of the colonized are often characterized as "primitive," "sub-political," and "ritualized," "at least in terms of the categories of Western social science." The effect, we may surmise, is not merely to make the practices of others objects of investigation, but also to place them as in some way inferior. In this sense ritual often carries a pejorative connotation, particularly when it is linked, as in the situation discussed here, to a practice like the *koutou*.

In the final section of this discussion, I shall develop this notion further and suggest why it is so. To accomplish this, it is useful to return to John Fairbank, primarily because from early in his work on "traditional" China Fairbank took up the subject of ritual and its relation to Chinese notions of rulership and external relations. He also frequently used the terms "symbolic" and "ceremonial" (both of which might be added to Comaroff's list) and deployed them in such a way as to distinguish between "traditional" and modern values and sensibilities.

Crucial to Fairbank's thinking, I believe, was a taken-for-granted distinction between culture and power,[10] a position authorized by the sociology and anthropology of the 1930s and 1940s. In one of his more classic formulations of this distinction, Fairbank contrasted the "power structure," the domain of civil and military administration, to "culture," the domain of "the ideology of imperial Confucianism, the underlying classical philosophy of social order, and the ritual observances and ceremonial forms."[11] The relationship between the two domains was one in which culture legitimated and sanctioned society's power structure. This, we may conclude, was a major difference between traditional and modern societies. In the latter, societies had evolved or developed so that legitimation was situated in the power structure itself and was embodied most prominently in rational, disinterested rules and laws.[12]

Offering an alternative to this interpretation of the relation between political power and culture is not a simple task, however, primarily because, as Comaroff suggests, the notions involved are deeply embedded within Western social science and, I would add, Euro-American intellectual practices. There are also difficulties because of "commonsensical" assumptions about how societies are more or less complex, more or less developed, primitive, premodern, and modern. In this sense, reworking the categories would probably do little more than legitimate them. A more fruitful way of proceeding, I believe, is to start by interrogating the division between power structure and culture.

Fortunately, there is now a rich literature that does just this. Catherine Bell (1992), for example, has recently pointed out that since the beginning of this century studies of "sacred kingship" have tied ritual, political power, and legitimation of that power closely together. More often than not, the relationship posed is one in which ritual is an "artifice" designed to disguise brute power. Building on the work of Geertz, Cannadine, and Bloch,[13] Bell rejects this instrumental notion of ritual, one that always seeks to find more basic purposes for ritual activity (1992:193). In its stead, she argues that ritual activities are "themselves the very production and negotiation of power relations." This insight then allows Bell to substitute for the authoritarian notion of power one that sees ritualization as "a strategic mode of practice" that "produces nuanced relations of power, relationships characterized by acceptance and resistance, negotiated appropriation, and redemptive reinterpretation of the hegemonic order" (196).

The reorientation that Bell has accomplished serves to dissolve the distinction between power structure and culture so that ritual practices themselves produce power relations. But the relations so produced are no longer unidirectional, nor are they reliant upon a domain external to them for their rationale. Moreover, by drawing attention to strategies, nuances, acceptance, resistance, and negotiation, Bell takes ritual out of the domain of an acted script and radically historicizes it. Among other things, this suggests that older ritual forms might be appropriated to say or do new things or might themselves be open to revision. Put another way, by questioning the division between power structure and ritual, Bell also disturbs the taken-for-granted division between "traditional" and "modern" societies and the comparative categories that continue to authorize this distinction.

Although space prevents a thorough consideration of the implications of Bell's insights for the formation of relations of power in Qing China,[14] I will use the rest of this essay to offer alternative interpretations for at least some Qing imperial rituals. My concern will remain with familiar figures, ones crucial to earlier interpretations. In this case I will consider the *koutou* and symbolic action in the form of "tribute" presented to the Qing emperor.

The scandal of the *koutou* lay, as Fairbank indicated, in the abject servitude of the subject performing the act in front of a ruler who supposedly demanded total submission (power structure) because that is what state ideology directed (culture). We may now see the distinction drawn by Fairbank as something more than merely analytic; it rehearses and repeats the precise theoretical structure that Bell questions, suggesting that a reconsideration of the *koutou* is in order. Recall, for instance, that during the performance of the *koutou* in court audience, the emperor is high and vertical (seated), his subject is low and horizontal, parallel to the earth. Surely this is an invocation of heaven, earth, and human intervention between them, an ancient tripartite organization of the cosmos familiar to students of Chinese philosophy. Neither emperor nor subject is ultimately high or low; they occupy positions less high than heaven and less low than earth and constitute a specific and thoroughly human relationship between these polar reference points. The *koutou*, as human bodily intervention on earth, brings to completion the generative acts of a superior (corresponding to heaven) and produces the conditions necessary for new acts of genesis (corresponding to earth). Another way of putting this is that the *koutou* empowers the lesser in a dependent relationship with a superior. In this sense the act is a nuanced negotiation of imperial power.

Such negotiation is further emphasized by the fact that not everyone is permitted to *koutou*. Those who do are significant in terms of circumstances and the conditions from which a specific relationship is being formed. This indicates, first, that the subject must be encompassable—that is the emperor can incorporate only the actors and conditions of his own time. Second, the subject must be powerful in the sense of having attributes and capacities desirable for incorporation into imperial rulership. On the other hand, what makes for encompassability lies outside the audience proper. In the case of guest ritual, it can be situated in the evaluation made by the court of the virtue they discern in the history of previous contact with particular kingdoms, in the inferior king's petition for entry, in the gifts or tribute (*gong*) presented to the emperor, and in the preparation for audience of the ambassador himself or of his embassy. All these elements manifest the power of an inferior king to command his own domain while embodying his capacity to complete the emperor's kingship.

The demonstration that an inferior king can command his own kingdom may, in other words, be manifested in a number of ways. Consider the gifts presented to the court. In Qing imperial records I am familiar with, especially ritual texts such as the *Comprehensive Rites, gong* may be glossed as *fangwu* (local products). *Fangwu* included things from other kingdoms as well as those from the imperial domain. But in the specific case of peripheral lords who wished to forge a relationship with the Manchu overlord, the prefatory comments in the "Guest Ritual" section of the *Comprehensive Rites* indicate that they were to offer the "most precious things" of the domain they commanded to the supreme lord.

Gong, therefore, signifies things brought to fruition as a result of the virtuous actions of a lord in his kingdom; the lord's ability to recognize these things as such; and his reverent offering of them up to the emperor. Put another way, local products had inscribed upon them those attributes of a sublord related specifically to those powers the Qing imperium wished to incorporate into the emperor's rulership as well as indicating the sublord's sincere desire to be included. *Gong,* however, is only one part of the picture. If the offerings of a sublord *open* the process of encounter between the Manchu court and other kingdoms, what brings the process to *completion* are the emperor's bestowals (*ci*) and rewards (*shang*) to his sincerely loyal inferior. And like those things offered up, the downward flow is also made up of precious things, things that the emperor commands in his own kingdom.

It is important, however, not to confuse this process of prestation (Mauss 1967), if it may even be called that, with familiar categories generated from the tradition-modernity model. I do not think it is helpful to think of these precious things as payment within an exchange model, because it enmeshes them in forms of value that seem to me highly inappropriate (market value or utilitarian value, for instance). Nor do I think it is especially helpful to characterize them as symbolic, because that interpretation repeats the dichotomy between political power and culture, making gift exchange a masking device for more real activities (recall Fairbank's assertion that tribute was an ingenious vehicle for trade).

Also worth consideration is how far offerings and bestowals came into play in forging other relationships. In his study of the Macartney embassy to China, J. L. Cranmer-Byng noted that bestowals to the British included Korean and "Mohammedan patterned cloth," and perhaps even Indian linen; and concluded that it is interesting to know "tribute once given might be distributed to other tributary states" (1957–58:166). Cranmer-Byng's observation directs our attention to issues surrounding the handling, storage, and the recirculation of *gong*, a subject we know far too little about. It also suggests, for example, that the ability to gather in the things of one sublord and bestow them on another might be a central realization of imperial power. In this respect it might be useful to think about the role of objects in the making of a universal moral order; that is, in the construction of Manchu imperial hegemony.

Conclusion

Reconsidering the *koutou* and tribute in the terms offered here reworks sovereignty and subjects in ways that return us to fundamental issues of power. For too long, the relations assumed by the tradition/modernity dichotomy have shaped the historical subject in China. That subject, put simply, has been repeatedly judged inferior, ill formed, misguided, pre- or semirational, caught up in a world of illusions—all characteristics generated in comparison with the presumably fully formed and free subjects of modernity. Once it is recognized that the material production of imperial sovereignty was inseparable from practices of ceremonial presentation, then we might better appreciate the historically specific and different ways subjects might be constituted and human agency enabled. For the whole point of working on attributes of generation and completion in imperial guest ritual was to produce subjects capable of extending Manchu rulership into the future. In this sense the human capacity to generate or complete might be seen as the historically contingent yang and yin of imperial power, the always risky means by which the Qing imperium, itself a complex agent made up of the powers of superiors and inferiors, extended the power of the exemplar outward in the world.

Notes

This chapter was originally written for a panel discussion organized by Angela Zito for the Association of Asian Studies meetings in 1989. I thank her for her many suggestions and unwavering support. Tani Barlow, Donald Lowe, Mark Elliot, Stephen Shutt, and the Chicago reviewers all made important contributions to this essay. As always, Judith Farquhar provided the necessary intellectual stimulation and support to begin, develop, and bring the project to completion.

1. Throughout this chapter I use pinyin romanization except where quoting directly from other sources. Those interested in the numerous variations on the spelling of *koutou* should see the *Oxford English Dictionary* under "kowtow," which at this point is an English loan word from the Chinese.

2. One of the earliest references I have found is to "abject submission," which

is also a reference to the *koutou*. Davis (1836, 1:53) links it to an idea of "profitless submission," by which he means that there has been no material gain for Europeans who performed the *koutou*. Also see Murray et al. (1843, 1:309–10), where a similar point is made about peoples other than Europeans.

3. For a discussion of the *koutou* and its central role in Euro-American perceptions of imperial China, see Hevia 1992b. The image was revived once again following events in Tiananmen Square in June 1989. Concerned that the president might veto a bill designed to provide safe haven to Chinese students currently in the United States, the editor of *Washington Post National Weekly Edition* (4–10 December 1989, 26) characterized the kowtow as the "deep servile bow, the ultimate gesture of deference and debasement," and warned that a "presidential veto of the visa bill would be a presidential kowtow." Here the editor provides a canonical version of "rituals of abject servitude." Also see "Major Must Not Kowtow in Peking," *Observer,* 1 September 1991, and William Safire's recent criticism of the China policy of the Bush administration, which he characterizes as kowtowing to Peking, see the *Raleigh News and Observer,* 15 September 1992. These representations of the "kowtow" are also present in the most mundane forms. See, for example, the comic strip "The Phantom," *Raleigh News and Observer,* 15 December 1991. Having been told to kneel before a Mongol khan, the Phantom responds, "I go to my knees for no man . . . only for my god."

4. I have found only a few exceptions to this pattern of interpretation. See, for instance, Carl (1907:147–48). In his reference to the "kowtow" Joseph Levenson (1968, 2:67–69) noted that a Chinese envoy once performed the act before the Russian czarina in 1731. This observation seems to call standard interpretations into question. Levenson did not do so, however. Rather, after noting that no record of this event was to be found in Chinese sources, he concluded that a fundamental distinction existed in imperial China between state power and Confucian beliefs. The division here between power structure and belief (culture) is one I will return to at the end of this chapter.

5. In suggesting that there is in fact a Qing notion of sovereignty, I am going against received wisdom. In the classic formulation by John Fairbank (1942), most recently repeated by Warren Cohen (1990:8), China's rulers perceived their territories as a cultural instead of national entity; hence "culturalism" rather than "nationalism" dominated their thinking. Just how this would preclude a notion of sovereignty is not clear.

6. Here I draw primarily on Marin 1988. For additional useful discussion of the European notion of sovereignty see Hinsley 1969, 1986.

7. There was another kind of irony as well. At the same time that British diplomats objected to Chinese practices on the grounds that they demeaned the British sovereign, other subjects of that king were extending and consolidating their own empire at the expense of other sovereignties in Asia and Africa. Space prevents my considering this issue here, but a comparison between the ways the

British insinuated themselves into the Mughal Empire before overthrowing it and their actions in China would be instructive. Similarities between the Qing imperial formation (a term I borrow from Inden 1990) and the British Empire in India might also be helpful.

8. See Rockhill 1905, Cooley 1981, and Wang 1971 for discussions of some of these issues.

9. This reorganization of senses, predicated on a mind/body dualism, stands in stark contrast to earlier European formations. In an example that Anthony Pagden (1982:138–39) provides from sixteenth-century Spanish discourse on the Americas, a hierarchy based on the senses appears absent. Rather, a determinative relationship was posited between sense organs and mental capacities in such a way that sensations influence intellect. As Pagden puts it, "Bodily sensations are the vehicle for communication between the 'real' outside and the intellectual 'inside'" of the body. This being the case, the nature of the outside, or in other words the environment (climate, terrain, and astrological disposition), could become a crucial causal element for explaining the wide variation in the developmental level of reasoning capacities among various human social groups. This argument was used by Bartolomé de Las Casas, for example, to account for the differences to be found both among various Amerindian groups and between Amerindian societies in general and European civilization.

10. At times Fairbank treats the distinction he draws between power structure and culture as real enough; at other times he treats it as an abstraction, "warranted only by its utility as an analytic device." See, for example, his discussions in 1969 on the political tradition and 1988 on "culturalism" and compare them to Fairbank (1968a:273). Mancall (1968b:63) makes a similar claim about the tribute system in the same volume, that it is merely a "Western invention for descriptive purposes."

11. The division between structure and culture drawn here by Fairbank is present throughout much of the work on "traditional" Chinese foreign relations. See, for example, the various pieces in the Fairbank 1968b and the various works of Mancall and Wills cited in the references. The distinction may also appear as that between ideology and reality or, as some have it, between appearances and reality. See my discussion of the appearance/reality divide common in nineteenth- and twentieth-century representations of China in Hevia 1989, 1990, and 1992a.

12. Fairbank's purpose in organizing matters in these terms was to take issue with the "theory of imperialism" (1969:468). Having separated power structure from culture, he then argued that Westerners were able to penetrate the Qing political order (synarchy), whereas the traditional culture remained sinocentrically impervious to Western penetration. The upshot was that "the 'Western conquest' proved abortive." Instead of the power structure's being rationalized in such a way that legitimacy could flow from it rather than from traditional culture, "the Chinese world order finally disintegrated" (1968a:275). The failure to rationalize

power, in other words, and not the Western assault on Qing sovereignty, was the cause of the dynasty's collapse. To paraphrase Joseph Esherick (1972), this is the sort of logic that produces apologetics for imperialism.

13. Here Bell cites Geertz (1980:122–136); Cannadine (1987:1–19); and Bloch (1987:271–97).

14. One way of addressing Bell's references to relations of appropriation, resistance, and nuance would be to look more closely at the Qing court's political relations with inner Asia. I have recently begun to do this by exploring encounters between emperors and Tibetan and Mongol lamas. These relations are particularly interesting because they are rife with claims and counterclaims to superiority in a variety of domains of practice. To provide only one example, it is useful to consider the implications for imperial power of subjects' participating in imperial audience rituals *and* Tibetan Buddhist initiation rituals, as seems to have occurred with a number of Qing emperors and Tibetan and Mongol lamas (see Hevia 1992c).

References

Adams, Charles, F., ed. 1853. *The works of John Adams*. 10 vols. Boston: Little, Brown.

Anderson, Benedict. 1983. *Imagined communities*. London: Verso.

Barker, Francis. 1984. *The tremulous private body*. New York: Methuen.

Bell, Catherine. 1992. *Ritual theory, ritual practice*. Oxford: Oxford University Press.

Bloch, Maurice. 1987. The ritual of the royal bath in Madagascar. In *Rituals of royalty: Power and Ceremonial in traditional societies,* ed. David Cannadine and Simon Price, 271–97. Cambridge: Cambridge University Press.

Cannadine, David. 1987. Introduction. In *Rituals of royalty: Power and ceremonial in traditional societies,* Cambridge: Cambridge University Press.

Carl, Katherine A. 1907. *With the empress dowager of China*. New York: Century.

Cohen, Warren. 1990. *America's response to China*. New York: Columbia University Press.

Comaroff, Jean. 1985. Bodily reform as historical practice: The semantics of resistance in modern South Africa. *International Journal of Psychology* 20:541–67.

Cooley, James. 1981. *T. F. Wade in China*. Leiden: E. J. Brill.

Cranmer-Byng, J. L., ed. 1957–58. Lord Macartney's embassy to Peking in 1793: From official Chinese documents. *Journal of Oriental Studies* 4, nos. 1–2: 117–85.

———. 1962. *An embassy to China: Being the journal kept by Lord Macartney during his embassy to the emperor Ch'ien-lung, 1793–1794*. London: Longmans, Green.

Da Qing tongli. 1756. (Comprehensive rites of the Great Qing). Beijing: Palace Edition.

Davis, John F. 1836. *The Chinese: A general description of the empire and its inhabitants.* 2 vols. London: Charles Knight.

Esherick, Joseph. 1972. Harvard on China: The apologetics of imperialism. *Bulletin of Concerned Asian Scholars* 4, no. 4:9–16.

Fabian, Johannes. 1983. *Time and the other.* New York: Columbia University Press.

Fairbank, John K. 1942. Tributary trade and China's relations with the West. *Far Eastern Quarterly* 1:129–49.

———. 1968a. The early treaty system in the Chinese world order. In *The Chinese world order,* ed. John K. Fairbank, 257–75. Cambridge: Harvard University Press.

———, ed. 1968b. *The Chinese world order.* Cambridge: Harvard University Press.

———. 1969. *Trade and diplomacy on the China coast: The opening of the treaty ports, 1842–1854.* Stanford: Stanford University Press.

———. 1988. Born too late. *New York Review of Books* 35, no. 2:14–16.

Foucault, Michel. 1973. *The birth of the clinic.* New York: Vintage Books.

———. 1980. *Power/knowledge: Selected interviews and other writings.* Ed. C. Goron. New York: Pantheon.

Geertz, Clifford. 1980. *Negara: The theatre state in nineteenth century Bali.* Princeton: Princeton University Press.

Hall, David L., and Roger T. Ames. 1987. *Thinking through confucius.* Albany: State University of New York Press.

Hay, John. 1983a. Arterial art. *Stone Lion Review* 11:70–84.

———. 1983b. The human body as a microcosmic source of macrocosmic values in calligraphy. In *Theories of art in China,* ed. Susan Bush and Christian Murck, 74–102. Princeton: Princeton University Press.

Hevia, James. 1989. A Multitude of lords: Qing court ritual and the Macartney embassy of 1793. *Late Imperial China,* 10, no. 2:72–105.

———. 1990. Making China "perfectly equal." *Journal of Historical Sociology* 3, no. 4:379–400.

———. 1992a. Leaving a brand on China: Missionary discourse in the wake of the Boxer Movement. *Modern China* 18, no. 3:304–32.

———. n.d. *The Macartney embassy in the history of Sino-Western relations.* Conference volume on the 200th anniversary of the First British Embassy to China. London: British Association for Chinese Studies, forthcoming.

———. 1992c. Qing emperors, Tibetan and Mongol lamas, and audience rituals: The political implications of Qing imperial ceremonies. Unpublished paper.

Hinsley, F. H. 1969. The concept of sovereignty and the relations between states. In *In defense of sovereignty,* ed. W. J. Stankiewicz, 275–88. New York: Oxford University Press.

———. 1986. *Sovereignty.* Cambridge: Cambridge University Press.

Hsü, Immanuel. 1960. *China's entrance into the family of nations: The diplomatic phase, 1858–1880.* Cambridge: Harvard University Press.

Inden, Ronald. 1990. *Imagining India.* Oxford: Basil Blackwell.

Judowitz, Dahlia. 1988. *Subjectivity and representation in Descartes.* Cambridge: Cambridge University Press.

Levenson, Joseph. 1968. *Confucian China and its modern fate: A trilogy.* Berkeley and Los Angeles: University of California Press.

Lowe, Donald. 1982. *History of bourgeois perception.* Chicago: University of Chicago Press.

Mancall, Mark. 1968. The Ch'ing tribute system: An interpretive essay. In *The Chinese world order,* ed. John Fairbank, 63–89. Cambridge: Harvard University Press.

———. 1971. *Russia and China.* Cambridge: Harvard University Press.

———. 1984. *China at the center.* New York: Free Press.

Marin, Louis. 1988. *Portrait of the king.* Minneapolis: University of Minnesota Press.

Mauss, Marcel. 1967. *The gift.* New York: W. W. Norton.

Murray, Hugh, et al. 1843. *An historical and descriptive account of China.* 3 vols. London: Simplin, Marshall.

Pagden, Anthony. 1982. *The fall of natural man.* Cambridge: Cambridge University Press.

Pritchard, E. H. 1943. The kotow in the Macartney embassy to China in 1793. *Far Eastern Quarterly* 2, no. 2:163–201.

Rockhill, William W. 1905. *Diplomatic audiences at the court of China.* Reprint ed. Taipei: Ch'eng Wen, 1971.

Ryan, Michael. 1982. *Marxism and deconstruction.* Baltimore: Johns Hopkins University Press.

Scarry, Ellen. 1985. *The body in pain.* New York: Oxford University Press.

Stallybrass, Peter, and Allon White. 1986. *The politics and poetics of transgression.* Ithaca: Cornell University Press.

Wang, Tseng-tsai. 1971. The audience question: Foreign representatives and the emperor of China, 1858–1873. *Historical Journal* 14, no. 3:617–33.

Wills, John E., Jr. 1984. *Embassies and illusions: Dutch and Portuguese envoys to K'ang-hsi, 1666–1687.* Cambridge: Harvard University Press.

Young, Robert. 1990. *White mythologies: Writing history and the West.* London: Routledge.

8

(Re)inventing *Li:*
Koutou and Subjectification
in Rural Shandong

Andrew Kipnis

In 1989 Party Secretary Feng was by far the most powerful man in Fengjia village.[1] He had been the secretary of the village for over twenty years and had held political posts at the township, county, provincial, and even national levels. He could be domineering at times, frequently lecturing other villagers and even yelling at them. His authority was solidly rooted both in the success to which he had led the village and in his official posts and unofficial connections in the Chinese Communist Party (CCP). Thus, when on Chinese New Year I saw him kneel and bow to women and men throughout the village, I was bewildered. What could it mean for such a powerful man to *koutou*[2] to villagers who were in many respects his underlings?

James Hevia (this volume) points out that many sinologists have interpreted *koutou* as displays of abject servility performed only by members of a subordinated group. Yet, as the example of Secretary Feng indicates, on occasion even the most powerful villagers *koutou*. Moreover, none of the villagers I spoke with were concerned with subordination when performing *koutou*. Though villagers refused to *koutou* at times, on other occasions those who wished to *koutou* were restricted from doing so. In Fengjia the "abject servitude" interpretation of *koutou* seemed to explain neither why rural Chinese men and women chose to *koutou* on many occasions nor why they were hesitant to *koutou* on others.

This reinterpretation presents the *koutou* as a form of *li* (ritual) that enables one to participate in the (re)structuring of social relations and hence the subjectivities that are caught up in these relations. I describe two interwoven processes of subject construction that villagers act on when performing *koutou*: intimate and imagined. "Intimate subject construction" creates subjectivities while forming, committing to, and participating in groups of people with whom one is personally linked. "Imagined subject construction" create subjectivities while forming, committing to, and participating in "imagined communities" (Anderson 1983) of people of similar religion, class, ethnicity, or nationality. Though I separate these two types of subject construction analytically, in practice most modern rural *koutou* contribute to both processes simultaneously.

Concepts of subjectivity are difficult to use cross-culturally. As Strathern points out (1988: 59), "Concern with identity as an attribute of the individual person is a Western phenomenon." Strathern's warning is useful at two levels. First, the subject construction undertaken in Fengjia should not be understood in terms of the Western identity project—answering the question, Who am I:? Subject construction there was related more to the question, To which groups of people should I, or is it possible for me to, commit myself? Second, the subjects constructed were neither unitary nor noncontradictory. Rather than creating singular agents committed to a single identity, Fengjia villagers constituted shifting, multiple actors whose agency was contradicted by the histories of their past construction.

Having emphasized that the subjects constituted in practices like the *koutou* are shifting and contradicted, however, I should caution that I do not see them, like so many images on an MTV screen, as ephemeral and infinitely malleable. Through *koutou,* villagers committed themselves to imagined and intimate subjects as they constructed them. In deciding when and how to commit themselves, villagers were keenly aware of how new or changing commitments might contradict existing ones. A villager's resistance to performing *koutou* often indicated ambivalence about the subject the given *koutou* would help to create. Villagers and their commitments did change. But this change occurred over months and years and thus cannot be imagined outside lived time.

Foucault's notion of "subjectification" clarifies both intimate and imagined processes of subject construction.[3] For Foucault, making persons into subjects involves both the dividing and labeling practices of state institutions (which often rely on the classificatory schemes of social scientists) *and* the techniques by which people try to mold themselves. Here I discuss how Chinese rural villagers form intimate and imagined subjects in reaction to (within and against) the classifying practices of the party-led state. In rural Shandong the ideological practices that define the place of "peasants" in Chinese society, and the labeling practice of the *hukou* (household registration) that classifies individuals and families as peasants or nonpeasants resident in specific villages, provide the context within which the subjectifying practice of the *koutou* takes its significance. Chinese rural people construct intimate subjects as members of a certain village or family and imagined subjects as peasants or nonpeasants, within and against state practices that define and delineate these entities.

Guanxi (in the sense of human relationships) are central to the process by which *koutou* constitute and reconstitute intimate subjects. *Guanxi* are simultaneously and to the same degree matters of *ganqing* (human feeling) and material obligation. Thus *guanxi* unify what often is (and even more often is imagined to be) separate in the West: relationships of economic exchange and friendship.[4] In addition, *guanxi* constitute both the individual and the social. In *Zhongguo wenhuade shenceng jiegou* (The deep structure of Chinese culture), Sun Longji (also romanized Sun Long-kee) provides a useful terminology for discussing this constitutive power.[5] For Sun, the *xin,* or heart-mind—the locus of individual motivation—is always defined socially through the *ganqing* of *guanxi.* In addition to constituting individual heart-minds, *guanxi* also define the boundaries (ever shifting) of the group of people whose "magnetic fields of human feeling" (*renqingde cilichang*) constitute individual heart-minds. In short, *guanxi* simultaneously define the individual and the social. Through managing *guanxi, koutou* participates in restructuring intimate subjects.

Bourdieu's (1977, 1990) notion of "disposition" also helps illuminate *koutou.* For at the moment of a *koutou* one embodies attitudes and inclinations (i.e., dispositions) both toward performing *koutou* in general and toward the specific relationship in which that *koutou* takes place. As Bourdieu points out, practices in which dispositions are embodied often simultaneously produce self and society.[6] In this case, the dispositions *koutou* embody participate in the production of *xin* (self), "magnetic field of human feeling" (intimate subject), and "peasantness" (imagined subject).

In brief, I argue that we should see *koutou* as a practice that allows one to participate in the construction of intimate and imagined subjects. As such, performing *koutou* can be a powerful act and is more likely a social initiative than a display of "abject servitude." By helping to produce *guanxi, koutou* allow one to participate in the construction of intimate subjects. By asserting a positive peasant ethos, *koutou* allow rural Chinese people to contest state objectifications of peasants and thus to participate in the construction of heterodox, imagined "peasant" subjects.[7] Conversely, we should view reluctance to perform a given *koutou* as resistance to creating a given intimate or imagined subject, not as the avoidance of a servile gesture.

Placing Fengjia

Fengjia is in northeastern Shandong Province. In 1989 more than 60 percent of the village's population of approximately 1,150 belonged to the four branches of the Feng family. Zhangs, Lins, Jias, and a few other family names made up the rest of the population. The village relied primarily on farming wheat, corn, cotton, mung beans, and (starting in 1989) potatoes. Fengjia also ran a cornstarch factory (over fifty employees) and a textile factory and contracted out several smaller sideline industries to individual households. Compared with neighboring villages, Fengjia was slightly wealthier and considerably more collectivized. Though land, in accordance with the responsibility system, was allocated to individual families, plowing, seeding, irrigation, and some parts of harvesting were still organized collectively. Consequently wealth was relatively equally distributed. Every family in the village owned a brick house. Politically the village had been (considering the rampages most of the countryside has gone through) comparatively stable, with Party Secretary Feng retaining power as village head for over twenty years. In addition, the village had a reputation for obeying party mandates. Though Fengjia was not a subsidized "model" village, its lack of any extremely impoverished families (at least during the 1980s), its political stability, and its willingness to follow party leadership were all factors in the selection of this village as a research site for foreign social scientists.[8]

The household registration (*hukou*) policy that labels villagers either peasants or nonpeasants (*nongmin* or *fei nongmin*) has been a relatively stable facet of CCP policy. All people allocated land in the land reform (undertaken in 1948 in Fengjia) became peasants in the new society. During the late 1950s, CCP concern about underemployment in the cities led to the *hukou* policy. "Peasants" were generally forbidden to migrate to cities. The state required every city, town, and village to keep records, called *hukou bu,* of their populations and required localities to use these records to restrict migration. Those born in peasant households inherited "peasant" status. Though there have been small revisions in *hukou* policy, and exceptions by which a few people manage to have their *hukou* changed, an enduring division between rural and urban populations has emerged.[9]

Whether one is a peasant is important to both family and ritual life. *Hukou* laws give children of mixed peasant and nonpeasant marriages peasant *hukou*. Several of the village's matchmakers told me that the first thing they consider in arranging matches is the potential mates' *hu-kou*—that they always match a peasant with a peasant and a nonpeasant with a nonpeasant. Several nonpeasants took pains to explain how "backward" and "feudal" certain customs (including those that employ *koutou*) were and how, not being peasants themselves, they would not deign to participate.

Though children receive the same *hukou* as their parents, peasant students can theoretically gain a nonpeasant *hukou* through success at school. During the 1980s 90 percent of Fengjia's children attended junior high school.[10] After junior high about 25 percent of Fengjia's children were able to test into a high school, the best of these going to the academic high school in the county seat or one of numerous nationally run technical high schools (*zhongzhuan*). Of those who made it to the academic high school, about 60 percent went to college. If one made it to college or a nationally run technical high school, one was assigned a job in a city after graduation and given a nonpeasant *hukou*. Of the approximately 160 students who graduated from Fengjia elementary school between 1975 and 1983, 13 made it to the academic high school, 8 to college, and between 10 and 15 to *zhongzhuan*. Thus, between 10 and 15 percent succeeded in becoming nonpeasants.[11]

Parents waited for children to complete their education before arranging their marriages. As a result, students did not worry about leaving fiancées behind when trying to test into college. The state encouraged this practice and claimed to refuse to allow romantic considerations to enter into the calculation of job assignments. Since most villagers got married as soon as they reached the legal age of twenty-two for men and twenty for women, students who left school after junior high were usually engaged several years before marriage (at the age of seventeen), while those who waited until graduation from high school—or rather until they failed to test into college—did not get engaged until the age of twenty, just before their marriages.[12] Thus, villagers who went to high school but not college received their peasant *hukou* just before their weddings, whereas those who left school after junior high passed several years as unmarried peasants. As I will argue below, the timing vis-à-vis marriage of the subjectification resulting from the postgraduation *hukou* designation of "peasant" influenced young villagers' dispositions at their wedding ceremonies.

Patrilineality, though certainly not traceable to the CCP's *hukou* policy, was legally confirmed in the official movement of a woman's *hukou* when she married. In general, at marriage women moved from their parents' home and village into those of their husband and parents-in-law.[13] Consequently, at marriage the bride's family separated themselves from the bride, while the husband and his family concentrated solely on building new relationships. The bride both built new relationships and separated herself from old ones. In Fengjia, the day before a daughter was to be married out, the family of the bride sponsored a gathering called a *song hezi* (literally, "delivery of boxes"). Friends and relatives of the bride's family came over and gave presents both to the bride's family and for the bride's dowry. Because they were about to "lose" a daughter, the bride's parents were usually very sad at this event.[14]

Although by 1990 patrilocal weddings and the CCP *hukou* policy had been fairly constant features of Fengjia life for several decades, ritual life, and the official objectifications of the classes created by the *hukou* policy, had changed radically. During the Cultural Revolution (GPCR), the Maoist state simultaneously directed red guards to "root out feudal custom" and glorified the revolutionary spirit of the worker and poor peasant, in part by ideologically embodying this spirit in Mao himself.[15] In Fengjia village this dual movement eradicated almost all of the rituals employing *koutou*[16] and encouraged a solidarity with Mao, evidenced by the continued presence of prominently displayed Mao portraits. After the Cultural Revolution the CCP reversed both of these movements. It tolerated a "comeback" of "feudal" custom and replaced the glorification of poor peasant revolutionary spirit with an ideology that conceives of peasants as "backward" (*luohou*). In the village, as one man put it, "traditional customs [*fengsu xiguan*] replaced revolutionary spirit [*geming jingshen*]." On the national level, plans to supersede the peasants replaced exhortations to learn from them. As Zhao Zi Yang put in his speech at the thirteenth party congress, "The primary stage of socialism is the stage for gradually casting off poverty and backwardness; it is the stage of gradually replacing a country where farming based on manual labor forms the basis and peasants constitute the majority, with a modern industrial nation where nonpeasant workers constitute the majority" (Zhao 1987:10–11). From this point of view peasants should get rich, thus eliminating that part of their identity (being poor) that was valued positively under Maoism. More important, peasants as a class should work for their own transformation into a proletariat, eliminating their "peasantness."

I do not wish either to extol the Cultural Revolution (it was certainly a negative experience from the point of view of most, though not all,

Fengjia residents) or to criticize post-1978 policy. Rather, I want to make two related points. First, the *koutou*, and all the rituals that surround it, should be viewed not as "survivals" from feudal times, but rather as modern, post-GPCR (re)inventions. Old villagers acknowledged that ritual life in the 1980s differed considerably from the pre-GPCR period. On one hand, many customs, notably those involving ancestral halls, had not been revived. On the other hand, increases in wealth[17] allowed for an expansion of banqueting and gift giving, and thus the invention of new ritual occasions when these activities could take place.

Second, during the GPCR there was both a positive valuation placed on being a peasant (especially a poor one) and a personage, Mao, with whom peasants could identify. After 1978 "backwardness" became the most salient characteristic of the peasantry. Instead of moving the Maoist revolution forward, the peasantry stood accused of slowing the nation's progress toward the socialist utopia of a teleological Marxism. Not only did the speeches of officials create this image, but the public media (television, radio, and newspapers) to which all villagers had access regurgitated it endlessly, and the speech of villagers reflected it.[18] This officially negative objectification and the reassertion of "tradition" (*chuantong*, as villagers say) by Fengjia peasants are, I will argue, related.

Koutou in Fengjia

In 1989 Fengjia villagers distinguished two types of bodily decorum: a bow (*jugong*) and *koutou*. A bow involved bending from the waist while standing. A *koutou* was a bow of the head while kneeling on one or both knees. Though any kneeling bow counted as a *koutou*, on at least two occasions I saw elder villagers do a fuller *koutou* that included three bows in each of three directions. When asked why younger villagers did not do this style of *koutou*, one old man responded, "because they never learned how," an explanation that can be accepted literally as far as it goes.

Before 1949 there were no bows in Fengjia, only *koutou*. When the CCP came to power, leaders wanted to end arranged marriages in the countryside. As part of this effort, they encouraged changes in the wedding ceremony itself, including the substitution of bows for *koutou*. In the post-1978 (re)invention of ritual, villagers continued to use bows in wedding ceremonies. Though it no longer demanded the substitution of bows for *koutou*, the post-1978 state still pronounced arranged marriages illegal. Thus parents needed to claim that the degree to which they controlled their children's spouse selection was not "arranging" a marriage.[19] In asserting that the marriage was a matter of free choice, bows by the bride and groom (as opposed to *koutou*) helped make this claim.

Other than the claim bows made about "free marriage," I view post-1978 bows and *koutou* as similar. Both constructed *guanxi* in a similar manner, and both were seen by local nonpeasants as "feudal" practices. Both counted as a type of *bai,* a verb I translate as "to embody respect for." In a wedding the bride and groom *bai* various groups of people by bowing; on other occasions people *bai* by performing *koutou*.

I observed bows in wedding ceremonies and *koutou* on four occasions: ancestral sacrifices, funerals, weddings, and the spring festival (*chunjie*). In the ancestral sacrifices of 1988–90 Fengjia, one or more adult members of a family, sometimes accompanied by a male child, walked out to a point near the site of that family's ancestral grave. They usually brought a basket containing yellow paper and some food and liquor, drew a circle with a cross in the middle, wrapped some of the food in the paper and lit it, then knelt down and performed *koutou* while saying the relational kinship names of those ancestors who were on their minds. After the paper was burned they got up, poured some liquor and scattered some of the remaining food on the crossed circle, then left.

A full analysis of funerary *koutou* would require another essay. For now it is enough to note that in most 1988–90 Fengjia funerals, male friends and relatives both performed *koutou* in family groupings in front of the deceased's memorial tablet and did so collectively at the place where the ashes were buried. In addition, the morning after the funeral the immediate family of the deceased (men and women) usually went door-to-door through the entire village performing a *koutou* to whoever happened to be at home. This latter occasion is the only time I heard of elders performing *koutou* to youth. Close relatives usually visited the grave again and did *koutou* three weeks, five weeks, one hundred days, and one year after the funeral.

In marriages there can be both bows and *koutou*. During most 1988–90 Fengjia wedding ceremonies, an offering table was set up in the courtyard of the groom's family home. Usually the father of the groom, or some other elder male relative if he was dead, first performed a *koutou* before the table. Then the text of the wedding ceremony was read: "Embody respect for heaven and earth, embody respect for your ancestors, embody respect for your father and mother, embody respect for your friends and relatives, embody respect for each other" (*bai tian di, bai zux-*

ian, bai dieniang, bai qinqi pengyou, huxiang bai). In the descriptions of
modern wedding ceremonies in older villages, after each "embody respect
for," the bride and groom should bow before the offering table. In the
eight ceremonies I saw, however, the bride never bowed, while some of
the grooms bowed and other did not.

No one forced either the groom or the bride to bow. After reading
the ceremony, firecrackers were lit and the couple was considered married,
koutou or not. In general there was no fuss over the issue. But in one
ceremony there appeared to be considerable tension. In this case the
groom's aged paternal grandmother was still alive. Out of respect to her,
throughout the day the family included in the wedding every custom and
symbolic display the old woman could remember. Other villagers constantly commented that they had never seen such and such before and had
no idea what it meant. When the time for the ceremony came, the old lady
first burned some paper and then did a full *koutou;* her son, the groom's
father, then also did a full *koutou*. As the ceremony was read, however, the
bride not only did not bow, but by wearing sunglasses and folding her
arms, managed to look defiant rather than embarrassed as most brides do.
The groom also just stood there, but in contrast he appeared mortified,
constantly glancing back and forth between his bride and his father. Perhaps in this wedding, because they were so consciously inventing tradition, the family elders especially hoped the young couple would bow.

The final *koutou* I will discuss are the *bainian* (embodying respect on
Chinese New Year). On New Year's Day in 1989 most families got up
before dawn. Upon rising, the younger generations performed *koutou* to
the older generations in the family. Then, at most houses, *jiaozi* (dump-
lings) were cooked, firecrackers were set off, some paper (with *jiaozi* in it)
was burned for the ancestors, and breakfast was eaten. After breakfast
people walked around the village performing *bainian* (i.e., *koutou*), to anyone in the village who was older by both years and generation.[20] People
went around the village both singly and in groups. Except for mothers
with small or infant male children, these groups were segregated by sex.
Unmarried women and girls (who were expected someday to marry out
of the village) did not participate.

I spent the Chinese New Year in the house of an elderly woman who,
either calculated by age or by generation, was one of the oldest people in
the village. Hundreds of people came to *koutou* that morning. The activity
ranged from ceremonious to rushed and superficial. One old man, almost
as old as this woman in years but a generation younger, came over and

talked for almost an hour (visitors who came during this interval also did *koutou* to him) before performing an elaborate *koutou*. At the other extreme was a group of about twenty high-school boys. The leaders rushed in, said "we've come to *bainian*," knelt down, and quickly left. The rest, unable to fit in the room, milled about the courtyard and in some cases even failed to *koutou*.

Although most of the villagers came to the old woman's house to *bainian,* some did not. One man who failed to appear was a township official who, though he held a peasant *hukou,* did not consider himself a peasant. Significantly, when his own sons married, this man did not include those elements of the ceremony he considered "feudal"—including the parts where bows or *koutou* would take place.

During the several days after spring festival villagers went to other villages to *bainian* their elder affinal relatives. They brought food gifts, performed a *koutou,* and were treated to a banquet. In all of these spring festival *koutou,* almost as soon as the performer touched his or her knee to the ground, the person to whom the *koutou* was directed would urge the performer to get up quickly (*kuai qilai*).

Koutou as Li

An old villager said to me of the *koutou* in the ancestral sacrifice, "Before it was a superstition, now it generates a meaning/feeling" (*Guoqu shi mixin, xianzai biaoshi yige yisi*). This statement, though apparently simple, says much about what *koutou* and *li* meant in 1988–90 Fengjia. Earlier, ancestor worship was efficacious because of the agency of dead ancestors. In the late 1980s, when most villagers dismissed (at least to outsiders) the agency of dead people, the *koutou* of the past was called a superstition.

The second part of the statement is more complex. The term, "to generate a meaning/feeling" was also used to describe what one did when giving a gift. What gift giving, the *koutou,* and ritual have in common is that they are all types of *li* (gift as *liwu, koutou* and ritual as forms of *lijie*) and are all ways of working on (creating, maintaining, and improving) interpersonal relationships (*guanxi*). Since *guanxi* involve both *ganqing* and social/material obligation, the translation "meaning/feeling" is necessary. The *yisi* generates both the idea of what the material obligation involved in the relationship is or should be and the feeling involved in the relationship.

Other villagers described the *koutou* as an embodiment of *jingyi,* a word commonly translated as "respect." However, this translation is accurate only if one emphasizes that this respect is not abstract admiration, but rather a *ganqing* that accompanies the social/material obligation extant within a concrete relationship. During the GPCR, villagers with rich peasant and landlord class labels were forbidden to perform *koutou* at the funerals of poor and middle peasants. If *jingyi* meant only an abstract sort of admiration, as we often take respect to mean, then during the GPCR landlords might well have been forced to *koutou* at poor peasants' funerals. But this "respect" implies a concrete relationship, and the expansion of it in a *koutou* helps constitute that relationship. The CCP's ban of landlord *koutou* at poor peasants' funerals was an attempt to prevent the formation of (and deny the existence of) cross-class relationships.

We must see the *koutou*'s *yisi* or *jingyi* as constitutive of relationships and hence, following Sun Longji, of both individual heart-minds and "magnetic fields of human feeling."[21] Performing a *koutou* can be a powerful assertion of social initiative. In fact, several villagers described both the prohibition of landlord *koutou* during the GPCR and the "tradition" of allowing only men to *koutou* at funerals as restrictions on privileges of the relatively powerless.

Understanding the *koutou* as a type of *li* that works on *guanxi* and thus on both the individual and the social allows us to consider exactly how *koutou* constitute the social world. I submit that *koutou* form relationships (*guanxi*) between people by declaring them members of the same (hierarchically constituted) group. Recall that *koutou* during spring festival were divided into separate periods for immediate family, village, and affinal relatives. This partition allows each group to be constituted separately. Unmarried women do not perform *koutou* at the village level, because no one knows what village they will belong to after marriage. Performing a *koutou* to one's dead ancestors (now deprived of extra-worldly agency), though clearly also a form of mourning and an expression of *xiao* (filial piety), is an affirmation of one's relationship to all living members of the family (i.e., the descendants). Likewise, performing a *koutou* to the recently deceased at a funeral is both mourning, *xiao,* and a reconstitution of the relationships among all of those who *koutou* at the same festival.

At weddings brides move from one family to another. Though women usually maintain strong affinal ties, at her wedding a bride's primary *guanxi* begin shifting from her family to her husband's. At weddings the bride should theoretically *koutou* (or at least bow) with her husband five times (to heaven and earth, to ancestors, to mother and father, to friends and relatives, and to each other). If carried out, these five bows would constitute the bride's relationship to her husband in five ways,[22] announcing them both to be members of the same five subgroups: the entire social world (*tiandi*), the husband's patrilineal family extended indefinitely in time toward both the past and the future (*zuxian*), the immediate family of the husband and his father and mother (*dieniang*), the living extended family of the husband projected outward in space by affinal ties and friendships (*qinqi pengyou*), and the immediate family to be constituted by the new bride and groom (*huxiang bai*). The husband's father's *koutou* before the offering table likewise reconstitutes his relationships within the extended patrilineal family.

The hesitancy of brides to *koutou* at their weddings is very ambiguous. Even within the context of a single wedding, multiple interpretations could be possible, and to force a single interpretation would be a grave ethnographic error. Most villagers said that brides do not bow at weddings because they are embarrassed (*buhaoyisi*). Some claimed that this embarrassment itself was a "traditional" disposition for brides to assume at weddings. I address this emphasis on tradition in the next section. Here let me discuss the only woman I met who, by self-assuredly bowing at her wedding, "violated" this "tradition." The young woman in question was highly educated (a high-school graduate), a hard and able worker, handsome and outgoing. She said in a boastful but jocular manner, "If you have no shortcomings you are not afraid to bow even if they [your new family and friends] are all strangers." This interpretation again portrays the *koutou* as more of a social initiative than a burden. Only the self-confident dare to boldly assert new relationships with people they do not know well.

Other interpretations of the wedding bows (or lack thereof) are possible, however. The timing of the husband's father's *koutou* and the resultant reconstitution of the extended patrilineal family are important. By performing a *koutou* just before the ceremony proper, the father focuses attention on the bride's changing membership in patrilineal units. In another interpretation, the wedding bows could be seen as asserting that the bride is now related to her original family only as an affine, not as a member of the same patrilineal unit. A bride's refusing to bow could be seen as resisting this assertion.[23] Remember that the day before the wedding the bride's family usually sponsors a *song hezi,* a sad event for the parents of most brides. Immediately after spending a day with parents expressing their sadness at "losing" their daughter, a bride may not be up to generating the meaning/feeling that would reconstitute her family membership. To do so would be a slap in the face to her parents.

In any case, whether one interprets a specific case of reluctance to bow at a wedding as the expression of a "traditional" disposition, as hesitancy to assert one's new relationships, or as resistance to the negation of one's natal (*niangjia*) relationships, the refusal to bow is only temporary. After a period that allows for a reconstruction of her *xin*, the new bride begins to participate in rituals that require performing *koutou* before the ancestors of her husband's family—now also her family.

In the village there are numerous points of view. Each vantage, I argue, corresponds to membership in a particular (though openly defined) social group, a particular "magnetic field of human feeling." At times there are contradictions among these groups that manifest themselves in a hesitancy to *koutou*. The organization of spring festival *koutou* (different times for constituting relationships with different groups), the five separate bows during the wedding ceremony, and the refusal of brides to *koutou* at their weddings all point to these distinct vantages.

So far I have described the *koutou* as a *li* that works by recreating the membership of social groups, thus acting upon both the group as a whole and the relationships among members of groups. However, performing *koutou* to live people (as opposed to ancestors and the recently deceased) adds another dimension. Here, Bourdieu's concepts of timing (1977: 5–15, 1990:98–111) and disposition clarify matters. When, during the village-level spring festival *koutou*, an old man spends an hour talking with an old woman and then performs a full *koutou*, he not only affirms a relationship as a fellow villager like any other fellow villager, but also works on his personal relationship with her. Likewise, when members of the younger generation of an immediate family *koutou* to their elders, and the elders urge them to rise quickly, individual relationships may be mended. Thus the following statement made to me by a township-level official at a spring festival banquet: "When a daughter-in-law performs a *koutou* to her mother-in-law over spring festival, and the mother-in-law tells her to rise quickly, all the year's contradictions can be resolved in one minute—the family can reunite and resume production."[24] With proper timing, the dispositions that *koutou* reveal can be artfully employed to mend *guanxi*.[25]

Koutou as Peasant Subculture

In addition to being a type of *li*, the *koutou*, along with various other recently reinvented "traditions," forms a sort of peasant subculture.[26] Recall the following two points: first, that peasants as a group are defined externally, by the state, through the bureaucratic subjectification of the *hukou;* and second, that the (re)invention of tradition by villagers coincides with the negative objectification of peasants as a group in the post-1978 propaganda.[27]

Peasant subculture and its opposition have different teleologies. Those who want to be "advanced" (*jinbu*), see this subculture as "backward" (*luohou*); those who value it see the subculture as a tradition (*chuantong*) that should be passed on to the future (*chuanxialai*) in order to respect (*xiaojing*) one's ancestors. One view presents the future as something to be filled with the re-creations of past practices; the other presents it as something to be filled with the new, thus necessitating the rejection of the past.

In Zhao Ziyang's "primary stage of socialism," peasants themselves are part of the "past" that needs to be replaced to form a new future. Local nonpeasants take up this objectification when they scorn the *koutou* and other (re)invented rituals of Fengjia peasants as "backward" (*luohou*) and "feudal" (*fengjian*).[28] In contrast, villagers who were "peasant and proud" contested this objectification by flaunting their new *li*. These villagers made constant efforts to explain to me (a nonpeasant outsider), the importance of *lijie* (etiquette and ritual) in village life. These same villagers showed great delight when I tried to observe various conventions of local etiquette.[29] Like so many other "subcultures," positive peasantness delighted in precisely those elements that outsiders scorned (Hebdige 1979).

In light of the "subcultural" implications of the *koutou*, we can now reexamine the hesitancy of some villagers to perform it. The villager who did not participate in the spring festival intravillage *koutou*, who also eliminated the *koutou* from his sons' weddings, and who identified himself as a nonpeasant (though technically a peasant) was clearly connected with these implications. The position of youth was more complex. Certainly some young villagers were less than enthusiastic about performing *koutou*. One older villager made this tendency a generality, saying, "Young people don't like formal ritual." It would be easy to posit that since young people were always on the less powerful end of the hierarchies that these rituals implied, they did not like to participate. But such a view does not explain those young people who did participate.

More central here is the relation of young people to schools. Recall that young people in school still have a chance of testing into a nonpeasant *hukou* classification. Even if a particular student's chances are not high, I speculate that the high schools and perhaps even the junior highs are dominated by an ethos other than that of peasant subculture. For one thing, these institutions are boarding schools situated in the towns and cities. Second, the students themselves can escape "peasanthood" through educational achievement. Moreover, since the schools as a whole and teachers individually are evaluated on the testing successes and failures of their students, the school's teachers and administrators (all nonpeasants) have institutional interests in fueling this ambition. In short, the schools are thoroughly nonpeasant institutions.

The two grooms I saw bow deeply at their wedding ceremonies had both left school after junior high and thus had both been "peasants" for at least four years. In contrast, two of the grooms who seemed most averse to bowing at their weddings had both gone to the academic high school and had only six months previous given up on testing into college and thus becoming nonpeasants. For these young men, marriage, residency in the village, and designation as peasants had all come at once.[30]

I do not want to oversimplify. Going to high school did not simply or directly "cause" a refusal to *koutou*. But an emergent peasant subculture did create contradictions for would-be nonpeasant youth and their parents.[31] Being designated a peasant and committing oneself to peasanthood resolved these contradictions. This reconstitution took time, and young villagers hesitated to wholly enact their "peasantness" while the memory of their dreams of becoming nonpeasants still lived.

One "youth" who chose to *koutou* was Secretary Feng. Though the most powerful person in the village, because his generational name was a young one and because his father was still alive, in 1989 Secretary Feng was by "traditional" reckoning a rather junior member of the village. At spring festival he dutifully paid his respects to his "elders" in his family and throughout his village. Why did such a powerful man acknowledge his "youth" in such an impotent hierarchy? The significance of Secretary Feng's *koutou*, I think, was not his subordination in a traditional hierarchy, but rather the affirmation of his peasant subculture and his reconstitution as a villager. As with other youths whose *xin* were constituted firmly as both peasants and villagers, the problems of hierarchy were secondary (at least in 1989) to the expression of a positive "peasantness" and to the reconstitutive power the *koutou* afforded.[32]

Conclusion

As a final example, consider the marriage *koutou* depicted in Carma Hinton's documentary *Small Happiness,* filmed in another northern Chinese village during the 1980s. In the wedding scene a relative of the groom reads aloud a list of the groom's ancestors' names. The bride and groom, standing side by side, kneel on a mat after each name is read. The groom kneels without assistance. The bride, in contrast, though seemingly willing to kneel on her own, is repeatedly pushed down. A rowdy crowd of the groom's relatives, friends, and neighbors watches, talks, and laughs. At the conclusion of this scene, Hinton cuts to a series of interviews with young local women. They assert that there is little choice but to *koutou* in one's wedding ceremony. If one did not *koutou* voluntarily and quickly, one would be pushed.

The scene is ambiguous. As part of a movie about the difficulties of rural Chinese women, however, Westerners might easily read these *koutou* as forced displays of servility. Certainly the violence of such forced *koutou* serves patriarchy by usurping the bride's *guanxi*-forming initiative. Yet I argue that the "abject servitude" interpretation of *koutou* is inappropriate even in this case. Note that the bride performs *koutou* not to but *with* her husband. The bride's *koutou,* whether forced or voluntary, do not declare her subservient to her husband or any members of his family. Rather, the *koutou* declare social commitments toward which the bride may have had contradictory feelings.

In conclusion, let me reemphasize two of the points made at the beginning of the chapter. First, since the act of performing *koutou* both reeks of "peasantness" and works on groups that are predominately made up of rural agriculturalists, the *koutou* can always be said to work on a double level. Those who *koutou* constitute their relationship to the members of the group to whose hierarchy they are performing *koutou, and* they claim a bond with these group members as fellow peasants. The two processes of subject construction posited at the beginning of this chapter—the intimate and the imagined—are always interwoven.

Second, the subjects created in these processes, though complex and contradictory, are not ephemeral. Subjectification is always a temporal process. Though a villager's *hukou* may be changed instantly from non-peasant to peasant or, in the case of marriage, moved instantly from one family and village to another, subjectification takes time. Subjectification is not merely a matter of institutional classification, but the creation of a subject within and against that classification. It is only after adapting to one's classification, and creating something positive within it, that people can make themselves and be made into specific kinds of acting subjects.

Notes

1. Fengjia village is in Zouping County, Shandong Province. My seven months of research in the village, undertaken in six trips to Zouping County between June 1988 and June 1990, would have been impossible without the supportive cooperation of the people of Fengjia village and the Zouping County Office of Foreign Affairs (*waiban*). The Committee on Scholarly Communication with the People's Republic of China of the National Academy of Sciences, as well as the University of North Carolina's off-campus dissertation grants, supported my research in Fengjia village. The Johns Hopkins–Nanjing University Center also provided support while I was in China. I finished writing this chapter during a postdoctoral fellowship at the East-West Center. James Hevia, Dorothy Holland, Angela Zito, and two anonymous readers made valuable suggestions on various drafts. Judith Farquhar provided guidance from beginning to end.

2. Two issues need clarifying here. First, to avoid the sycophantic implications of the English word "kowtow," I will use the Mandarin *koutou* (from which kowtow is derived) to describe the kneeling bows of rural Chinese villagers. Second, the exact form of bodily motion to which *koutou* refers differs in varying Chinese contexts. The definition of what counts as a *koutou* in Fengjia village is not the same as in imperial ritual. Though the details of court protocol are beyond the scope of this chapter, one old villager claimed that any kneeling bow counted as a koutou in rural northern China during the late 1980s, whereas the Qing court version required "knocking" one's head on the ground three times in each of three directions while kneeling. Like the English "kowtow," *koutou* may be used as a noun or a verb.

3. Though much of Foucault's work may be cited here, the most explicit formulations of "subjectification" occur in Foucault 1982 and in Rabinow's (1984: 7–13) introduction to *The Foucault Reader*.

4. For other pertinent (but in some cases divergent) discussions of *ganqing* and *guanxi* see Fried 1953, Jacobs 1979, King 1991, Oi (1989:131), Walder (1986:179–85), and Yang 1988, 1989a.

5. I use Sun's (1987) terminology with some reservations. Sun uses an essentialized, psychologized notion of Chinese culture, of which *guanxi* subject construction is the central component, to paint a negative picture of Chinese the world over. Sun describes a series of "Chinese characteristics," including an underdeveloped sexuality, an inability to control bodily fluids and functions in public, a sycophantic personality, a rejection of rationality, and political despotism as entailments of a desire to construct and be constructed by *guanxi* subjects. Sun sees

these characteristics as psychologically engraved on the individual brain of anyone raised in a Chinese family. I believe neither that any of these characteristics are entailments of the *guanxi* construction of subjects nor that such construction is primarily a matter of psychological desire. However, I do find the language he uses to describe *guanxi* subject construction enticing.

6. However, I should emphasize that my use here reflects only Bourdieu's most fluid moments. I am not comfortable with Bourdieu's theoretization of "the habitus," defined "as a system of dispositions" (1977:214, 1990:54). The singularity with which Bourdieu asserts *the* habitus as *a* system, isomorphic with a group of people, problematizes his own critique of "objectivism." I would prefer to envision many unsystemized "habitus" whose mutual contradictions open possibilities for a critically self-aware agent. For a similar critique see Certeau 1984. In any case, I use the word "disposition" to refer to an attitude, an inclination, a stance, and so on that may or may not be explicit, conscious, or well thought out.

7. I take the term "objectification" from Dominguez's (1989) book *People as Subject, People as Object*. It refers to the process of making an "imagined" community "real" by the very act of characterizing it. For example, by describing peasants as "backward" one not only characterizes peasants but also implies that they exist as a coherent, unitary group.

8. I address the question of how official CCP selection of research site influenced my ethnography at greater length in my dissertation (Kipnis 1991). I believe, at least with regard to the topics addressed in this chapter, that I would have reached similar conclusions in other villages in the same area. I was allowed to interview anyone in the village without official supervision. More important, the variety of conflicting voices I heard regarding *koutou* in Fengjia convinced me that I was not being presented with a prefabricated "party line."

9. For a more detailed history of *hukou* policies see Huang 1990, Kipnis 1991, Potter and Potter 1990, and Whyte and Parish 1984. The rights and obligations of peasants and nonpeasant citizens also differ. Under the post-1978 responsibility system (*zeren zhi*), peasants receive land that they must farm to feed themselves and their dependents and to pay grain taxes to the state. They are not given jobs by the state. Nonpeasants are assigned to work units (*danwei*) by the state and are eligible to buy grain from the state at subsidized prices.

Many cases have been reported of peasants' buying grain at the market (not state subsidized) price to pay their taxes and feed their families. However, I did not hear of this in Fengjia village. Since some nonpeasants (particularly rural teachers) continue to live in villages and some peasants move into the cities with friends and relatives, the peasant/nonpeasant split is not strictly a village/town one. In Zouping County (where Fengjia is situated), only about 7 percent of the population have nonpeasant *hukou*.

10. The Sunzhen Township Educational Committee plans to make junior

high school compulsory after 1992. During the 1980s there were not enough teachers and classrooms to go around.

11. This percentage was more than twice as high as that recorded for the province as a whole in the 1990 *Statistical Yearbook of Shandong*.

12. Two factors exacerbate the tightness of the timing here. First, local officials allowed those wishing to marry to add a year to their ages after passing 1 January (thus allowing marriages to occur before spring festival, an agricultural slack season). Consequently many peasants married at the age of twenty-one for men and nineteen for women. Second, students who failed to test into college often stayed in high school an extra year to try the test again. Consequently, many did not quit school until the age of twenty—often, for both men and women, the summer before their winter marriages.

13. Local officials claimed to encourage equally both patrilocal and matrilocal (*nan dao nüjia luo hu*) marriages, but in fact in Fengjia and environs almost all marriages were patrilocal. Upon marriage a woman's *hukou* was moved to her husband's village, thus legally encoding her new identity. The general pattern was that of village exogamy. Yet somewhat more common than matrilocal marriages were marriages of a daughter to a family of a different surname within the same village. However, these marriages were still a minority. Friedman, Pickowicz, and Selden (1991) also suggest that the implementation of Maoist socialism tended to reinforce patriarchy.

14. In those cases there the daughter was already "lost," that is, where either through attending college or manipulating connections the daughter had found work outside the village and thus had effectively moved out of her home, the *song hezi* became a relatively cheerful event.

15. Mayfair Yang (1989b) discusses the subject construction that resulted from Mao worship.

16. During the GPCR, a few villagers claim to have secretly continued to *koutou,* but only on limited occasions, within the privacy of their immediate families.

17. In contrast to many other villages, the increase in wealth in Fengjia is not entirely traceable to the post-1978 responsibility system. Rather, it began with improvements in agricultural methods that were adopted in the early 1970s.

18. In 1989 almost every household in the village had both a television and a radio. About half of the households subscribed to newspapers.

19. Croll 1981 presents a general discussion of arranged versus free marriage in the PRC.

20. For each surname there is a set of generational names. For example, in 1989 for the surname Feng, the Ru, Da, Yue, Yong, and Chang generations still had living members. Generational names come after the surname when writing or speaking a person's name. Thus a member of the Ru generation with the given

name Hai would be called Feng Ru Hai. In theory, members of the Ru generation are two generations older than a person named, for example, Feng Yue He. However, because there are four branches of the Feng family in the village, and because this set of generational names has been in use for twenty generations, some with the generational name Yong are older than the youngest Da's. All the different branches of all the different surnames in the village have worked out generational equivalencies among each other, so that a Zhang of a certain branch can also extend kinship names to, and pay generational respects to, the appropriate Fengs. For an interesting discussion of the extension of kinship terms throughout a village regardless of surname, see Fei Xiao Tong (1939:90–91).

21. As in Hevia's description of Qing court ritual (this volume), the *koutou* is a constitutive rather than a representational use of the body. By embodying meaning/feeling, the motion of the body helps constitute relationships.

22. Clearly the bride's *koutou* would constitute relationships to others besides the husband, but no one else would share all five groups.

23. In her recent research in the same area of Shandong, Judd (1989) emphasizes the competing claims on a woman's work, resources, and person by her mother's family (*niangjia*) and her mother-in-law's family (*pojia*). In Fengjia these claims are staked in part through the contributions each family makes to the dowry. Stockard (1989:22) also speaks of this tension in the Canton delta.

24. The words in Chinese for the last phrase here were *tuanjie shengchan*, an example of how the language of political propaganda has entered everyday speech.

25. In the somewhat divergent context of Qing dynasty imperial funerals, Rawski (1988:248) likewise notes the importance of *koutou* as a disposition-displaying practice. She describes how the dispositions revealed by the emperor's *koutou* helped construct a hegemonic cultural politics of proper filiality.

26. I take the concept of subculture from Hebdige 1979. He uses the term to describe symbolic practices that undermine the assumptions of hegemonic ideologies. In a later self-critique Hebdige (1988:212) abandons the concept because of the historical closure and negativity he then felt the term implied. I rescue the term on the following grounds. First, I do not think one need assume that the term culture (and by extension subculture) implies closure either in the historical sense or in the sense of evenly belonging to a single group of people. Cultures and subcultures always exist in overlapping and contradictory relations to various groups of people. In addition, to build on the biological metaphor (i.e., a bacterial "culture"), we can assume that cultures are always developing, dying, or mutating—somehow changing over time. If one allows the term this flexibility, then Hebdige's second misgiving is more easily handled. As Hebdige so powerfully described in 1979, during certain historical moments some cultural practices derive their power from their ability to undermine more hegemonic understandings. To point at this critical destructive power with the word *sub*culture is not to deny

these practices either their productive aspects or their potential to develop into something positively or even hegemonically "cultural." Indeed, in the present analysis I try to demonstrate that *koutou* are simultaneously subcultural and productive of subjectivities. See Hobsbawn and Ranger 1983 for the seminal conceptualization of the political importance of invented traditions.

27. There also exists a thriving "*guanxi* ethics" among city dwellers (Yang 1988, 1989a). However, this "tradition" revolves around the practices of gift giving and banqueting (also important among villagers, but in a different form) and does not include rites like the *koutou*.

28. Here it is interesting to note that the language of scorn echoes both the state ideology of the Cultural Revolution (in the criticism "feudal"), and the present ideology (where the peasants are "backward").

29. Some of these same villagers remembered Mao in quite a positive light. Arguably this relates to the more positive imagery of rural people during the Cultural Revolution.

30. I spoke at length with one of these young men. He was very pleased about his marriage but disappointed at not being able to test into college and uncertain about his future.

31. Including—to name a significant contradiction that is not fully resolved upon becoming a peasant—that between a desire to respect (through etiquette) peasants and their work and a desire for more open and equal interaction between the sexes (which is possible at school but restricted and hierarchized in some of the [re]invented etiquette). However, I should also point out that in reference to the *koutou*, this contradiction is not relevant. If women are older than men, men *koutou* to them; it is age, not gender, that is important.

32. Somewhat similarly Zito 1987 describes the pivotal and powerful positions that "sons" occupied by performing ancestral sacrifice during the Qing dynasty. A full comparison would take another essay; here I will lay out my position briefly. Following more structuralist leads, Zito explores the paradoxes of identification and differentiation that hierarchizing rituals like the *koutou* entail. Such simultaneous identification and differentiation integrate social wholes. In contrast, my more poststructural interpretation primarily emphasizes the identifying aspects of *koutou*. Since identification without a linking differentiation implies the formation of separate and opposing groups, my analysis points toward the disintegration of social wholes. The continuity and difference of our analyses should be understood in relation to the historical periods we analyzed. The Qing dynasty rituals Zito describes occurred in a context where filiality was a hegemonic ideology and the agency of ancestor spirits was taken for granted—that is, where the substance of heaven and earth and the state and the family was asserted as a single whole. In the 1980s the agency of ancestor spirits was problematic and filiality (in relation to the ideology of modernization the CCP espouses) was subversive. That I find

poststructural theory more illuminating than structural theory in the analysis of modern *koutou* perhaps reflects the disintegration of Qing dynasty ideological hegemony.

References

Anderson, Benedict. 1983. *Imagined communities: Reflections on the origin and spread of nationalism.* London: Verso.

Bourdieu, Pierre. 1977. *Outline of a theory of practice.* Trans. Richard Nice. Stanford: Stanford University Press.

————. 1990. *The logic of practice.* Trans. Richard Nice. Stanford: Stanford University Press.

Certeau, Michel de. 1984. *The practice of everyday life.* Trans. Steven F. Rendall. Berkeley and Los Angeles: University of California Press.

Croll, Elizabeth. 1981. *The politics of marriage in contemporary China.* New York: Cambridge University Press.

Dominguez, Virginia R. 1989. *People as subject, people as object.* Madison: University of Wisconsin Press.

Fei Xiaotong. 1939. *Peasant life in China.* London: Routledge and Kegan Paul.

Foucault, Michel. 1982. The subject and power. In *Michel Foucault: Beyond structuralism and hermeneutics,* by Herbert Dreyfus and Paul Rabinow, 208–26. Chicago: University of Chicago Press.

Fried, Morton H. 1953. *Fabric of Chinese society: A study of social life of a Chinese county seat.* New York: Praeger.

Friedman, Edward, Paul G. Pickowicz, and Mark Selden. 1991. *Chinese village, socialist state.* New Haven: Yale University Press.

Hall, David L., and Roger T. Ames. 1987. *Thinking through Confucius.* Albany: State University of New York Press.

Hebdige, Dick. 1979. *Subculture: The meaning of style.* New York: Methuen.

————. 1988. *Hiding in the light: On images and things.* New York: Routledge.

Hobsbawm, Eric, and Terence Ranger, eds. 1983. *The invention of tradition.* New York: Cambridge University Press.

Huang, Philip C. C. 1990. *The peasant family and rural development in the Yangzi delta.* Stanford: Stanford University Press.

Jacobs, Bruce J. 1979. A preliminary model of particularistic ties in Chinese political alliances: *Kan-ch'ing* and *Kuan-hsi* in a rural Taiwanese township. *China Quarterly* 78 (June): 237–73.

Judd, Ellen R. 1989. Chinese women and their natal families. *Journal of Asian Studies* 48 (August): 525–44.

King, Ambrose Yeo-chi. 1991. *Kuan-hsi* and network building: A sociological interpretation. *Daedalus* 120 (Spring): 63–84.

Kipnis, Andrew. 1991. Producing *guanxi:* Relationships, subjectivity and ethnicity in a rural Chinese village. Ph.D. diss., University of North Carolina at Chapel Hill.

Oi, Jean. 1989. *State and peasant in contemporary China: The political economy of village government.* Berkeley and Los Angeles: University of California Press.

Potter, Sulamith H., and Jack M. Potter. 1990. *China's peasants: The anthropology of a revolution.* New York: Cambridge University Press.

Rabinow, Paul. 1984. Introduction. In *The Foucault reader,* ed. Paul Rabinow, 3–29. New York: Pantheon.

Rawski, Evelyn. 1988. The imperial way of death. In *Death ritual in late imperial and modern China,* ed. Evelyn Rawski and James Watson, 228–54. Berkeley and Los Angeles: University of California Press.

Statistical yearbook of Shandong. 1990. Beijing: Zhongguo Tongji Chubanshe.

Stockard, Jamie E. 1989. *Daughters of the Canton delta.* Stanford: Stanford University Press.

Strathern, Marilyn. 1988. *The gender of the gift.* Berkeley and Los Angeles: University of California Press.

Sun Longji. 1987. *Zhongguo wenhuade shenceng jiegou* (The deep structure of Chinese culture). 2d ed. Hong Kong: Ji Xian She.

Walder, Andrew G. 1986. *Communist neo-traditionalism: Work and authority in Chinese industry.* Berkeley and Los Angeles: University of California Press.

Whyte, Martin King, and William L. Parish. 1984. *Urban life in contemporary China.* Chicago: University of Chicago Press.

Yang, Mayfair Mei-hui. 1988. The modernity of power in the Chinese socialist order. *Cultural Anthropology* 3 (November): 408–27.

———. 1989a. The gift economy and state power in China. *Comparative Studies in Society and History* 31 (January): 25–54.

———. 1989b. Three constructions of the subject in socialist China. Paper presented at the 1990 American Asian Studies meetings in Washington, D.C., 17–19 March.

Zhao Ziyang. 1987. *Zhongguo Gongchandang dishisanci quanguo daibiaodahui wenjian huibian* (Edited documents from the thirteenth party congress of the Chinese Communist Party). Beijing: Renmin Chubanshe.

Zito, Angela. 1987. City gods, filiality and hegemony in late imperial China. *Modern China* 17 (Summer): 333–71.

Gendering
Bodies

9

The Classic "Beauty-Scholar" Romance and the Superiority of the Talented Woman

Keith McMahon

Introduction

In the middle decades of the seventeenth century a type of vernacular novel appeared in China that in both literary and colloquial parlance is called the story of "the beauty and the scholar" (*jiaren caizi*). One of the most prominent features of such works is their portrayal of smart, capable, chaste young women who are equal to and in some cases better than their male counterparts in terms of literary talent, moral fiber, and wit. The woman is so important that the habitual word order of "scholar-beauty" (*caizi jiaren*), the predominant usage then and now, deserves to be changed to the less common but also acceptable "beauty-scholar."

The prominence of such portrayals of women in Qing fiction is part of a deviation among highly literate circles from the discourse of obligatory male and female roles. The beauty-scholar romances were a playing ground for positions already expressed since the late sixteenth century by literati critical of certain norms governing women and marriage, especially the value of widow chastity or the opinion that it is virtuous for a woman to be silent and uneducated (Ropp 1981:128–30; Mann 1987:50; Ko 1992). Statements by sixteenth-century thinker Li Zhi and others that women are as intelligent as men or that women should be allowed their own choice in marriage bear a definite connection with the way such statements are played out as themes in these romances (Ropp 1981:129–30).[1] The concurrent appearance of this fiction and the increasing recognition of women's literary and artistic activity in the late Ming and Qing likewise cannot be accidental (Ko 1992; Widmer 1989, 1992; Robertson 1992). Paul Ropp notes the early Qing author Pu Songling (1640–1715), who uses literary Chinese to create many of the same portraits met in the vernacular beauty-scholar romances; for example, women more "strong-willed, . . . intelligent, and . . . courageous" than men, or lovers choosing their own partners and being monogamously equal in marriage (Ropp 1981:130–31). Patrick Hanan writes of another famous early Qing writer, Li Yu (1611–79/80), whose drama and fiction are full of clever women with brilliant schemes, "enterprising and ingenious women" (also "bold, resolute, and resourceful"), who are more active than men in pursuing goals of self-interest, which they put ahead of the traditional goals of self-sacrifice (Hanan 1988:103–4, 151). Similar views on women continue in the mid-Qing among male literati such as Wu Jingzi (1701–54), Yuan Mei (1716–98), Dai Zhen (1724–77), Ji Yun (1724–1805), Li Ruzhen (ca. 1763–1830), and Yu Zhengxie (1775–1840), who variously take up the criticism of such things as foot-binding, widow chastity, or concubinage (Ropp 1981:132–40, 140–51; Lin 1935).

As part of this trend, the beauty-scholar romance portrays chaste women who, like a small but significant number of their real counterparts in the mid-seventeenth century, are active in social and literary spheres normally off-limits to them. The romance can be seen as displaying an alternative aspect of the equation between chastity and female excellence that Susan Mann has discussed in terms of Qing propaganda on widow chastity. Public honoring of chaste widows in China suggested that "female chastity was a metaphor for community honor." The upward mobility of a family supposedly had to do with keeping widows chaste (Mann 1987:43, 49). The moral imperative of such propaganda seems capable of producing merely the emblematic image of woman as passive sufferer. In the situation described in the beauty-scholar romance, however, the aura of chastity goes beyond the narrow frame of widowhood and provides female characters with a power of self-determination and self-invention that exceeds not only normal female roles but male ones as well. In other words, although self-sacrificing chastity still dominates the moral discourse and is the main model for female excellence, another type of chastity is shown to exist that allows for active female self-direction, at least in the imaginary realm created by the beauty-scholar romances and other works of Qing fiction such as the stories of Li Yu, Pu Songling, and the novels *Rulin waishi* (Wu 1984) and *Jinghua yuan*.[2]

The chaste early Qing romance must also be seen against the tendencies of previous fiction, in particular the late Ming erotic story, with its portrayals of both men and women easily given to consuming passion and illicit sex. The romances covered in this chapter, especially the "classics" of the early period such as *Haoqiu zhuan, Ping Shan Leng Yan,* and *Yu Jiao Li,* clearly react against the "decadence" of late Ming fiction, but at the same time they continue the liberationist trend of the late Ming works on a more rational and self-controlled level.[3] The liberation I refer to in the chaste romance is the lovers' freedom to choose their marriage partners themselves rather than acquiesce to parental arrangement; the woman in particular is given a greater privilege of choice and is often allowed a monogamous marriage. The price of this freedom, however, is the rationalization and deerotization of love: although the lovers have more choice than usual in selecting each other, they must promise, as it were, not to indulge themselves before marriage; above all, the woman must remain chaste. In addition, superior man and superior woman must wend their way through a complex series of obstacles before they attain union in the end.

My interest below will be to describe the characteristic way the beauty-scholar romance balances woman and man. As formulaic and predictable as these novels may be, they always construct a tension between (1) the normal way marriages are arranged, with partners chosen by the parents and with talented women often married to boorish or profligate men, and (2) the ideal, nonconformist way being played out in the story. Idealism is grounded in a formulaic symmetry or equivalence that patterns the lovers' path to marriage. Yin and yang interchange; woman impersonates man, and man resembles woman. Such similarity and mirror opposition imply a perfect dovetailing of male and female, sometimes neutralizing sexual difference and at other times creating an outright exchange of sexual characteristics. As a genre, these novels work toward a self-definition whereby they are about a man and woman who are not really male and female and who, in particular contrast to the erotic works of the period, avoid having sex. The chaste couple replaces sex with words: poems, letters, and polite conversation. They end up as *zhiji*, "intimate companions" or "knowers-of-each-other's-innermost," not as *yuanjia*, "enemies enamored," the term used for infatuated lovers, like those in the late Ming story, whose capsule of passion explodes in the end because of the inevitability of excessive indulgence. In the late Ming erotic story, passion tends to exceed the capacity to fulfill it; in the chaste Qing, the lovers contain their passion and achieve everlasting harmony.

Definition of the Beauty-Scholar Romance

The "classic" or what I will also call "chaste" beauty-scholar romance—to be distinguished from the male-centered erotic romance of the same period—can be defined as a novel of some ten to twenty chapters about a young man and woman who represent the best in intelligence, looks, and moral character that civilization has to offer (Lin 1988:57). They chance to meet and then get to know each other, often through the exchange of literary messages, especially poetry. It becomes spontaneously apparent that they are meant for each other. Mean people (*xiaoren*) try to steal the woman away or otherwise prevent the two from uniting, but they fail because the youths are so much cleverer and more virtuous. Their love exists just outside—but not too far outside—the traditional system of marriage according to "ritual," *li*—that is, according to such things as arrangement by the parents and the matching of the wealth and rank of the two families. They match for their own benefit rather than their parents', although ultimately they obtain their parents' blessings as well as conform to the ideal that the man should pass the official exams before marrying the woman. The classic romances are devoid of descriptions of sex, although they vary in whether they allow the still unmarried lovers to embrace or hold hands. Realistic detail is extremely sparse. For example, in one work the lovers elope, but the precise steps they take are completely omitted (see *Zhuchun yuan xiaoshi*, chaps. 16 and 17). The language is correspondingly polite and formulaic, rarely obscure or colorfully colloquial as in other fiction of the period. These are the works the great eighteenth-century novel *Honglou meng* (Dream of the red chamber) makes fun of for being all alike in plot and written in pretentious literary language.

That these romances are "chaste" is significant because of their contrast with the erotic romances, which share the generic features of length and plot outlined above but differ in two main respects: they contain explicit sexual detail, and they give the man multiple partners. More precisely, the chaste romances at most allow him two wives and perhaps an additional maid as concubine; the erotic romances tend to allow him three or more. These works continue the erotic trend in vernacular fiction that began in the sixteenth century, but they differ from the earlier erotic fiction in centering on ultimately conjugal, not adulterous or otherwise illicit, sex. Although I will not discuss them at length in this essay, their contrast with the chaste romances is essential in defining the theme of the superiority of women. That theme is attenuated in the erotic romances because of the "recentering" of the polygynous man and the sexualization of his "superior" women. In the erotic works, which can be called "scholar-beauty" romances, the man becomes the center of a polygynous marriage in which he has premarital sex with some or all of his wives and concubines. He occasionally saves sex with his premier wife until their marriage, thus allowing her the honor of the well-kept chastity that is so valued in the classic romances. She and the other women, however, retain fewer superior qualities than the heroines of the beauty-scholar novel; sometimes several of the unchaste women split between themselves the superior features of the one chaste woman; that is, one might be intelligent, another beautiful, and a third valiant.[4] At the same time, despite the lesser stature of the women, the man is always a talented and benevolent husband whom the women gladly and unjealously serve. In the end, the chaste and erotic romances are alike in the way they instance fulfilled love in a civilized marriage of scholar and beauty or beauties.

The *Caizi Jiaren* Romance as a Genre of Vernacular Fiction

Before discussing the way these novels work out male/female relations, I must further elaborate how and why *caizi jiaren* fiction can be seen as a genre of literature. The origin of the *caizi jiaren* type of story can be taken back to the famous Han love affair between Zhuo Wenjun and Sima Xiangru, or Tang tales such as *Yingying zhuan* or *Liwa zhuan*, or Yuan and Ming plays such as *Xixiang ji* (in which the term *caizi jiaren* itself appears)[5] or *Mudan ting*. The lovers in these stories eloped, met secretly, or simply were a "true" match in spite of parental opposition (Cheng 1984:34; Lin 1988:61–65).[6] Such stories are extremely common in the Ming and Qing in both operatic and fictional forms, one often being an adaptation from the other. As comic romances (although some of the antecedents above are not comic), the *caizi jiaren* stories differ little from those in any culture about a young man and woman who have an incontrovertible necessity to be together; they meet, encounter blocks to their union in the form of villains, social pressures, or their own failure to recognize their destiny; they finally break through the obstacles and unite in marriage. As a group of like books, not simply stories with universal features, however, the *caizi jiaren* romances constitute a genre that attains a specific historical and cultural identity because of its appearance in twenty-chapter (or so) form about the early Qing. This identity has been noted since works like Lu Xun's *Brief History of Chinese Fiction* in the 1930s (Lu 1973:245–55).[7] I will follow Lu Xun's path and give my own and recent Chinese scholars' observations on the subject of seventeenth- and eighteenth-century beauty-scholar romances.

The mainland scholar Lin Chen has written one of the most comprehensive studies of the genre in recent years, based on his own research as well as that of scholars who throughout the 1980s have communicated with each other about *caizi jiaren* fiction personally, at conferences, or through publications. Many have noted the obvious prominence of remarkable women in these novels, a subject I will treat below (Lin 1988: 55–84; Lu 1973; Li 1984:59; Cao 1984:45). Many have also observed the formulaic quality of character portrayal and plot. In his seminal work of 1934, Guo Changhe dismissed the genre for its lack of imagination and thus killed the topic of *caizi jiaren* fiction for the next fifty years (Lin 1988:54). Recent scholarship has redeemed the works mainly by celebrating their promotion of self-determination in marriage. Lin Chen says that the term *caizi jiaren* was in common use by the early Qing and at that time already carried the notorious connotation of the self-determined marriage between two talented and good-looking youths (1988:56). Some of these works, however, such as *Haoqiu zhuan* and *Xing fengliu,* eschew the appearance of free choice, so that this feature, like any other single one, is not universal for this genre.[8]

Identification of the existence of the "scholar-beauty book," or *caizi jiaren shu* (also *caizi jiaren xiaoshuo,* or novel), must have come about shortly after the fiction started being written in the late Ming to early Qing. The term *caizi jiaren* (or *jiaren caizi,* since it occurs both ways) appears in the romances themselves in both positive and negative senses, but in neither sense very often; authors perhaps avoid the expression because of its negative connotations.[9] An important early example of the recognition of this group of books is Liu Tingji's derogatory reference in about 1715. For him these "recent" books are a nuisance, but he judges them not as bad as some of the obscene novels and stories that the late Ming produced in great numbers (although he has high praise for *Jin Ping Mei;* Lin 1988:56–57; Liu 1985:1284).[10] Another famous reference is the one in *Honglou meng* about "beauty-scholar and other such books" (*jiaren caizi deng shu,* perhaps significantly putting "beauty" before "scholar"), which were well established by *Honglou meng*'s time in the mid-eighteenth century; they are said to be all alike, of inferior literary quality, and obscene.[11] A passage at the beginning of one of the later romances itself reflects these critical opinions and states that its story attempts to be something different (*Zhuchun yuan xiaoshi*).

Lin Chen provides a short account of the evolution of *caizi jiaren* fiction: in the early period, from the Shunzhi reign into the Kangxi (ca. 1640s to ca. 1670s), the love story is intertwined with episodes about national events, contains many coincidences and twists and turns in plot, and shows little development of the realistic concerns of everyday life. From the 1670s on, *caizi jiaren* fiction divides into those works that continue as before with minor variations and those that have a greater variety of content, including episodes about demons and people with fantastic powers, about the exam system, court cases, monks and nuns, prostitution, illicit romance, and so forth (Lin 1988:81–84). At some point in this continuum the vicissitudes of the scholar and the beauty go from being the core of the story to being just another part of the variety.

The Remarkable Woman and Her Relationship with the Man

The talented and independent woman is not new in Chinese literature, nor is her attachment to a handsome scholar. Her concentration in beauty-scholar romances of the early to mid-Qing, however, is a clear identifying feature of these novels.[12] Able to do as well as or better than the man, such a woman often dresses as a man in order to move about more freely than custom ordinarily allows; she goes out to get what she wants rather than waiting for things to come to her in her inner chambers.[13] One of her mottoes is, "Though in body I am a woman, in ambition I surpass men" (BGZ, chap. 1, 6).[14] Dressed as a man, she can say what she wishes, even set up her own marriage. She is typically an only child cherished by her parents, especially her father, who educates her as if she were a boy (YZJ, YJL, DQR, SHS, LEB, WRY). She helps her father and her lover out of predicaments (YZJ, YJL, and others). Her poetic skill startles even the emperor (PSLY). She is worth ten sons (YJL). But in the end all she wants is the man she has chosen for herself, the one worthy of her; she does not even mind if, as often happens, he takes a second wife.

Her alleged superiority over her husband is part of a symmetry of mutual correspondence or complementarity that extends to numerous areas in the relationship of girl and boy, beyond mere talent and will-power.[15] For example, if she is an only daughter with a father and no mother, then he is an only son with a mother and no father (YJL).[16] They are monogamous and sexually balanced, for "man and woman are the same as concerns the great desire" (DQR, chap. 3, 23). All she wants is for them "to be equal husband and wife" (*pingdeng fuqi;* DQR, chap. 12, 112). In one work, symmetry of plot development also helps establish that they absolutely match each other; that is, they run into parallel sequences of difficulties that demonstrate their fates are intertwined (FHY).

When they are together, they conduct discussions in which the

woman has as much input as the man, or more. The men do not conde-
scend to the women. Certain deprecating expressions found in many other
fictional male characters—for example, the derogatory reference to the
"woman's way of thinking" (*furen jianshi*)—are not part of the handsome
scholar's vocabulary.[17] We may even imagine that the couple will die at the
same moment in old age, seated peacefully with smiles on their faces, as
do an elderly well-matched husband and wife in *Baigui zhi,* whose corpses
never rot (chap. 16, 118).

The presence of cross-sexual characteristics is a major aspect of the
lovers' complementarity. The young man and woman look alike or at least
easily pass as members of each other's sex (Hessney 1979, 1985:223–
24). In *Haoqiu zhuan* and *Xing fengliu* the young man is "just like a beautiful woman" (XFL, chap. 1, 2; HQZ, chap. 1, 2). In *Feihua yong* it is said
that the young hero would be beautiful if he dressed as a woman, although
he does not actually do so (chap. 5, 45). Usually only the woman dresses
as a man; the other half of the cross-dressing story is not written except in
Ming and Qing erotic works in which a man disguises himself as a woman
either to seduce unsuspecting women[18] or to have homosexual liaisons
with men who like female impersonators.[19] The classic beauty-scholar romance is the story of the upward mobility of the woman, so that a man's
dressing or acting like a woman would be not only illogical but perverse.[20]
The romance does suggest permeability of gender boundaries, as with the
notion that the woman is "as good as" a son. But perfect symmetry of
male and female cross-dressing would have to occur in a context devoid of
the gender hierarchy that dictates that women must act like men in order
to prove their superiority.

Besides the lack of true symmetry in cross-dressing, there is often a
similar inequality in the ratio of sexual partners. Although the famous
early works such as *Haoqiu zhuan* and *Ping Shan Leng Yan* feature monogamous relationships, in many other romances the author allows the
man one more wife and perhaps a maid as concubine. But the story always
carefully works out that the two wives, often good friends, are equal in
rank and are not jealous of each other or of the maid.[21] The maid herself
is the close companion of one of the wives (also often a go-between for
the man and woman) and therefore mercifully kept in the family by this
strategy rather than being married off and never seen again. As indicated
above, however, if there are any more than these two wives, then the novel
is usually erotic and the plot is a series of sexual adventures in which the
man collects one woman after another, to end up as the successful and

benevolent polygynist found in Qing novels like *Shenlou zhi, Wushan yan-shi,* or *Xinghua tian.*

§

The points above about the talents of the woman, the suggestion of symmetry between man and woman, and the asymmetry of one scholar married to two beauties must now be fleshed out by looking at individual novels. The theme of the talented woman is taken to extremes in *Baigui zhi,* a sixteen-chapter novel of the late eighteenth or early nineteenth century (Lin 1988:401–5).[22] Here all together five women disguise themselves as men in order either to get an education and take the exams or to meet face-to-face with men they hope to marry—dressed as a man, each avoids openly breaking the rule of no contact between unmarried men and women. One of the women even impersonates the man she eventually marries (chaps. 7, 8). No mention is ever made of the women's bound feet, which in reality would make long-term disguises as men utterly impossible.[23] At the end of the novel, the emperor is about to marry two of the highest examinees to his daughter and the daughter of a prince, but then he learns that the two examinees are women. He forgives them, saying that it is too bad such talented women cannot be put to use serving the state: "Alas, what can be done about it?" (chap. 16, 117).[24]

Although disguising oneself as a man is a breach of propriety—and deception of the emperor is the highest crime of all—the women are ultimately forgiven because they are seen to have no other way and to mean no harm. At first, however, when the father of one of the women discovers she has secretly arranged her own betrothal, he tries to have her buried alive. Later another man orders the arrest of his daughter and her secret lover. In both cases the women are forced to fend for themselves and perceive that the best way of doing so is to disguise themselves as men. Their spectacular success is what finally gains them their way.

In *Baigui zhi* there are no "bad" women, only "bad" men: the two fathers mentioned above, whose wives openly oppose their husbands' harshness, and a young scholar who has as much talent (*cai*) as the other youths but who lacks virtue (*de*). He impersonates one of the heroes in order to marry one of the beauties; failing that, he tries to elope with another of the beauties, fails again, and dies in prison (chaps. 5 and 6). The same two beauties eventually become the wives of the man the impostor tried to impersonate. The moral of the impostor's case is that talent and virtue must go together (as the commentary at the end of the fourth chapter states). In another part of the novel, the "bad" man is one who blithely promises his sister to another man without consulting her or other family members; his wife upbraids him and has him undo his promise (chap. 12, 84).

§

The early Qing novel *Feihua yong*, in sixteen chapters, takes the principle of symmetry to another height of artificiality by making the fates of the two lovers precisely parallel (Lin 1988 : 85–98, 261–63). Two seven-year-olds, a boy and a girl, spontaneously exchange couplets as they and their parents are watching a festival; the two are matched then and there. Misfortune causes the families to be split up, and both children end up with adopted parents. As adopted children they meet again without recognizing each other, secretly exchange poetry, and make a marriage pact. Circumstances separate them once more, and each eventually is adopted by the other's father, again without recognition. The play of symmetry is such that the man and woman must exchange not only matching poetic couplets but family units as well to show that they properly correspond to each other. This notion is restated in terms of yin and yang toward the end of the novel when their trading of surnames is compared to "yin changing into yang, yang changing into yin" (chap. 15, 141). Since it is too improbable for them actually to exchange sexes, they merely exchange parents. They approximate switching sexes in two places where such switches are imagined: First, as a youngster, she is said to be so bright that "if she were a boy" she could certainly gain fame in the literary world (chap. 3, 25). Later, when they meet for the second time, she remarks to herself how beautiful he would be if he dressed as a woman (chap. 5, 45).

The reference to the exchange of yin and yang in *Feihua yong* is not very remarkable in light of the commonness of that idea in parts of the Chinese tradition, especially Daoism and the arts of inner and outer alchemy. But among the works of the beauty-scholar genre, it is remarkable in its passing evocation of the formulaic operations of symmetry. As it applies in these novels, symmetry means both formal equivalence or even distribution (of talents, attractiveness, and so on) and complementarity. The lovers are "equal" in that they have like abilities and are evenly balanced in status and power in their marriage. They are complementary in that they mirror but reverse each other (e.g., the girl's mother is dead and so is the boy's father), and they alternate attributes and situations (e.g., she impersonates a man, he is like a woman; they exchange families, etc.).

Sometimes they are equal in the sense of being identical, but only temporarily or ephemerally, such as when the woman disguises herself or duplicates a man and the man looks like a woman; in these situations the symmetry is skewed, since social norms make it unlikely that a man would care to pass as a woman in order to better himself. Still, the possibility of one-for-one exchange is held out and is essential to their love equation.

The combination of identity and complementarity is most apparent in their quintessential mode of interaction, the exchange of matched poetry. In this activity symmetry is the truest, in the sense that each lover's poetry is the mirror image of the other's; that is, they use the same tonal pattern, rhyme, and syntax, in which, for example, the classes of empty and full words in one's couplet match those in the other's. At the same time, of course, they use complementary, not identical, imagery; they use words and images that are sometimes antithetical, sometimes analogous, but not exactly the same.

In sum, symmetry as I use it here is a general term that includes such functions as equivalence, identity, and complementarity. It refers to a mirroring—that is, the reflection of you in me and me in you—and connotes parallelism, the idea of similarity and analogy across an intermediate distance. The lovers are equal in capacity, sometimes to the extent that they can duplicate or be mistaken for each other, though such plays on gender identity mainly are left to the imagination or form part of a temporary ruse.

Asymmetry in the Polygynous Romance

The principle of symmetry still applies even when the man marries two women; in this case the equivalence may apply between him and one or both of the women or between the women themselves. In such stories the scholar wins two talented beauties instead of one; the two women are close friends and glad to stay together in a two-wife polygynous marriage. Theirs is like a marriage of three people to each other rather than one man to two women.[25]

The twenty-four-chapter *Yu Jiao Li* of the early Qing provides one of the best known examples of the kind of two-wife polygynous marriage I am describing.[26] As in other romances featuring such a marriage, it is made clear very early that the man never intended to have more than one wife; at the start he had his heart set on one and only one. As if to enforce this unitary determination, the author of *Yu Jiao Li* constructs a system of equivalences in which both the scholar and the first beauty are only children, the man fatherless and raised by his mother, the woman motherless and raised by her father. When her parents fail to have a son, her father takes a series of concubines, all of whom fail to have children, although when he remarries them to other men they then bear sons. He and his wife finally have a daughter; soon after, the wife dies. Having only a daughter turns from a misfortune into a blessing, because it is a situation so signally intended by fate. She is so special that she is said to be more talented than "ten sons" (chap. 6, 68).[27]

Being so special, she is allowed the superior position when it comes to selecting a husband, who must first win her in a poetry contest (chaps. 6, 7). When the hero's poetry proves the best, their match is established. Villainous plots separate the lovers, however, and he by chance falls in with another woman who eventually becomes his second betrothed. The second woman and he meet when she dresses as a man, having gone out, as it were, to get what she wants—a husband of her own choice. To achieve her goal, she stages a clever deception by inventing a "sister"—herself—and promising this "sister" to the man, withholding the truth from him until a later moment.

In other words, the careful machinations of plot make it such that the hero does not appear to agree easily to take on another woman. When the woman in disguise realizes that he is already betrothed, she tests him by asking him what he would do if a second woman were available for him. He replies that he could not be of "two hearts" (chap. 14, 155). But after becoming bosom friends with this "man," the hero is delighted to accept the offer of betrothal to the man's "sister." He reasons that since he has lost contact with his first love, this second offer is something within reach. When the "man" asks what he would do if his first love reappeared, he says that he would marry both women and make them equal in status (chap. 14, 158). Later the double marriage is legitimized by reference to the precedent of the ancient emperor Shun, who married two sisters (the two women in *Yu Jiao Li* are cousins). In addition, having themselves become friends, the two women feel that by being married to the same man they will always have each other and thus will not have to worry about "boredom" in the "inner chambers" (chap. 16, 181). In the end he also takes as concubine one of his wife's maids who helped them in their efforts to arrange their marriage.

In *Yu Jiao Li* the play of symmetry is at work to some degree between the man and each of the women: the man and the first woman mirror each other in being only children raised by one parent of the opposite sex; the man and the second woman match in both having widowed mothers and complement each other in her switching of sex roles, although in this case he is never said to resemble a woman. The two women match as well, since they are cousins, each of whom has a widowed parent, one male, the other female, and they become special friends when they display their talent through an exchange of matched poetry (chap. 15).

The cross-dressing episode in this case includes an element found in other romances, the ploy of the woman's dividing herself in two, her own self disguised as a man and her fictitious "sister" self whom "she" betroths to the scholar-hero.[28] In other works of the genre, the man also splits himself up to assume a disguise allowing him better access to the woman, but in these cases he ends up turning to humbler social versions of his own gender; for example, he becomes the gardener or scholar's servant (*shu-tong*) in the woman's house. In such disguise he is unlike the cross-dressed woman because he lacks the status to be able to arrange a betrothal between the heroine and a fictitious self. In works like *Fenghuang chi* and the erotic romance *Qingmeng tuo,* both beauty and scholar disguise themselves, thus acting out a symmetry of bisection, the woman going up the social ladder, the man going down.

§

Other novels feature two-wife marriages with similar types of equivalences at work. In the early Qing *Lin er bao,* of sixteen chapters (ca. 1672), the man and his first wife are only children; he and his second wife have the same birth date (Lin 1988:267–70). He is the son of a commoner; both wives are daughters of officials. After promising herself to the hero, the second woman disguises herself as a man to flee a forced marriage to another man, takes refuge in the first woman's family, and, in male disguise, marries the first woman. On the wedding night she briefly fondles the other woman before going to sleep (chap. 11, 118). Afterward she invents an excuse to delay consummation until she can get the man to marry both of them; she herself takes second rank in deference to the first wife, whose family took care of her during her hardship (chap. 16 works out the settlement of rank).

In contrast with *Yu Jiao Li, Lin er bao* has one of the women playing a greater role in arranging the marriage, which both the man and the other woman must accept as a fait accompli. *Lin er bao* also contrasts with *Yu Jiao Li* and other chaste romances in that it contains two scenes of light eroticism: the two women in bed, the one caressing the other, and the consummation between the man and the first woman. In the latter scene, which is slightly censored in the 1983 Shenyang edition, the second woman reveals her disguise to the man but not to the first woman; in the dark she puts the man in her place in bed and lets him make love to the first woman, who does not discover the identity of her partner until the next morning. Although angry, the first woman is soon mollified, and the second woman finally removes her disguise (chap. 16, 166–69).

§

In *Wan ru yue,* sixteen chapters, also of the early Qing,[29] the symmetry works mainly between the two wives: they are born on the same date with only a two-hour difference, which thus determines their ranking; they have the same last name—Zhao—and first names with the same meaning, Ruzi and Wanzi ("Like a Son"); they are both talented only children, and as other only-child daughters in such novels, are cherished "as if" they were sons. One is a poor southerner (though her ancestors were once illustrious officeholders), the other a rich northerner.

In contrast to the heroes in *Yu Jiao Li* and *Lin er bao,* the man in *Wan ru yue* is more consciously involved in the process by which he ends up marrying two wives. Having already declared loyalty to the first woman, whom he met when she was disguised as a man, he becomes irresistibly attracted to the second woman and allows himself to betroth her. Since the two women have the same surname, he figures that marriage to both is "heaven's intent" (chap. 7, 65). Like other works, *Wan ru yue* has the women help him reach his conclusion. The first woman, whom he leaves in the south, worries that he will abandon her for another, secretly follows him northward, and discovers his liaison with the second woman. Deciding not to interfere and thus show unseemly jealousy, the first woman again disguises herself as a man, this time to serve as a go-between to arrange the hero's marriage to both women. She reckons that, with two wives, the man will be happier anyway, and the women will have each other as "good friends" (*hao pengyou;* chap. 10, 92, 95). The mutual consideration between the wives, who discuss the problem of their ranking at length (chap. 14), is based on the same logic of reciprocity and deference that the poor woman had used: any jealousy one might feel can too easily incite jealousy in the other; since in the end the love one has for the man is the same as the other's, his rejection of one is just as bad as his rejection of the other (chap. 10, 91–92). In their decision to rank the poor woman first, the wives clearly choose as the criterion of precedence their slight difference in age, not social status or beauty, which would be considered too crude for such a chaste situation (chap. 14, 132–33).

Whether symmetry applies between man and woman, woman and woman, or man and man, whether it applies in the case of one-wife or two-wife marriage, it suggests that everyone can be of the same gender and can cross with the other gender. In one sense beauty and scholar are both men, as when she is disguised as a man betrothing herself to the scholar; in another sense beauty and scholar are both women, as when she is disguised as a man married to the other beauty. In *Wan ru yue* it is even such that all three are men, since both women are "like sons." The symmetry is always skewed, of course, since a beauty never marries two scholars, although she almost does in a brief scene of *Qingmeng tuo* (chap. 17) because of the confusion created by multiple disguises. But her excellence so overshadows the man that his role as dominant mate is thrown into abeyance. Women are portrayed as the main directors of action in the beauty-scholar marriage, whether there is one wife or two.

§

The mid-Qing novel *Zhuchun yuan xiaoshi*, in twenty-four chapters, was written perhaps a century or so (mid- to late eighteenth century) after the "classic" beauty-scholar romances *Ping Shan Leng Yan, Haoqiu zhuan,* and *Yu Jiao Li,* which it praises in its prologue (Lin 1988:234–39).[30] Like *Yu Jiao Li,* it features a polygynous marriage with a maid added as a "side chamber" (*ceshi*). As in other romances, the efforts and planning of the women bring about the man's union with two wives. He and the first woman are betrothed as children, but then are separated because of unforeseen complications. She never forgets the original arrangement; he does, however, and goes on to meet another woman, whom he gets to know through an exchange of poetry. By chance the two women end up living in the same home and become good friends. In pursuing the second woman, the man sends a message that is accidentally picked up by the first, whose existence is unknown to him and who had not known about his relationship with her friend, the other woman. The same careful maneuvering occurs here as in *Yu Jiao Li* and other works to open up a way for the man to have two wives without his seeming to be an intentional, premeditated polygynist. The first woman, hoping there will be room for her in the man's future family, uses hints and insinuations to gradually pry open the second woman's secret love and include herself as well. She wishes to find a "way for both women to be satisfied" (chap. 10, 64). A whole chapter is spent in which the first woman's cryptic remarks mystify and alarm the second woman, who is already moody and depressed from having failed to hear from her lover, whose latest message was intercepted by the first woman (chap. 10). When the truth finally emerges, the two women become close allies, and their next job is to inform the man, who now remembers his first betrothed and promises loyalty to both her and the second woman (chaps. 12, 13).

As in many of these novels, the two women make skillful use of their wits to arrange affairs the way they want. But in *Zhuchun yuan xiaoshi* they are more traditionally feminine in behavior in that they largely confine themselves to the inner chambers and do not disguise themselves as men.[31] Their moodiness, their use of subtle hints, and the man's "melancholy" (*chouchang;* chap. 11, 71) suggest the convoluted emotional world of *Honglou meng* of the same period rather than the more straightforward and robust world of the early classic beauty-scholar romances in which women disguise themselves as men or boldly compose poetry before the emperor (as in *Ping Shan Leng Yan*).[32]

§

My last and brief example of two-wife polygyny is from *Dingqing ren,* in sixteen chapters and probably of the mid- to late seventeenth century (Lin 1988:271–75; Zhang 1985:124–37). In this case, when it seems the hero will never be able to marry the heroine, he marries her maid instead, as the heroine had instructed him, but he refuses to consummate the marriage (chap. 15, 135–36). Then, when the heroine shows up after all, he sleeps with her the first night and her maid the second. The story furthermore insists that neither woman "is in the least bit jealous" (chap. 16, 152). In *Baigui zhi* the husband resolves the problem of priority by sleeping with both at once, for a scene of "many varieties of love" (chap. 16, 113). But in that case it is a matter of two women of the same class, not a woman and her maid.

Three versions of the superior woman appear in *Dingqing ren:* the heroine, the talented and assertive maid who stands in for the heroine, and a third woman who is forcibly married to a villain. The third woman's superiority emerges in the form of her shrewish temper, which enables her to subdue the villain, whom she literally rides like a horse by trapping him beneath her and sitting astride him (chap. 9, 84; chap. 10, 85). She eventually causes his death from *junei,* "fear of the inner one"—being hen-pecked (chap. 12, 106). Other novels, including ones not in this genre, feature such foil characters as well, often as depicted here for the comic relief of portraying a wife prevailing in a conjugal quarrel.[33] Of all women in Chinese literature, the shrew (*pofu*) demands monogamy the most loudly; in *Dingqing ren* she is posed against two "better" women who unjealously marry the same man.

The Riddle of Two-Wife Polygyny

The recurrence of marriage to two women in so many of these stories suggests several possible interpretations. Historical precedent has the legendary emperor Shun marrying two sisters, as mentioned in *Yu Jiao Li*. In literary history, the bigamous man typically marries his first wife while he is still poor and has not yet passed the imperial exams; he then travels to the capital, succeeds in the exams, and is offered the beautiful daughter of a high official—thus the story of the famous Ming opera *Pipa ji* (The lute), for example. He may attempt to refuse the offer, but that risks the wrath of the high official, who may threaten to ruin the man's future (as found in the Qing novel *Jin lan fa*, chaps. 12, 13). The hero may fail to reveal the existence of his "husk wife" (*zaokang zhi qi*), the term used for the woman he leaves behind, and marry the official's daughter. In some stories the "husk wife" dies of poverty and grief; in others, the second wife helps him reunite with his first wife by bringing her into the marriage. The "bigamy" of the beauty-scholar romance may be looked at, then, as a kind of happy resolution of the problem of the man's pre- and postexam pursuits.

Along the same line, other explanations might say that for the man bigamy bridges the gap between initial fate and subsequent revision, which are parallel to arranged versus self-determined marriage; the man marries a woman from each of two such categories. Two-wife polygyny is also perhaps a compromise between monogamy, demanded by superior women, and polygyny, wished for by even superior men. Having two wives is as far as the decent man dares to go; in other words, bigamy is like a chaste abbreviation or metaphor for polygyny.[34]

As a manifestation of the principle of symmetry, the three-person marriage may play out the mirroring of twos. That is, the female pole in the pair of the beauty and scholar simply folds out in mirrorlike reduplication into a doubling of the woman. We are still left with the riddle, however: Why, if the woman is so superior, does she allow her husband such advantage in the marriage (aside from material reasons such as the woman's desire for economic security or the need for male progeny—real factors in the Ming, Qing, and after, but not so much in the romances)? Given the superiority of the woman and the exchangeability of sexual characteristics, one might argue that the unit of two women and one man in fact does not reflect an imbalance in favor of the man but rather a dynamic triangle in which all three are of the same sex; neither the man nor either of the two women is the stable pivot; each can mediate between the other two. Indeed, the strong friendship between the women invites such a suggestion. The problem with this line of reasoning, as I have already established, is that the stories always illustrate the woman's upward mobility based on an assumed gender hierarchy. That is, the woman must always dress as a man in order to exercise her superiority and be rewarded for it. Another possible reason for doubling the woman is the implication found in the romances themselves that there are not enough good men in the world to match the number of good women; in the end, two superior women married to one superior man is better than one of the women married to a superior man but the other to a boor or no one at all.[35] The paucity and thus preciousness of good men is also the message of *Honglou meng,* whose hero Jia Baoyu seems to wish he could have all the women of the garden to himself; he is miserable about the prospect of their marriage to far-off and unknown men, most of whom he despises as inferior and "muddy" creatures (chap. 100). Like the hero of the beauty-scholar romance, of course, Baoyu presumes that he is somewhat better than other men and thus more deserving of female company. Furthermore, although men in general may indeed be "muddy," it is never suggested that they abandon the real powers that readers assume they possess or that they might want to exchange places with their female counterparts in the long term.

Whatever the interpretation, it is significant that in these works two-wife polygyny marks the limit of maintainable chastity. To repeat, once the man goes beyond two wives or has sex with them or others before marriage, then the novel becomes erotic. The sexual interchangeability of the polygynous threesome breaks down once the marriage contains four or more, in which case the man returns to being the center and the women to being subordinate stations for his revolving visitation. The erotic romances sometimes have the man declaring his three or more wives to be "equal" in rank, but in the end he grades the women according to both social class and personal qualities, including quality of sexuality (with the chaster ones at the top, the sexier at the bottom; see, for example, *Xiuping yuan* and *Taohua ying*). The chaste or classic romances scrupulously avoid ranking women according to quality; the characters carefully maintain a civility that is part of a general attempt to avoid any more embarrassment than already exists because of the man's marriage to two women, who help by being so superior as to be above jealousy.

In sum, the prescriptions of the classic romances state that a chaste family must not have too many excellent women. Otherwise it must face the unpleasant prospect of ranking the wives and thus reducing their aura of superiority. Furthermore, women and men can maintain this parity only when they are chaste before marriage and form a group of no more than three partners—or three and one-half, the half being the maid who is taken as concubine.

Conclusion

Regardless of single or multiple marriage, the scholar and the beauty are as pure as can be and tower above all other couples. Their marriage is based on love between two individuals who want each other, not on the contract between two sets of parents who choose partners for their children. But although the couples of the Qing romances base their relationship on love, they still behave rationally. They discipline lust; they obtain the blessing of their parents and, for that matter, match themselves according to the same standards of class and good training that their parents would have used. The *caizi* and *jiaren* are still a special case within the "old" system and not representatives of some new "democracy," although they may be on the way to some such future. They operate according to the ancient rule of "expediency," *quan*, to which these novels occasionally refer when young people, especially women, act more boldly than usual.[36] That is, within a habitually rigid framework, they "expediently" bend the rules of ritual because of the extraordinary circumstances of their absolutely perfect match. In fact, the woman's cleverness allows her to bend the rules so far that she climbs to the top of the social order and fools even the emperor, who is so impressed that he forgives her and lets her marry the man she wants. Expediency in these cases shows how easily rules can be bent "after all."

Many recent Chinese scholars have labeled these works "progressive" (*jinbude*) for promoting freedom of choice in marriage and granting women a greater sphere of self-determination than male views of women normally allow. This positive version of female subjectivity has the woman competing in the man's world (which means skillfully using his language, especially in writing), proving herself superior, and then winning the right to marry the man of her choice. Her final goal throughout is not to serve in office but to win the recognition that love should be the premise for marriage. Love, or *qing*, however, refers not to consuming sexual passion but to the self-evident "meant for each other" quality that the young man and woman have both from the traditional objective perspectives of fate (as in "match made in heaven") and parental blessing and from their own (now also emphasized) subjective perspective. This new perspective gains validity because of the extraordinary capabilities of the youths, especially the woman, who is often bolder than both her father and her husband. Such superiority "deserves" to have its way. The word "subjective" must be further qualified so that it does not connote anarchic or indomitable will; the *caizi* and *jiaren* are only tactically or "expediently" rebellious. The privilege of superior class combined with superior virtue and innate capability are as conventional as can be and are still central factors in the lovers' match; those who possess such privileges and capacities will have their way.

A more precise label than progressive would be "rational optimism," as in: the world is full of opportunists and schemers who measure others according to benefits to themselves; but villainy can be outwitted and good marriage matches can be had as long as one is talented, good-looking, and virtuous oneself and capable of steadfast devotion to another. The rationalism of these works comprises civility, meaning the proper channeling of passions, and symmetry, the mirrorlike balance of yin and yang. The play of alternating polar effects breaks down the normally over-determined roles of male and female and allows sexual identities to cross over and contain each other. Instead of being sexual, the intercourse of the lovers is verbal, modeled on the polite medium of the written word, through which the youths pass the test of marriage by the time-honored means of establishing one's worth—poetic expression.

In short, the beauty-scholar romance is dedicated to the notion that one man and one woman can achieve perfect symmetry in love fate and actually consummate their love on earth, however little attention is actually given to consummation; for that one must consult the erotic romances. No one is punished for his or her brazenness, as in the late Ming story, or left unrequited, as in *Honglou meng*. The woman and man live to old age and die in short succession, without illness (FHY, chap. 16, 155), proving that theirs is the best way to live.

Appendix: Abbreviations

BGZ: *Baigui zhi*
DQR: *Dingqing ren*
FHC: *Fenghuang chi*
FHY: *Feihua yong*
HQZ: *Haoqiu zhuan*
LEB: *Lin er bao*
PSLY: *Ping Shan Leng Yan*
SHS: *Sai hong si*
WRY: *Wan ru yue*
XFL: *Xing Fengliu*
YJL: *Yu Jiao Li*
YZJ: *Yu zhi ji*
ZCY: *Zhuchun yuan xiaoshi*

Notes

This essay is an abridged version of a chapter in my forthcoming book *Misers, Shrews, and Polygamists,* a study of polygamy, sexuality, and male/female relations in eighteenth-century Chinese fiction, where it precedes a chapter on erotic romances in the Qing. I have benefited from the editorial suggestions of Tani Barlow and two anonymous reviewers.

1. Another sixteenth-century thinker, Lü Kun, also wrote about the talent and independence of the woman (Handlin 1975, 1983, chap. 6).

2. The ideas in this paragraph and numerous paragraphs below were stimulated by the generous comments of Tani Barlow.

3. The reaction against "decadence" begins as early as the 1640s in story collections such as *Zui xing zhi* and *Qingye zhong* (Hanan 1985:189–213). See the preface to *Hua tu yuan,* for example, which criticizes illicit love and calls for love based on true *yuan,* or destiny. See McMahon (1988, chap. 5), on *Haoqiu zhuan* and the reaction against late Ming decadence.

4. This is also found in Li Yu's works (Hanan 1988:95).

5. According to Yao 1987, the terms *caizi* and *jiaren* have been linked since the Tang to refer to three types of love stories: love between a gifted man and a courtesan, love between man and ghost or spirit, and premarital affairs between young men and women from upper-class families.

6. Lin Chen notes that the formulaic plot of the beauty-scholar romance can be found in early Ming literary tales. Ming works such as Xu Wei's *Nüzhuangyuan* and Wu Bing's *Lümudan* supply the *caizi jiaren* story with the themes of the remarkable woman and replacement of passion by wit (Hessney 1979:94–95, 107–9).

7. Lu Xun discusses *Yu Jiao Li*, *Ping Shan Leng Yan*, and *Haoqiu zhuan*. The fullest treatment in English of these romances is Hessney 1979, which discusses *Yu Jiao Li*, *Haoqiu zhuan*, *Ping Shan Leng Yan*, *Hua tu yuan*, and others. Chap. 1 and pp. 29–37 discuss the question of genre. See also Zhou 1990.

8. On *Xing fengliu*, see Lin (1988:214–18). The collection of homoerotic stories *Bian er chai* contains *caizi jiaren*–like characters who are both male (McMahon 1988:73–78).

9. The term appears, for instance, in the infamous late Ming pornographic novel *Langshi qiguan*, chap. 13, 4b, in which it is applied to adulterous lovers just before they begin oral-genital intercourse. The term can also be found, for example, in *Wan ru yue*, 23, 56, 145, the latter occurrence in the title of the final chapter: "The beauties and the scholar unite in grand union"; in *Yanzi jian*, chap. 1, 1b; *Fenghuang chi*, chap. 2, 8b–9a; in the prefaces to *Feihua yong* and *Tiehua xianshi;* and in *Xing fengliu*, chap. 1, 1. In the last two cases the term has a negative connotation: in the former because such stories are considered clichés, in the latter because they are thought to lead to immorality.

10. Liu Tingji puts the erotic romance *Qingmeng tuo* in a list with *Ping Shan Leng Yan*, *Fengliu pei*, *Chunliu ying*, and *Yu Jiao Li*, which he finds inferior but still not to the point of "greatly corrupting public morals" like *Rouputuan*, *Bian er chai*, and numerous others.

11. Liu Tingji also says *jiaren caizi*. See *Honglou meng*, chaps. 1 and 54. Many scholars discuss *Honglou meng*'s reference to *caizi jiaren* fiction (Lin 1988:65–74); Li 1984:79–80; Miao 1984:214–31). *Rulin waishi* does not mention scholar-beauty books, but it makes satirical use of the term "scholar-beauty"; see, for example, chap. 8, 156; chap. 28, 382; and chap. 34, 469.

12. She also appears in drama of the preceding period; see especially the late Ming Xu Wei's *Nüzhuangyuan*, in which the heroine impersonates a man and becomes a *zhuangyuan* (Hessney 1979:94–95). The story of Xiaoqing, the "female talent" (*nücaizi*) of late Ming fame, perhaps had a strong influence on the development of the theme of talented women writers in seventeenth-century fiction, as suggested by Widmer (1992:120).

13. Dressing as a man occurs in many earlier stories, those of Hua Mulan and of the failed lovers Liang Shanbo and Zhu Yingtai, both of the Six Dynasties, being two of the most famous.

14. See the appendix for a list of abbreviations. Because of the difficulty of establishing standard editions for fiction, my convention will be to give title of work, chapter number, then the page number of the edition I used. Providing the

chapter number gives those with different editions a better chance at locating the quotation. See references for details on the editions used; all romances are listed by title, since none have known authors.

15. Hessney (1979:166–69), also discusses geniuses in pairs and the complementarity of their union.

16. Other stories with just an only son/only daughter are ZCY, YZJ, DQR, FHY, XFL, FHC.

17. But such derogatory words may be uttered by other male characters (LEB, chap. 1, 5).

18. In Ling Mengchu's *Pai'an jingqi*, story 34, the man infiltrates a harem; in *Xingshi hengyan*, story 8, the man seduces a young woman. In the Qing, see *Yu Lou Chun* and *Naohua cong*.

19. See Li Yu's *Wusheng xi*, story 6; *Bian er chai*, stories 3 and 4; and the Qing novel *Pinhua baojian*.

20. The evidence that Charlotte Furth gathers on androgynous males in the Ming and Qing parallels this conclusion in that physically androgynous men were also seen as subversive and as having "erotic motivation and moral complicity" (Furth 1988:18).

21. Lin (1988:80), notes this point, especially the women's punctiliousness in demonstrating mutual respect, in the following novels: YJL, *Chun liu ying*, YZJ, LEB, DQR. See WRY, chap. 10, for a lengthy working out of ranking.

22. Its earliest edition is that of 1805.

23. See *Qingmeng tuo*, however, a semierotic romance in which the disguised woman's bound feet do give her trouble (chap. 12). To disguise herself, she wraps cloth around her normal shoes, then puts on socks and men's shoes (4a). In the erotic *Wufeng yin*, the woman stuffs the front of her shoes with foot-wrapping material, then sews her shoes to her socks to keep her feet from slipping out (chap. 12, 7a) In *Fusheng liuji* a biographical account is given of a woman's disguising herself as a man to accompany her husband on an outing. Her feet are a problem, but not an insurmountable one in the contained situation of the episode; see Shen (1980:12); and in English, Shen (1983:44–45).

24. In the *Tanci Zaisheng yuan*, the woman Meng Lijun becomes *zhuangyuan*, then prime minister, and even when discovered to be a woman, she refuses to give up her post.

25. See Hanan (1988:58–62) about a play of Li Yu's in which the man's two wives are lovers themselves.

26. Scholars from Lu Xun onward have written about this "classic." See Lu (1973:246–48); Lin (1988:139–43, 242–44); Zhong (1984:159–73); Chen (1984:174–89); and Hessney (1979).

27. In *Fenghuang chi*, her talent is "ten times better than a man's" (chap. 4, 8b).

28. The same situation occurs in BGZ, chap. 3.

29. Lin Chen and Xiao Xiangkai say that this novel was written after YJL and PSLY (Lin 1988:184–90; Xiao 1987:166–75).

30. The prologue also mentions the erotic *Qingmeng tuo* and *Xiuping yuan,* criticizing both as inferior works.

31. At one point one of the women goes out to make an appeal at court, doing so as herself, not in man's disguise.

32. Lin (1988:238) notes that despite the unclear dating of this book, this kind of indirect communication between moody women could not have been found in the early Qing.

33. See WRY, chap. 14 and following, *Wufeng yin,* chaps. 5, 7, and BGZ, chap. 12. The shrew is central in numerous works of fiction and drama (Wu 1988:363–82).

34. It does not hurt to cite here the statement from the Zhou annals in the *Shiji* to the effect that taking three wives is considered an excess (Sima 1972:140). Also recall that the character *jian,* composed of three woman radicals, means "evil."

35. Widmer suggests that "acceptable sons-in-law [were] hard to come by" and cites an instance of a mother's marrying her two highly accomplished daughters to the same man (Widmer 1989:30).

36. See HQZ, chap. 8, 101; YJL, chap. 5, 62; XFL; chap. 8, 65; and DQR, chap. 6, 49. Also see the discussion of "expediency" in Hessney (1979:194–96).

References

Primary Sources

Since none of the romances have identifiable authors, I give only the titles and omit the pseudonyms. I have included only those titles most central to my analysis. The many other works mentioned in passing are listed in the glossary of Chinese characters in the back of the book.

Baigui zhi. 1985. Shenyang: Chunfeng.
Bian er chai. Microfilm of edition in Palace Museum, Taipei.
Dingqing ren. 1983. Shenyang: Chunfeng.
Feihua yong. 1983. Shenyang: Chunfeng.
Fenghuang chi. Genshu Wu edition in Beijing University Library.
Haoqiu zhuan. 1981. Zhengzhou: Zhongzhou Shuhuashe.
Hua tu yuan. 1983. Shenyang: Chunfeng.
Jin lan fa. Edition in Beijing University Library.
Jinxiang ting. 1984. Shenyang: Chunfeng.
Langshi qiguan. n.d. Zhongguo Guyan Xipin Congkan, no. 5.
Lin er bao. 1983. Shenyang: Chunfeng.
Ping Shan Leng Yan. 1983. Shenyang: Chunfeng.
Qingmeng tuo. Buyue Zhuren Ding edition in Beijing University Library.

Sai hong si. 1983. Shenyang: Chunfeng.
Wan ru yue. 1987. Shenyang: Chunfeng.
Wufeng yin. Fengyin Lou edition in Beijing University Library.
Xing fengliu. 1981. Shenyang: Chunfeng.
Yanzi jian. Edition in Beijing University Library.
Yu Jiao Li. 1981. Shenyang: Chunfeng.
Yu zhi ji. 1983. Shenyang: Chunfeng.
Zhuchun yuan xiaoshi. 1985. Shenyang: Chunfeng. Also in Van Gulik Collection, Princeton University, Gest Oriental Library microfiche.

Secondary Sources

Caizi jiaren xiaoshuo shulin. 1985. *Ming Qing xiaoshuo luncong,* vol. 2. Shenyang: Chunfeng.
Cao Bisong. 1984. Caizi jiaren xiaoshuode jinbu yiyi he xiaoji yiyi. In *Ming Qing xiaoshuo luncong,* 43–48. Shenyang: Chunfeng.
Chen Tiebin. 1984. Lun *Yu Jiao Li.* In *Ming Qing xiaoshuo luncong,* 174–89. Shenyang: Chunfeng.
Cheng Yizhong. 1984. Lue tan caizi jiaren xiaoshuode lishi fazhan." In *Ming Qing xiaoshuo luncong,* 34–42. Shenyang: Chunfeng.
Furth, Charlotte. 1988. Androgynous males and deficient females: Biology and gender boundaries in sixteenth- and seventeenth-century China. *Late Imperial China* 9, no. 2 : 1–31.
Guo Changhe. 1934. Jiaren caizi xiaoshuo yanjiu. *Wenxue Jikan* 1, nos. 1–2 : 194–215, 303–23.
Hanan, Patrick. 1985. The fiction of moral duty: The vernacular story in the 1640s. In *Expressions of self in Chinese literature,* ed. Robert Hegel and Richard Hessney, 189–213. New York: Columbia University Press.
———. 1988. *The invention of Li Yu.* Cambridge: Harvard University Press.
Handlin, Joanna. 1975. Lü K'un's new audience: The influence of women's literacy on seventeenth-century thought. In *Women in Chinese society,* ed. Margery Wolf and Roxanne Witke, 13–38. Stanford: Stanford University Press.
———. 1983. *Action in late Ming thought: The reorientation of Lü K'un and other scholar-officials.* Berkeley and Los Angeles: University of California Press.
Hegel, Robert, and Richard Hessney, eds. 1985. *Expressions of self in Chinese literature.* New York: Columbia University Press.
Hessney, Richard. 1979. Beautiful, talented, and brave: Seventeenth-century scholar-beauty romances. Ph.D. diss., Columbia University.
———. 1985. Beyond beauty and talent: The moral and chivalric self in *The fortunate union.* In *Expressions of Self in Chinese Literature,* ed. Robert Hegel and Richard Hessney, 214–50. New York: Columbia University Press.
Ko, Dorothy. 1992. Pursuing talent and virtue: Education and women's culture in seventeenth- and eighteenth-century China. *Late Imperial China* 13, no. 1 : 9–39.
Li Sai. 1984. Shi lun caizi jiaren pai xiaoshuo. In *Ming Qing xiaoshuo luncong,* 49–83. Shenyang: Chunfeng.

Lin Chen. 1988. *Mingmo Qingchu xiaoshuo shulu*. Shenyang: Chunfeng.

Lin Yutang. 1935. Feminist thought in ancient China. *T'ien Hsia Monthly* 1, no. 2:127–50.

Liu Tingji. 1985. *Zaiyuan Zazhi*. In *Liaohai congshu*, vol. 2. Shenyang: Liaoshen Shushe.

Lu Xun. 1973. *A Brief History of Chinese Fiction*. Trans. Hsien-yi Yang and Gladys Yang. Westport, Conn.: Hyperion Press.

McMahon, Keith. 1988. *Causality and containment in seventeenth-century Chinese fiction*. Leiden: E. J. Brill.

Mann, Susan. 1987. Widows in the kinship, class, and community structures of Qing dynasty China. *Journal of Asian Studies* 46, no. 1:37–56.

Miao Zhuang. 1984. *Honglou meng* yu caizi jiaren xiaoshuo, In *Ming Qing xiaoshuo luncong*, 214–31. Shenyang: Chunfeng.

Ming Qing xiaoshuo luncong. 1984. Vol. 1. Shenyang: Chunfeng.

Robertson, Maureen. 1992. Voicing the feminine: Constructions of the gendered subject in lyric poetry by women of medieval and late imperial China. *Late Imperial China* 13, no. 1:63–110.

Ropp, Paul. 1981. *Dissent in early modern China*. Ann Arbor: University of Michigan Press.

Shen Fu. 1980. *Fusheng liuji*. Beijing: Renmin Venxue Chubanshe.

———. 1983. *Six episodes of a floating life*. Trans. Leonard Pratt and Chiang Su-hui. Harmondsworth, Eng.: Penguin.

Sima Qian. 1972. *Shiji*. Beijing: Zhonghua Shuju.

Widmer, Ellen. 1989. The epistolary world of female talent in seventeenth century China. *Late Imperial China* 10, no. 2:1–43.

———. 1992. Xiaoqing's literary legacy and the place of the woman writer in late imperial China. *Late Imperial China* 13, no. 1:111–55.

Wolf, Margery, and Roxanne Witke, eds. 1975. *Women in Chinese society*. Stanford: Stanford University Press.

Wu Jingzi. 1984. *Rulin waishi*. Shanghai: Guji Chubanshe.

Wu, Yenna. 1988. The inversion of marital hierarchy: Shrewish wives and hen-pecked husbands in seventeenth-century Chinese literature. *JHAS* 48, no. 2: 363–82.

Xiao Xiangkai. 1987. Bie kaile yige shengmiande yibu caizi jiaren xiaoshuo—*Wan ru yue*. Postface to *Wan ru yue*, 166–75. Shenyang: Chunfeng.

Yao, Christina Shu-hwa. 1987. *Cai-zi Jia-ren:* Love drama during the Yuan, Ming, and Qing periods. Ph.D. diss., Stanford University.

Zhang Jun. 1985. Man shuo *Dingqing ren* zhongde qing. In *Caizi jiaren xiaoshuo shulin*, 124–37. Shenyang: Chunfeng.

Zhong Ying. 1984. Ping *Yu Jiao Li*. In *Ming Qing xiaoshuo luncong*, 159–73. Shenyang: Chunfeng.

Zhou Jianyu. 1990. Caizi jiaren xiaoshuo yanjiu. Ph.D. diss., Chinese Academy of Social Sciences, Beijing.

10

Theorizing Woman: *Funü, Guojia, Jiating* (Chinese Woman, Chinese State, Chinese Family)

Tani E. Barlow

> The generic *woman*, like its counterpart, the generic *man*, tends to efface
> difference within itself. . . . Woman as subject can only redefine while
> being defined by language.
>
> Trinh, "Difference"

> What narratives produce the signifiers of the subject for other traditions?
> Spivak, "The Political Economy of Women"

> The cause of the origin of a thing and its eventual utility, its actual em-
> ployment and place in a system of purposes, lie worlds apart.
>
> Nietzsche, *On the Genealogy of Morals*

The theorizing part of my argument revolves around points expressed
in the three aphorisms above. First, in T. Min-ha Trinh's words, "Woman
as subject can only redefine while being defined by language." *Funü* or
"Chinese women," the object of my genealogical attention, is a subject in
Trinh's sense; to this day the politics of *funü* involve "redefinition while
being defined," as I will illustrate. But though language situates and constitutes, it does so within the constraints of canon, text, and tradition.
Gayatri Spivak's "What narratives produce the signifiers of the subject for
other traditions?" compels a situated, historical response. Finally, distilled
in my assertions (that Chinese intellectuals' appropriation of the imperialists' sex binary in their struggle against patrilineally expressed difference
opened the bodies of peasant women to the state's restructuring) is a particular view of history: in Nietzsche's motto, "The cause of the origin of a
thing and its eventual utility, its actual employment and place in a system
of purposes, lie worlds apart" (Nietzsche 1969:76; Minson 1985).

Attention to these three points allows me to argue here that hege-

---

Chinese is not inflected. All nouns are both singular and plural and read according to
the sense of the English syntax.

monic *funü*/women, the principal female subject position available to women under Chinese socialism, took shape in "a system of purposes" that constitutes a genealogy. One kin-inflected category, *funü*/kinswomen, became the tradition against which cultural revolutionaries in the 1920s posed a colonial sign, Woman, that they called *nüxing*. Political *funü*/women, an element of Chinese Communist Party (CCP) *nomenklatura*, contested "Westernized" *nüxing*/Woman, redesignating it "bourgeois," and marked it off as normatively forbidden. The Revolution resituated *funü*/women inside *guojia* (state) and thus by synecdochic logic, inside *jiating* (family) under a Maoist inscription. Modern *funü*/women thus provided a staging ground, offering the sexed bodies of peasant women as a space of modernization.

That is to say, despite their common roots, contemporary official language marks a discontinuity in Chinese women's history. *Funü*/women actually belongs in a discursive constellation not with older female subjects, but with other modern state categories, like worker (*gongren*) and youth (*qingnian*) and proletariat (*wuchanjieji*). Eighteenth- and nineteenth-century *funü*/kinswomen and Maoist *funü*/women are linked tangentially.[1] Only in relation to modern *nüxing*/Woman did the old compound *funü* relinquish its previous connection to female kin and relocate itself as a state category representing all Chinese women rather than merely one's own kin. Since sex-identity politics first entered Chinese political discourse in the May Fourth movement of 1919 and the neologism *nüxing*/Woman emerged as a trope of colonial realist literature, *funü* has been a statist (and under the CCP out of power, a protostatist or what I call "fugitive state") category, with all the prerogatives of a statist subjectivity. It was part of the "system of designations" that until the overthrow of Maoism "regulate[d] all important social relationships" (Billeter 1985:138). Indeed, more than any state category I can think of, *funü*/women and the government bureaucracy that enabled it, the Women's Federation, or Fulian, "construct[ed] the interests it represents" (Laclau and Mouffe 1985:120). Over the course of nearly fifty years, the 1940s to the mid-1980s, Fulian has sustained *funü* and so ensured that gender inscription remained a province of the state.[2]

This critique and the alternative genealogies that follow are rooted in a debt I owe to an earlier generation of innovative scholars: Marilyn B. Young, Phyllis Andors, Margery Wolf, Kay Anne Johnson, Wolfgang Kubin, and Charlotte Beahan. Their historiography assumed a relatively undivided subject of global feminism; it predated, in other words, recent contests over gender theory and postcolonial criticism. Their research made my own thinkable. My debt to them is very great, and so is my gratitude.

Producing Virtuous Mothers and Good Wives

In late imperial Chinese discourses *funü* signified female family members.[3] In his *Jiaonü yigui* (Inherited guide for educating women), the eighteenth-century scholar Chen Hongmou neatly illustrated what I mean.

> When *fu*[a] [persons, sages, women of rank] are in the *jia* [lineage unit] they are *nü* [female, woman, daughter]; when they marry they are *fu*[b] [wives], and when they bear children they are *mu* [mothers]. [If you start with] a *xiannü* [virtuous unmarried female], then you will end up with a *xianfu* [virtuous wife]; if you have virtuous wives, you will end up with *xianmu* [virtuous mothers]. With virtuous mothers there will be virtuous descendants. Civilizing [*wanghua;* literally, transforming through the influence of the monarchy] begins in the women's quarters. Everyone in the *jia* benefits from female chastity. That is why education for women is so important. (Chen, n.d., 1b–2a)

Chen's statement invites analysis because it demonstrates so well why later cultural radicals found colonialist categories worth borrowing and even, perhaps, why the Maoist state's recuperation of *funü* had nativist overtones.

The first point I want to raise involves categories. The citation presents a *fu*[a] who marries a husband, has children, is "her" father's daughter (her in quotation marks because pronouns in Chinese are not inflected for gender). Chen says that the *fu*[a] is a person of rank within the differential kinship sublineage group, *jia*. The point, however, is that the text's very specificity concerning *fu*[a] forecloses a general category of "generic woman," a category that would incorporate *fu*[a] (woman of rank), *nü*, *fu*[b] (wife), *funu* (female kinfolk), *xiannü* and all poor women of no rank. In other words, I could translate the passage as follows: "Before [women] are married they are *nü*/female/daughters, when they get married they are *fu*/wives, and when they give birth to children then they are *mu*/mothers." But to do so would involve substantiating a category of woman, Trinh's "generic woman," that does not appear in the syntax of the sentence.

A lot rests on this reading, because in contemporary standard Chinese *nü* (in its cognates *nüzi, nüren, nüshi,* etc.) is almost always translated as "woman," "female," or "women." Indeed, in Chen Hongmou's own text there appear innumerable instances in which *nü* should indeed be translated as "woman"—usually instances in which *nü* appears in a pair with *nan,* meaning "male," "men," or "man," as part of a parallel or multiple homology of gender domains (Yanagisako 1987:109). Why the binary *nan/nü* is subordinated to other signs is not my concern here. It is pertinent, however, that the syntactical habit I have cited appears throughout Chen's text. It is so prevalent that it forecloses transcendent framing of female persons as generic women.

"Inherited Guides" also does not support a transcendent agent called Woman. The subjects Chen's passage addresses, primarily wives and daughters (*funü*), are "women," of course. But they are women, as I will demonstrate momentarily, because they enact protocols specific to their subject positions. *Funü* acts as a frame of differential *jia* relation, not as a transcendent category. In fact, there exists no moment in Chen's text where "woman" operates as a framing category beyond *jia* or relationality. (That is why I am claiming that the *funü* whose referent is "the masses of Chinese women" has no late imperial antecedent). Another way to phrase this point is that Chen Hongmou assumes no foundational status for Woman. Rather than noting certain kin-specific situations, actions, and responsibilities as instances of "things that women do," Chen explains that acting within the boundaries of ethical-practical kin relations makes a person recognizably female.

Thus differential kin linkages are for Chen the agent that positions people in relation to one another—what makes them who they are and therefore what genders them. Chen Hongmou did not have to provide his readers with charts of quotidian differential positions, since these had long been normalized into the primary categories of personal experience and common sense.[4] Here I want to focus on that older, discursive system. A decade ago Elizabeth Cowie argued, against prevailing wisdom, that rather than theorizing women as women *situated in the family* we ought to grasp that it is "in the family—as the effect of kinship structures—that women as women are produced." Cowie sought to understand "kinship" not as a system of exchange but as a production line for subjectivities. I quite agree. Part of my reason for invoking Cowie is to ratify the notion that kinship nomenclature is productive discourse that constructs by virtue of its effects. But just as significant was Cowie's conclusion that "the sign 'woman' in exogamy is not exchanged but produced in the exchange of actual women" (Cowie 1978:61–62).

Cowie showed how the forces in anthropological discourse that produced Lévi-Strauss as a theorist of kinship had also appropriated adjacent theories about language, and had introjected these into sexist notions like the belief that Woman and Man consist of different, unequal substances. Her insight helps me argue that *the exchange of actual women in patrilineal, patrilocal Chinese kinship produced not the sign "woman," but a profusion of signs with one thing in common: though they all accommodated "real" women, none could be reduced to a prediscursive category Woman.* The process of exchange of women in the late imperial Han Chinese contexts was a social discourse for the production of persons. By its very syntax and inscription, it provided multiple subject positions and diverse, complex protocols of practice. But it did not produce Woman as a hegemonic sign.[5]

Under these conditions, gendering in Chen Hongmou's world proceeded as a cosmological activity whereby differential relations on the analogy of yin/yang established and positioned subjects normatively on the primary sites of the *jia*, in constantly reinscribed taxonomies that included protocols of (gender and positionally appropriate) behavior.[6] Chen Hongmou's texts do not refer to women's bodies. They do not designate as women those persons whose bodies exhibit specific markings, like bound feet or large breasts (Carter 1980). Other contemporary texts also seem relatively uninterested in conflating gender and body (McMahon, this volume). Particular cosmological ordering made engendering one of many activities that contributed to the coherence of human culture.[7]

I want to reinforce one last point about gendering, and to do so I cite Judith Butler (1990:111):

> Gender is not a culture as sex is to nature [nor is sex] prior to culture, a politically neutral surface on which culture acts. . . . Simone de Beauvoir wrote in *The Second Sex* that "one is not born a woman, but rather *becomes* one." The phrase is odd, even nonsensical, for how can one become a woman if one wasn't a woman all along? And who is this "one" who does the becoming? Is there some human who becomes its gender at some point in time? How does one "become" a gender? What is the moment or mechanism of gender construction? And, perhaps most pertinently, when does this mechanism arrive on the cultural scene to transform the human subject into a gendered subject?

I use Butler's point to suggest that as gender is to culture, so sex is to culture. Cultural codes and discursive traditions turn out genders, which have in common the fact that they possess different foundations. It becomes clear why I might argue that *all* formations of "woman," not just *funü* and *nüxing*, possess multiple, complex genealogies. Because the instability of gendering is historically so pronounced, it makes as little sense to conflate women and bodies in old China as it would to do so in pre-Enlightenment Christianity (Castelli 1991). Indeed, historically bodies are as easily the ground of similarities between women and men as they are the first ground of their difference (Flax 1990:51). Since Chen Hongmou's texts do not refer to women's bodies or designate as women those whose bodies exhibit specific markings, and since other contemporary texts also tend not to conflate gender with body, I have turned elsewhere for the apparatus of gendering.

When I name the processes of gendering in Chen Hongmou's world social cosmology enacted primarily on the (never stable or fully bounded) site of the *jia*, I am rendering into my own language the point the late sixteenth-century physician Li Shichen made in his *Materia Medica*. "Normally *qian* and *kun* make fathers and mothers; but there are five kinds of non-males [*feinan*] who cannot become fathers and five kinds of non-females [*feinü*] who cannot become mothers" (Furth 1988).[8] *Qian* and *kun* are the first and last hexagrams of the *Ijing*, or *Book of Change*, the foundational text of Confucian studies since the Song dynasty (Smith et al. 1990). *Qian* and *kun* refer to forces operating in *tiandi*, the realms extrinsic to human culture, as well as the realm of *wen*, human social life.

The forces of yin and yang are many things: logical relationships (like up and down, in and out, husband and wife), practical forces, "designations for the polar aspects of effects," and in a social sense, powers that inscribe hierarchy (i.e., yang subordinates yin because it encloses the lesser force into itself), but yin/yang is neither as totalistic nor as ontologically binary as the Western stereotype would have it (Porkert 1985:13). What Li Shichen says, then, is that the dynamic forces of yin/yang do "produce"—only not anatomical women and men, but father subject positions or hierarchical, relational, subjectivities named mother and father, husband and wife, brother and sister, and so on.

Li understood yin/mother and yang/father (or yin/wife and yang/husband, yin/junior brother and yang/senior brother and so on) as agencies by which cosmic order established itself.[9] "Father/mother" is a differential relation, structured on the analogy of yin/yang, possessing temporality that exceeds that of the bodies of the specific person answering to the name "father" or "mother" at any given moment. Yin/yang does not produce women and men. It produces mothers and fathers, wives and husbands—capable, in turn, given fertile human material (aided by medical practitioners, if necessary) of (re)producing sons and daughters.

The anomaly confronting the physician, the problem that has forestalled cosmological production of "father" and "mother," in the cases Li cites, is derived from a general instability of bodies in most Confucian discourse. Here the nonman and the nonwoman, whose defective bodies forestall reproduction, as well as the castrated, the impotent, the vaginally impenetrable, and bodies known to change from female to male and from male to female, all present to the physician surfaces that are neither stable nor automatically "gendered." For Li Shichen's and Chen Hongmou's time, Simone de Beauvoir's peculiar notion that "women are not women but become women" makes sense. Why? Because the surfaces onto which eighteenth-century Chinese subjectivities were inscribed (Li Shichen's fecund organ system) were more flexible than the (gendering) subject positions that producing sons and daughters actually enabled women to occupy and possess.

The instance cited could be joined by myriad others. Gendering proceeded in late imperial China not at the level of one but in multiple discourses beyond my present scope—many, like *I* commentary, not directly addressing immediate persons, yet others appropriating "female" for subversive purposes. Its processes changed under different social and discursive conditions, and it produced bodily effects—the bound foot, for instance—marking the body as feminine.[10] But at no time was gender ever "a property of bodies or something originally existent in human beings"; it was always "the set of effects produced in bodies, behaviors, and social relations" through deployment of "complex political technolog[ies]."[11]

What appear as "gender" are yin/yang differentiated positions: not two anatomical "sexes," but a profusion of relational, bound, unequal dyads, each signifying difference and positioning difference and analogically. A *nü* is a daughter, unequally related to parents and parents-in-law. A *xiaozi,* or filial son, is differentially unequal to mother and father, yin to their yang. A *fu*[b] is a wife, tied in a secondary relation to her husband. A *xianfu* is a wife who, grasping the powers visited upon the secondary yin term, masters through familiarity with protocol (Porkert 1985:22–23). Obviously (invoking Cowie's point), subjects got produced within the *jia* (more properly *jia*-ist or familial discourses). Chen Hongmou's definition of *nü, fu*[b], and *mu* makes it clear that while (good) women in the *jia* did effect social relations outside the family, no position existed for female persons (or male persons, for that matter) outside the *jia*'s boundaries.

The *fu*ᵃ exists within the kin world of reciprocal inequality by virtue of her father's high standing.¹²

Chen Hongmou sought to educate women in order to produce more *xiannu* or virtuous women and thereby to enhance the *jia*—that is all. Learning to act virtuously is coterminous with acting "like a woman" in Chen Hongmou's view, and "acting like a woman" required maintaining difference. "[Just as] the yin and the yang are different natures [*shuxing*], so males and females [*nan/nü*] should act differently," as Chen's text puts it. In the view of Lu Jingxi, Chen Hongmou's own authority, "there is a difference between the *li* [ritual] of men and women [*nan/nü*]. If you do not maintain the distinction, then you will cause gossip" (Chen, n.d., 15). *Li*—behaviors, rituals, or normative manners—were what, for the most part, protocol consisted of; they provided guidance for appropriate, proper, good, and efficacious self-presentation. Prescribed, normative be-havior and gendered experience were inextricable (Chen, n.d., 9b). When the daughters act on the *li* of daughterhood, married women act on the *li* of wives, and so on, then the distinction between men and women is ac-complished and gendering is effected.¹³

Lest the reader get the wrong impression, these protocols took virtu-ally everything into consideration. "As a kinswoman [*nüzi*], you must es-tablish yourself in life [*lishen*]," one reads, for instance. "In behavior don't turn your head from side to side; if you wish to speak do so without moving your lips; if you wish to sit, do so without moving your knees, and if you stand do not wiggle your skirt. If you are happy do not giggle, if you are unhappy, do not yell aloud. Inside and outside [*nei/wai*] [the *jia*] women and men [*nan/nü*] should be separate" (Chen, n.d., 6b). Chen Hongmou cited reams of text from ancient times describing in minute detail the *lishu* (body etiquette) he felt would allow people in the present, through their physical actions, to resurrect the splendid world of the Con-fucian past.

These texts produced "gender" relationally by linking good behavior to correct enactment of written protocols that inscribe kin difference. "The father-in-law [*aweng*] and mother-in-law [*agu*] are the heads of the husband's family," a typical specimen reads. "You are their daughter-in-law when you marry your husband, so you must support them as you supported your own parents." What that requires is service of a specific order enumerated in concrete detail: serve parents only when properly dressed, listen attentively while remaining in a standing posture, prepare their wash water and towels in the morning, premasticate their food, prepare their bedding, and avoid disorder, criticism, or neglecting their comfort.

This is precisely what I am calling protocol.[14] It is neither a mere code, nor a map, nor a "role." It rests on a shifting foundation, the cosmic activity of yin/yang, yet it provides advice and counsel on achieving naturalized, normative, gendered relational subjects. Protocols instruct. They provide a continuity and reinforce subject positions by linking the archaic past in which these protocols were first established to contemporary texts. They stand as a bulwark of order against the undoing of gender distinction that Daoist practices threatened.[15] A protocol models in a bare-bones narrative fashion.

By the nineteenth century these protocols, or what Gary Hamilton calls "codification[s] of the roles of family members," had become completely embedded in a wider system of abstract allegiances, "loyalty to [the monarchy's] symbols and philosophic principles" (1984:417–18). I substitute "protocol" for Hamilton's "role," since the latter suggests an ontological status, but overall I think Hamilton is correct. His insight is particularly valuable in that it points to the power of narrativity. If kinship, or differential positionality, became metaphor (or strategy), if protocols stood for subjectivities that were rooted in the old textual heritage, then change required, among other things, strategic reinvention and retelling of protocol and stories (Lauretis 1984:106). Such indeed did occur, as I will argue shortly.[16]

Producing *Nüxing*/Woman

Under Western imperialism efforts began to retheorize the figures (*fu*[b], *nü, funü, mu,* and so on) populating texts like Chen Hongmou's. The Manchu dynasty's long, slow implosion and the imperialists' relentless penetration of the heartland via "treaty ports" transformed the political elite's social configuration and powers. The "high centre" of kingship, in Benedict Anderson's beautiful phrase, receded, and sacral legitimacy was at its end (Anderson 1983:25). Whereas texts coded with meaning and associated with the monarchy had enabled Confucian officials to regulate the meaningful world, gargantuan pressures dispersed the older stacked powers; they collapsed in 1905 when the Qing throne abolished the civil service examination system. Where once a Chen Hongmou could hegemonize Confucian textual production of gender, there emerged a modern, post-Confucian, professionalized intellectual who oversaw the transcription of foreign signs into the new domestic, urban, mass market, mechanized print economy—an "intellectual" who signaled a shift from the widely diffused textuality of the old society to the scriptural economy of realist representation in a modern peripheralized world economy.

In the early twentieth century a new social formation arose calling itself *zhishi jieji*, or intellectual class, later to become *qiming xuezhe* (enlightened scholars), and finally, under the same forces that produced *funu*/women as a political category, *zhishifenzi*, or Chinese intellectual under Maoist inscription (Certeau 1984). *Zhishifenzi* were the educated element of the tiny, exceedingly significant new commercial bourgeoisie that monopolized the appropriation of Western ideas, forms, signs, and discourses (Bergere 1990). In their hands, peripheralization of signs proceeded as new missionary-educated and college-graduate professionals imported, translated, republished, and commented on texts in foreign languages (Barlow 1990). Historically this group constituted itself as a colonialized elite, meaning two things: that the imperialist semicolonization of China forced into existence "new intellectuals," and that these elements did not just passively import neologisms from Japan and the European West, but actively redrew the discursive boundaries of elite social existence. In this way the *zhishifenzi* occupied (thereby further valorizing) new, modernist social fields like *shehui*, or "society" (Woodside 1976:54). Situated inside the treaty ports in a crude material sense—the Palladian English banks, French boulevards, German beer, American YMCAs, and Japanese factories—neologisms like *shehui* acquired increasingly concrete referents. The powerful older terms *guan* (official), *gong* (public), and *si* (private) from Chen Hongmou's time increasingly gave ground. Once-robust conventions were reduced to something intellectuals of the 1920s would call "tradition" (*chuantong*) and would regard either with painful nostalgia or with contempt and fear.

A larger project would require far more comment on colonialist discourse among the treaty-port *zhishifenzi*. Here let it suffice that the discourses of semicolonialism had an effect on older Chinese gendering practices at many levels. A rash of masculinist interest in the universal sign of woman had surfaced as early as the 1830s, when there occurred what Mary Rankin (1975) calls an efflorescence of "pro-feminine" male writing. Male reformers in the 1860s spoke admiringly of "enlightened" relations between women and men in Western countries. Anti-foot-binding and pro-female academy arguments held key positions in the late 1890s and first decade of the twentieth century, in the work of major male new-style intellectuals.

Indeed, masculinist recycling of *nü* initiated, according to the Charlotte Beahan (1975a), an unprecedented female journalism within the slackening Confucian discourses between 1890 and 1910. Calling themselves sisters (*jiemei*), female writers reversed the strategy Chen Hongmou had adopted when he argued for female literacy on the grounds that ethical women in families produced strong states. "Why isn't China strong?" one asked. "Because there are no persons of talent. Why are there no persons of talent? Because women do not prosper."[17] Late Confucian women, as Beahan carefully points out, sought liberty on nationalist grounds. The sisters' publications contributed part of what emerged rapidly as a "myth of the nation" (Brennan 1990:44). That is to say, writers positioned themselves as citizens of the Chinese nation, as advocates of national emancipation from Western imperialism and Manchu occupation, and as constitutionally different from men of their own Han Chinese nationalist group.[18] On those unimpeachable grounds they sought to mobilize China's "beloved but weak two hundred million women . . . the direct slaves of slaves" (Beahan 1975a:384).

The expression "slaves of slaves" as a term for Chinese women signified a change in the theorization of *nü*. "Slave" referred to Han Chinese males "enslaved" to the Manchu monarchy and thus signaled democratic patriotism. "Slaves of slaves" recategorize all Chinese women into a patriotic unity against the myriad imperialists seeking to "divide China up as though it were a melon," as people put it then. The kin-inflected category of *funü* began the referential shift. Writers made Chinese *nüren* (female person) one specific instance of a universal category consisting of all women, and they did it under a patriotic inscription.

An example of the mechanics of the referential shift comes from Zhen Ziyang's *Nüzi xin duben* (New study book for women), a collection of stories about virtuous women linked generically to narratives in the Chen Hongmou book I cited earlier. The older text celebrated "just mothers," "ethical stepmothers," and other situated kinswomen who had managed the *jia* sphere well, thereby affecting, through their adept use of protocol in difficult circumstances, the space beyond their own *jia*—the *gong* or general world. Indeed, Chen Hongmou's use of narratives of contradiction applauded the discipline and far-sighted judgment required of "good" kinswomen. The modernist text, in contrast, provided not one but two sets of ethical narratives about good women, set off from each other in two separate books (Zhen 1907). Book 1 retold stories familiar to readers even before Chen Hongmou's time, such as the story of Mencius's mother, who sacrificed to provide her son an appropriate ethical environment, Yue Fei's wife Liang, who personally fought the Nuzhen barbarians on behalf of the Song dynasty, and Hua Mulan of the Liang dynasty, who masqueraded as a filial son and fought as her father's proxy for twelve years. It also included examples of women who had, in the hoary past, transgressed unfairly gendered boundaries or had been ignored in masculinist histories. Huang Zongjia, for instance, "was born a girl but did not want to be a woman/*nüzi*," so she masqueraded as a man and served as an official; Suo Maoyi taught the master calligrapher Wang Xizi his calligraphic style; and so on.

Book 2 assembled a set of parallel stories about famous women of the West who matched or exceeded Hua Mulan's filial devotion because they served not father, husband, or patriline but the nation. "Sha Latuo" or Charlotte Corday, according to this version of the story, studied at a nunnery for six years and became engrossed in a particular book about national heroes (I cannot figure out who the author "Puluhua" might have been in a European language). The book's inspiration sent Sha Latuo to Paris, where she surprised the tyrant Mala (Marat) while he was with his concubine. In prison for his murder, she sent her father a filial letter declaring that tyrannicide was not a crime, and she met her death with "Puluhua's" book clutched in her hands. Another narrative venerated Madame Roland, who studied "the Confucianism of her country" but preferred the example of the Greeks and Romans. After marrying Roland for his politics, she inspired her timid husband to resist Robespierre's "People's Party" (*mindang*). When Robespierre executed Madame Roland, her husband committed suicide and their servants, overcome, also petitioned for execution. Their requests were carried out! (Zhen 1907, 2.10:7b–9a).[19]

The juxtaposition of "Chinese" and "other" stories engendered meaning in two significant ways. First, obviously the reworked "Chinese" stories and the "Western" parallels jointly showed female heroes shifting their loyalties from husband or father to "nation," without directly requiring that they abandon the prior object. A certain "Frances" (Frances Willard, perhaps) appears to have been selected because, following her father's death, she remained unmarried and devoted herself to the improvement of North America through a renovation of the family, the nation, and finally the entire world. Nation rose up to peripheralize father, without necessarily precluding his importance (Zhen 1907, 13:10a–12a).

Second, the bilateral mutual exchange of "Western" signs and "Chinese" narrative had the effect of producing a category of universal womanhood. ("Chinese" narratives changed in a generic sense when the subjects of their interest became "Western" women.) When Zhen situated Chinese female heroes in the company of European women of the state like Joan of Arc, Charlotte Corday, and Madame Roland, the effect was to legitimate and universalize *nüzi* within a statist, universal (i.e., Europeanized) world history. Zhen sought to conjoin bourgeois state revolutions like the Glorious Revolution, the French and Italian revolutions, to the expected Chinese revolution (the Xinhai Revolution occurred a few years later, in 1911). Giving such remarkable prominence to Western women in their national revolutions, moreover, also granted universality to heroic female actions of whatever kind, at whatever time. Remarkably, the "Chinese" section of the text went so far as to legitimate Wu Zetian of the Tang dynasty, a woman previously reviled as a female usurper and defiler of her husband's throne. Before the 1920s, though, female heroes rested securely in the inherited binary division familiar from Confucian contexts of the filial hero and the just throne.

The term *nüxing* (literally, female sex) entered circulation during the 1920s when treaty-port intellectuals overthrew the literary language of the Confucian canon. Critics replaced the *wen* (culture) of the old world with *wenxue* (literature), inscribed in a hybrid literary language (part colloquial Chinese, part "European" syntax garnered from reading Western fiction in Chinese translation; Huters 1984, 1988). *Wenxue* consisted of an appropriated realist representationalism, an insight that has produced a good deal of focus on the production of modernist subjectivities (Anderson 1990). The field of *wenxue* unfolded in the 1920s as a general terrain of combat for intellectuals. The May Fourth movement of 1919 established *wenxue* as primarily governed by realist referentiality: the second most significant major figure within that new textuality, after the "hypertrophied self" (Huters 1984) of the writer, of course, was the figure of *nüxing*.

Nüxing was not a self-reference. It was not initially an "identity" for women at all. Like the recuperation of *nü* as a trope of nationalist universality in masculinist discourses, *nüxing* was a discursive sign and a subject position in the larger, masculinist frame of anti-Confucian discourse. When intellectuals overthrew the Confucian canon they sought the total transformation of "Chinese culture." The same modernist revolution that invoked new, modern signs like society (*shehui*), culture (*wenhua*), intellectuals (*zhishifenzi*), individualism (*geren zhuyi*), and innumerable other modern Chinese neologisms gave *nüxing* or "Woman" wide discursive powers. *Nüxing* played a particularly significant role in two separate textual streams, literary representation and the body of the writing known as Chinese feminism. Historically speaking, women writers did not predominate in either one.

"Historical languages constitute classes," as Talal Asad has argued; "they do not merely justify groups already in place according to universal economic structures" (1987:606). *Nüxing* coalesced into a category in Asad's sense when, as part of the project of social class formation, Chinese moderns disavowed their older literary language of power. After the May Fourth movement of 1919, Chinese writers wrote in a newly modernized, Westernized, semicolloquial language in which *nüxing* played the part of a subject of representation and an autonomous agent. *Nüxing* was one half of the Western, exclusionary, essentialized, male/female binary. Within the *zhishifenzi* as a class, the sign of the sex binary had enormous utility. *Nüxing* (and to a lesser extent its correlate *nanxing*, male sex) was magnetic, attracting around its universal, sexological, scientistic core a psychologized personal subject position that made it the fulcrum for up-ending Confucianism and all received categories. Chinese translations of European fiction and social theory also relocated agency in the individual at the level of sex opposition and sex attraction. In particular, colloquial fiction made sex the core of an oppositional personal identity and Woman a sexological category.[20]

The career of *nüxing* firmly established a foundational womanhood beyond kin categories. It did so on the ground of European humanism. That is, when it introduced the category "Woman" (*nüxing*), Chinese feminist writing also flooded texts with representations of women who were the "playthings of men," "parasites," "slaves," and so on—dependents of men or simply degraded to the point of nonexistence. Feminist texts accorded a foundational status to physiology and, using monolithic forms of Victorian ideology from nineteenth-century Europe, they grounded sexual identity in sexual physiology. Indeed, the most shocking of all Chinese feminism's arguments substituted sexual desire for reproductive service to *jia* as the foundation of human identity. The secret attraction of European texts was their emphasis on what Foucault has called "sexuality" and has excavated as though it were any other historical artifact (Foucault 1979; Weeks 1986). Yet when the leading male feminist Yeh Shengtao spoke of women, even while he granted foundational status to male/female, it was often in terms of Chinese women's lack of personality or human essence. In other words, when Chinese translators invoked the sex binary of a Charles Darwin they valorized notions of female passivity, biological inferiority, intellectual inability, organic sexuality, and social absence through reference to the location of these "truths" in European social scientism and social theory. Thus Chinese women became *nüxing* Woman only when they became the other of man in the Victorian binary. *Nüxing* was foundational when she became *nanxing*'s (man's) other.

Ching-ku Stephen Chan's recent exploration of *nüxing* in the literature of major male May Fourth realist writers makes this point at the level of the high literary text. When the *zhishifenzi* turned to European-style realism, Chan argues, "the classical mimetic function of realism" required that the writer represent himself through his own representations of the other, and the other of male realist choice was Woman. *Nüxing* was first and foremost a trope in the discourses of masculinist, Europeanist, Chinese realist fiction. As Chan puts it, "Textually speaking, where is *she* to be found?" *Nüxing* appears in a literal, representational sense, "but [always] as an innocent scapegoat, paying for the crimes that society has committed day after day, generation after generation." Semicolonial Woman made her appearance in a cruel equation that held that "the root of *your* [female] suffering is to be found in *my* [male writer's] inability to right the wrongs that society has done *me*" (Chan 1988 : 26–27).

Chan's point can also be made in a slightly different way. When the modernist female writer Ding Ling began producing texts in the late 1920s, she too had to struggle with the self/other oppositional dynamic coded into the sexual equation of Man/Woman. Ding Ling's texts sought to make Woman a subject position and they read like explications of modern Chinese woman's social psychology. Yet the texts Ding Ling produced during that period of her career invoke a *nüxing* who must either die, commit suicide, or lose herself in a sexual excess, and mental disorder. No positivity, no universal woman independent of man could exist under the terms of the recoded Victorian sex binary. In the end Ding Ling, who continued to write, but not as a woman, simply abandoned psychological realism (Barlow 1982).

The social history of the trope *nüxing* requires more space than I am allotted here. Once it entered elite *zhishifenzi* discourses, *nüxing* the representation took on a life of its own. Her image appeared in popular movies and pulp fiction, in photographs and fashion magazines and strolled the schools, boulevards, and parks. These indigenous representations of *nüxing* constructed a universal category Woman in the image of an object of consumption, to paraphrase Annette Kuhn, and *nüxing* eventually "enter[ed] cultural and economic circulation on [its] own accord" (Kuhn 1985:19, cited in Hutcheon 1989:22). She ceased to be a "Western" sign and became instead a sign of Westernization. *Nüxing* was never a disfigured or unsuccessful replication of Victorian woman; she was always a recoding of modernist discourse on the sexual construction of gender, situated in a semicolonial contest. Once recontextualized, the sign *nüxing*/Woman, had a career and politics of its own. In this respect Nietzsche's point that "the cause of the origin of a thing and its eventual utility, its actual employment and place in a system of purposes, lie worlds apart" is, historically speaking, literally correct (1969:66).

Producing *Funü*/Women

The sex-binary of Man/Woman and the sign *nüxing*/Woman never went uncontested. Carolyn Brown has vividly shown Lu Xun criticizing the formulation and arguing that the physical body of modern Chinese women "had become the repository of a meaning—the signified, that it did not rightfully bear" (1988:68). Social criticism from Chinese Communist Party theorist Xiang Jingyu, who employed *funü*/women as a figure in Marxist writing on women, contested the cultural world's pervasive irrationalization of *nüxing* (Leith 1973:50–51, 61). Xiang lost no time classifying *nüxing* as a product of bourgeois women's preoccupations, and her comments in the early 1920s set the tone for Communist theorizing for decades. Nonetheless, Xiang's early Communist *funü* had entered modern Chinese discourse the same way as sex-opposed *nüxing* had, through *zhishifenzi* appropriation. In the process of transmitting social theory, Communists retranslated out of the European revolutionary heritage a Woman they called *funü* to distinguish it from the febrile *nüxing*. The bourgeois social sciences, political rights theory, and nineteenth-century patriarchal theory that left-wing *zhishifenzi* found so valuable also shared elements of the sex essentialism manifest in contemporary realist fiction. But appropriators shaped their critique to emphasize social production, thus weighing historical and institutional teleology over organic, biogenetic time.[21] Moreover, the *funü*/woman of early Chinese Marxist thought was always insufficient because the all-encompassing revolutionary equation, theory and praxis, held that she would come into her own only in the future when the proletariat gained the ascendency. Unlike *nüx-*

ing, Marxist *funü* was the product of revolutionary practice and existed in a future world, after the revolution.

The Chinese translation of August Bebel's *Women and Socialism* established *funü* in its political usage (Beibeier 1949). The translation's chiliastic tone and systematic use of *funü* as the figure par excellence of general social revolution relied on a conjuncture of woman and society that had attracted Chinese Marxists from the start. Joining it later in CCP theory were Engels's "Origins of Family, Private Property and the State,"[22] Lenin's "The Soviet Political Power and Women's Status," "International Women's Day," and "On the Freedom to Love," and Stalin's "International Women's Day."[23] *Nüxing* had taken over the foundational sex binary Man/Woman from Victorian literary texts and feminist theory in translation. The Communist inscription of *funü* engaged other discourses, most obviously Euro-Marxist notions of production/reproduction, teleology, stage theory, state/society binarism, and of course woman's universal, international referentiality.

Chinese Marxist discourses on *funü* clarify how thoroughly the history of women in China had become, by the early 1950s, a subsidiary of the history of the European working class. Du Zhunhui's 1949 *Funü wenti jianghua* (Lectures on the woman problem) exemplifies how, when Europe gets placed at the hegemonic center of "universal" theories of capital, Chinese history is inevitably reduced to being a subsidiary, local growth, possessing historical significance only as a semicolony of Europe, following a two-thousand-year dark night of "feudalism." Du's sophisticated historical critique insists that *funü* forms a social category (*fanchou*). Still, the final chapters find her berating the Chinese women's movement for its failures, using as her measure the "universal" European women's movement (Du 1949).[24]

State building supplanted bourgeois consolidation in both "white" and Communist camps as the Japanese advanced in the late 1930s. Socialist *funü* obviated *nüxing* once the Right allowed the discourses of national salvation (*jiuguo*) to become the special preserve of the Left. The reactionary Right rescinded its pallid remaining feminist-rights arguments and dissolved the women's movement into a "feminine mystique" (Diamond 1975; Croll 1978; Kruks, Rapp, and Young 1989). Socialist mobilization politics targeted *funü* as a tactical object and eventually made her a triangulating category mediating between modern state and modern Chinese family. But in the provinces during the late twenties and thirties an increasingly Maoist CCP began grafting local practices onto its international Marxist teleology of women in the discourse of social production/reproduction.

§

"Keep in mind," said a 1932 activists' organizing manual for Party cadres doing women's work under the auspices of the Jiangxi Soviet, "what world revolutionary leader Lenin said [to the effect that] 'socialism cannot succeed without the participation of women.' At the same time we ought to keep in mind *that the Liberation of Chinese women and the victory of Soviet state power are inseparable* (my emphasis; JF 1932, 3.2.2: 53–54).[25] The Communist Party's fugitive state project ("fugitive" in the sense that between 1930 and 1940 each state apparatus the CCP established decamped under pressure) made the *funü* of Chinese Marxism into a category of political praxis. In so doing it reversed and canceled the earlier relationship of theory and practice.

Not only did the "universal" woman of Euro-Marxism, an agent in the "universal" history of capital, relinquish her theoretical centrality to the women of practical village mobilizations, but Chinese Communist practices canceled out the existence of that older European woman so that she simply vanished. The peripheralized sign of woman realized its own independent local politics, to put it another way. Context revised text. The Jiangxi Soviet (1930–34) described *funü* as a political subject who was over fourteen years of age; had been emancipated from the *tongyangxi* (infant brides by purchase), prostitution, and female slave systems; had recourse from family violence; did not bear the bodily marks of "feudalism" (no earrings or foot-binding); called herself *funü;* and took part in liberating political praxis (JF 1932, 3.2.2:21).

This subject existed within a structured sphere of politics beyond the rural calendar of field work and beyond village social relations. She labored according to schedule (JF 1931, 11, item 1–7:38) and according to protective laws (JF 1931, 12:231). A rudimentary bureaucracy concerned itself with her welfare (JF 1932, 2, 1:46) and ensured her freedom of marriage.[26] Political networks, such as the Working Women's Congress (JF 1932, 2.1:43), operated to rationalize her political outlook (JF 1932, 1.2:44–45).[27] The symbolic center of this woman as a subject was undoubtedly the effort to propagandize "Women's Day."[28]

Discourses of woman under the fugitive state had a proto–mass line function that allowed activists, the Party Central Committee, and local women to speak in different voices and that opened a large range of positions to local people.[29] These subject positions included *qingfu* (young women), *nücdai de tongyangxi* (oppressed wives by virtue of infant bride sale), *da pinku laodong funü* (the large suffering masses of laboring women), *nongcun zhong di laodong funü* (laboring women of the rural villages), and *nügong nongfu* (women workers and peasants). Even the heterogeneous *funü* of this period, however, was always a subject-effect of state discourses and a by-product of its legal, ideological, and organizational apparatus. It is just that before 1949 the mass line did not attempt political closure. *Funü* appeared in the form of a range of subject positions residing in the Soviet state, beyond the reach of family and feudalism. As one document put it, village women do not understand the agitation for liberation and need to have explained to them the link between victory in class struggle and the liberation of women. They must be taught that their self-interest is concerned to the state and not the family (JF 1932, 6:20).

The ideological ideal was a healthy, semiliterate woman of eighteen to thirty-five who could "destroy her familist outlook and serve [the state even when called upon to make] government transfers" (JF 1933, 8.31:104). She was expected to act out of self-interest (*benshen liyi*) for her personal rights (*quanli*), "representing" herself through grass-roots mass organizational work (JF 1933, 3.14 87).[30] The *funü* encountered in these texts appeared never to have understood what was meant by "women's self-interest" until propagandists explained the stakes in concrete detail.[31] The natural interests women theoretically possessed, in other words, had first to be inscribed via the actions of recruiting, educating, nurturing, and mobilizing. *Funü*'s proper field was "the organizational sphere of the party [*dang di zuzhi fanwei*]," where she sustained herself in the political space of the CCP through election (*xuanzhi*), mobilization (*dongyuan*), and various organization (*zuzhi*) practices (JF 1933, 3.28:89).

Maoism in the late thirties and forties constantly reformulated *funü*, always retaining the statist slant (Stranahan 1981, 1983). The formula that emerged in the early 1940s consequently involved a synecdochic process of exchange between two interpenetrating objects of political discourse, the state (*guojia*) and the family (*jiating*) (Lu Fu 1949). Rather than posit independent *funü* as an agent of politics outside the domestic closure, as the brief earlier experiments had done, later Soviet practices emphasized production of *funü* through political processes that retained women and men in a sphere of politicized domestic relations.

After 1943 the CCP turned to transformation of the family itself. By

1947 Maoist state policy had shifted—in contradistinction to Marxist theory and socialist practices elsewhere—toward a strategically reinvented family that appears in these texts as *jiating*. The homily of the Zhu Fusheng family conference, for instance, treated the history of domestic politics as a party historiographer might chronicle a Central Committee meeting. The women of the Zhu family, though oppressed, did not have the habit of democracy; they did not know how to speak, ask questions, or actually say a thing. After Zhu Fusheng explained democratic procedure to them, they collectively transformed themselves from an autocracy (*jiazhang zhuanzhi*) into a democratic family (*minzhu jiating*). In the subsequent months family members instituted political-democratic policies such as self-criticism (*ziwo piping*), domestic production of thread and cloth, and scheduled planning, all activities related to the kinds of domestic production the CCP was promoting at the time. The homily of the Zhu family shows very economically how the state's political practices interpenetrated family relations, lodging *funü* through democratic rhetoric within a renovated statist *jiating* or nucleating family (Lu Fu 1949).

The recuperation required that the politicized new family reconstitute itself in the language of politics. Leading party officials promoted domestic political construction, as Zhou Enlai did, for instance, when he argued that women did not really need emancipation from family so much as men needed to take family responsibilities as seriously as women did. Not just mothers, but fathers too had a substantial political obligation to be the best parents possible (Zhou 1942). As Patricia Stranahan has argued, it was precisely this reorientation of woman policy that provided the stable base peasant women eagerly accepted; the resulting line both reflected peasant common sense and achieved revolutionary transformation through social production.[32] The resulting collaboration of village women and the Central Committee was, I want to stress, neither "traditional" nor "Marxist" in a simple, universalist sense. It was syncretic and as modern as any other practical Marxism.[33]

The newly minted Maoist family formation that rested on this interpenetration of state and family made the body of a woman a realm of the state at the same time as it opened the state to inflection by kin discourses and kin categories (Fulian, n.d., 7–11). The entry point was reproductive science. Woman-work *ganbu* (cadres; particularly nurses, who were known as "Nightingales" in honor of Florence Nightingale) brought to political activity the powerful new scientific knowledge of sanitation, physiology, and scientific midwifery. Texts drilled village women in reproductive physiology ("it's just like your farm animals") and dispensed information on bodily functions like the menstrual cycle and hygiene (don't borrow pads, don't drink cold water, stay away from dirty menstrual blood, which carries diseases, don't have intercourse during your period, visit the doctor for irregularities, etc.) (Lu Fu 1949:74–77). Scientific midwifery connected reproduction to politics (ibid., 78, 80).

The dawning of the golden era of Chinese Communist familism in the 1950s found the modern Chinese *jiating* sandwiched between the pre-1949 peasant-inflected formation and idealized revolutionary images flooding in from the more advanced socialist USSR. By that time the *jiating* had become the modernized, bourgeois family of *zhishifenzi* idealization: mommy, daddy, and me.[34] *Jiating* grounded social production in a context heavily marked with the traces of older cultural codes and ideological formations, just as the modern nation did. The modern socialist *jiating* and Maoist *guojia* coexisted in unity—as concept metaphors of each other. This is how I interpret mobilizations like the 1957 campaign "Industrious and Frugal in Establishing the Nation, Industrious and Frugal in Managing the Family," where state and family are virtually synonymous; what operated in one sphere translates directly into the other (Fulian 1958:27). "The material and cultural life of our state's [*guo*] masses of people has improved substantially in the past few years. But the lives of many families [*jiating*] are still not comfortable," the text reads. To raise the *jiating*'s level the masses must "industriously develop our state's industry and agriculture." The work of housewives (*jiating zhufu*) must exactly mirror the work going on outside the *jiating* in the *guojia*. "Every housewife could be industrious and frugal in managing the family affairs, if she institutionalizes a rational planning schedule. . . . *Industriousness and frugality in the family labor strengthens industriousness and frugality in the nation*" (my emphasis; Fulian 1958:2).

Women's Federation and *Funü* as a State Category

William Parish and Martin Whyte once commented that after socialist Liberation in 1949 the Chinese state took no clear measures to transform family structure, and that Fulian, the state's Women's Federation, was an "amorphous" government bureaucracy, the only mass organization that people belonged to by virtue of physiology (Parish and White 1978:39). This does not explain the very real powers of the Women's Federation. The importance of Fulian lay in its power to subordinate and dominate all inscriptions of womanhood in official discourse. It is not that Fulian actually represented the "interests" of women, but rather that one could not until recently be "represented" *as a woman* without the agency and mediation of Fulian. That fact is a measure of its success and its importance.[35]

In late 1948 the government commissioned its leading female officials, dignitaries, and luminaries in the liberated areas to plan the All-China Democratic Women's Association's (later simply Women's Association) first meeting as soon as Beijing fell.[36] With formal gravity the planning committees and standing committee began directing the installation of new bureaucratic frameworks charged with deciding national policy and convening the association's first representative congress (Fulian 1949:5). In these initiating moments Fulian consolidated its power as a national state organ for responsibly representing "new China's women." With mechanical deliberation the bylaws connect representation of "female masses" to the international socialist women's movement, through the accumulating processes of representation (Fulian 1949:94–100). "What deserves most pride," one document read, "is that the representatives [*daibiao*] from the liberated areas are elected from the local area women's congresses. . . . We have been commissioned by the female masses. We must loyally represent their opinions" (Fulian 1949:20–21). They added an important proviso: "Representation [*daibiao*] means representing the masses; [it does] not [mean] controlling [*guan*] the masses."

This bureaucratization and Fulian's transformation from actively producing *funü* to formally representing them in Beijing relied on the CCP's history of struggle. But it radiated a new sort of definitional power. Representative bodies like congresses and the Federation itself not only "represented the masses," they also consolidated and mediated internal differences (*tuanjiele gezhong butong de funü*), homogenizing political subjects into a representable mass, so to speak, through an elaborate machinery of political democracy. The inception of Fulian initiated for *funü* unprecedented participation in the rituals of state formation and promised the newly minted subjects bureaucratic powers: but only so long as it—Fulian, the government—retained the power to determine what, in fact, constituted a *funü* (Fulian 1949:73–74).

Deng Yingchao, speaking to this issue, laid out the official view when she argued that woman in the discourses of the state had achieved "political, economic, cultural and social elevation and elevation of herself in the family" (Fulian 1949:28). Fulian's charge involved consolidating and expanding the political sphere carved out earlier under the fugitive state: a process, the document argued, that ensured equal status for women by transforming them from consumers into producers (Fulian 1949:31). By its third congress Fulian spoke in even broader, less autonomous terms, the dialect of the state:

> The All China Women's Federation is, under the leadership of the Chinese Communist Party, an organization for the basic organization of every strata of laboring women. The All-China Women's Association has achieved enormous work success since the Second National Congress. In the new period of history the organization of the All-China Women's Federation wants to expend even greater energy in the task of better organizing all the country's women in the social reconstruction, so it must improve and strengthen its mass viewpoint and its mass line work methods. It must be concerned with and reflect the real interests and demands of women, and it must struggle energetically to end discrimination and the harming of women; [it must guide] the attitudes and activities of children; it must serve the masses of women with enormous energy at every turn, particularly in [child welfare] . . . so that Fulian and the mass of women have an even more intimate relationship (Fulian 1958:3).

The founding of the Fulian, however, was *not* specific to women. The same ritual unfolded in the mass groups that "reflected and represented" youth, trade unions, and other politically delineated constituencies. The Fulian organization (and its replicas) took part in a reinscription of the national body, and thus it represented at a subordinated level the processes of state building commencing at levels superior to itself.

At the beginning of this chapter I argued that sex identity (the commonsense notion that what makes women female is their sex and more specifically the influence of their indisputably physiological sex organs on themselves) grounded on anatomical difference had not held a central place in Chinese constituting discourses before the early twentieth century. I concurred with Mark Elvin, who suggested that when the late imperial state rewarded virtue it was surprisingly blind to anatomical difference and rewarded people according to coded social, kin-anchored behaviors that I called protocols. A Confucian like Chen Hongmou wrote as a father-official and not as a CCP state bureaucrat like Cai Chang, whose job was to instruct, represent, and produce women as *funü* (Fulian 1988:247–54). This suggests to me that although the old imperial state had actively intervened in social formations related to gender, it never saw fit to cast male/female in essentialist binary terms.

The socialist state did consolidate gender difference on the material ground of scientific physiology. Scientism has been part of modern Chinese reformist and revolutionary rhetoric since the May Fourth movement. Part of scientistic discourse, clearly reflected in Fulian documents, is the idea that people are in literal fact material because their organic reproductive capacity makes them like animals (Kwok 1965). Thus, gendering under Maoist inscription unfolded within the tradition of scientific socialism and its emphasis on reproduction. The fusion of peasant realism and socialist scientism gave rise to texts like "People and Wealth Flourish" (*Ren yu cai wang*) that "encourage the people of the liberated areas not merely to work hard to get enough to wear and eat, but also to have more children, which, once born, must be supported [*yanghuo*]." Lyrically conflating "production" and "reproduction," the state vowed to train midwives, investigate infant mortality, propagandize for scientific sanitation, oppose feudal superstition, and publish popular chapbooks on infant care, all predicated on popularizing a modern understanding of reproductive physiology and sanitary childbirth practices.[37]

Much work among women aimed at producing people who would collaborate in the state's biopolitical agenda.[38] Before the twentieth century, of course, birth and death had possessed no direct link to the throne, or state political economy. Life and death commenced in the spatial boundaries of *jia* and organized themselves around such matters as pollution, temporality, rupture, and consolidation (Ahern 1975). Although late imperial domestic and popular medical practices regarding menstruation, conception, parturition, suckling, and so on were historically sophisticated, they participated in the same neo-Confucian epistemic order that gendered people; and that meant reference to the state through dyadic obligation to father, husband, and monarch. The socialist state, on the other hand, popularized a direct linkage between state's needs and modern obstetric practices. *Study Guide for the New Woman* very straightforwardly declaimed that "the twenty-seven lessons in this book, all told 30,000 words, are for the exclusive use of village women in their study [*xuexi*] and in [female] literacy classes and political lessons [which the CCP attempted to organize at the village level whenever possible]. It is very appropriate as a refresher for teachers and active elements [activists representing the CCP's agenda at the village level] in studying self-discipline" (Lu Fu 1949: 1). The book concluded each of its lessons ("The ritual [*lijiao*] etiquette of the feudal society is the source of women's suffering," "The inharmonious family causes great harm," "Pay attention to menstrual sanitation") with an attached series of study questions: "How does the old power of feudalism in your village oppress women? Do we still have feudal ways of thinking?" and "What is the source of family unhappiness? How can we make the family a happy place?"

This process of study (*xuexi*), or learning the correct mass line, transmitted the notion that physiology was the foundation of gender difference. It inscribed the difference between women and men in terms of scientific fact, and it understood the baseline of reproductive physiology to be the basis of social reproduction. Thus, as has been the case in modernist discourses elsewhere, the CCP's statism made anatomical difference into the key factor in social life. It also assumed that male and female were essentially different organisms (What else do the "physiology of the human female" and the "physiology of the human male" do but inscribe difference on a surface of similitude?) and on that basis made reproductive biology and physiology its scientific foundation. But the inscription of gender difference at the level of reproductive physiology elided something very interesting. It made material reproduction the site of gender difference, but it did not reduce personality to physiological terms. That is to say, although biology may be destiny, it did not appear to directly determine gender-appropriate psychology. In Fulian writing particularly there is a tendency to attribute difference to physiology while curtailing attributions of difference at the level of personality. This latter, the realm of feeling and character, remained until recently bound to conventions of Maoism that emphasized social class, not sex anatomy or "gender."

It is easier to see the statist construction of *funu* under Maoism now that Maoism is a dead letter (Billeter 1985). One of the most interesting parentheses closing the Maoist period has been the recurrence of writing about sexuality, subjectivity, romantic love, gender psychology, and feminism (*nüxing zhuyi*) in fiction, cultural criticism, and social theory (Barlow 1994). The collapse of political *funü* loosed a torrent of writing about *nüxing*, who, under the present formulation, now endures new and compound indignities. Not just physiologically distinct but biologically inferior, post-Mao *nüxing* exhibits "natural" emotions that clarify her essential endocrinal difference (Honig and Hershatter 1988). "Class" as a frame of personality has given way to sexual physiology as a frame of identity. Certainly the present barrage of *nüxing wenxue*, or women's literature, has rekindled the battle that in 1942 set Cai Chang and Ding Ling at odds over how to fill up the empty category of woman (Dai Jinhua & Meng Yue 1989).

The resurgence of a subversive *nüxing* helps clarify the contradictory formation of *nüxing/funü* from a final angle. Under the previous statist protocol, *funü* allowed for the social production of woman in politics but disallowed any psychology of gender difference. The even older initial May Fourth literary inscription of *nüxing* made Woman the "other" of man but proved insufficiently stable to resist statist inscriptions of *funü*. The recuperation of *nüxing*'s heterosexual male/female binary does enable difference as femininity and does provide a position of great potential for resistance (Barlow 1994). Post-Mao *nüxing*, however, has rendered itself powerless in the face of clearly prejudicial "scientific" claims to female inferiority.

Given that *funü* offered a way of opening village women to statist operations and *nüxing* has provided an oppositional personal identity for urban educated classes, how Chinese intellectuals will process issues of sex identity and subjectivity in the next decade depends on many factors. Of course, although it was intellectuals who initially constructed the originary colonialist categories of modern Chinese gender politics, there is no guarantee that as a class they will continue to monopolize its potential. Whether writers and resisters relocate the contest in sexuality and gendered identity or whether the struggle shifts to other sites will decide the future of *funü/nüxing*. That is because at another level altogether these terms are simply the vocabulary of everyday life in the People's Republic of China. As such they form a reservoir for usages, in Certeau's sense, vastly different from the designs of those who appropriated them long ago or those who employ them now. As such they also offer prolific opportunity for contest. The "presence and circulation of a representation," to echo Certeau, echoing Nietzsche, "tell us nothing about what it is for its users" (Certeau 1984:xiii). Users, not makers, speakers, not historians will decide.

Notes

1. The same is true of *guojia* (postmonarchy nation/state), which partakes of an older social formation, *guo* (empire), and *jiating,* meaning a contemporary domestic unit that formed in part as a reaction to *jia* (patriline). (*Guojia* is translated as nation or state depending on context.) These powerful terms all show the marks of intense political struggle yet are obviously different from their predecessors.

2. See Anagnost 1989 for an example of the discursive powers of the state's propaganda.

3. For what follows I am indebted to Joanna Handlin's classic article "Lu K'un's New Audience: The Influence of Women's Literacy on Sixteenth-Century Thought" (1975), particularly pp. 36–38, which concern Chen Hongmou.

4. It is a commonplace of Western studies of Chinese society that sacral relationships, specifically the "Three Bonds" (*sangang*) and "Five Human Relations" (*wulun*), structure all human experience. That is why I claim later in this chapter that the social space signified by the neologism "society" (*shehui*) was new and part of a general discourse of Chinese modernity. The semicolonial *shehui* of neutral meeting places and autonomous individuals did not yet exist before the Unequal Treaty System erected European-style cities in China's hinterlands. The texts and artifacts of the old society are the "signifiers of the subject" for the earlier tradition and can be read as such.

5. It situated men (*nan/ren*) that way too. For a good discussion of the tensions between personal morality and sacral kinship see Lau 1985. No subject dressed as female could take the civil service examination or serve the monarch in an official capacity, it is true. Yet, as Keith McMahon has found, a persistent literary tradition existed that toyed with the fantasy of the superior woman who, masquerading as a man, outshines her male relatives and competitors at their own game (McMahon, this volume). His work reinforces my point; it was not so much that "women" were categorically unequal to "men" (neither of these categories was cast as a stable, exclusionary bodily trap) or that women's essence precluded service, since at least in theory female gendering practices allowed for transgender masquerade. Rather, subject positionality required people to execute different tasks inside which personal effort and adherence to service ideals differed greatly.

6. Both Judith Butler and Teresa de Lauretis point out that gender for post-Cartesian Western subjects originated on the privileged site of heterosexuality, itself a disciplinary discourse. Indeed, this insight has become a commonplace in much feminist theory. Women become women in the compass of masculine, heterosexual desire. My object in focusing on the *jia* as and considering it the privileged site under most Confucian discourses is to suggest (1) that heterosexuality, sexuality as an institution à la Foucault, and sexual identities in the European metaphysical sense have no particular historicity here, and (2) that the sexed body of "Western" gender processes does not obtain. An interesting but rather brief reference to the taxonomic range possible within the yin/yang dynamic in the feudal past is Wang 1989.

7. Many people have made the point that civilization (*wen*) serves as the basis of existence in a late Confucian episteme, but none so eloquently as Angela Zito (1989).

8. Furth translates *feinan* and *feinü* as "false" women and men. I overtranslate these terms slightly to convey my point about the literalness of language. The foundational or categorical figure is mother/father, not woman/man.

9. See, in this volume, Judith Farquhar, John Hay, James Hevia, and Angela

Zito. Forthcoming work by Farquhar particularly emphasizes the nonfoundational elements of body discourses in Chinese medical practice.

10. Though as McMahon points out in this volume, even bound feet could be concealed! The bodily sign never fixed identity.

11. The first quotation is from Lauretis (1987:3). The second is from Foucault, as cited in Lauretis (ibid.).

12. There is an important respect in which women (daughters, mothers, etc.) and men (sons, fathers, etc.) are the same. All kinds of women and all kinds of men, depending on the specifics of birth order and generational relations, still strive to be people (*ren*) of benevolence (*ren*). Neither being a person nor acting out the cardinal virtue of *ren* is essentially gendered. In this, Confucian practice resembles similar arguments about the woman's soul in forms of puritanism. It is rather that what is important is the execution of one's given tasks as a mother, a father, a daughter, or a mother-in-law (and combinations of these behaviors, since ego exists in multiple relationships). Gender is accomplished not so much through female virtues per se as through the behaviors of persons in specific subject positions of kin relation. This sense is made explicit in Joseph Lau's discussion of *dayi* (public virtue), but Lau does discuss *ren* (benevolence). Tu Wei-ming provides an important discussion of *ren* in "The Creative Tension between *Jen* and *Li*" (Tu 1979), but Tu does not talk about women's possessing *ren* (benevolence) as Lau does.

13. It is not clear to me whether establishing oneself *lishen* as a mother was considered equivalent to the requirements exacted of male Confucianists: filial behavior, examination preparation, reading and writing inside the canon, and producing filial sons. The extension of *lishen* to well-behaved women is probably part and parcel of the eighteenth-century movement Susan Mann (1987) has written about in her discussion of widow suicide.

14. Protocols are similar to what Spivak calls "regulative psychobiographies" (1989:227). I agree with Spivak, having reached a similar conclusion independently, that the history of women must rely on the excavation of the narratives that have effected our construction, though I regret her choice of the term "regulative psychobiographies," since to me it conjures up memories of the "psychohistory" movement of the 1970s. For a moving instance of narrative's effect on a working-class English girl's subjectivity, see Steedman 1986.

The ancient times Chen refers to go back to the Zhou (twelfth to third century B.C.E.) period. Contemporary compilers selected texts from older books that expressed particularly well the point the compiler wished to make. Because Chen's was a period of Han revival, interest in ritual and the codification of ritual was widespread.

15. The specific Confucian lineage I am analyzing equates "being a person" with realizing orderly relations between kin and establishing kin rhetoric as the metalanguage of social relations generally. Let Daoism stand as a counterexample,

the exception that "proves" the rule. Daoist discourse makes the dissolution of this economy of inequality its objective. Roger Ames suggests that Daoism pivots around an ideal axis or "third" gender, that of the ruler whose person reconciles both male and female actions. For Ames's Daoists the ideal Daoist person resides beyond the distinctions Chen Hongmou is drawing between relations with mother-in-law, relations with son, relations with husband, and so on. *In not taking a position, the ideal Daoist person becomes androgynous.* Objecting to distinctions, the Daoist refuses the marks that masculine or feminine behavior would inscribe onto the person. Physically, the Daoist sage must shrink his penis or stop her menstruation to achieve sagehood. They do not act within the protocols of gendered position and therefore are neither one "sex" nor the other (Ames 1981).

16. Hamilton's point about codification is also useful in the sense that since "[fictive] kinship [became] a metaphor for putting groups together and for determining hierarchies of all types" (1984:417), then it is not so startling that essentialization of sex/gender in Marxist liberationist discourse in the twentieth century got fixed in hierarchical stone at the same moment it offered the "liberation of women from men." My grateful thanks to Hamilton for his stimulating interventions during my graduate-school days.

For an excellent mammoth discussion of how retheorizing female subjectivity became so important in the late nineteenth and twentieth centuries, see Roxane Witke's venerable and still unsurpassed narrative history (Witke 1970). Also see the work of Michel de Certeau (1984) on the scriptural economy and Marie-Claire Bergere (1990) for a sociological discussion of class formation in the interwar years.

17. *Nüxuebao* (Women's study journal), cited in Beahan (1975a:383).

18. The myth of Chinese homogeneity and the exclusion of Manchus, indigenous peoples, Mongols, Uighurs, and other Moslem subgroups, and so on was as much a part of Chinese nationalism as such exclusions and differentiations have been elsewhere. See Bennington (1990:132). Benningston states what most of the contributors to Bhabha's *Nation and Narrative* assume—and I along with them—that "the idea of the nation is inseparable from its narration."

19. Mark Elvin argued that the hallmark of Chinese dynastic practice insofar as women are concerned was the throne's decision to reward women for their acts of resistance to family. He cites a remarkable number of instances in which women kill their own sons. The transfer of the female hero's attention from her father to the democratic West reinforced a statist strain in Han Chinese gender constructing practices therefore (Elvin 1984). Of course, women in the cases of chaste-widow suicide that Elvin cites did not really act on behalf of the state. Although the throne might have arbitrated in a sense, the suicide's object was never to protect the state qua state.

For a text showing that Westerners sacrifice to the state whereas Chinese are bound by the particularism of the Five Bonds—see Zhen (1907, vol. 2, chap. 12,

"Lu Zhi," 9a). The notion that Westerners sacrificed to the state was widespread, as was another equivalence—female body mutilation—between foot-binding and corseting.

20. This is the thesis of my forthcoming book, in a chapter titled "Chinese Feminism" (Barlow, n.d.). Mei Sheng's compendium and key articles (1929) allow the reader a marvelous overview of the debate over the Chinese woman question.

There exist extensive analyses of modern fiction for reference. The most productive critical commentary so far has come from Marsten Anderson, Ching kiu Stephen Chan, Chen Yu-shih, Rey Chow, Theodore Huters, and Wendy Larson, critics who all take seriously the generativity of the texts they read. Major Chinese texts that reinscribed the oppositional construction of male/female are, Ba Jin's (Family), Ding Ling's "Shafei nushi riji" (Miss Sophia's diary), and the novels of Mao Dun. Male/female was not, it should be noted, an exclusive or hegemonic formation, even during the May Fourth era. Lu Xun and Ling Shuhua appear to have found such reductionist terms for engendering untenable (Brown 1988; Chow 1988). See also Shen Zhiyuan 1936.

21. Social theory retained physiology as a sign of its materialism (Barlow, n.d.). And it never unpacked the inherent logical contradiction, of course. This is not at all surprising. The physiological anchor in our own essential notions of womanhood has coexisted quite happily with constructivist notions for decades (Butler 1990). This is particularly true in Chinese feminism, since the category itself was relatively novel and so the unpacking received even less attention.

22. Zhongguo Minzhu Funuhui (1949: 1–38).

23. Fulian (1949a). This collection has a slightly different composition.

24. My criticism of Du echoes the critiques that the Subaltern Studies group has leveled at the universal Marxisms (Chatterjee 1986; Chakrabarty 1988).

25. Jiangxi Fulian, ed., *Jiangxi suchu funü yondong shiliao xuanpian* (Selected materials for the Jiangxi Soviet women's movement) is a compilation of documents that I will cite hereafter as JF. The accompanying dates, however, are the dates of the documents' initial publication.

26. See JF (1932, 2:52) for the statement that "marriage is a relationship of two persons, male and female."

27. This is a splendid document detailing instructions governing women's organizations. It clarifies how women's work should model itself on established forms, possess an established work plan, and fix a topic for each meeting (for instance, "opposing feudal bonds" or "enlisting men, comforting troops, doing mass work, becoming literate").

28. See JF (1932, 3.2:53) and many subsequent documents. Women's Day and propaganda for the marriage law are the two major work areas for *ganbu* (cadres) undertaking women's work. JF (1933, 2.7) uses it to demonstrate why Woman is connected to state and suggests that workers use magazines, newspa-

pers, and storytellers to spread the word. The effort is also reflected in regional document JF (1933, 2.10:77). The document paraphrased here offers the flavor of the propaganda language. "March 8 is nearly here. March 8 is International Women's Day. It has the same significance as Labor Day and Youth Day. All over the world, laboring women demonstrate and march in parades on this day to oppose the oppression of capitalist landlords, the feudal restraints of the old society and old family. But our demand for thorough liberation as laboring women is undertaken under the leadership of the proletariat to overthrow the feudal restrictions of society and the old family. . . . If we look, what is life like for women in the Soviets who have already been liberated? They no longer have landlords, capitalists, destroying or oppressing them; they've already got independence and freedom. They've been liberated from deep family anxieties and live a happy life with a high degree of political culture" (JF 1933, 2:15): "Laboring women! Arm yourselves to protect the Soviet." It is significant that the international demonstrations are conceived to precede those taking place in the local context, but the local instantiation of this universal process exceeds even those global demonstrations assumed to be unfolding simultaneously!

29. The provisional nature of the laws and the multiplicity of voices are clear in JF (1932, 6.20:60–65), which talks about the resistance to certain laws. Its self-critical tone is significant.

30. The document gives instructions on the mechanics of representation. For example, set a time for conference, locate the laboring women's congress inside the system of other mass organizations, recruit according to certain forms, get ten to twenty women, establish a representative, elect a presidium and such capped by a party member, and so on. See p. 88 for good discussion of how representation works.

31. JF (1933, 6.25:95) suggests that quite strongly.

32. Stranahan's are the best empirical studies available in English (1981, 1983). Her work supports that of Phyllis Andors (1975, 1983), arguing that given the material and cultural context the CCP's policy on women's affairs was remarkably fair and productive both in party terms and in the view of the woman policy effected.

33. Examples are the case histories and subject biographies in Fulian 1949c.

34. At least this is how I interpret the writing on love and family construction that the state issued in the 1950s (Dan Fu 1956; Li Di 1955). An example of the style of writing comes from Lo Fu: "In the Soviet Union the new family of socialism has become the organizational basis of society, the major reason for the strength of the society. The party, the government, youth organizations, and all the collective organizations of Soviet society that organize and teach mass work, all are aimed at strengthening without stop the Soviet family as the base. The basic utility of the Soviet family is the education of children [zinü] to become people active with communist consciousness. This is the most important responsibility of

the citizen who is a parent, the responsibility for raising children in the society. . . . Husband and wife have extremely important responsibilities to society and to their children, and these feelings will insure the happiness of family life (1956:19).

35. To my knowledge there is no institutional history of Fulian yet available. The following supply partial information on founding and early propaganda/literary outreach: Croll 1974, 1978; Hemmel and Sindbjerhg 1984.

36. These luminaries and dignitaries were, in descending order: Cai Chang, Deng Yingchao, Zhang Chinqiu, Li Dechuan, Chen Shaomei, Kang Keqing, Ding Ling, and Ho Xiangning (Fulian 1949b:102–8). The only real surprise here is Ding Ling, who had been purged from her women's work following the publication of her "Thoughts on March 8" essay in 1942.

37. Much public health writing took birth and female physiology as its starting point. Take for instance:

> LECTURE 22 "WE WANT TO STUDY NEW METHODS OF CHILDBIRTH"
> Giving birth and raising children [*shenger yangnü*] is a glorious event. Also, it is a great event in terms of the fate of the laboring mother and infant. But in the old society this greatness was not appreciated. Using ignorant midwives and allowing them to manage the birth has mortally wounded untold numbers of adults and children. In this lesson we want to study new methods, tell everybody about it, so they won't be afraid and will help out others.

and

> When the pregnant woman reaches term, prepare a place for her to deliver and implements such as . . . yarn, cloth, cotton, a towel . . . oilcloth, clothing for the child and so on. . . . When the woman goes into labor have her pace up and down on the ground . . . piss and shit at her leisure . . . take a look at the cervical opening when it is as big as a silver ingot [etc. etc., in pedagogic detail]. (Lu Fu 1949:78–80)

38. Foucault 1978. For explication of biopolitics, specifically chapter 5, "Right of Death and Power over Life."

References

[Ahern], Emily Martin. 1975. The power and pollution of Chinese women. In *Women in Chinese society*, ed. Margery Wolf and Roxane Witke. Stanford: Stanford University Press.

Ames, Roger. 1981. Taoism and the androgynous ideal. In *Women in China: Current directions in historical scholarship*, ed. Richard Guisso and Stanley Johannesen. Historical Reflections, Directions 3. Boston: Philo Press.

Anagnost, Ann. 1989. Prosperity and counter-prosperity: The moral discourse of wealth in post-Mao China. In *Marxism and Chinese experience: Issues of social-*

ism in a Third World socialist society, ed. Arif Dirlik and Maurice Meisner. Armonk, N.Y.: M. E. Sharpe.

Anderson, Benedict. 1983. *Imagined communities: Reflections on the origin and spread of nationalism.* London: Verso.

Anderson, Marsten. 1990. *The limits of realism: Chinese fiction in the revolutionary period.* Berkeley and Los Angeles: University of California Press.

Andors, Phyllis. 1975. Studying Chinese women. *Bulletin of Concerned Asian Scholars* 7, no. 2:41.

———. 1983. *The unfinished liberation of Chinese women, 1949–1980.* Bloomington: Indiana University Press.

Asad, Talal. 1987. Are there histories of people without Europe? A review article. *Comparative Study of History and Society* 29 (July): 594–607.

Barlow, Tani E. 1982. Feminism and literary technique in Ding Ling's early work. In *Women writers of twentieth century China.* Eugene: University of Oregon, Asian Studies Publications.

———. 1989. Asian perspective: Beyond dichotomies. *Gender and History* 1, no. 3:318–30.

———. 1990. *Zhishifenzi* (Chinese intellectuals) and power. *Dialectical Anthropology* 16:209–32.

———. 1994. Politics and protocols of woman. In *Engendering China: Women, culture and the state,* ed. Gail Hershatter et al. Cambridge: Harvard University Press.

———. n.d. *Imagining woman.* Durham, N.C.: Duke University Press. Forthcoming.

Barlow, Tani E., and Gary Bjorge, eds. 1989 *I myself am a woman: Selected works of Ding Ling.* Boston: Beacon Press.

Beahan, Charlotte. 1975a. Feminism and nationalism in the Chinese women's press, 1902–1911. *Modern China* 1, no. 4:379–417.

———. 1975b. Mothers of citizens: Feminism and nationalism in the late Ch'ing. Photocopied manuscript.

Beibeier [August Bebel]. 1949. *Funü yu shehui* (Woman and society). Trans. Shen Ruixian. Shanghai: Kaiming Books.

Bennington, Geoffrey. 1990. Postal politics and the institution of the nation. In *Nation and narration,* ed. Homi K. Bhabha. London: Routledge.

Bergere, Marie-Claire. 1990. *The golden age of the Chinese bourgeoisie, 1911–1937.* Trans. Janet Lloyd. New York: Cambridge University Press.

Billeter, Jean-François. 1985. The system of class status. In *The system of state power in China,* ed. S. R. Schram. Hong Kong Chinese University Press.

Brennan, Timothy. 1990. The national longing for form. In *Nationalism and narrative,* ed. Homi K. Bhabha. London: Routledge.

Brown, Carolyn T. 1988. Woman as a trope: Gender and power in Lu Xun's "Soap." *Modern Chinese Literature* 4, nos. 1–2:55–71.

Burton, Antoinette. 1992. British feminist identity and the Indian woman. In *Western women and imperialism: Complicity and resistance,* ed. Nipur Chaudhuri and Margaret Strobel. Bloomington: Indiana University Press.

Butler, Judith. 1990. *Gender trouble: Feminism and the subversion of identity*. London: Routledge.

Carter, Angela. 1980. *Sadeian woman and the ideology of pornography*. New York: Harper Colophon.

Castelli, Elizabeth. 1991. "I will make Mary male": Pieties of the body and gender transformation of Christian women in late antiquity. In *Body guards: The cultural politics of gender ambiguity*, ed. Julia Epstein and Kristina Straub. London: Routledge.

Certeau, Michel de. 1984. The scriptural economy. In *The practice of everyday life*. Berkeley and Los Angeles: University of California Press.

Chakrabarty, Dipesh. 1988. Conditions for knowledge of working-class conditions. In *Selected subaltern studies*, ed. Ranajit Guha and Gayatri Spivak. New York: Oxford University Press.

Chan, Ching-ki Stephen. 1988. The language of despair: Ideological representations of the "new woman" (*xing nüxing*) by May Fourth writers. *Modern Chinese Literature* 4, nos. 1–2:19–39.

Chatterjee, Partha. 1986. *Nationalist thought and the colonial world: A derivative discourse*. Tokyo: United Nations Books.

Chen Hongmou. n.d. *Wuzhong yigui* (Five posthumous regulations). In *Jiaonü yigui* (Posthumous regulation on educating women). Sibubeiyao ed., vol. 3, N.p.: Zhonghua Shujyu.

Chow, Rey. 1988. Virtuous transactions. *Modern Chinese Literature* 4, nos. 1–2: 71–87.

Cowie, Elizabeth. 1978. Woman as sign. *m/f* 1:49–63.

Croll, Elizabeth. 1974. *The women's movement in China: A selection of readings, 1949–1973*. Modern China Series 6. London: Anglo-Chinese Educational Institute.

———. 1978. *Feminism and socialism in China*. London: Routledge and Kegan Paul.

Dai Jinhua and Meng Yue. 1989. *Fuchu lishi dibiao* (emerging from the horizon of history). Zhengzhou: Henan Renmin Chubanshe.

Dan Fu. 1956. *Mantan liangxing guanxi zhong de daode wenti* (Conversation about moral question concerning relations between the sexes). Shanghai: Xuexi Shenghuo.

Diamond, Norma. 1975. Women under Kuomintang rule: Versions of the feminine mystique. *Modern China*, 3–46.

Du Zhunhui. 1949. *Funü wenti jianghua* (Lectures on the woman problem). Hong Kong: New China Books.

Elvin, Mark. 1984. Female virtue and the state in China. *Past and Present*, no. 104:111–52.

Flax, Jane. 1990. Postmodernism and gender relations in feminist theory. In *Feminism/postmodernism*, ed. Linda Nicholson. London: Routledge.

Foucault, Michel. 1978. *The history of sexuality*. Vol. 1, *An introduction*. New York: Pantheon Books.

Fulian, ed. 1949a. *Makosi, Engesi, Liening, Sidalin lun funü jiefang* (Marx, Engels, Lenin, and Stalin on women's liberation). Beijing: Renmin Press.

———. 1949b. *Quanguo funü diyici quanguo daibiao dahui* (First congress of the All-China Women's Association). Hong Kong: Xinmin Press.

———. 1949c. *Zhongguo jiefangchu nongcun funü fanshen yondong sumiao* (A rough sketch of the *fanshen* movement among rural women in the liberated regions of China). N.p.: Xinhua Books.

———. 1958. *Zhongguo funü diansi quanguo daibiao dahui huizongyao wenxuan* (Selected key documents of the Third National Congress of Chinese Women). Beijing: Zhongguo Funu Zazhi Press.

———. 1988. *Cai Chang, Deng Yingchao, Kang Keqing funü jiefang wenti wenxuan* (Cai Chang, Deng Yingchao, and Kang Keqing's selected works on the question of women's liberation). Beijing: People's Press.

———. n.d. *Zhongguo jiefangchu funü canzhan yondong* (Political participation movement of the women of the Chinese liberated areas). Hong Kong: New People's Press.

Furth, Charlotte. 1988. Androgynous males and deficient females: Biology and gender boundaries in sixteenth and seventeenth century China. *Late Imperial China* 9, no. 2:1–30.

Hamilton, Gary. 1984. Patriarchalism in imperial China and Western Europe: A revision of Weber's sociology of domination. *Theory and Society* 13, no. 3:393–425.

Handlin, Joanna. 1975. Lu K'un's new audience: The influence of women's literacy on sixteenth-century thought. In *Women in Chinese society,* ed. Margery Wolf and Roxane Witke. Stanford: Stanford University Press.

Hemmel, Vibeke, and Pia Sindbjerhg. 1984. *Women in rural China: Policy towards women before and after the Cultural Revolution.* Curzon: Scandinavian Institute of Asian Studies.

Honig, Emily, and Gail Hershatter. 1988. *Personal voices: Chinese women in the 1980s.* Stanford: Stanford University Press.

Hunter, Jane. 1984. *The gospel of gentility: American women missionaries in turn-of-the-century China.* New Haven: Yale University Press.

Hutcheon, Linda. 1989. *The politics of postmodernism.* London: Routledge.

Huters, Theodore. 1984. Blossoms in the snow: Lu Xun and the dilemma of modern Chinese literature. *Modern Chinese Literature* 10, no. 1:49–79.

———. 1988. A new way of writing: The possibilities for literature in late Qing China, 1895–1908. *Modern China* 14, no. 3:243–77.

Hyatt, Irwin T., Jr. 1976. *Our ordered lives confess: Three nineteenth-century missionaries in east Shangung.* Cambridge: Harvard University Press.

Jiangxi Fulian (JF), ed. 1982. *Jiangxi suchu funü yondong shiliao xuanpian* (Selected materials for the Jiangxi Soviet women's movement). Jiangxi: Jiangxi Renmin Chubanshe.

Kruks, Sonia, Rayna Rapp, and Marilyn B. Young, eds. 1989. *Promissory notes: Women in the transition to socialism.* New York: Monthly Review Press.

Kuhn, Annette. 1985. *The power of the image.* London: Routledge and Kegan Paul.

Kwok, David. 1965. *Scientism in Chinese thought.* Berkeley and Los Angeles: University of California Press.

Laclau, Ernesto, and Chantal Mouffe. 1985. *Hegemony and socialist strategy.* London: Verso.

Larson, Wendy. 1988. The end of "funü wenxue": Women's literature from 1925–1935. *Modern Chinese Literature* 4, nos. 1–2: 39–55.

Lau, Joseph. 1985. Duty, reputation, and selfhood in traditional Chinese narratives. In *Expressions of self in Chinese literature,* ed. Robert Hegel and Richard Hessney. New York: Columbia University Press.

Lauretis, Teresa de. 1984. *Alice Doesn't: Feminism, semiotics, cinema.* Bloomington: Indiana University Press.

———. 1987. The technology of gender. In *The technology of gender.* Bloomington: Indiana University Press.

Leith, Suzanne. 1973. Chinese women in the early Communist movement. In *Women in China,* ed. Marilyn Young. Ann Arbor: Michigan Papers in Chinese Studies.

Li Di. 1955. *Zhufu shouji* (Handbook for housewives). Beijing: Tongsu Weni Press.

Lo Fu. 1956. *Funü wenti jiben zhishi* (Basic knowledge on the woman question). Beijing: People's Press.

Lu Fu [pseud.]. 1949. *Xinfunü duben* (Study guide for the new woman). Hong Kong: Xinminzhu Press.

Mann, Susan. 1987. Widows in the kinship, class, and community structures of Qing dynasty China. *Journal of Asian Studies* 46, no. 1: 37–56.

Mei Sheng. 1929. *Zhongguo funü wenti taolunji* (General discussion of the Chinese woman question). Shanghai: Wenhua Books.

Minson, Jeff. 1985. *Genealogies of morals: Nietzsche, Foucault, Donzelot and the eccentricity of ethics.* London: Macmillan.

Mohanty, Chandra. 1984. Under Western eyes: Feminist scholarship and colonial discourses. *Boundary 2* 12, no. 3. 13, no. 1: 333–58.

———. 1987. Feminist encounters: Locating the politics of experience. *Copyright* 1 (Fall): 30–44.

Nietzsche, Friedrich. 1969. *On the genealogy of morals.* Trans. W. Kaufman. New York: Vintage Books.

Parish, William, and Martin Whyte. 1978. *Village and family in contemporary China.* Chicago: University of Chicago Press.

Porkert, Manfred. 1985. *The theoretical foundations of Chinese medicine: Systems of correspondence.* Reprint ed. Cambridge: MIT Press.

Rankin, Mary Backus. 1975. The emergence of women at the end of the Ch'ing. In *Women in Chinese society,* ed. Margery Wolf and Roxane Witke. Stanford: Stanford University Press.

Riley, Denise. 1988. *"Am I that name?" Feminism and the category of "Woman."* Minneapolis: University of Minnesota Press.

Shen Zhiyuan. 1936. *Funü shehuikoxue changshi duben* (A general primer in women's social science). Shanghai: Shenghuo Books.

Smith, Kidder, Jr. et al. 1990. *Sung dynasty uses of the "I ching."* Princeton: Princeton University Press.

Spivak, Gayatri. 1989. The political economy of women. In *Coming to terms: Feminism, theory, politics,* ed. Elizabeth Weed. New York: Routledge.

Steedman, Carolyn. 1986. *Landscape for a good woman: A story of two lives.* London: Virago.

Stranahan, Patricia. 1981. Changes in policy for Yanan women, 1935–1947. *Modern China* 7, no. 1:83–112.

———. 1983. *Yan'an women and the Chinese Communist Party.* Berkeley, Calif.: Center for Chinese Studies Press.

Strand, David. 1990. *"Civil society" and "public sphere" in modern China: A perspective on popular movements in Beijing, 1919–1989.* Chapel Hill, N.C.: Duke University Press Asian Pacific Studies Institute.

Trinh, T. Min-ha, ed. 1986–87. Difference: A special Third World women issue. *Discourse* 8 (Fall–Winter).

Tu, Wei-ming. 1979. *Humanity and self-cultivation in Confucian thought.* New York: Asian Humanities Press.

Uhlig, Elizabeth. 1989. The culture of women: American missionaries and their daughters in China. Unpublished manuscript, University of Missouri at Columbia.

Wang, Yeujin. 1989. Mixing memory and desire: *Red Sorghum,* a Chinese version of masculinity and femininity. *Public Culture* 2, no. 1:31–54.

Weeks, Jeffrey. 1986. *Sexuality.* London: Tavistock.

Witke, Roxane. 1970. The transformation of attitudes of women during the May Fourth era. Ph.D. diss., University of California, Berkeley.

Wolf, Margery. 1985. *Revolution postponed.* Stanford: Stanford University Press.

Woodside, Alexander. 1976. *Community and revolution in modern Vietnam.* Boston: Houghton Mifflin.

Yanagisako, Sylvia Junko. 1987. Mixed metaphors: Native and anthropological models of gender and kinship domains. In *Gender and kinship: Essays toward a unified analysis,* ed. Jane Collier and Sylvia Yanagisako. Stanford: Stanford University Press.

Zhen Ziyang. 1907. *Nüzi xin duben* (New study book for women). 6th ed. N.p.

Zhongguo Minzhu Funuhui, ed. 1949. *Makesi, Liening, Engesi, Sidalin lun funu jiefang* (Marx, Lenin, Engels, and Stalin on women's liberation). Hong Kong: New People's Press.

Zhou Enlai. 1942. Lun xianqi liang mu yu muzhi. (On virtuous wife, good mother, and the mother's responsibility). *Jiefang Ribao* (Liberation daily), 20 November.

Zito, Angela. 1989. Grand sacrifice as text/performance: Ritual and writing in eighteenth-century China. Ph.D. diss., University of Chicago.

Glossary of Chinese Characters

agu	阿姑	Chengye	成業
aweng	阿翁	*couchang*	惆悵
Ba Jin	巴金	Chu	楚
bagang	八綱	"Chu dong"	初冬
bai	拜	*chuangzaole*	創造了
Baigui zhi	白圭志	*couantong*	傳統
bainian	拜年	*couanxialai*	傳下來
bazi	八字	Chun liu ying	春柳鶯
Bayue de	八月的鄉村	*counjie*	春節
xiangcun		*ci*	賜
bei	備	*cunmin jiaoyu*	村民教育活動組
benshen liyi	本身利益	*huodongzu*	
Bian er chai	弁而釵	*da pinku*	大貧苦勞動婦女
bianhua	變化	*laodong funu*	
biaoshi	表示	*Da Qing tongli*	大清通禮
bimo	筆墨	*da yi*	大義
bingyin	病因	Dai Zhen	戴震
Bowu zhi	博物志	Dai Jinhua	戴錦華
buhaoyisi	不好意思	*daibiao*	代表
cai	才	*dangde zuzhi*	黨的組織范圍
Cai Chang	蔡暢	*fanwei*	
caizi jiaren	才子佳人	*dangqun*	黨群關系
caizi jiaren shu	才子佳人書	*guanxi*	
caizi jiaren	才子佳人小說	*danwei*	單位
xiaoshuo		*dao*	道
Cao Zhi	曹植	*de*	德
ceshi	側室	Deng	鄧穎超
Chao Meng-fu	趙孟頫	Yingchao	
chaofu	朝服	*dianli*	典禮
chen	陳	*dieniang*	爹娘
Chen	陳弘謀	*dli*	地理
Hongmou		Ding Ling	丁玲

Dingqing ren	定情人	Gu Kaizhi	顧愷之
Dong Zhongshu	董仲舒	guan	觀
		guan	管
dongyuan	動員	*Guangya*	廣雅
fa	法	*guanxi*	關系
fanchou	范疇	*guo*	國
fangwu	方物	Guo Xi	郭熙
fanwang	藩王	*guojia*	國家
fei	肺	*guoqu*	過去
Feihua yong	飛花詠	Han	漢
feinongmin	非農民	*Hanshu*	漢書
feinan	非男	*haopengyou*	好朋友
feinu	非女	*Haoqiu zhuan*	好逑傳
feng	風	Hong gaoliang	紅高梁
Feng jia	馮家		
Feng shou	手收	*hongbai xishi lishihui*	紅白喜事禮事會
Fenghuang chi	鳳凰池		
fengjian	封建	*Honglou Meng*	紅樓夢
Fengliu pei	風流配	*houjin fenzi*	后進分子
fengshui	風水	Hsieh Yu-yu	謝幼輿
fengsu xiguan	風俗習慣	Hu Feng	胡風
fu	富	*hua*	華
fu[a]	夫	Hua Mulan	花木蘭
fu[b]	婦	*Hua tu yuan*	畫圖緣
Fuchu lishi dibiao	浮出歷史地表	Huan K'uan	桓寬
		Huang Zongjia	黃崇嘏
Fufa	福發		
Fulian	婦聯	*huangdi*	皇帝
funü	婦女	Hui Zong	徽宗
Funü wenti jianghua	婦女問題講話	*hukou*	戶口
		hukou bu	戶口簿
furen jianshi	婦人見識	*Hulan he zhuan*	呼蘭河傳
Fusheng liuji	浮生六記		
Fuyi	父乙	*huqin*	胡琴
ganbu	干部	*huxiang bai*	互相拜
ganqing	感情	Ji Yun	紀昀
ganying	感應	*jia*	家
geming jingshen	革命精神	*jian*	奸
		jiao	郊
Geng	庚	*jiaozi*	餃子
geren zhuyi	個人主義	*jiating*	家庭
gong	公	*jiating zhufu*	家庭主婦
gong	貢	*jiaren caizi deng shu*	佳人才子等書
gongren	工人		

niangjia	娘家	*Qingye zhong*	清夜鐘
Nongcungongzuo tongxun	農村工作通訊	*qinqi*	親戚
		Qiu Jin	秋瑾
nongcun zhong de laodong funü	農村中的勞動婦女	*quan*	權
		quanli	權力
nongmin	農民	*ren*	仁
nü	女	*ren*	人
nücaizi	女才子	Ren Xiong	任熊
nüdangjia	女當家	*Ren yu cai wang*	人與才旺
nügong nongfu	女工農婦	*Renmin ribao*	人民日報
nüren	女人	*renqing*	人情
nüshi	女士	*renqingde cilichang*	人情的磁力場
nüxing	女性		
nüxing wenxue	女性文學	*renwu*	人物
nüxing zhuyi	女性主義	Renwu zhih	人物志
nüzhi	女子	*Rouputuan*	肉蒲團
Nüzi xin duben	女子新讀本	Ruan Yuan	阮元
Nüzhuangyuan	女狀元	*Rulin Waishi*	儒林外史
Pai'an jingqi	拍案驚奇	Ruzi	如子
Pan Jinlian	潘金蓮	*Sai hong si*	賽紅絲
pengyou	朋友	*sangang*	三綱
pian	篇	*sanjiao*	三焦
Ping Shan Leng Yan	平山冷燕	*sanxian*	三獻
		Sha Lutuo	沙魯脫
pingdeng fuqi	平等夫妻	"*Shafei nushi riji*"	沙非女士日記
Pinhua baojian	品花寶鑒		
pofu	潑婦	Shang	商
pojia	婆家	*shang*	賞
poulian	剖臉	*shanshui*	山水
Pu Songling	蒲松齡	*shanshui hua*	山水畫
Puluha	樸路哈	*shehui*	社會
Qi	齊	*shehui daode pingyi hui*	社會道德評議會
qi	氣		
qi	器	*shen*	神
qian	乾	*sheng*	生
Qiao	橋	*Sheng si chang*	生死場
qiming xuezhe	啟明學者	*shenger yangnü*	生兒養女
qimo	氣脈	*Shenlou zhi*	蜃樓志
Qing	清	*shenqi*	生氣
qing	情	*shi*	是
qingfu	青婦	*shi er zhang*	十二張
Qingmeng tuo	情夢柝	Shi Kuang	師曠
qingnian	青年	*shi/fei*	是非

Shiji	史記	*wenming zu*	文明組
"*Shimian zhi ye*"	失眠之夜	*wenren*	文人
		wenren hua	文人畫
Shisan jing zhushu	十三經注疏	*wenxue*	文學
		Wu	吳
Shuo Maoyi	鑠茂漪	Wu Bing	吳炳
Shuowen	說文	Wu Jingzi	吳敬梓
shutong	書童	Wu Zetian	武則天
shuxie	疏瀉	*wuchan jieji*	無產階級
shuxing	屬性	*Wufeng yin*	五鳳吟
si	私	*wuguan*	五官
si	死	*wulun*	五倫
Sima Qian	司馬遷	*Wushan yanshi*	巫山艷史
Sima Xiangru	司馬相如	*Wusheng xi*	無聲戲
song hezi	送盒子	*wushi*	五事
Sun Longji	孫隆基	Xi	析
Sun Muzi	孫穆子	(Duke) Xiang	襄公
Taisu	太素	*xiang*	象
Tanci Zaisheng yuan	彈詞再生緣	Xiang Jingyu	向警予
		xianggui minyue	鄉規民約
tanxin	談心	*xianfu*	賢婦
Taohua ying	桃花影	*xianjin fenzi*	先進分子
ti	體	*xianmu*	賢母
tiandi	天地	*xiannü*	賢女
Tiehua xianshi	鐵花仙史	*xianzai*	現在
tongyangxi	童養媳	*xiao*	孝
tuanjie shengchan	團結生產	Xiao Hong	蕭紅
tuanjiele gezhong butong de funü	團結了各種不同的婦女	Xiao Jun	蕭軍
		Xiao qing	小青
		Xiao Zhong	小鐘
		xiaojing	孝敬
Two-and-a-Half-Li	二里半	*xiaonü yigui*	孝女遺規
		xiaoren	小人
wai	外	*xiaozi*	孝子
waiban	外辦	Xie Youyu	謝幼嬛
Wan ru yue	宛如約	*xieyi*	寫意
Wang Xizhi	王曦之	Xifu	媳婦
Wanghua	王化	Ximen Qing	西門慶
Wanzi	宛子	*xin*	心
Wangzhi	王制	*Xin Funü duben*	新婦女讀本
wei qi ying xue	衛氣營血	*Xing fengliu*	醒風流
wen	文	*Xinghua tian*	杏花天
wenming	文明		

Xingshi hengyan	醒世恆言	*zaokang zhi qi*	糟糠之妻
		Zeng Jing	曾鯨
Xinhai geming	辛亥革命	*zeren zhi*	責任制
Xiuping yuan	繡屏緣	Zhang Hong	張宏
xiyi	西醫	Zhang Hua	張華
Xu Wei	徐渭	(Duke) Zhao	昭公
xuanze	選擇	Zhao Mengfu	趙孟頫
xue	穴	Zhao San	趙三
xuexi	學習	Zhao Zi Yang	趙紫陽
yang	陽	Zhen Zeyang	震澤楊
Yang Shangshan	楊上善	Zheng	鄭
		Zheng Xuan	鄭玄
yanghuo	養活	*zhengqi*	正氣
Yantie lun	鹽鐵論	*zhi*	質
Yanzi jian	燕子箋	*zhi bing bi qiu yu ben*	治病必求于本
Ye Zi	葉紫		
Yeh Shengtao	葉聖陶	*zhiji*	知己
Yi	夷	*zhishi jieji*	知識階級
yige	一個	*zhishifenzi*	知識分子
Yijing	易經	*zhi-wen*	質文
(duke) Yin	隱公	*zhong*	中
Yin (wind name)	因	*zhongyi*	中醫
		zhongzhuan	中專
yin	陰	Zhou Chen	周臣
ying	應	Zhou Fang	周昉
yisi	意思	*zhu*	主
"*yongjiu de chongjing hezhuiqiu*"	永久的憧憬和追求	Zhu Yingtai	祝英台
		Zhuang Zhou	莊周
		zhuangyuan	狀元
Yu Jiao Li	玉嬌梨	Zhuangzi	莊子
Yu Lou Chun	玉樓春	*Zhuchun yuan xiaoshi*	駐春園小史
Yu Zheng Xie	俞正燮		
Yu zhi ji	玉支璣	*zhuguan*	主觀
yuan	緣	Zhuo Wenjun	卓文君
Yuan Mei	袁枚	*zhuren*	主人
yuanjia	冤家	*zhuti*	主題
yuanming [*fen*]	元明 [粉]	*zinü*	子女
Yueying	月英	*ziwo piping*	自我批評
Yue Fei	岳飛	Zouping	鄒平
yun	韻	*Zui xing shi*	醉醒石
yunhua	遠化	*zunji shoufahu*	遵紀守法戶
zang	臟	*zuxian*	祖先
zangxiang	臟像	*zuzhi*	組織

C O N T R I B U T O R S

Ann Anagnost is assistant professor of anthropology at the University of Washington in Seattle. Her current research is on constructions of civility and the issue of population quality in post-Maoist China.

Tani E. Barlow is associate professor of history at San Francisco State University and senior editor of *positions: east asia cultures critique*. Her forthcoming book *Imagining Women: Dingling and the Category "Woman" in Chinese Modernity* (Duke University Press) rethinks gender history in the revolutionary period.

Judith Farquhar, associate professor of anthropology at the University of North Carolina, Chapel Hill, is author of *Knowing Practice: The Clinical Encounter of Chinese Medicine* (Westview, 1993) and of articles on problems of knowledge and embodiment in Chinese medicine appearing in *Social Science and Medicine* and *Medical Anthropology Quarterly*. She has coauthored with James Hevia a critique of the concept of culture in American historiography of China (*positions* 1993).

John Hay teaches the history of Asian art at the university of California, Santa Cruz. He received a B.A. in Chinese studies at Oxford University and a Ph.D. in Chinese art history at Princeton. He has written on Chinese figure and landscape painting, art theory, and rocks.

James L. Hevia is an assistant professor of history at North Carolina A&T State University in Greensboro. His most recent publications have appeared in *Modern China*, the *Journal of Historical Sociology*, and *positions*. His current research interests focus on European colonialism in nineteenth-century China. He is at present completing a book on the Macartney embassy to China in 1793.

Andrew Kipnis received his Ph.D. in anthropology from the University of North Carolina at Chapel Hill in 1991. He is an assistant professor of anthropology at Northern Kentucky University. He is working on a book on the forms and practices of sentimentality and relationship in modern China.

Shigehisa Kuriyama teaches in the Graduate Institute of the Liberal Arts at Emory University. He is currently completing a comparative study of conceptions of the body in classical Greek and Chinese medicine.

Lydia H. Liu is assistant professor of Chinese and comparative literature at the University of California, Berkeley. She is currently working on a book on translingual practice between East and West. Her recent publications include "Translingual Practice: The Discourse of Individualism between China and the West," *Positions* 1 (Spring 1993), and an essay titled "Invention and Intervention: The Making of a Female Tradition in Modern Chinese Literature," in *From May Fourth to June Fourth: Fiction and Film in Twentieth Century China* ed. Ellen Widmer and David Der-wei Wang (Cambridge: Harvard University Press, 1993).

Keith McMahon is associate professor of Chinese language and literature at the University of Kansas. He is the author of *Causality and Containment in Seventeenth-Century Chinese Fiction* (Brill, 1988) and a study of polygamy and male sexual privilege in Qing novels, *Misers, Shrews, and Polygamists* (Duke, forthcoming).

Angela Zito, assistant professor of Chinese religion at Barnard College of Columbia University, has published on ritual and power in Chinese society in *Modern China* and *positions.* She is completing a book on the relations between writing and ritual in Grand Sacrifice in eighteenth-century China.

INDEX

acupuncture, 27, 32, 37, 40n. 22, 82–87, 96n. 7, 110
agency, 9, 120
All China Democratic Women's Association, 273, 275
Anagnost, Ann, 7, 12–14, 15n, 278n. 2
anatomy, 81, 82, 83, 92, 110
ancestors, 213–14; curse by, 25–27; sacrifice to, 208, 210, 213; spirits of, 221n. 32; veneration of, 114; worship of, 121, 209–11
Anderson, Benedict, 157, 163, 202, 261
art, 184; body in, 42–44, 46, 51–52, 56; Buddhist, 43; criticism, 42; European, 4; Greek, 4; Japanese, 43; nudity in, 44–46, 51–52, 56; painting, 42, 189; sculpture, 42, 53

Barlow, Tani, 10, 12–14, 124n. 11, 176, 195n, 253, 262, 267, 277–78, 282nn. 20, 21
Barthes, Roland, 146, 149
Baudrillard, Jean, 4, 79
Beahan, Charlotte, 254, 263, 281n. 17
beauty-scholar, 227–29, 231, 233, 236, 242–44, 246; classic, 242
Bell, Catherine, 192–93, 198nn. 13, 14
Bernini, Gianlorenzo, 53–54, 57
Bertolucci, Bernardo, 181, 190
binary, 253, 255–56; code, 134; division, 265; essentialist terms, 275; male/female, 278; ontological, 258; sex, 269
biology, reproductive, 277
body, 32, 34, 44–46, 48, 51, 53, 55–56, 58, 70, 101, 107–13, 117–19, 121–22, 125nn. 17, 23, 25, 131, 164–66, 168–69, 173, 183–84, 186–90,

217n. 5, 220n. 21, 258, 279n. 6; affliction of, 23; anatomy of, 92, 110, 165; animal, 164; appearance of, 1; as metaphor for polity, 65; nude, 42; and rocks, 68; as social, 62–63, 64, 65, 134, 137, 139, 150; as system of experiences, 45; as unstable, 13, 31, 36
body/self, 110; Chinese, 12, 23, 67, 78; consciousness, 28, 31; Daoist, 64; embodiment as *ti*, 63–64; female, 13, 72n. 10, 158, 161–66, 170, 173–75; gendered, 162–70; human, 164, 170; and ideology, 122; imagery of, 50; male, 168; and medicine, 11, 13, 31, 82, 93; natural, 8; in painting, 10; passion and decorum, 183, 207–10, 260; of peasant women, 162; personal, 122; physical, 268; politicized, 12, 131–56; power of, 122; ritual bodies, 184; in society, 4; studies of, 1, 4, 43; Western, 79, 80; and yang, 122
boundaries, 103, 106, 110–12, 114–15, 117, 127n. 33, 163, 183–84; gendered, 264; politics of, 103, 120–22
bound feet, 71n. 9, 120, 122
Bourdieu, Pierre, 6, 139–41, 203, 213, 218n. 6
bourgeois, 254, 262, 265, 268–69; family, 273; social science, 150, 268; society, 3
bowing, 183, 187, 208, 211–13, 217n. 2; and decorum, 207; by groom, 215; refusal of, 212–13
British, 181–83, 191, 194; Crown, 184, 187; diplomats, 196n. 7; East India Company, 182; embassy, 187; king, 187, 196n. 7